Psychoanalytic Perspectives on Art

P P A

Editor | Mary Mathews Gedo

The Analytic Press
1985

Distributed by
Lawrence Erlbaum Associates, Publishers
Hillsdale, New Jersey   London

The Analytic Press

Distributed solely by

Lawrence Erlbaum Associates, Inc., Publishers
365 Broadway
Hillsdale, New Jersey 07642

Library of Congress Cataloging in Publication Data
Main entry under title:

Psychoanalytic perspectives on art.

Bibliography: v. 1, p.
1. Psychoanalysis and art—Periodicals. I. Gedo,
Mary Mathews.
N72.P74P78   1985   701'.05   85–9212
ISBN 0–88163–030–6 (v. 1)

Printed in the United States of America
10 9 8 7 6 5 4 3 2 1

Contents of Volume 1

About the Authors

William Conger received his M.F.A. from the University of Chicago in 1966; earlier, he had studied at the School of The Art Institute of Chicago and at the University of New Mexico. Conger's abstract paintings have been exhibited widely in museums and galleries during the past decade. He is represented in the collections of The Art Institute of Chicago and The Illinois State Museum, as well as in numerous private and corporate collections in the United States and abroad. This year, Conger will serve as visiting professor of Art at Northwestern University, on leave from De Paul University, where he is professor of art and had been department chairman for ten years. Conger is represented by the Roy Boyd Gallery, Chicago and Los Angeles.

John E. Gedo, M.D. has practiced psychoanalysis for more than 25 years and has written extensively about the theory, technique, and intellectual history of the discipline. His works include: *Models of the Mind* (with A. Goldberg, 1973); *Freud: The Fusion of Science and Humanism* (co-editor, 1976); *Beyond Interpretation* (1979); *Advances in Clinical Psychoanalysis* (1981); *Portraits of the Artist* (1983); *Psychoanalysis: The Vital Issues* (two volumes, co-editor, 1984); and *Psychoanalysis and its Discontents* (1984). He is training and supervising analyst at the Institute for Psychoanalysis, Chicago, and past president of the Chicago Psychoanalytic Society.

Mary Mathews Gedo obtained her M.A. in psychology from Wellesley College and her Ph.D. in Art History from Northwestern University. In addition to her book *Picasso, Art as*

Autobiography and articles on the psychology of art, she has published extensively on the pioneer American modernist Manierre Dawson as well as on contemporary art in Chicago. She is currently engaged in research for a book on the theme of "The Artist and Death."

Donald Kuspit is professor of art history at the State University of New York at Stony Brook. He holds two Ph.D.s, one in philosophy from the University of Frankfurt, the other in art history from the University of Michigan. The College Art Association awarded him the Frank Jewett Mather Award for Distinction in Art Criticism for 1982. His books include: *The Philosophical Life of the Senses* (1969); *Clement Greenberg, Art Critic* (1979); *The Critic as Artist: The Intentionality of Art* (1984); and *Leon Golub, Existentialist/Activist Painter* (to appear in the spring of 1985). Kuspit is also the author of over 350 articles and reviews. He is a contibuting editor to *Art in America,* a staff reviewer for *Artforum,* and he has curated 25 exhibitions.

Steven Levine is associate professor in the Department of the History of Art, Bryn Mawr College. He received his Ph.D. from Harvard and published his dissertation as *Monet and His Critics* (1976). He is currently completing a monograph with the tentative title: "Reflections and Repetitions: Meanings in the Water Paintings of Claude Monet." The book treats Monet's work in the joint perspectives of the traditional iconography of Narcissus and the contemporary psychoanalytic analysis of narcissism. Levine has lectured on this and related subjects at the Institute for Advanced Study, Princeton, New Jersey, the Free University of Berlin, the University of Virginia, and the Philadelphia Association for Psychoanalysis, where he has twice led a series of seminars on art and psychoanalysis.

Robert S. Liebert, M.D. has taught in the Department of Art History at Columbia University and is associate clinical professor of psychiatry at the College of Physicians and Surgeons, Columbia University; adjunct associate clinical professor of psychiatry at Cornell University Medical College; and training and supervising psychoanalyst at the Columbia University Psychoanalytic Center for Training and Research. Liebert has also taught a variety of courses at Columbia, with which he has been associated for many years. His first book, *Radical and Militant Youth: A Psychoanalytic Inquiry,* evolved from his research on the 1968 student rebellion at Columbia. His most recent book, *Michelangelo: A Psychoanalytic Study of His Life and Images,* is reviewed in this issue of *PPA.*

Francis V. O'Connor is an independent historian of art who holds a Ph.D. from The Johns Hopkins University. He specializes in American art and art patronage since 1930, has published four books, and is co-author of a catalogue raisonné of Jackson Pollock. He lives in New York and is director of Raphael Research Enterprises, a fine arts counseling service. He is currently working on a history of the American mural. His essay in this issue of *PPA* is drawn from a work in progress on the psychodynamics of the creative and patronage processes.

Jerome D. Oremland, M.D. obtained his psychoanalytic training at the San Francisco Psychoanalytic Institute. He has held numerous teaching and professional positions; he is currently clinical professor of psychiatry at the University of California, San Francisco, and is on the editorial boards of the *International Journal of Psychiatry in Medicine,* the *Journal of Preventative Psychiatry, Psychoanalytic Inquiry,* and *Samiksa, Journal of the Indian Psychoanalytic Society.* He has published numerous papers, including several devoted to Michelangelo. His most recent essay about art is "Empathy and Its Relation to the Appreciation of the Formative Arts, Painting and Sculpture," in *Psychoanalytic Inquiry.*

Gilbert Rose, M.D. is a practicing psychoanalyst and lecturer in psychiatry at Yale University. Rose has contributed a number of original articles and reviews to the interdisciplinary literature of psychoanalysis and the humanities. His book *The Power of Form* (1980) is the first full-length psychoanalytic exploration of the nature of aesthetic form. It suggests that all art forms share a common biological function: orientation in an ambiguous reality. In addition to his full-time private practice, Rose is a member of several editorial boards.

Earl E. Rosenthal is professor of the history of art at the University of Chicago. Among his courses in Italian and Spanish Renaissance art and architecture, he has offered since 1954 a seminar on the art of Michelangelo, and in 1964 he published an article titled "Michelangelo's *Moses — dal di sotto in su."* His other publications include studies on Renaissance sculpture, emblems, and architecture. His most recent book is *The Palace of Emperor Charles V in Granada,* which will be published by Princeton University Press.

Laurie Schneider is professor of art history at John Jay College (CUNY), as well as a psychoanalyst in private practice. She took her Ph.D. in art history at Columbia University and her M.A. in developmental psychology at Columbia Teachers College. She is a psychoanalyst at the New York Center for Psychoanalytic Training, and the author of numerous interdisciplinary papers and of the book *Art on Trial* (1976).

Jack J. Spector is professor of art history at Rutgers University. He has specialized in 19th-century French Romanticism and is the author of *Delacroix's Murals at Saint-Sulpice* (1967); *Delacroix's Death of Sardanapalus* (1974); and *Les Écrits de Delacroix sur l'art* (in press). He has written also in the fields of psychoanalysis *(The Aesthetics of Freud,* 1972–78), Surrealism, and art criticism. He has increasingly sought to combine an understanding of the artist's period and social environment with insights into the artist's psychology.

Ellen Handler Spitz holds a degree in art history and Ph.D. in philosophy from Columbia University. She has published in journals of aesthetics, psychoanalysis, psychiatry, and education, and her forthcoming book, *Art and Psyche,* will be published by Yale University Press. She is a special candidate at the Columbia University Center for Psychoanalytic Training and Research, and teaches at Columbia.

Michele Vishny obtained her Ph.D. from Northwestern University. She is an art historian, lecturer, critic, and contributor to *Arts Magazine, Gazette des Beaux-Arts, Art International,* and other journals. She is the author of *Mordecai Ardon* (1975) and *Maryan's Personages* (1983). She continues to be engaged in research on Paul Klee and is also working on aspects of contemporary art in Chicago; she has curated several exhibitions.

Laurie Wilson is director of the New York University Art Therapy Program. She received her Ph.D. in Art History from CUNY and published her dissertation, *Louise Nevelson: Iconography and Sources* (1981), which is reviewed in this volume of *PPA*. She has published a number of articles on Nevelson and on various subjects in art therapy. She is now a research candidate in psychoanalysis at the Psychoanalytic Institute of New York University Medical Center and is an art therapy consultant in the Department of Child and Adolescent Psychiatry at St. Luke's Hospital.

Psychoanalytic Perspectives on Art

Introduction

Volume I of *Psychoanalytic Perspectives on Art* inaugurates not only a new journal but an entirely new species of art periodical. Until now, no publication in the visual arts has addressed itself primarily to exploring the meaning of the work—its style as well as its iconography—as a reflection of its creator's inner world. This relative neglect of the psychological approach probably reflects some concern that psychoanalytic interpretations may distract the viewer away from contemplation of the work to preoccupation with the personality of the artist. By contrast, many art historians have seemed more receptive to—or at least tolerant of—a variety of other new causal critical approaches, such as the fashionable Marxist politico-economic interpretations of art.

As Leon Edel (1982) pointed out, using a metaphor borrowed from Yeats, arguments against psychoanalytic interpretations of art ignore the fact that one cannot separate the dancer from the dance. Every sincere work of art inevitably reflects the character, personality and thought processes of its creator. Although we ordinarily think of nonobjective art as devoid of referents, even works of this type may be—and frequently are—suffused with intense personal significance for the artist. The reluctance of art historians to avail themselves of this rich field of interpretations suggests that resistance to the psychoanalytic approach transcends the threat of distracting the viewer or the disadvantages of our inability to "put the artist on the couch."

Perhaps this reluctance often springs, instead, from the discomfort of the necessary self-exposure implicit in resonating to the inner life of the artist in question. But ignoring the psychological aspects of creativity does not negate their importance. All of our judgments as art historians and critics reflect not only technical knowledge and expertise, but our personalized response to the artist in question—precisely the resonances which echo between the personality of the artist and our own. Even such seemingly "objective" questions as the decision concerning whether a given work should be considered as an autograph production of a given artist depends on many subtle psychological factors in addition to the more objective and readily definable criteria. Perhaps in the not-too-distant future, technological breakthroughs will render such decisions infallible and irrefutable. Until that day, we will continue to base such judgments not only upon such conscious factors as whether we consider the composition and execution of the work worthy of the master in question, but upon subtle perceptions outside of conscious awareness. In order to comprehend the artist more completely, to control our critical decisions more effectively, we need to master, rather than to avoid, psychoanalytic avenues to art.

But if we, as art historians, have often been overly timid about applying psychoanalytic perspectives to art, psychoanalysts have often been too bold. Brashly rushing in, certain analyst-critics have based far-reaching conclusions concerning the interconnections between an artist's character and his career on an insufficient sample of his work and a superficial knowledge of the cultural matrix which gave rise to it. *PPA* hopes to address itself both to art historical sins of omission and to psychoanalytic sins of commission by promoting the kind of interdisciplinary dialogue that will permit us to develop a sound, useful methodology for applying psychoanalytic insights to art and artists.

Volume I of *PPA* contains four separate sub-sections, devoted respectively to aesthetics and art theory, self-portraiture, sculpture, and book reviews. In view of Freud's own interest in applying his insights to the visual arts, it seems especially appropriate to begin this volume with a review of Freud's aesthetics, contributed by aesthetician-philosopher Ellen Handler Spitz, who is currently engaged in studying psychoanalytic theory. Steven Levine's essay, "Monet, Fantasy and Freud," offers additional provocative suggestions concerning the origins of Freud's aesthetics in the common Northern European cultural matrix he shared with his near contemporary, Claude Monet. Levine's essay also indirectly calls attention to another issue to which art historians have generally seemed unresponsive: the manner in which our own experiences and pre-conscious motivations shape and direct our scholarly interests. Levine originally intended to contribute an essay on Monet's self-portraits to *PPA,* only to find himself, instead, writing about the aesthetic milieu which gave rise to Freud's publications on art. Levine's article also gave rise to a feature which we hope to expand greatly in successive issues: the interdisciplinary dialogue, here contributed by psychoanalyst Gilbert Rose, who offers a brief, but poetic, response to Levine.

Section I closes with Donald Kuspit's brilliant definition of 20th-century Expressionism as a kind of psychic flirtation with chaos. Drawing on the most recent publications in psychoanalysis, Kuspit offers provocative suggestions which seem especially timely in view of the current vogue for Neo-Expressionist painting.

The heart of Volume I is composed of a long special section devoted to the examination of the psychodynamics of self-portraiture. The essays have been organized in a progression from those that deal with the most symbolic to those that explore the most direct self-images. The editor's essay about Francisco Goya scrutinizes the symbolic self-references he made in 14 small paintings that he created as a series immediately after recovering from the life-threatening illness of 1792–93, which left him permanently deaf. Jack Spector's contribution examines a single work of art, Eugène Delacroix's painting *Michelangelo in His Studio,* a picture that reveals the French master's intimate identification with his great Renaissance predecessor. Michele Vishny, in her discussion of Paul Klee's self-imagery examines a wide variety of his self-portraits, from the most indirect "encrusted" examples to the most direct self-representations. Vishny provides detailed evidence concerning Klee's personality as expressed through these pictures and emphasizes the formidable nature of the artist's characterological defenses, which effectively shield him from our view.

Francis V. O'Connor's lyrical piece, "The Psychodynamics of the Frontal Self-Portrait," focuses on the most direct and searching of all self-images, the absolutely frontal self-representation. His conclusion that the incidence of such frontal self-images invariably coincides with a period of crucial change or special stress in the artist's life has far-reaching implications. For example, the first overt self-portrait that Goya executed after his recovery from the illness of 1792–93, the highly romantic drawing today in the collection of the Metropolitan Museum of Art was the only *fully* frontal self-image he ever created—an unique self-representation which certainly substantiates O'Connor's thesis.

Section III of the volume includes essays about two significant 20th-century sculptors, Louise Nevelson and Henry Moore, contributed, respectively, by Laurie Wilson and Laurie Schneider. These young scholars personify the interdisciplinary thrust of *PPA,* for they are both active as teaching art historians and have simultaneously obtained training at psychoanalytic institutes. Among our contributors, Schneider makes the most explicit connections between an artist's oeuvre and aspects of psychoanalytic tenets, for she perceives many of Moore's mother-child sculptures as excellent illustrations for analytic theories on child development. Wilson demonstrates that one can illuminate the psychological aspects of an artist's oeuvre without sacrificing discretion or giving offense.

The fourth section of the volume features reviews of Robert Liebert's *Michelangelo: A Psychoanalytic Study of His Life and Images* and Laurie Wilson's *Louise Nevelson: Iconography and Sources.* Both books have been selected for review because they emphasize the personalized roots of creativity, the inseparable relationship between the dancer and the dance. Art historian Earl Rosenthal and psychoanalyst John Gedo both discuss Liebert's book. Gedo's detailed critique coincidentally inaugurates another feature which we hope to continue in future volumes: the exploration of methodological problems and the examination of the author's attitudes toward his artist subject. The section also includes Liebert's response to these two essays. Perhaps in subsequent volumes we will be able to expand this feature to include three-way conversations among the principals involved in reviewing a book. This would be a more complex undertaking, but one which the greater lead time for subsequent volumes should make possible.

Psychoanalyst Jerome Oremland and artist William Conger each consider Wilson's study of Nevelson from the unique viewpoint of his own discipline. Conger is the only professional artist who contibuted an essay to this volume; once again, we hope to expand the participation of those who create art in subsequent issues, even including autobiographical accounts of their creative efforts by those willing to cooperate.

Volume II of *PPA* will be devoted entirely to 19th-century art, primarily painting. Essays by a number of the art historians who contributed to the first volume will again be featured. In addition, Henry Adams, Reinhold Heller, Joel Isaacson, Norma Lifton, and Thomas Sloan will provide fresh viewpoints and insights. The volume will also contain an interdisciplinary dialogue between the noted Cézanne scholar Theodore Reff and psychoanalyst John Gedo concerning the relationship between Cézanne's art and personality. Several psychoanalysts who did not contribute to this volume will appear in Volume II, including Aaron Esman, George Moraitis, Harry Trosman, and Lawrence Warick, the latter writing in collaboration with Elaine Warick. Jay Martin, a practicing psychoanalyst as well as Leo S. Bing Professor of Literature at the University of Southern California, will contribute an essay on "The Death of Beautiful Ladies in 19th Century Painting."

I would like to end this introduction on a more personal note, with special thanks to both John Gedo and Terry Ann R. Neff for their substantial help in bringing Volume I of *PPA* to fruition. The publisher actually invited my husband to serve as my co-editor of *PPA*. Although he formally declined to undertake this role, he gave me his generous help along every step of the way, sharing his much greater experience and expertise in editorial matters with me. I was equally fortunate to have Mrs. Neff as copy editor. She, too, brought both vast experience and good judgment to her task, which involved giving far more help than mere corrections of grammar and syntax. Thanks also to Paul Stepansky, editor in chief of TAP for his unlimited good advice and reassurance, and to Eva Sandberg for cheerfully undertaking the typing chores.

Mary Mathews Gedo, Editor

Section One   Aesthetics and Art Theory

Ellen Handler
Spitz, Ph.D.

A Critique of Pathography, Freud's Original Psychoanalytic Approach to Art

Freud's psychoanalytic investigations growing initially out of his dissatisfaction with the use of hypnosis as a method for treating neurotic patients in the last decade of the 19th century[1] have given rise to widespread cultural changes in our actual institutions and overt behavior as well as in our mental life itself, i.e., in the ways in which we think about many aspects of human functioning. Insights into the structure and workings of the psyche gleaned from psychoanalysis have in our time been applied to nearly every aspect of human experience and, with respect to art, the influences have been pervasive, not only on art itself but on artists, audiences, and critics.

To attempt the task of tracing the myriad paths by which Freud's ideas have found their way into the aesthetic realm in and since his own time would thus be rather like trying to trace the fluff of a dandelion after a child has blown it from its stem. Within the field of literary criticism, for example, Freud's ideas on parapraxes and jokes, dream symbolism, myth of the primal horde, Oedipus complex, and concept of overdetermination have all been used by critics at various times as ways of approaching poems and novels. In this paper I am concerned with one model of the Freudian approach to art. This is the model that Freud himself developed in his book *Leonardo da Vinci and a Memory of his Childhood* (1910) and to which he gave the name "pathography." Clearly, Freud did not limit his applications of psychoanalysis outside the clinical setting to just this model. He also, for example, applied his ideas directly to the texts of certain of Shakespeare's major plays (including *Hamlet, King Lear,* and *Mac-*

This paper was awarded the Fritz Schmidt Prize in 1983 by the Seattle Psychoanalytic Society. It appears in expanded form as chapter 2 of the author's forthcoming book, *Art and Psyche* (Yale University Press).

beth) as well as to myths, nursery rhymes, fairy tales, etc. These intratextual applications of psychoanalytic theory will not be considered here. I will be concerned solely with the pathographic paradigm, *which treats each work of art as an outgrowth of the internal and external biography of its creator.*

It is important to realize at the outset that Freud's tastes in art were limited and conservative, albeit enthusiastic. He did not enjoy music, for example (Freud, 1914a), and took no interest in the stirring avant-garde movements of his time in visual arts, music, theater, or dance. He ignored such contemporary geniuses as Kandinsky, Picasso, Schoenberg, Joyce, Isadora Duncan, and likewise avoided 20th-century European philosophy. Thus, supremely gifted, original, and daring as he was in developing within his own bailiwick, his cultural preferences were derived from the world of the 19th century.

My first task here will be to show a continuity between Freud's model of pathography and the 19th-century critical tradition to which he was heir. Needless to say, the parallel point, namely, that Freud was importantly successor to a specific 19th-century medical and scientific tradition, has been much stressed elsewhere. After demonstrating important links between pathography and Romantic criticism, I turn to a discussion of pathography in terms of the ongoing debate in aesthetics on problems of intention and expression. Finally, I shall suggest that psychoanalysts have much to gain by considering their projects from both the relevant historical and philosophical perspectives and that to do so is to enrich pathography as a mode of psychoanalytic criticism as well as to bring it more focally into the mainstream of critical inquiry.

Freud and the Romantic Critical Tradition

The views on art that formed the background for Freud's work have been characterized as the Romantic or expressive critical tradition. Although Abrams (1953) opines that to fix a *terminus a quo* for this tradition would be tantamount to determining the precise point at which yellow turns to orange on the rainbow, nevertheless, he offers the year 1800, which is among other things the year of publication of Wordsworth's *Preface to the Lyrical Ballads,* generally considered the prototypic document of Romantic criticism.[2] In this work Wordsworth defines poetry as "the spontaneous overflow of powerful feelings,"—feelings, that is, *of the poet*—thereby shifting dramatically the focus of critical attention from audience or work of art to the psyche of the artist who created it.

My claim is that Freud's approach, pathography, may be seen as emerging from this larger context. Seen in this manner, rather than as an isolated phenomenon, we can perhaps better understand some of the possibilities and limitations attendant upon it. In describing this Romantic context, Abrams (1953) points out that, when art is viewed as "the expression or uttering forth of feeling" (as John Stuart Mill put it in his essay on poetry of 1833), certain questions and notions follow from this. A critic will want to ask, for example, how and to what extent a particular work yields insights into the psyche of its creator: whether it be genuine, spontaneous, sincere.[3] Furthermore, if the external world is depicted in art or described in poetry, it must under this approach be seen primarily as a *projection* of the artist's state of mind, an idea that eventually finds its most felicitous formulation in T. S. Eliot's notion of the "objective correlative" (1932). Aspects of works of art as externalizations of psychic states paved the way for the advent of late 19th-century Symbolism and a host of other styles including Post-Impressionism, Expressionism, Fauvism, Surrealism, and Abstract Expressionism,[4] the relevant question for the critic in each case being: what is the underlying feeling, psychic state, conflict, or desire that is finding expression here, possibly disguised? A model such as this necessarily implies an interpretative mode that involves a "looking through." Abrams's metaphor for this is that the mirror that the artist had formerly held up to nature, in the Romantic model becomes transparent (1953), thus enabling an audience to look through this tinted glass to the mind and heart of the artist himself.

This Romantic viewpoint, with its attention centered on the way in which an artist's inner life of feeling finds expression in his works, informed the climate into which Freud's first writings were released, and it may have played a role in shaping both the reception of his ideas and their development. Kris (1946) reports, for example, the intriguing phenomenon that, when Freud first published his *Studies on Hysteria* in 1895, reviews from the scientific and medical communities were mixed; *one* reviewer only, not a clinician but a literary critic and poet—Alfred von Berger, director of the Imperial Theater in Vienna—recognized the significance of the new work and saw it as a "herald" of a new psychology. Kris believes it no accident that the greatness of Freud's discoveries should thus have been first recognized by a literary rather than a scientific scholar since "Freud's predecessors in the study of man were not the neurologists, psychiatrists and psychologists, from whom he borrowed some of his terms, but rather the great intuitive teachers of mankind [i.e., the artists]" (1946, p. 265). Yet, and this is a point I want to emphasize here, Kris further states that "Their influence [i.e., the influence of Freud's discoveries] on the literary mind would be inexplicable had not the previous development of literature turned in a direction which created favorable predispositions for this influence" (p. 270).

Thus, the Romantic tradition that Freud inherited not only provided fertile soil for the reception of his ideas but also nourished, it seems, the growth of these very ideas, particularly as Freud began to apply them directly to the arts.

This Romantic or expressive mode which found its way in various guises into European fine arts, literature, music, and criticism of the 19th century, gave rise by its focus on the artist to myths and cults of the artist,[5] to views of the artist as different from others, as hypersensitive, fragile, "possessed," etc., thus reviving in modern times Plato's notion of the artist's madness. Indeed it is not uncommon today for psychoanalysts (and others) to regard artists as persons with particularly intense or persistent conflicts, as the very term "pathography" connotes.

Actually, after coining this term in his study of Leonardo da Vinci and promising to "stake out in a quite general way the limits which are set to what psycho-analysis can achieve in the field of biography" (1910), Freud in fact defines pathography only by making exclusions. He says, for example, that "we should be glad to give an account of the way in which artistic activity derives from the primal instincts of the mind if it were not just here that our capacities fail us" (p. 132), and that "pathography does not in the least aim at making the great man's achievements intelligible." He tells us what pathography cannot (yet) do and what psycho-analysis cannot (yet) explain. Hence, in the absence of a clear, positive account of either his aims or the supposed value of his work, we must fall back on the obvious connotations of the word. A less inclusive term than biography, pathography seems to imply writing about suffering, illness, or feeling, with important over-tones of empathic response on the part of the author for his subject. It suggests *selected* aspects of a life, precisely in fact those aspects pertaining to (mental) disease, to intrapsychic conflict, its symptoms, and their etiology. My point here is that the conception of the artist implicit in Freud's term grows solidly out of the Romantic tradition in which artistic creativity is variously associ-ated with moments of intense emotion, altered states of con-sciousness, and pain.

Such a view of the artist as uniquely endowed emotionally, as chosen or cursed, can be seen as leading to speculations about what possible therapeutic value the making of art might have for its creator. Psychoanalysts in recent years have debated this issue, and the very term "art therapy" betokens a positive side to the controversy. Most pathographers tend, however, to see the solu-tion of artistic problems as contributing little of lasting value to the resolution of intrapsychic conflict; in fact, this viewpoint is fundamental to their interpretative method, which depends on the repetition, the reappearance of certain persistent motifs through-out the artist's lifespan. For example, Liebert says:

> We expect that the underlying forces [of conflict] will be expressed repeatedly as a reflection of continuous internal pressure within the artist. This expectation grows out of the view that the manifest solution of the latent and unconscious conflict in the artist, the work of art, does *not* have the effect of "working through"—that is, of permanently altering the central mental representation of himself and others and bringing about basic changes in other aspects of his internal psychological organization and outlook. Thus, as each artistic endeavor inevitably fails in this respect, the underlying con-flict will reappear. Each new artistic solution to it will be somewhat different from the previous one, but still motivated toward a similar end (1982, p. 18).

A further discussion of the issues involved in this controversy would be out of place at this point. Suffice it to say that the entire matter presupposes a view of art and artists that derives from the Romantic critical tradition.

Abrams offers one passage in which he attempts to characterize the overall approach common to this tradition. One is struck by its similarity to Freud's views which, I propose, take Romanticism as their point of departure, going on then to develop and refine it by offering hypotheses concerning the nature and origin of "perceptions, thoughts, and feelings."[6] Abrams's summary follows:

> A work of art is essentially the internal made external, resulting from a creative process operating under the impulse of feeling, and embodying the combined product of the poet's *perceptions, thoughts and feelings*. The primary source and subject matter of a poem, therefore, are the attributes and actions of the poet's own mind; or if aspects of the external world, then these only as they are converted from fact to poetry by the feelings and operations of the poet's mind (1953, p. 22, my italics).

Freud's pathographic approach—minimally (or only secondarily) concerned with the ways in which art either mirrors the outside world per se or affects its audience or possesses its own internal formal structure, but maximally concerned with the narrative of an artist's inner life as it can be inferred from a careful study of his works (and other biographical material)—thus represents a final flowering in the 20th century of Romantic criticism. Before asking how pathography has furthered, advanced, or contributed to this particular mode of criticism, I would like to spend another moment on Freud's predecessors and then turn to a discussion of the way in which pathography poses problems that coincide with problems aestheticians have considered under the categories of intention and expression in art.

Although Romantic critics generally viewed the work of art as an expression of the artist's feeling, it is interesting to note that, even before Freud's seminal work of the 1890s, there were literary critics who understood that works of art may function not merely to express feelings but also to disguise and conceal them. One such critic was John Keble, a leader in the Oxford movement and holder of the Oxford Chair of Poetry; in the 1840s Keble had formulated a theory of poetry which—dedicated appropriately to Wordsworth, who can also be seen as proto-Freudian in his developmental thinking—embodies the notion that art is an *indirect* expression of "some overpowering emotion, or ruling taste, or feeling, the direct indulgence whereof is somehow *repressed*" (Abrams, 1953, p. 145). Keble speaks of art as giving "healing relief to secret mental emotion" (p. 145), of art as "paint[ing] all things in the hues which the mind itself desires" (p. 147), and as "a safety-valve, preserving man from actual madness" (p. 146). Thus, for Keble, art involves not simply the direct, spontaneous expression of feeling but rather internal *conflict* between the artist's need to give utterance to his emotions and his "instinctive delicacy which recoils from exposing them openly" (p. 147).

Although my research has not unearthed any *perfectly* parallel passage in Freud's oeuvre to juxtapose with the above quotations, it must be clear to any reader of Freud how close Keble's (and other Romantics')[7] views are to those of classical psychoanalysis. I offer the following excerpts from Freud which at least presuppose Keble's views and are perspicuously consonant with the Romantic theory of art:

> Creative writers are valuable allies and their evidence is to be prized highly, for they are apt to know a whole host of things between heaven and earth of which our philosophy has not yet let us dream. [Freud's point is underscored by his literary paraphrase from Act I, scene 4 of *Hamlet*.] In their knowledge of the mind they are far in advance of us everyday people, for they draw upon sources which we have not yet opened up for science (1907, p. 8, my insert).

Here Freud indicates his agreement with the Romantics that artists are uniquely endowed with an ability to tap into the powerful emotions and hidden secrets of the human heart.

> In my opinion, what grips us so powerfully can only be the artist's *intention,* in so far as he has succeeded in *expressing* it in his work and in getting us to understand it. . . . what he aims at is to awaken in us the same emotional attitude, the same mental constellation as that which in him produced the impetus to create . . . [Freud goes on to say that a work of art should admit of the application of psychoanalysis] if it really is *an effective expression of the intentions and emotional activities of the artist* (1914, p. 212, my italics).

Here Freud agrees with the Romantic position that the work of art is the result of an artist's need or intent to express some aspect of his emotional life or a certain intrapsychic "constellation."

In the above passages, Freud indicates that what the artist finally creates is a compromise resulting from his inner conflict between wanting to express certain feelings directly and not being permitted to do so. His mode of compromise is to express his fantasies in altered form in his works of art, a mode which, although Freud does not indicate it here, he considered less than entirely satisfying. The parallel with Keble's views is apparent; although Keble seemed to feel by contrast that poetry possesses for the poet a healing power akin to prayer.

In the second passage quoted above, Freud uses the words "intention" and "expression." If we acknowledge that pathography emanates from the matrix of Romantic criticism, as I have tried to demonstrate, then we may expect it will admit of the same sort of philosophical critique as does that approach to art. Before considering this critique as it is found in some aestheticians' arguments against intention and expression, I would like to pause to (1) distinguish pathography from Romantic criticism on the one hand and (2) argue that pathography *can* function as a critical mode on the other. For it is clear that unless we can establish pathography as at least potentially a critical mode, the arguments of the aestheticians will be irrelevant to it.

First I must acknowledge having blurred certain distinctions between pathography and Romantic criticism in the foregoing pages in order to establish parallels between the two. However, whereas the Romantic critic employs biographical and other information in order to interpret the work of art, his prime object of inquiry; in pathography the movement is reversed: according to Freud, the works of art or aspects thereof are taken as starting points "for discovering what determined [the artist's] mental and intellectual development" (1910, pp. 130–131). Thus, in pathography, the psyche is the prime object of inquiry. As such it might be possible to rule out pathography as a critical mode entirely, to see it as a purely psychological study, as the search for a man. In mocking a quest of this sort and dismissing it as not only extraneous to critical inquiry but also as quite absurd, the aestheticians Wimsatt and Beardsley (1954) offer a mischievous quote from Thomas Hardy: "'He's the man we were in search of, that's true,' says Hardy's rustic constable, 'and yet he's not the man we were in search of. For the man we were in search of was not the man we wanted'" (p. 295).

I want, however, to argue that pathography *may* be seen as a viable critical mode. My reasons seem to fall spontaneously into metaphoric language. While in pursuit of pearls, because he is looking so intently about him, a diver may discover many beautiful coral reefs and underwater flora. Arnold Isenberg (1948), arguing for a somewhat different point, uses a similar figure (which may have been my inspiration): "It is as if we found both an oyster and a pearl when we had been looking for a seashell because we had been told it was valuable. It *is* valuable, but not because it is a seashell" (p. 163).

The idea is that, in order to *do* pathography, one must *look* carefully and read slowly. One must dwell on detail. One must attend with utmost sensitivity. Since something of the artist has found its way into each work of art (and this is granted even by Wimsatt & Beardsley, 1954), then to seek the former, we must deal with the latter. Hence, if my analogy holds, pathography in its effort to penetrate to certain sorts of psychic meaning in works of art is bound to attend to these works aesthetically and—if well done—even to contribute to our awareness and understanding of them. I am suggesting that, in other words, although the directions of emphasis are different, the lines do run parallel and, since works of art are perceived as wholes, since what the artist meant by the poem *is* in some sense the poem, the pathographer-psychoanalyst may be considered as partaking in critical inquiry, as contributing (even if he conceives this as only a minor or secondary function) to the critical enterprise.[8]

It is also worth noting that, contrary to Freud's formulation in the *Leonardo* (as quoted above), in actual practice, pathography works both ways: works of art are used to penetrate the psyche of the artist, but hypotheses about the artist's inner life are also used to interpret his works. In the latter case, certainly, the analyst can be seen as speaking with a critical voice. One important way of judging the value of such remarks is to return to the works of art in question and reexperience them in the light of the proffered psychoanalytic interpretation. Such a reexperiencing or "second moment" is fundamental to the concept of criticism held by at least some philosophers (cf. Isenberg, 1948), and its centrality to the pathographic approach is manifest by the usual inclusion in pathographic texts of reproductions of the works of art under consideration. Note the inclusion of at least several plates in Freud's *Leonardo*. More tellingly, however, with respect to literature, Freud specifically instructs his readers "to put aside this little essay and instead to spend some time in acquainting themselves with *Gradiva* . . . so that what I refer to in the following pages may be familiar to them" (1907, p. 10). We might compare this passage with the following from Isenberg: "Reading criticism, otherwise than in the presence, or with direct recollection, of the objects discussed, is a blank and senseless employment" (1948, p. 164).

A counter-argument to my claim that pathography be considered at least potentially capable of functioning as a critical mode could be made by citing differences between psychoanalysts and critics with respect to their techniques of listening, looking, or reading. Such differences certainly do exist, and the issue bears further study. I want to maintain, however, that such variations are no different in kind from those one might encounter among individual critics or representatives of particular schools. For example, it might be argued that a psychoanalyst approaches a text with an eye or ear for only certain sorts of psychosexual allusions, for certain sorts of gaps or inconsistencies. Yet, similarly, the formalist critic may approach a painting oblivious of its iconography, his eye attuned merely to nuances of line, shape, and color, to perhaps a "steeply rising and falling curve" (Isenberg, 1948, p. 162). A drama critic may be principally concerned with language rather than with psychological subtlety or dramatic fulfillment. One music reviewer may listen for the guest conductor's particular interpretation of tempo and dynamics and attend to his rapport with the orchestra; whereas another critic attending the same concert may have score in hand, intently listening for the balance of sound, his focus on the internal arrangement of voices within the music. In each case, and I include the psychoanalytic, what is seen, read, or heard will be somewhat different but may, under particular circumstances and for a particular audience, become critically relevant.

The circumstances under which remarks become critically relevant can be highly variable. For example, even an art dealer's pronouncement about the relative worth of two seemingly fine impressions from the same lithographic plate *could* become critically relevant to the prospective buyer if such a pronouncement spurred him to look more carefully and "critically" at the two prints in question. On the other hand, comments on the monetary value of works of art are generally taken to be critically irrelevant and usually are. As was mentioned earlier, such factors as conscious and unconscious need and motive, knowledge, familiarity, and curiosity all play a role. The best definition I have encountered for what actually happens when a remark does become critically relevant is to be found in Isenberg, where he says that the essential condition of the aesthetic experience is that attention should rest on a certain content (1944). Any remark that contributes to this, which serves "to expand the field on which attention rests," would seem to me critically relevant.

Thus, I can find no better reason for excluding any one of these approaches (i.e., the formal, historical, psychoanalytic, etc.) than any other. It even seems plausible that under most circumstances, except in the case of normative criticism, these modes would come into conflict only when exponents of one or another claim to have exclusive or prior hegemony over a work or works of art, to possess, in other words, the *true* interpretation."[9]

Intention, Expression, and Pathography

Granted then that we can, at least under some circumstances, consider pathography a critical mode with respect to art, we must now raise the issues that have been advanced by modern aestheticians with respect to Romantic theories of art. Broadly speaking, the critique falls into two parts: (1) It accuses Romantic criticism of incorporating the so-called "intentional fallacy," that is, of assuming unjustifiably that knowledge of the artist's intentions is (a) available and (b) desirable as a standard for how a work of art should be interpreted, read, responded to; and (2) It claims that Romantic theory takes a wrong-headed view of the expressive qualities of art. In what follows, I shall draw upon the work of Wimsatt and Beardsley as representatives of the first of these critiques (with Cioffi as their principal opponent), and Bouwsma, Tormey, and Kivy as exponents of the second critique.

The psychoanalyst writing on art using Freud's *Leonardo* as a model may be unaware of the ways in which such aestheticians have called into question the validity of his enterprise. If, in addition to advancing or illustrating some aspect of psychoanalytic theory for an audience of peers, he seeks to make an interdisciplinary contribution to our understanding of the works discussed and be taken seriously outside his own domain, the analyst is bound to entertain the arguments of such philosophers as the above—not so much with the end of refuting them as of understanding and attempting to incorporate the valid insights they possess.

My aim in this section, therefore, will be to summarize some of the arguments and counter-arguments that bear on issues already in part discussed. My own view is that the anti-intentionalist arguments have sufficient weight to be taken seriously; they offer (at least) good reasons why intentionalist critics (pathographers) cannot pretend to have both necessary and sufficient claims on the way in which works of art ought be read. By insisting on the autonomy of the art object, they provide an important caveat for the pathographer and point out at least one direction in which he might look for what he senses might be missing in his approach. On the other hand, the arguments in favor of intention and expression are strong enough to establish these modes as viable, critically relevant ways of approaching works of art.

The first charge that is made against the intentionalist critic is that an artist's intention, defined as other than or more than, in some sense, the resultant work of art, is ultimately unknowable and hence a rather poor criterion on which to hang an interpretation. This charge bears on the problem of freedom and determinism in human behavior, an issue on which Freud, as we have seen, wavered, though usually holding to the view that even if intention could not be entirely explained by current theory, it is determinate and hence susceptible of full explanation at some future time.[10] In the *Leonardo,* which came under heavy attack when first published and which has provoked periodic attacks ever since, he demurs, however, on this point:

> But even if the historical material at our disposal were very abundant, and if the psychical mechanisms could be dealt with with the greatest assurance, there are important points at which a psycho-analytic enquiry would not be able to make us understand how inevitable it was that the person concerned should have turned out in the way he did and in no other way. . . . We must recognize here a degree of freedom which cannot be resolved any further by psycho-analytic means. Equally, one has no right to claim that the consequence of [a particular] wave of repression was the only possible one (p. 135).

Yet, further on in the same work he stresses an opposite claim, namely, that a person's fate is ultimately determined by "the accidental circumstances of his parental constellation." In any case, his ambivalence aside, Freud would certainly have argued, against Wimsatt and Beardsley, that we can know *something* about the artist's intentions from sources external to the work of art and that this "something" will be not only relevant but central to our understanding of the work in question.

Wimsatt and Beardsley, however, want to define intention in terms of the work the artist has created. They justify this by pointing out that a work of art is usually defined by what it excludes as well as by what it contains (1954). Therefore, intention must be equated with result and, if so, we are free to deal exclusively with the latter on its own terms. If, however, pursuing some alternative chimera of intention, we are driven outside the work into a morass of conflicting, incomplete, and altogether troublesome data, none of this will have critical bearing on the work of art which, by definition, we have already claimed as the embodiment of intention.

Thus, Wimsatt and Beardsley seek to argue, whereas a designing intellect caused the work of art to come into being, we cannot turn back and make that designing intellect (or whatever we can fathom of it) into the standard by which we interpret the work. The poem must "work" like a pudding they claim: all lumps have to be stirred out before the dish is served and, to elaborate on their image, I would add that to offer the lumps or the recipe or some information about the past personal circumstances and present humor of the chef would not improve the flavor of the pudding. They draw a sharp line between what they call "personal and poetic studies," between "internal and external evidence." Internal evidence is public and discoverable through *reading* the poem;[11] therefore, it is admissible; whereas, external evidence is private and not a part of the work itself (it may be found in journals, letters, etc.). To follow it is to be led away from the work of art and thus to make extra-critical judgments that devalue the existing body of the work as a sufficiently rich source of immanent consistent suggestive meanings. To do pathography as criticism, would be for these authors to violate the given boundaries of the work of art, to fail to respect it as a realized whole.

Wimsatt and Beardsley clearly base their anti-intentionalist protest on the grounds that to do pathography is to reduce the work of art to a window, or to tamper with its frame, or to treat it as if it were an ordinary message, thus to deprive it of its special ontological status in the culture. I believe it important for psychoanalysts to confront this particular issue and to recognize that for most aestheticians and art critics, even amateurs of art, and above all for artists, the work represents an end and not a means. It is importantly bracketed or framed. Consequently, there is a necessity in doing pathography for returning frequently to the work of art. For example, one must return to Leonardo's *Madonna, Child, and St. Anne* to reexperience the painting in the light of Freud's hypothesis about the artist's two mothers. One must test the interpretation by seeing whether the painting *looks* different, whether new aspects of it come into focus, whether in Wimsatt and Beardsley's jargon it *works* differently. In this sense the anti-intentionalist argument must be taken seriously by the pathographer: his interpretations must bear the test of a second moment of aesthetic experience or else he cannot claim, whatever else he may be doing, to be making critical statements about works of art.

An intriguing point to consider here is whether what "works" aesthetically is sometimes, always, or never what "works" psychodynamically. My hunch is that the aesthetic solution must work psychologically, but that a given work may admit of more psychological possibilities than aesthetic ones. I am not prepared to argue this point here, and whether or not I am correct, it is clear that the anti-intentionalists make sense when they challenge us to show the *coincidence* of aesthetic and psychological needs. We need to question, for example, the relationship between the psychological and aesthetic demands which a piece in progress places on the artist as he works. When a pathographer attempts to discuss intention, he must not neglect this aspect of intention, that is to say, the needs, dictates, strictures, and seductions of the work of art itself—its form, its own internal structure. The pathographer must, in short, remember that the artist is after all an artist, and that in the process of creation, the created work enters into its own dialogue with its creator. Moreover, as Gay (1976) points out, in some cases the imperatives of "craft" take precedence over other (psychic) considerations.

Returning to Wimsatt and Beardsley, their distinction between internal and external may be difficult to uphold. They reluctantly admit to cases where it is hard to draw lines between the public history of a word or phrase and the usage or associations of that word for a particular author. Rebutting them, Cioffi (1964) points out that when we know something (biographical) about a poem, we often tend to read it into the poem; the intended meaning thus seems to inhere in the poem (work of art). Likewise, when we learn that something was *not* intended, we are apt to reject an interpretation that ignores this even though such an interpretation may previously have seemed legitimate.[12] In other words, what we know about a given work of art tends to become "unobtrusive" for us as regards that work (Stern, 1980). In Cioffi's words, "A reader's response to a work will vary with what he knows; one of the things which he knows and with which his responses will vary is what the author had in mind, or what he intended" (1964, p. 315). Cioffi goes on to make the point I stressed above: namely, that you cannot know whether remarks are merely biographical or whether they are critical

> until after you have read the work in the light of them. . . . If a critical remark fails to confirm or consolidate or transform a reader's interpretation of a work it will then become for him just evidence of something or other, perhaps the critic's obtuseness. Biographical remarks are no more prone to this fate than any others (p. 316).

Hence, Cioffi attempts to collapse Wimsatt and Beardsley's distinction between internal and external evidence by translating it into the problematic distinction "between what we can and cannot be expected to know" about a given work of art. He claims that, since art is (importantly) a human product, "there is an implicit biographical reference in our response to [in his example] liter-ature," and that this "is, if you like, part of our concept of literature [art]" (p. 318).

Furthermore, for Cioffi, as for me, interpretation arises in a heterogeneity of contexts.[13] He speaks of throwing a "field of force" around the work of art such that, once certain biographical data are known, it becomes increasingly perplexing to discern the boundaries of the work. An ontological problem now appears: how can we "appeal to the text" when its edges have become blurry? Cioffi's argument runs into difficulties, however, when it comes up against certain sorts of familiar counter-examples in which what we know about the author seems to have minimal or zero effect on our perceptions of the work of art.

Are we justified in assuming "a necessary link between the qualities of the art work and certain states of the artist" is the way the question is put by Tormey (1971, p. 350). He then answers with a resounding "no" but proceeds to draw his examples exclusively from the art of music, a tack also taken by Bouwsma (1954) in his paper on the theory of art as expression. Because music is perhaps the most difficult art to discuss biographically,[14] it well serves the anti-expressionists' cause. In any case, Tormey claims that his arguments hold for the other art forms as well, and I would expect Bouwsma to claim the same. Tormey asserts:

> the expressive qualities of a work of art are logically independent of the psychological states of the artist, and humor (or sadness) in a madrigal is neither necessary nor sufficient for amusement (or despair) in a Monteverdi . . . the presence of an expressive quality in a work of art is never sufficient to guarantee the presence of an analogous feeling state in the artist (p. 358).

Tormey bases his argument in part on a distinction he draws between the transitive and intransitive uses of the term "expressive." He points out that performances are noted as "expressive," that "espressivo" is a commonly met marking on musical scores, that a human face can be called "expressive," in each case without the implication of an intentional object, without in other words an expectation of the further question "of what?" His claim is that for a work of art to be expressive, it need not imply a prior act of expression, and that to conflate these two usages is the fundamental error of the Romantic theory of art. For Tormey, "acts of expression" are common to all forms of human behavior so that to discuss art in such terms is to say something trivial at best since it is to say nothing that can distinguish a work of art from any other product of human activity. To say, however, that a work of art or a performance is expressive in the former sense is quite different. Expressive in this sense implies that the work in question possesses certain aesthetic qualities our perception of which depends on our ability to discriminate among a "highly complex set of predicates and . . . their logical relations to one another."

Tormey offers an example in which knowledge of the personal tragedy of a composer's life "has little to do with the aesthetically relevant expressive qualities of the music itself." If we, for example, should discover that a certain composer was, at the time of writing a certain piece, both anxious and even humiliated though his music when played sounds spritely, carefree, and tuneful (as was so often the case with Mozart), we might infer perhaps that the composer in question was, in creating such a piece, attempting to distance himself from his pain. From a psychoanalytic point of view, we might suggest that the gaiety of the music served as a defense against the fear and depression of the composer. However, what Tormey urges is that we may not claim on that account to *hear* the music differently, to hear it as "humorous but disguisedly bitter," etc. It is not clear, in the case of music at any rate, that, except in cases where music is integrated with a verbal text, extra-musical information of a biographical nature can make us hear the music differently at all. What we hear when we are sensitive to music are the aesthetic qualities of a particular composition in performance.

And performance is important here, especially if, with Susanne Langer (1953), we conceive it as a "completion" of the musical work. Langer says that "real performance is as creative an act as composition . . . a logical continuation of the composition, carrying creation through from thought to physical expression" (pp. 138–139). Thus, she gives full homage to the "sonorous imagination" of the performer who must give "utterance" to the "conceptual imagination" of the composer. According to this view, we must extend the notion of expression to cover the feeling-states of performers. Clearly, this is untenable.[15] To say, for example, that a rendition of the Tchaikovsky *Violin Concerto in D* by Jascha Heifetz was more expressive than a performance of the same work by Isaac Stern is to make no psychological statement about either of the two men involved. Tormey's point is that to speak about a work of art is not necessarily to speak about a person and vice-versa. Peter Kivy (1980) has written recently on expression in music and borrows heavily, I feel, from Bouwsma's earlier paper. Kivy quotes Bouwsma to the effect that "the sadness is to the music rather like the redness to the apple, than it is like the burp to the cider" (Bouwsma, 1954, p. 265). Kivy's own images of this difference in the ways we understand expression include a man with a clenched fist, and the face of a St. Bernard dog. Commonly, we would describe the former as "angry," and the latter as "sad." Kivy argues that when we say that the dog has a sad face we do not mean that his face expresses sadness in the same way in which we mean that the fist-clenching man expresses anger. Kivy holds that, similarly, when we refer to a passage in a musical composition as sad, we mean it in the former rather than in the latter sense. His thesis thus involves an effort to divorce biographical reference from musical criticism, though not absolutely, for, as he says, music *can* occasionally express genuine sadness or terror on the part of a composer. What he claims is that, generally speaking, when we characterize a piece of music as "brooding" or "spritely" we do not mean to so characterize its composer, nor do we mean that the music causes us to brood or to caper. We are rather, by using such predicates, Kivy asserts, describing qualities inherent in the music, and he endeavors to offer historical, physiological, and iconographic accounts for such qualities that are not only possible but plausible.

Tormey agrees that there must be some connection between what an artist does and the resulting expressive qualities of the work of art. What he wants to preserve is precisely what Wimsatt and Beardsley want to protect, namely, the uniqueness of the aesthetic object; what these philosophers assert is that there is no simple, logical, or consistent relation between what an artist feels or thinks or knows or does and the resulting expressive qualities of the work of art. The artist, Tormey insists, is, over and above expressing himself, "making an expressive object" (1971), an object that has the power to make others feel. This may involve even in a nontrivial sense some expression of the artist's state of mind, but to say this is scarcely to begin to address the complexity of the creative act which results in what we perceive as an "expressive" work of art.

Freud himself had some awareness of this problem in the theory of art, as the following quotes will evince. At the end of his *Moses of Michelangelo* (1914a) after initially claiming that "it can only be the artist's intention, in so far as he has succeeded in expressing it in his work and in conveying it to us, that grips us so powerfully" (p. 212), he concludes with doubt:

> What if we have taken too serious and profound a view of details which were nothing to the artist, details which he had introduced quite arbitrarily or for some purely formal reasons with no hidden intention behind? What if we have shared the fate of so many interpreters who have thought they saw quite clearly things which the artist did not intend either consciously or unconsciously? I cannot tell (pp. 235–236).

In this passage Freud implies that it is not only possible but even likely to find in a work that which the artist did not in some sense intend; he therefore betrays his awareness that intention alone may not provide an adequate theory of art.

There are two issues here: one is whether psychoanalysis can adequately account for the artist's intention, and the other is whether we must allow for aspects in a given work of art that are extra-intentional, even given the psychoanalytic concept of intention, which is far more inclusive than the artist's conscious purpose or design. We are returned here to an ontological question. If, with Wimsatt and Beardsley, we define the work of art as equivalent to the artist's intention, then we must interpret Freud's passage above to mean that psychoanalysis simply fails to give a complete account of intention, of the internal workings, dynamics, structure of the work of art. If, on the other hand, we conceive the work of art as a cultural object existing in its own space and time and continuously affected by forces outside the artist's purview (cf. Cioffi), then we can interpret Freud's passage as indicating his awareness not of the limits of psychoanalytic theory to account for works of art as intentional objects but rather its limitations vis-à-vis art seen as that which transcends intention.

Freud's equivocation here has to do partly with his emphasis, in the early stages of the development of psychoanalytic theory, on the investigation of the id. In the years prior to 1923 (with publication of *The Ego and the Id,* which established a new direction for psychoanalytic investigation)—that period in which Freud's major contributions in the direct application of psychoanalysis to the arts were written—his primary focus was on the nature of repressed wishes and drives: he saw this as the "real" material for interpretation. The countervailing forces were acknowledged, but only one side of the intrapsychic conflict was deemed important. Hence, his view of intention was strongly weighted towards id-dominated unconscious factors. Not yet having developed his structural theory into its final form, he was not interpreting from a perspective that included in fair measure accounts of the forces of id, ego, superego, and reality on behavior. Only later, with the work of Anna Freud (1936), Hartmann (1939), Rapaport (1967), and Kris (1952), was a balance established, a more equal distribution of interest, so that some of these issues which seemed so doubtful with respect to art have come more recently to be addressed somewhat differently by the so-called ego psychologists. (See also Waelder, 1965.)

I am suggesting here that, in part, the reason for Freud's view of art as puzzling and for his at times rather baffled attitude towards it lies in the narrowly focused perspective he took on it during the early years of the development of psychoanalytic theory. As this next quote testifies, he seemed to sense this:

> It may be that we have produced a complete caricature of an interpretation by introducing into an innocent work of art purposes of which its creator had no notion, and by so doing have shown once more how easy it is to find what one is looking for and what is occupying one's own mind—a possibility of which the strangest examples are to be found in the history of literature (1907, p. 91).

A few lines later, however, Freud reasserts his faith in the explanatory value of the psychoanalytic notion of unconscious intention, and hence in the deterministic intentionalist theory:

> Our opinion is that the author need have known nothing of these rules and purposes, so that he could disavow them in good faith, but that nevertheless we have not discovered anything in his work that is not already in it. . . . He need not state these laws [of unconscious intention], nor even be clearly aware of them; as a result of the tolerance of his intelligence they are incorporated within his creations (pp. 91–92).

He again equivocates in his famous line from *Dostoevsky and Parricide* (1928), when he exclaims: "Before the problem of the creative artist analysis must, alas, lay down its arms" (p. 177); and in the same work he refers to the artist's "unanalysable gift."

In yet another work, Freud (1908) again expresses his inability to explain both the artistic (creative) and aesthetic experience but indicates as well his awareness of the transforming power of art. He begins by asking how the artist manages to impress us and arouse in us emotions of which we had not realized ourselves capable. He notes that querying the artist will not result in any satisfactory explanations. Then he offers the following formulation:

> [The artist] creates a world of phantasy which he takes very seriously—that is, which he invests with large amounts of emotion—while separating it sharply from reality. . . . The unreality of the writer's imaginative world, however, has very important consequences for the technique of his art; for many things which, if they were real, could give no enjoyment, can do so in the play of phantasy, and many excitements which, in themselves, are actually distressing, can become a source of pleasure for the hearers and spectators at the performance of a writer's work (1908, p. 144).

In this passage Freud comes close to a classical view of art as imitation. In the course of this particular work, *Creative Writers and Day-Dreaming,* he develops a connection between art and children's play, emphasizing the seriousness, the value to the child/artist of his illusory, make-believe world. Thus, he paves the ground for some of the more recent psychoanalytic authors such as Winnicott who have greatly elaborated on the derivation of artistic activity from childhood play.[16]

Having presented these specimens of Freud's shifting views on art, we must return to our original problem, asking now both how psychoanalytic interpretation of art [in the pathographic mode] can respond to the anti-intentionalist and anti-expressionist critiques that have been leveled against it and also what specific contribution psychoanalysis can make to the debate between intentionalists and anti-intentionalists. I have tried in the text to indicate some answers to the first of these questions. The psychoanalytic interpreter must (1) seek to respect the integrity of the work of art, remembering that it is consciously framed and holds a special status within the domain of cultural objects; (2) attend to the way in which it, as an autonomous object, exerts its own pulls upon the artist—pulls that may be technical, aesthetic, and not necessarily traceable to depth psychology; (3) bear in mind that the work of art is a real object apart from the psyche of its creator and that thus to make statements about its creator is not necessarily to make statements about it and vice-versa.

With respect to the second question, clearly the most obvious contribution psychoanalysis can make to the debate on intentionalism is the notion of the dynamic unconscious. This construct significantly broadens the concept of intention. By appeal to unconscious motivation, the most apparently far-fetched intention may be attributed to an artist, his strenuous denial only serving, in the case of resistance, to support rather than disprove the allegation. Theoretically, it becomes possible for the psychoanalyst to claim as the result of intention all aspects of the work of art considered as a psychic product. Since psychoanalytic theory offers no clearly designated limits as to what can and cannot be ascribed to unconscious intention (each case must be treated individually), the analyst is free to press for as inclusive an interpretation as he can supply by, for example, tracing specific imagery to universal unconscious fantasy, etc. Interpretations of this sort cannot be falsified or refuted by recourse to the sorts of confirmatory evidence we would produce in the case of conscious intention. Hence, if we accept it, the concept of unconscious intention adds weight to the old Platonic claim that artists do not stand in any privileged position with respect to the criticism of their own works, while at the same time it supports the intentionalist doctrine. I do not think, however, that psychoanalysis can bolster the intentionalist cause in any other sense than in thus expanding the kinds of intention we may expect to find embodied in works of art. For if, with Wimsatt and Beardsley, we are prone to rule out as critically irrelevant all external evidence of artistic intention, we will be even less apt to be convinced by descriptions of hidden or disguised intention than by that which is openly avowed. On the other hand, Wimsatt and Beardsley's position may be reconciled with other psychoanalytic approaches to art—beyond pathography—which lie outside the scope of this paper.

In the case of expressionism, however, psychoanalysis has perhaps somewhat more to offer. The philosophers (Tormey, Kivy, etc.) who wish to deny simple or direct relations between what, for example, a piece of music expresses and the feeling-state of its composer are nevertheless willing to grant that *some* connection does exist. Psychoanalysis, by giving a complex account of intrapsychic processes, can contribute towards an understanding of the way in which an artist's changing moods, thoughts, and percepts are transformed in the process of creation into what finally emerges in the completed work of art.[17]

Ultimately, the debate turns on the ontological issue. Is the work of art to be seen as a psychic product, the infant-child of its parent-creator whose mind, whose fantasies, we must know in order rightly to fathom it? Or is the work of art to be viewed as semi-autonomous—even, for some critics and philosophers, fully autonomous—an artifact that can and should be judged for itself alone without external reference? Clearly, the pathographer takes the former stance and, although he does not claim exhaustive authority for his interpretations, he is reluctant to define limits for them. What the philosophers point out is that works of art are more than psychic products though they are certainly that. They exist in historical time; they partake of cultural traditions and technical conventions; they frequently outlive their creators and change in response to the new contexts that spring up around them; and they have in some sense a life of their own, a life that grows in part out of the mind of their creator but that may take on overlays of meaning and significance beyond what could ever have been intended either consciously or unconsciously by the artist who created them.

Thus, in conclusion, I suggest the following: although psycho-analytic criticism (pathography) has at least partially fulfilled its tacit promise to penetrate more deeply into the psyche than any previous approach, it seems clear that a serious dialogue with contemporary aesthetics can promise further refinements both of its goals (possibilities and limitations) and possibly even of its methodology. Therefore, it is in the best interests of both disciplines and of the humanities in general to foster this ongoing dialogue.

Notes

1 See Freud (1894) and Freud and Breuer (1893–95) in which the neurophysiological theory of the mind is presented with its concepts of repression, cathexis, mobile and bound energy, and the splitting of idea from affect. Shortly after this, Freud developed the notion that the repressed idea could be a fantasy rather than a memory and developed the technique of "free association" as opposed to "suggestion."

2 My examples of Romantic criticism will be drawn largely from English sources. My point here is not that Freud read these authors (he probably did not) but rather that we can analogize the interests and emphases of these writers with those of Freud. My effort is to draw a parallel rather than merely to make a specifically historical statement.

3 Obviously for a psychoanalytic critic, these categories must somehow expand in meaning to include unconscious intention as well, e.g., the artist's unconscious wish to hide certain things from himself.

4 Apropos of these styles, we might also note the connection between the "stream of consciousness" novel and the psychoanalytic notion of "free association."

5 See Kris and Kurz (1979) for a fascinating excursion into this topic which traces its roots back to ancient history.

6 For Freud and Romanticism, see Trosman in Gedo and Pollock (1976, pp. 46–70).

7 Note also the views of other Romantic critics of the same period, especially Hazlitt, who compared poetry with dreams and even suggested that art may arise from a need to compensate for physical deformity: "Do you suppose we owe nothing to Pope's deformity? He said to himself, 'If my person be crooked, my verses shall be strait'" (in Abrams, 1953, p. 142).

Note further the following passage by De Quincey: "In very many subjective exercises . . . the problem before the writer is to project his own inner mind; to bring out consciously what yet lurks by involution in many unanalysed feelings; in short, to pass through a prism and radiate into distinct elements what previously had been even to himself but dim and confused ideas inter-mixed with each other" (in Abrams, 1953, p. 144).

8 To grasp the poet, one must undergo the poem. Note the convergence between this view and Kris's ideas of the progressive identifications in aesthetic experience.

9 Note Stuart Hampshire's (1966) argument against such a notion. Monroe Beardsley rebuts Hampshire on the grounds of what he calls "critical rationality" and "public semantic facts" that antecede interpretation in "The Testability of an Interpretation," 1970.

10 Freud deals with this issue of determinism and predictability in "The Psychogenesis of a Case of Homosexuality in a Woman" (1920), where he points out that although with hindsight the results always seem inevitable, the reverse is not obvious: ". . . in other words, from a knowledge of the premises we could not have foretold the nature of the result" (p. 167).

11 Beardsley describes what is admissible as evidence for interpretation of works of art in a later paper (1970): ". . . public semantic facts, the connotations and suggestions *in* poems, are the stubborn data with which the interpreter must come to terms . . ." (p. 382, my italics).

12 A classic example of this phenomenon is Freud's mistaking "vulture" for "kite" in Leonardo's report of his dream. Knowing the word was mistranslated cannot help but affect our attitude towards the interpretation. As Cioffi said, "There are cases in which we have an interpretation which satisfies us but which we feel *depends* on certain facts being the case" (1964, p. 311, my italics).

13 On the importance of context, see also B. Lang (1982, p. 411), where he points out that fundamental elements of style are *context-bound,* that they reveal themselves only by acting with and on other units within a (fluctuating) whole or context chosen by creator and then by audience.

14 Although I am not prepared to argue this point here, I would point out the relatively smaller numbers of pathographies of composers and musicians than of writers and artists. One noteworthy pathographer working in the area of music is Stuart Feder, however, and a list of his recent works is included in my references.

15 For a recent, interesting discussion of the way in which biographical knowledge about the composer *can* affect performance, see Rothstein (1983).

16 Bouwsma seemed to have understood this derivation too, for he says: "In art the world is born afresh, but the travail of the artist may have had its beginnings in children's play" (1954, p. 265).

17 For an excellent discussion of these issues, see Kris (1952, pp. 302–18).

References

Abrams, M. H. (1953). *The mirror and the lamp.* New York: Oxford University Press.

Beardsley, M. (1970). The testability of an interpretation. In J. Margolis (Ed.), *Philosophy looks at the arts.* Philadelphia: Temple University Press, 1978.

Bouwsma, O. K. (1954). The expression theory of art. In M. Philipson & P. J. Gudel (Eds.), *Aesthetics today.* New York: New American Library, 1980.

27 Cioffi, F. (1964). Intention and interpretation in criticism. In J. Margolis (Ed.), *Philosophy looks at the arts*. Philadelphia: Temple University Press, 1978.

Dutton, D. (1982). Why intentionalism won't go away. Paper read before the American Society for Aesthetics, 40th Annual Meeting, Banff, October 29, 1982.

Eliot, T. S. (1932). Hamlet. In *Selected essays, 1917–32*. London.

Feder, S. (1980). Decoration day: A boyhood memory of Charles Ives. *The Musical Quarterly*, 46(2): 234–261.

_____ (1978). Gustav Mahler, dying. *The International Review of Psychoanalysis*, 5: 125–148.

_____ (1980). Gustav Mahler um mitternacht. *The International Review of Psycho-analysis*, 7: 11–26.

_____ (1981). Gustav Mahler: The music of fratricide. *The International Review of Psycho-analysis*, 8: 257–284.

Freud, A. (1936). *The ego and the mechanisms of defense*. New York: International Universities Press, 1966.

Freud, S. (1894). The neuro-psychoses of defense. *S. E.*, 3: 43–68.

_____ (1907). Delusions and dreams in Jensen's "Gradiva." *S. E.*, 9: 3–95.

Freud, S. (1908). Creative writers and daydreaming. *S. E.*, 9: 141–53.

_____ (1910). Leonardo da Vinci and a memory of his childhood. *S. E.*, 11: 57–137.

_____ (1914a). The Moses of Michelangelo. *S. E.*, 13: 211–38.

_____ (1914b). On narcissism. *S. E.*, 14: 73–102.

_____ (1920). The psychogenesis of a case of homosexuality in a woman. *S. E.*, 18: 145–172.

_____ (1927). Fetishism. *S. E.*, 21: 149–157.

Freud, S. & Breuer, J. (1893–95). Studies on hysteria. *S. E.*, 2.

Gay, P. (1976). *Art and act*. New York: Harper & Row.

Hampshire, S. (1966). Types of interpretation. In W. E. Kennick (Ed.), *Art and philosophy*. New York: St. Martin's Press, 1979.

Hartmann, H. (1939). *Ego psychology and the problem of adaptation*. New York: International Universities Press, 1958.

Isenberg, A. (1944). Critical communication. In M. Mothersill, et al. (Eds.), *Aesethetics and the theory of criticism*. Chicago: University of Chicago Press, 1973.

Kivy, P. (1980). *The corded shell*. Princeton, NJ: Princeton University Press.

Kris, E. (1952). *Psychoanalytic explorations in art*. New York: International Universities Press.

Kris, E. & Kurz, O. (1979). *Legend, myth and magic in the image of the artist: A historical experiment*. New Haven & London: Yale University Press.

Lang, B. (1982). Looking for the styleme. *Critical Inquiry*, 9: 405–13.

Langer, S. (1953). *Feeling and form*. New York: Charles Scribner's Sons.

Liebert, R. (1982). Methodological issues in the psychoanalytic study of an artist. *Psychoanalysis and Contemporary Thought*, 5: 439–65.

Mill, J. S. (1833). What is poetry? In J. M. W. Gibbs (Ed.), *Early essays by John Stuart Mill*, London, 1897.

Rapaport, D. (1951). *Collected papers of David Rapaport*, M. Gill (Ed.). New York: Basic Books.

Rothstein, E. (1983). Discovering the Beethoven inside the monument. *New York Times* (Jan. 23), 2: 1–24.

Stern, L. (1980). On interpreting. *The Journal of Aesthetics and Art Criticism*, 39, 2: 119–29.

28   Tormey, A. (1971). Art and expression: A critique. In J. Margolis (Ed.), *Philosophy looks at the arts*. Philadelphia: Temple University Press, 1978.

Trosman, H. (1976). Freud's cultural background. In J. E. Gedo and G. Pollock (Eds.), *Freud: The fusion of science and humanism. Psychological Issues*, Monographs 34/35.

Waelder, R. (1965). *Psychoanalytic avenues to art*. New York: International Universities Press.

Wimsatt, W. K. & Beardsley, M. L. (1954). The intentional fallacy. In J. Margolis (Ed.), *Philosophy looks at the arts*. Philadelphia: Temple University Press, 1978.

Wordsworth, W. (1800). *Preface to the lyrical ballads*.

Steven Z.
Levine, Ph.D.

Monet, Fantasy, and Freud

Fig. 1. Claude Monet, *Water Lilies*. c. 1925. Oil on canvas, 51¼ × 79½". The Art Institute of Chicago, gift of Mrs. Harvey Kaplan. Photo courtesy of the Art Institute of Chicago.

After 30 years of largely unrewarded and much reviled labors within the art world of Paris, Claude Monet (1840–1926) finally saw the public triumph of his paintings in 1889. Several months before the retrospective exhibition which he shared with the sculptor Auguste Rodin and which consolidated the reputations of both artists, Monet was interviewed at length by a journalist for a widely circulating Paris newspaper. In response to a question concerning the painter's place of origin, the interviewer quoted Monet as affirming his Norman, and especially his maritime, sources: "I have remained faithful to that sea in front of which I grew up" (Geffroy, 1922, p. 7). Later interviews reiterate the crucial role of the sea in Monet's reminiscences of his childhood, but the key quotation for my purposes comes from the artist's friend and authorized biographer. Using the iterative voice of the imperfect, Geffroy has Monet make an extraordinary statement about the sea as though such had been his recurrent habit: "I would like, he used to say to me, to be always before or upon it, and when I should die to be buried in a buoy" (p. 5). Monet's terminal fantasy of permanently returning to his maternal maritime matrix confirms the lifelong fidelity of which he spoke in 1889; moreover, his letters repeatedly reaffirm it and his paintings continuously reenact it. In a forthcoming book I analyze Monet's relationship to the sea, and more generally to the physical phenomena and symbolic features associated with water, as it is reflected and refracted in the texts and pictures of Monet's art, life, and age.

The principal objects of my scrutiny are, of course, the paintings themselves. To be sure, these paintings are the artifacts of conscious craft and are not reducible to authorial intentions and cultural paradigms that will be supposed by some of my critics to hover in an indistinct zone of unconscious tendencies. Knowing that my method of analysis will not satisfy those who require the rehearsal of a series of irrefrangible connecting links between image and meaning, I nevertheless hope that others will be persuaded by the accretion of comparative material (letters, criticism, poems, paintings) around the core of Monet's art. Why does his art look as it does and what did his art mean to him and his contemporaries? And what might it mean to us? Monet is not here to answer these questions, and even if he were present his answers could not be other than partial, both biased and incomplete. His letters can help us form an opinion about what may have motivated and determined the shapes and subjects of his art, as can other writings that take up the same tropes and themes. These texts come from the writers who responded directly to Monet's paintings at the time of their exhibition and from writers, whether critics, poets, novelists, or psychologists, who did not. As I seek to show throughout my book, what articulates this textual and pictorial morass into a coherent body of thought is a preoccupation with the structures of reflection and repetition, or, to put it only somewhat metaphorically, with the legacy of Narcissus. From Ovid to Freud, then, by way of Monet, this story is yet another version of the individual's obsessive quest for the elusive and fragmented image of the self. And this paper is a fragment of that story.

*   *   *

It's terrifying what I see in my head.

—C. Monet (1864)

With more time before me I would be able to make and bring to fruition the beautiful things that I have in my head.

—C. Monet (1896)

One is no artist . . . if one doesn't carry a picture in one's head before executing it.

—C. Monet (1921)

Throughout Monet's long career, critical response to his art turned on the vexed issue of the relationship between the external world and the artist's interior vision: were Monet's paintings mundane transcriptions or dreamlike transfigurations? In *Monet and His Critics* (1976) I traced the fault lines of this interpretive dispute in the overlapping contours of numerous objectivistsubjectivist oppositions such as truth and dream, work and sketch, expression and impression, permanence and change. One of the most important distinguishing oppositions within this loose constellation of critical terms is reality and fantasy, and it is with respect to this crucial dyad that I have chosen the three utterances of the artist that precede this paragraph. Like that of his critics, Monet's own voluminous discourse may be read in terms of a precarious and shifting oscillation between the psychic demands, allures, and consequences of fantasy on the one hand, and on the other hand the practical deferrals, approximations, and compromises necessitated or facilitated by reality. The form of Monet's negotiation between demand and deferral is the work of art itself; not altogether external reality nor interior fantasy, the work of art is now assimilated to the objective pole, now to the subjective pole, by the variously worldly or withdrawn partisans in the debate. Within each alternative position there is the potential for positive as well as negative assessment of the appropriateness of Monet's alleged strategy. Not all critics, however, insist on the polarization of fantasy and reality, and some will seek out a conceptual model that is mediate to both.

For the purposes of this paper the coincidence of the critical debate with the emergence of a psychoanalytic theory of art and fantasy permits me to consider the degree to which the Freudian framework may help to organize our reading of this largely unself-conscious critical formation. In the generations before Freud the interior region of fantasy, reverie, and dream was the privileged terrain of Romantic and Symbolist artists (Ellenberger, 1970), and it would be surprising if the critics of the period around 1900 had not appropriated the analogy of daydreams and dreams in order to explicate Monet's pictures. Near the outset of Monet's career, Jules Castagnary, a well-known advocate of artistic naturalism, complained that the painter had left reality behind for pure idealism; Monet rendered "not the landscape, but the sensation produced by the landscape." In 1874 Castagnary used a series of highly charged terms in order to characterize what he took to be the dangerously irreal mental products of Monet and his Impressionist colleagues:

> From idealization to idealization they will arrive at that degree of romanticism without brake, where nature is no more than a pretext for reverie and where the imagination becomes impotent to formulate anything but personal, subjective fantasies without echo in general reason, because they are without control and possible verification in reality (Levine, 1976, pp. 16–17).

The ascription of fantasy continued to be made throughout Monet's career, but not always with the opprobrium implied by Castagnary and other veristic interpreters of Monet's paintings. If in 1887 Monet's own coworker Camille Pissarro declared the pictures "an incomprehensible fantasy" and in 1896 the minister of public instruction decried Monet's "fantasies in which he audaciously mocks the public," already in 1886 the widely read critic of *Le Figaro* praised the "charming" fantasy of Monet's seascapes and a decade later a Symbolist writer admired the *Cathedrals* as "almost fantastic" (Levine, 1976, pp. 71, 79, 202, 225). At the time of Monet's death a young art historian summed up the "fantasy" position as follows:

> One might say that a leaf interests him as much as or more than a dress, a dress more than a face. Thus begins to be manifest a sort of indifference in regard to the relative value of objects, an indifference that seems at the time of his beginnings to be a realist's submission to all the spots that affect his retina and which, by an imperceptible and logical evolution, will become a fantastic visionary authority that lends to things the aspects he wishes them to have (Levine, 1976, p. 409).

Between 1909 and 1927, Louis Gillet, art historian, musicologist, museum curator, and French academician, developed a sophisticated defense of the artist's "realm of fantasy" which we will consider in detail. As we will see, Gillet's discourse of fantasy bears remarkable similarities to that of Freud.

Gillet's article of 1909 is an account of the "subjectivism" of Monet's art. Gillet wrote of the pictures as a substitution for the natural world that is also its negation: "Never has a painter more resolutely denied matter." The canvas is a screen for projections of Monet's "interior spectacle," states of his sensibility, "mirages that have no existence but in himself." Monet's affect before nature is said to be indifferent and apathetic; his cognitive position is that of the extreme skeptic who knows only his own experience of a world that inevitably eludes possession. In the face of "universal nothingness,"

> the world is no more than evanescence and fantasmagoria: something suspect, uncertain, ephemeral and sparkling, an empire of nacre and opal, a world of gleams and apparitions. There is nothing more inconsistent and fugitive, nothing more audacious and intoxicating than this absolute nihilism that takes refuge in pure art and creates for itself in the imaginary a realm of fantasy, where, like the nuance of the neck of a dove, the jewel-box of dreams of the *Thousand and One Days* passes by (1909, p. 409).

Here Gillet's daytime transformation of "thousand and one nights" wittily relates the paintings to waking fantasy rather than the dreams of sleep.

Gillet's description refers to Monet's *Haystacks, Poplars,* and *Cathedrals,* pictures more than a decade old in 1909. Although overawed by their willful negation of reality, the critic concluded that "as fantasies, reality is always there to belie and compromise all." An irreducible "debris of form" remains behind in spite of Monet's desperate dematerialization of the world. The obduracy of objects and the materiality of paint together defeat the fantasmatic effort in the name of a reality that will not be suppressed. But Gillet was not here proclaiming the ineluctable triumph of reality over fantasy, for in the recent *Water Lilies* the critic found the natural equivalent to Monet's immaterial derealization of the objective world.

In front of the displayed series of 48 pictures of the watergarden at Giverny, Gillet saw "a painting without bounds, a liquid sheet, a glass without frame": "There is no more here than the play of the imaginary faculties, the simple combination of forms for pleasure in the category of art." Subjective play and pleasure rather than objective presence and possession constitute the paradigm of art, an art in which the fantasy of limitless extension displaces the centered complacency of the objectivist cognition of the discrete world of things. Even the artist's solid self is subverted in this flux of reflections and projections; insisting on the Nietzschean principle of *Allzumenschliches* (all-too-humanness), Gillet conferred on Monet the poetic intuition of the German philosopher's radical epistemological doubt. Of the *Water Lilies* Gillet wrote,

> in front of these motifs of unlimited fantasy one smiles at the good nature of the naive Aryan, always persuaded that man is the center of things. What lack of discretion, of true education! How much better company are effacement, Oriental impersonality! Water and reflections, an exchange of imponderables across fluids, the play of the ether and the wave glimpsed one through the other, a tangling up of slight errors, shadows playing on a mirror, what spectacle more worthy of the mortals that we are (p. 412).

For Gillet, then, the interior spectacle of fantasy was the distinctive feature of the mortal condition, and the externalization of fantasy in art takes on the consoling and redemptive character of self-conscious philosophy. Moreover, Gillet's understanding of the individual's ec-centricity to the world anticipates Freud's later presentation of the three cosmological, biological, and philosophico-psychological blows to human narcissism which expel us from the center of all things and even from the full mastery of our own minds (Freud, 1917).

The demystifying "Nietzscheanism" of psychoanalysis has often been pointed out, not leastwise by Freud himself (1914c). Whatever Freudian flavor there may be in Gillet's text is thus most likely attributable to an affinity of thought rather than any precise influence, for indeed in 1909 Freud was still very little known in France (Régis & Hesnard, 1914). Synchronism is the merest scholarly pretext for the juxtaposition of Monet, Gillet, and Freud *circa* 1910, but perhaps the common link to Nietzsche will redeem the transition to Freud that I will now make.

Freud's first major paper on these matters is "Creative Writers and Day-Dreaming" (1908 [1907]). Subsequent contributions recast this early formulation in the terms of the revised metapsychology, but Freud retained the core of his argument intact and applied it as well to artists other than writers. Here Freud correlated the adult's activity of art with the child's activity of play and proposed that the mediating mechanism within this developmental series is the making of fantasy:

> The creative writer does the same as the child at play. He creates a world of phantasy which he takes very seriously— that is, which he invests with large amounts of emotion, while separating it sharply from reality (1908 [1907], p. 144).

Reality comes into the story not merely as the outside limit of the work of art; reality has also been a precipitating factor in the genesis of the work, for "every single phantasy is the fulfillment of a wish, a correction of unsatisfying reality." Here we may begin to consider the critical understanding of Monet's art as a repudiation of reality and a celebration of fantasy in relation to the dynamic concept of the wish. For Freud, in 1908, the wishes that might have impelled Monet to improve upon unsatisfactory reality by way of fantasy derived from ambitious or erotic motives. (As an example of the fusion of these trends Freud cited the many altarpieces in which "the portrait of the donor is to be seen in a corner of the picture," the ambition of self-exaltation being here coupled with a component of erotic adoration.) Freud stressed that as far as the artist is concerned the wish is not a timeless stereotype but is triply marked by the present, past, and future periods of the individual's life-history and trajectory:

> A strong experience in the present awakens in the creative writer a memory of an earlier experience (usually belonging to his childhood) from which there now proceeds a wish which finds its fulfillment in the creative work. The work itself exhibits elements of the recent provoking occasion as well as of the old memory (1908 [1907], p. 151).

According to this scenario, the work also represents the future fulfillment of the wish.

A passage from *The Interpretation of Dreams* (1900) further illuminates the present context. There Freud associated fantasies, daydreams, and hysterical symptoms inasmuch as they are all erected upon a substrate of childhood memories. In order to illustrate the point Freud made characteristic use of an arthistorical analogy. Fantasies, Freud claimed,

> stand in much the same relation to the childhood memories from which they are derived as do some of the Baroque palaces of Rome to the ancient ruins whose pavements and columns have provided the material for the more recent structures (1900, p. 492).

Not only then do Monet's fantasies enclose a past history of desire within a present perception, Monet's paintings themselves constitute in their very structure a fantasylike reelaboration, or "secondary revision," of art-historical forms of the past. Although Freud nowhere pursued the implications of his analogy, just such a move is at the center of Richard Kuhns's *Psychoanalytic Theory of Art* (1983).

Unlike the child's play, the artist's wishful fantasy is addressed to an audience and enrobed in a medium. Given the often shameful nature of the ambitious or erotic wish, the public's acceptance of the fantasy must depend on the overcoming of its feelings of repulsion by way of what Freud at this time could only call the artist's "innermost secret":

> The writer softens the character of his egoistic day-dreams by altering and disguising it, and he bribes us by the purely formal—that is, aesthetic—yield of pleasure which he offers us in the presentation of his phantasies (1908 [1907], p. 153).

Freud had previously developed this notion of an aesthetic bribe, or "incentive bonus," in his book on jokes (1905a); although it provides an explanation for the willing seduction of a responsive spectator such as Gillet, so that in front of Monet's paintings he too can enjoy his own daydreams "without reproach or shame," the doctrine of the formal bribe fails to explain the equally persistent resistance to the work by other beholders. For example, the distinguished critic of the *Gazette des Beaux-Arts,* Roger Marx, was initially put off by what he saw as Monet's unbridled egotism. Of the *Water Lilies* he wrote,

> There is here an affirmation of authority and independence, a supremacy of the ego [*moi*], which offends our vanity and humiliates our pride. M. Claude Monet has no care but to satisfy himself; . . . such are the ends, egotistical in appearance, of his art, and it is fitting that everything is subordinated to them (Levine, 1976, pp. 307–308).

In the last phrase the writer acknowledged the aesthetic gain entailed by the acceptance of the forms of the artist's egotism, but many other beholders do not. Indeed, it was not until some while after the period of Freud's early writings that psychoanalytic theory developed a solution to the problem of a viewer's indignant resistance to the formal blandishments of a self-displaying art such as that of Monet (Fairbairn, 1938–39).

In the *Five Lectures on Psycho-Analysis* delivered at Clark University (1910a [1909]), Freud generalized the gist of his paper on "Creative Writers and Day-Dreaming." As a result of "the high standards of our civilization and under the pressure of our internal repressions," Freud argued that we all turn to fantasy by way of compensation for an unsatisfactory reality. He sketched out three possible paths, those of the normal individual, the neurotic, and the artist:

> The energetic and successful man is one who succeeds by his efforts in turning his wishful phantasies into reality. Where this fails, as a result of the resistances of the external world and of the subject's own weakness, he begins to turn away from reality and withdraws into his more satisfying world of phantasy. . . . If the individual who is at loggerheads with reality possesses an *artistic gift* (a thing that is still a psychological mystery to us), he can transform his phantasies into artistic creations instead of into symptoms. In this manner he can escape the doom of neurosis and by this roundabout path regain his contact with reality (1910a [1909], p. 50).

In all three cases a transformation of fantasy is at stake, but the media of transformation vary. One takes the world and remolds it to suit his or her desires; another remolds the interior constellation of the self and through regression repeats in neurotic form the repressed infantile wish. The artist is clearly a special type, for although the remodeling of the world proves to be unviable, there is no converse fall into neurotic illness. Yet much remains unclear concerning just how it is that artistic creativity manages to stave off regressive neurotic symptoms and reestablish productive links with that reality that endures beyond fantasy's embrace.

Leonardo da Vinci and a Memory of His Childhood (1910b) represents Freud's attempt to apply the model of wish-fulfilling fantasy to a particular art-historical case. Much has been written about this important text that need not concern us here (Farrell, 1963, offers the best introduction to the notorious subject of Leonardo's "memory" of the vulture-kite). Of particular interest to the art-historical biographer beyond the empirical specificities of Freud's account is the manner in which an apparent childhood memory of the mature artist is translated into a fantasy "which he formed at a later date and transposed to his childhood" (1910b, p. 82). Underlying this fundamental Freudian transformation is the abandonment of the theory of infantile seduction—still a topic of intense controversy in object-relations theory today—and its replacement by the interlocking notions of infantile sexuality, the Oedipus complex (first named in 1910), and unconscious fantasy. Although rooted in the clinical treatment of hysterical symptoms, the heuristic mechanism of fantasy is also elaborated by way of analogy with the allegedly historical recollections of nations. Thus, apropos of Leonardo, Freud wrote that "the memories he has of his childhood correspond, as far as their origins and reliability are concerned, to the history of a nation's earliest days, which was compiled later and for tendentious reasons" (p. 84). It is for this reason that great interpretive care must be exercised with respect to the retrospective recollections of Monet's childhood which were increasingly published in interviews with the artist from 1900 on. Monet recalled a ferociously unsupportive father and insufficiently nurturing mother, but rather than consider these problematic utterances of memory/fantasy here, I will continue to focus on the understanding of Monet's art as fantasy on the part of his critics. How did they use the concept and how might we?

In *Leonardo* Freud tentatively suggested an interpretation of the artist's later works as fantasies. In this respect he was very cautious:

> Kindly nature has given the artist the ability to express his most secret mental impulses, which are hidden even from himself, by means of the works that he creates. . . . Yet if one considers the profound transformations through which an impression in an artist's life has to pass before it is allowed to make its contribution to a work of art, one will be bound to keep any claim to certainty in one's demonstration within very modest limits (p. 107).

Later Freud confessed that he might merely have written "a psychoanalytic novel"—in other words, a fantasy of his own—but his findings are all the more interesting for the responsibility he took in relation to the projective, transferential lenses through which we cannot help but regard the world.

Having adduced from the so-called vulture memory or fantasy of the bird's tail being beaten about in the child's mouth a veiled reminiscence of sucking at the breast; and having discerned an iconographical correlate to this regressive oral fantasy in the form of Mona Lisa's smile and the subsequent and similar smiles of St. Anne, the Virgin, Leda, John the Baptist, and Bacchus, Freud concluded his discussion of Leonardo's art with a sentence that belies the reductionist implications of the model of the daydream-like release of pent-up psychological tension. In this sentence Freud also anticipated the nonregressive and sublimatory role of the ego-ideal which would explicitly appear in his writings in the paper on narcissism (1914b) before taking its place as the super-ego in *The Ego and the Id* (1923). Here then is the sentence that I have deferred quoting for a bit, because of my sense of its importance for the post-Freudian, and especially Kleinian (i.e., reparative), psychoanalytic theory of art:

> These pictures breathe a mystical air into whose secret one dares not penetrate; at the very most one can attempt to establish their connection with Leonardo's earlier creations. . . . It is possible that in these figures Leonardo has denied the unhappiness of his erotic life and has triumphed over it in his art, by representing the wishes of the boy, infatuated with his mother, as fulfilled in this blissful union of the male and female natures (1910b, pp. 117–118).

There is much to remark here, including the assumption of psychological bisexuality which Freud shared with both Fliess and Jung. What is especially interesting to me in the light of Gillet's insistence on the mechanism of denial in Monet's art is Freud's hint (indeed, if it is that) of a kind of therapeutic achievement in art that is unlike the regressive flight of neurotic denial and yet unlike, too, the working through and de-cathecting of the re-pressed affect that is the ostensible goal of psychoanalysis itself. Leonardo's triumph is precisely nowhere but in his art, nowhere but in the forms of his figures' smiles, and the fact of this triumph is not reducible to the fantasmatic release of libidinal frustration (Ricoeur, 1970).

A curious coincidence encourages me to link Leonardo's Freudi-an smile with Monet in 1910. In honor of Monet's 70th birthday Geffroy published a reminiscence in which he recalled with special pleasure a landscape painting of the Seine that Monet had once given the poet Mallarmé. The river view was a mere decorative meander, an aquatic arabesque "which Mallarmé used to compare to the smile of the *Mona Lisa*" (reprinted in Geffroy, 1922, p. 323). If in Leonardo's repeated smiles Freud had seen the artistic materialization of a repressed residue of early oral bliss, we may also choose to see, along with Mallarmé perhaps, an embedded erotic fantasy in Monet's most often repeated motif of reflections along the Seine. The meanings of this motif comprise the main matter of my forthcoming book; the painting in question, dated 1884, is number 912 in the catalogue of Monet's works (Wilden-stein, 1979a).

To return to Freud. At play in the texts *circa* 1910 is the controversy over the relative roles of reality and fantasy in the etiology of psychic productions ranging from neurotic symptoms to dreams, daydreams, and works of art. In 1911 Alfred Adler seceded from the psychoanalytic movement because of his empha-sis on the origin of individual neurosis in social reality rather than in intrapsychic conflict (Ellenberg, 1970). Freud's paper "Two Principles in Mental Functioning" (1911) may be read as a polemical riposte to Adler, but it is also important in the present context for its formulation of a metapsychological account of the functioning of fantasy in art. Freud imagined that the individual is originally governed solely by the tendency to gratify his or her inner needs, i.e., to gain pleasure and avoid pain; this is according-ly known as the pleasure-principle. As long as the individual is positioned vis-à-vis reality so that all needs are instantaneously gratified there is no apparent necessity for an appreciation of reality as something separate and apart. When, however, disap-pointment intervenes through deferred, defective, or deficient gratification, a new mental principle comes to be developed by which reality is recognized as the alternative bearer of pleasure and unpleasure alike. As a result of this reality-principle, then, Freud postulated the differentiation of the faculties of con-sciousness, memory, and thought.

But the recognition of reality does not render the drive for pleasure obsolete. Here is where play, fantasy, and art come in:

With the introduction of the reality-principle one species of thought-activity was split off; it was kept free from reality-testing and remained subordinated to the pleasure-principle alone. This activity is *phantasying,* which begins already in children's play, and later, continued as *day-dreaming,* abandons dependence on real objects (1911, p. 222).

The fantasy of self-sufficient independence from objects in the real world must be given up if the self-preservative instincts of the nascent ego are to thrive. On the other hand, fantasy continues to flourish with respect to sexuality; there the pleasure-principle may operate auto-erotically, free of the painful unreliability of object-dependence. Fantasy and sexuality thus develop hand in hand, and art retains much of this libidinal quotient in Freud's view.

In 1908 it was Freud's hypothesis that "a piece of creative writing, like a day-dream, is a continuation of, and a substitute for, what was once the play of childhood" (1908 [1907], p. 152); in 1911 he provided for the first time a theoretical picture of the dynamic forces whose continuous distribution and redistribution constitute the inner stuff of mental life. Art is once again of special interest to Freud for it illustrates the application of his theories beyond the restricted realm of the psychoneuroses, and thus tends to make good his claims for psychoanalysis as a general psychology of mind:

> *Art* brings about a reconciliation between the two principles in a peculiar way. An artist is originally a man who turns away from reality because he cannot come to terms with the renunciation of instinctual satisfaction which it at first demands, and who allows his erotic and ambitious wishes full play in the life of phantasy. He finds the way back to reality, however, from this world of phantasy by making use of special gifts to mould his phantasies into truths of a new kind, which are valued by men as precious reflections of reality (1911, p. 224).

In terms of the later metapsychology, what we see Freud doing is moving from the id-psychology of libidinal release to the ego-psychology that is perhaps first announced in the notion of Leonardo's artistic triumph. The spectator no longer needs to be bribed into permitting the shameful display of erotic and ambitious fantasy under the "disguise" of aesthetic form. Repressed infantile wishes are now complemented by mature judgment concerning the value of art as a reflection of reality. But this is still not Adler's social reality. This is the reality of an intrapsychic mode of thought, a reality that never ceases to be a projection, a reflection. And it is because this reality—the product of the dissatisfying displacement of the pleasure-principle—is itself "a part of reality" that spectators may share in the artist's triumph:

> Thus in a certain fashion he actually becomes the hero, the king, the creator, or the favourite he desired to be, without following the long roundabout path of making real alterations in the external world (1911, p. 224).

In 1908 art is seen as a substitute for children's games and adult fantasies; it is a mode of escape from reality. In 1911, on the contrary, art is a way of return. Freud's oscillation on this issue is continued in his essay "Animism, Magic, and the Omnipotence of Thoughts" in *Totem and Taboo* (1912–13). Here Freud emphasized the pole of fantasy at the expense of the emphasis on reality of just a year or two before:

> In only a single field of our civilization has the omnipotence of thoughts been retained, and that is in the field of art. Only in art does it still happen that a man who is consumed by desires performs something resembling the accomplishment of those desires and that what he does in play produces emotional effects—thanks to artistic illusion—just as though it were something real (p. 90).

In introducing illusion here Freud muddied the waters of formal beauty which had been seen as the spectator's vital "incentive bonus" in the period 1905–1908. It is now illusion that commands the acquiescence of the beholder in the power of the work, and it is precisely with respect to the dispute over formal *versus* illusionistic criteria that Monet's art had always risen and fallen. Form and illusion correspond to the libidinal bribery of the pleasure-principle and the objectivist judgment of the reality-principle; so far it seems that Freud cannot coherently account for the appeal and disappeal of an art such as Monet's to its disparate beholders, but he does consistently proclaim that it is desire, play, fantasy, and omnipotence of thought that characterize the internal relationship of the artist to the work.

This trend in Freud's theory of art is further continued in his first paper translated into French, "The Claims of Psycho-Analysis to Scientific Interest" (1913). Art is now said to be "an activity intended to allay ungratified wishes—in the first place in the creative artist himself and subsequently in his audience or spectators." In this account Freud amalgamated the pleasure and reality principles that receive correspondingly greater emphasis in the two scenarios of "Creative Writers and Day-Dreaming" and *Totem and Taboo*. To begin, Freud claimed that the artist "represents his most personal wishful phantasies as fulfilled." This, however, will not suffice:

> they only become a work of art when they have undergone a transformation which softens what is offensive in them, conceals their personal origin and, by obeying the laws of beauty, bribes other people with a bonus of pleasure (1913, p. 187).

This is a near-repetition of the text of 1908; in 1913, however, the interests of the reality-testing ego are acknowledged alongside those of the pleasure-ego of the earlier metapsychology. Accordingly, art is now seen as:

a conventionally accepted reality in which, thanks to artistic illusion, symbols and substitutes are able to provoke real emotions. Thus art constitutes a region halfway between a reality which frustrates wishes and the wish-fulfilling world of the imagination—a region in which, as it were, primitive man's strivings for omnipotence are still in full force (p. 188).

This, also, is a near-repetition of a prior text, but in distinction to the parallel passage in *Totem and Taboo,* Freud here for the first time explicitly related symbols to works of art. The pictorial aspect of dream-symbolism which is known under the rubric of "considerations of representability" is of course for Freud one of the distinguishing features of dream-work. A certain understanding of pictorial semiotics on Freud's part thus may be said to underlie the entire apparatus of dream-interpretation and the theory of the unconscious which is its corollary and consequence, but it was not until this paper of 1913 that Freud hinted at the converse kinship between dreams and art. Freud appears to have confirmed this linkage in the following year (1914c, p. 36), but as he elsewhere insisted (1916–17, p. 166), not all symbols in literature and art function in the way that dream-symbols do. Nevertheless, in footnotes added to *Leonardo* in 1919 and 1923 Freud described the compositional fusion of the bodies of St. Anne and the Virgin in Leonardo's painting and cartoon as "badly condensed dream-figures" and "the dream-like fusion of the two women—a fusion corresponding to his childhood" (1910b, pp. 114–115). Freud's analogy of the syntax and symbolism of dreams provides yet another bridge to the discourse of art criticism in the decades around 1900.

In the 1890s a wave of Schopenhauerian idealism swept across intellectual life in Europe, and art criticism in France was no exception in registering this impact in the form of a pervasive discourse of mental representations. Freud frequently acknowledged the psychoanalytic prescience of Schopenhauer on such subjects as repression, sexuality, and death (1914c, 1933), and once again the quasi-Freudian flavor of much of the criticism of the period is to be attributed to a general interest in German idealist thought. Thus in 1892 one critic alluded to Schopenhauer's famous mentalist dicta in writing that "the world is as we create it." With respect to Monet this is taken to mean that his pictures are affectively laden symbols of a suprasensible realm (Platonic or Freudian?) rather than mere perceptual registrations of material reality:

Even these realities find themselves thereby suddenly transfigured into the ideal, lose their value as real sensorial notions in order suddenly to double themselves, by the fantasmagorical vision of the master, with a mysterious *meaning* which suddenly makes them take part in the symbolic universe dreamed by the poets (Levine, 1976, p. 151).

Even more than the philosophers, Freud frequently acknowledged the poets as his precursors in the discovery of the symbolic structures of psychic reality. Freud's last words in his last book, *An Outline of Psychoanalysis* (1940), seek support from Goethe for a claim concerning our putative phylogenetic inheritance of symbols in works of culture as well as dream-work; in so doing Freud repeated a central preoccupation of more than 40 years. Thus it is once again with a Freudian ear that I would have you listen, for example, to a critic in 1893 who progressively discovered behind the ostensible reality of Monet's *Haystacks* and *Poplars* an interior realm of symbol and dream (Levine, 1976, p. 175).

In 1909 Roger Marx imagined a dialogue in which Monet takes issue with the picture of a dreamlike artwork that I have sketched above. The critic himself had just concluded that Monet's *Water Lilies* "open up to the mind the world of the illusion and infinity of dream." This conforms to Freud's sense of the observer's second-order participation in the artist's fantasy, but Marx's Monet is made to speak out against this notion:

> What ideal demon torments you . . . and what good is it to tax me as a visionary? Is it thus to other-wordly fantasies [*féeries d'au-delà*] that have led that exaltation and ecstasy of senses through which my devotion to nature is translated, satisfied, and appeased? At any rate, do not attribute to me the roundabout paths of chimerical schemes. The truth is simpler; my only virtue resides in my submission to instinct; it is for having rediscovered my intuitive and secret forces and having permitted them to predominate that I have been able to identify myself with creation and absorb myself in her (Levine, 1976, p. 304).

The denial of fantasy by which Monet is here characterized merely begs a further question in the Freudian theory of art that unfortunately is nowhere treated in an adequate fashion. This is the question of identification, namely, of the intrapsychic process by which the particular artist chooses, indeed often repeatedly chooses, a particular segment of nature or repertory of images into which to project the repressed materials that have motivated the wish, the fantasy, and the work. To put it more simply, this is the question of narcissism, and this question has only begun to be adumbrated in the papers that we have so far considered.

Freud introduced the mythological figure of Narcissus in his discussion of Leonardo's alleged homosexuality. Freud imagined that Leonardo chose to love beautiful young boys by way of a process of identification with his mother who had loved him when he himself had been a beautiful young boy. Although Narcissus was "a youth who preferred his own reflection to everything else" (1910b, p. 100), this reflection had first appeared to him in his mother's loving gaze. Thus Freud's concept of narcissism is from the first a theory of intrapsychic identification or introjection, that is, a theory of the ego-ideal; it is also an interpersonal theory, that is, a theory of the object-relations that are undergone from childhood to adulthood which variously connect us to others and to the world. Marx's Monet may deny the conscious intention of projecting his fantasies and speak instead of mere identification and absorption in nature, but this is simply to resituate the work of fantasy from the external realm in which Marx encountered it as the viewer of the paintings to the internal realm of the narcissistic omnipotence of thoughts in which Freud placed the creative artist.

In *Leonardo* Narcissus is the metaphor of one artist's sexuality; in later papers, however, Narcissus may be seen as the figure of the artist as a type. In *Totem and Taboo* (1912–13) and in "A Difficulty in the Path of Psychoanalysis" (1917), Freud implicitly associated the narcissistic omnipotence of thoughts of primitive humans and children with the psychic overvaluation that is typical of both neurosis and art. Whereas, however, primitive society gradually shed its narcissistic animism through the development of religion and science, and whereas the child grows from narcissistic cathexis of its self to the cathexis of first parental and then nonparental objects, the narcissistic artist is able to maintain these phylogenetic and ontogenetic positions without incurring the painful regressions of neurosis. In spite of frequent disclaimers that the artist is not a neurotic, Freud's correlation of art and neurosis is nevertheless very close in both directions; in another passage in *Totem and Taboo* Freud hazarded the thought that "a case of hysteria is a caricature of a work of art" (1912–13, p. 73). This peculiar image has its origin in what Freud called the mimetic imagination of hysterics according to which an apparent, physical symptom is substituted for an invisible repressed wish (1919, p. 261).

Just as the reality-principle of 1911 may be seen in relation to the challenge of the sociologically oriented individual psychology of Adler, so too the famous formulation of "On Narcissism" (1914b) is at least in part a reply to the schismatic analytic psychology of Jung. In response to Jung's desexualization of the libido and its reconceptualization as an all-pervasive life force, Freud not only reaffirmed the determinative role of sexuality in the etiology of the psychoneuroses (and art) but also sexualized the hitherto separate ego-instincts as well. Unlike the usage in *Leonardo* where narcissism is related to homosexuality, in 1914 narcissism is understood as "the libidinal complement to the egoism of the instinct of self-preservation, a measure of which may justifiably be attributed to every living creature" (pp. 73–74). Adapting a central Jungian concept to his own libido theory, Freud insisted that the hysterical cathexis of objects in fantasy is the only phenomenon properly described as introversion, whereas narcissism would denote the withdrawal of libido from objects altogether—whether in reality or in fantasy—and the consequent re-cathexis of the ego as its own object.

Freud called this form of pathology "secondary narcissism," the regressive recrudescence of the normal "primary narcissism" of early childhood. But narcissism finds a place in the dynamics of the normal adult in the form of an introjected ideal:

This ideal ego is now the target of the self-love which was enjoyed in childhood by the actual ego. . . . What he projects before him as his ideal is the substitute for the lost narcissism of his childhood in which he was his own ideal (p. 94).

Freud related this process of idealization within the ego to instinctual sublimation, a socially acceptable rechanneling of erotic or ambitious drives that he had earlier compared to artistic activity. In *Leonardo,* however, prior to the development of the full concept of narcissism, sublimation is not linked to trends in the ego but rather to the libidinal vicissitudes described in *Three Essays on the Theory of Sexuality* (1905b). Thus, it is in "The Moses of Michelangelo" (1914a) that we find Freud's most notable effort to incorporate into his theory of art the new metapsychological notions of narcissism and the ego-ideal.

In front of Michelangelo's *Moses* Freud adopted the attitude of the psychoanalyst to whom no manifestation of the psyche is without meaning. The interpretation of the work of art is here likened to that of the dream. Without wishing to rehearse Freud's complicated (and, in particular details, probably erroneous) argument, I will simply indicate that the sculpture is seen as a sublimation of narcissistic trends rather than object-libido, "a concrete expression of the highest mental achievement that is possible in a man, that of struggling successfully against an inward passion for the sake of a cause to which he had devoted himself" (1914a, p. 233):

And so he carved his Moses on the Pope's tomb, not without a reproach against the dead pontiff, as a warning to himself, thus, in self-criticism, rising superior to his own nature (p. 234).

The self-superiority of self-criticism is what Freud later codified as the introjected function of the superego. In addition to the recognition of the importance of the artist's inner objects—a concern that was subsequently developed by Klein (1929) and Kohut (1980)—there is a great deal of self-projection, of personal fantasy, in Freud's portrayal of Michelangelo; for this reason perhaps, Freud was very tentative in presenting his findings, which he first published anonymously. Nevertheless, his interpretive rigor is exemplary:

But what if . . . [we] have strayed on to a wrong path? What if we have taken too serious and profound a view of details which were nothing to the artist, details which he had introduced quite arbitrarily or for some purely formal reasons with no hidden intention behind? What if we have shared the fate of so many interpreters who have thought to see quite clearly things which the artist did not intend either consciously or unconsciously? I cannot tell (1914a, pp. 235–236).

Perhaps Freud could not tell because in 1914 his economic theory of art and fantasy as libidinal release was in disarray. The old separation of ego and libido that had served him in "Creative Writers and Day-Dreaming" and *Leonardo* had become fused in the concept of narcissism, but as yet no new dualism of drive had been formulated to explain psychic conflict. The new antagonist of libido or Eros, the so-called death instinct, was only incorporated into the metapsychology after 1920, but already in "Moses" we may glimpse the role that the inner agency of self-criticism and the trend of sublimated aggression would play in the later psycho-analytic theory of art. (As a parenthetic aside I would add that in my view it is the expression of aggression in Monet's art which explains, perhaps even more than sexuality, the resistance which so many beholders have continued to experience upon viewing the palpably mauled material substances of his art.)

In 1917 Freud produced his most elaborate theoretical treatment of art. This came at the end of the chapter on symptom-formation in the *Introductory Lectures on Psychoanalysis* (1916–17) in which Freud recapitulated and extended his theory of fantasy. Although reminiscent of the papers of 1908–13 that I have already discussed, the new discussion benefits from a more concise exposition and also introduces material on "primal" fantasies of both a sexual and aggressive nature that will serve as the theoretical basis for the development of Kleinian aesthetics in the later 1920s. But for Freud in 1917 the role of aggression in art still remained not much more than a veiled hint. For example, the category of megalomanic wish was now added to the earlier ones of ambition and eroticism.

For Freud, fantasy was the redemptive core of daily experience. In fantasy, "human beings continue to enjoy the freedom from external compulsion which they have long since renounced in reality" (1916–17, p. 372). This freedom from necessity—*Ananke,* as he called it—may take the form of daydreams, night-dreams, or neurotic symptoms. Freud once again referred to Jung's concept of introversion in order to distinguish healthy fantasy from mental illness:

> We will continue to take it that introversion denotes the turning away of the libido from the possibilities of real satisfaction and the hypercathexis of phantasies which have hitherto been tolerated as innocent. An introvert is not yet a neurotic, but he is in an unstable situation: he is sure to develop symptoms at the next shift of forces, unless he finds some other outlets for his dammed-up libido (p. 374).

And as one may have expected, for Freud the path that led from fantasy not to neurosis but back to reality was the path of art.

Here, then, is Freud's most extended passage on the personality and creative processes of the artist:

> An artist is . . . in rudiments an introvert, not far removed from neurosis. . . . Like any other unsatisfied man, he turns

away from reality and transfers all his interest, and his libido too, to the wishful constructions of his life of phantasy, whence the path might lead to neurosis. . . . An artist, however, finds a path back to reality in the following manner. . . . In the first place, he understands how to work over his day-dreams in such a way as to make them lose what is too personal about them and repels strangers, and to make it possible for others to share in the enjoyment of them. He understands, too, how to tone them down so that they do not easily betray their origin from proscribed sources. Furthermore, he possesses the mysterious power of shaping some particular material until it has become a faithful image of his phantasy; and he knows, moreover, how to link so large a yield of pleasure to this representation of his unconscious phantasy that, for the time being at least, repressions are outweighed and lifted by it (1916–17, p. 376).

In comparison to earlier formulations Freud here insisted on the energic or economic considerations that permit the artist to escape neurosis through a process of "working over" the unconscious fantasy. This recalls the important technical paper on psychotherapy with the title "Remembering, Repeating and Working-Through" (1914d). Although the psychic nature of the artistic process is stressed, Freud did not neglect the institutional aspects of art as so many commentators have alleged. The artist after all makes something real, and it is only in the interpersonal arena of artist and audience that this achievement is possible:

If he is able to accomplish all this, he makes it possible for other people once more to derive consolation and alleviation from their own sources of pleasure in their unconscious which have become inaccessible to them; he earns their gratitude and admiration and he has thus achieved *through* his phantasy what originally he had achieved only *in* his phantasy—honour, power and the love of women (pp. 376–377).

The particular goals that Freud specified may not strike us as sufficiently comprehensive to fit the implications of the theory, but we are now in a considerably stronger position to understand the artist than when we merely attended to the work of art as a formal bribe in the aim of libidinal release.

That motives other than pleasure may be at stake in the work of art becomes apparent in 1920 in Freud's most far-reaching revision of his metapsychology to date. In *Beyond the Pleasure Principle* (1920) Freud postulated the existence of a regressive trend to repeat, even compulsively and unpleasurably, a prior action or state of existence. His examples of compulsive repetition are traumatic dreams and certain anxiety-filled children's games; taken to its extreme in the so-called Nirvana principle, the repetition-compulsion reconstitutes the quiescence and animation of the earliest infantile, intra-uterine, and even (!) pre-uterine states prior to the irritations and exacerbations of life. The final term in this narcissistic withdrawal of affect is death. As Freud wrote, "we have unwittingly steered our own course into the harbour of Schopenhauer's philosophy" (pp. 49–50), and indeed here metapsychology joins metaphysics. How unwitting this was I cannot tell, but for me I can add that for the purposes of this paper we have now steered our course into the aqueous realm of Monet's nihilistic fantasy of self-dissolution as preserved in the form of the oceanic fantasy recorded by Geffroy in 1922, in the Nietzschean and Schopenhauerian discourse of his critics, and in the void and limitless extension and dispersion of the monumental *Water Lilies* of *circa* 1920–26.

As Eros seeks out stimulation and conjugation, the death instinct seeks out enervation, isolation, annihilation. However, just as the phenomenon of narcissism had convinced Freud of the inseparability of ego and libido, so too the repetitions of art and children's play convinced the later Freud of the fusion of the instincts of life and death. Here "the compulsion to repeat and instinctual satisfaction which is immediately pleasurable seem to converge . . . into an intimate partnership" (1920, p. 23). An implicit recollection of Aristotelian catharsis and the Kantian sublime allowed Freud to maintain that art does not necessarily spare the spectators "the most painful experiences and can yet be felt by them as highly enjoyable" (p. 17). Melanie Klein and not Freud was shortly to pursue this notion of reparative pleasure born of dissociative pain, but here in Freud's text we may glimpse the initial elements of a super-ego or restorative theory of art.

In 1922 Geffroy published his massive biography of Monet with a reproduction of the artist's self-portrait of 1917 or 1918 on the cover. Monet wrote that he smiled on seeing the photographic proofs of his portrait (1922), the lone bodily self-representation to survive the lacerations and incinerations that annihilated other contemporaneous painted reflections of himself. Monet's great friend Georges Clemenceau, the wartime prime minister of France, saved this one self-portrait from destruction, later bequeathing it to the Louvre and commenting upon it at length in his book on the artist. In a chapter of my forthcoming book entitled "Monet, Narcissus, and Self-Reflection" I deal further with the psychology and iconography of this portrait in which Monet is seen by his intimate friend as in the grips of an "inner dream" (Clemenceau, 1928, p. 26).

From 1889 to 1926 the dream was a familiar metaphor in the description of Monet's art. "It's his dream of light," "his dream that he deciphers along the banks of the Seine," Geffroy had written earlier (1895); and in the 1922 biography many of his and his colleagues' dream and daydream analogies of the preceding 30 years are interspersed throughout the text.

Geffroy's final chapter is called "Last Reverie Before the Water-Garden." If this is meant to indicate the daydream of the artist, it is the critic's fantasy as well. Monet is described in the pantheistic and even Buddhist position of adoring contemplation, and yet the critic also speaks of the painter's self-obstination, self-hypnosis, anxiety, and torment. The compulsive repetition of Monet's artistic bouts with extension and reflection recalls not only the psychic mechanism of *Beyond the Pleasure Principle* but also its psychic goal. Geffroy was at particular pains to combat the ingrained notion that Monet's art was unreflective, spontaneous, and improvised. On the contrary,

> this man was in reality . . . a perpetually anxious person, a daily tormented person, at the same time a solitary person with an *idée fixe,* racking his brains into exhaustion, forcing his will to the fixed and desired task, pursuing his dream of form and color almost unto the annihilation of his individuality in the eternal nirvana of things at once changing and immutable. This endless measure of his dream and of the dream of life he formulated, reprised, and formulated anew and without end in the mad dream of his art before the luminous abyss of the *Water Lilies* pool (1922, p. 335).

Geffroy's text is certainly a welter of fashionable ideas of the turn of the century. Neurasthenic exhaustion had been mentioned in connection to Monet as early as 1879 and most notably in reference to the artist's long-deferred exhibition of *Water Lilies* (Alexandre, 1909). The *idée-fixe*—mentioned by Monet himself in his private correspondence (1884)—is to be traced to the psychological works of Pierre Janet such as *Névroses et idées fixes* (1898), *Les Obsessions et la psychasthénie* (1903), and *Les Névroses* (1909; see Ellenberger, 1970). Nirvana and self-annihilation are artifacts of an orientalizing vogue that flourished around 1900 in the wake of Schopenhauerian idealism and the Nietzschean demystification of positive science. But Freud was a product of these cultural trends in psychology and philosophy as well, and his deathly economic principle of Nirvana offers an explanatory psychoanalytic framework for much that is groping yet insistent in the discourse of Monet's critics.

For Freud, Nirvana was the homeostatic principle of constancy according to which the human organism tends to the reduction of stimuli. This is the pleasure-principle of 1911; but the postulation of the death-instinct forced Freud to recognize that the incremental stimulation of the organism in the repetitions of traumatic dreams, children's play, sexual foreplay, and artistic creativity points to a non-quantitative principle of psychic life. The object of the drives now comes to be more complexly differentiated. For example, projected outward, the death-instinct is manifest in aggression and sadism; directed inward it is apparent in melancholia and masochism. On the one hand we find Monet's obsessive reworking and undoing of his canvases; on the other hand we find an attendant hypochondria and depression. Nirvana's deathly pull is, however, everywhere contravened by a life-sustaining impulse from Eros in a dialectical series that is further modified by the exigencies of reality. In "The Economic Problem of Masochism" (1924) Freud reconsidered the complex fusions and de-fusions of the life and death instincts and found that the quantitative distribution of cathexis cannot adequately account for what is experienced as pleasurable or unpleasurable. We have seen that earlier Freud described the artistic disposition in terms of a quantitative deployment of counter-regressive cathexis (1916–17); now Freud introduced a qualitative consideration of rhythm and periodicity which for the first time permitted a tentative approach to the relative successes and failures of particular artworks in mobilizing pleasurable or unpleasurable affect in their beholders.

In 1909 Gillet entitled his article on Monet "The Epilogue of Impressionism"; 15 years later, on the occasion of a large retrospective exhibition of the painter's works, the critic published an essay called "The Testament of Impressionism" (1924). After the deaths of van Gogh, Seurat, Gauguin, Cézanne, Renoir, Rodin, and Degas, Monet had now come to seem as having outlived his age. Fauvism, Cubism, and Dada were yesterday's news, and still Monet was not dead. His monumental *Water Lilies* decorations were begun during the war after the deaths of his wife (1911) and eldest son (1914); more and more the projected mural paintings for the Orangerie came to be perceived as a living epitaph. Gillet seems to have understood the dialectical motives of archaic regression and ultimate restitution that were embodied in these final works:

> All his life M. Claude Monet has been a sort of genius of water. From his childhood passed at Le Havre, and from his first master Eugène Boudin, he retains a nostalgia for the water, a love for the liquid element, multiple and feminine, for that which slips, ripples, reflects, sparkles, ruffles, and becomes convulsed; river or ocean, he always adored the siren or the nymph (1924, pp. 669–670).

In erroneous anticipation of an installation that the painter continually deferred up until the moment of his death in 1926, Gillet expected that in but a few months from the time of writing Monet's "immense circle of dreams" would take on the tangible reality of an architectural environment. This tangibility would nevertheless be equivocal for in the paintings "the things of life exist no longer but in the state of images, of memories, on an irreal plane in funereal shades":

> It is, as one sees, the river of existence, all the dreams of childhood, of youth—of love, of death, the whole history of a soul. . . . (p. 672).

As Bruno Bettelheim (1982) has recently insisted, Freud's *Psychoanalyse* is the story of the soul; and for Freud, as for Gillet, the protagonists of that story are Love and Death.

Monet's paintings are his dreams of Love and Death, and in *An Autobiographical Study* (1925 [1924]), written in the same year as Gillet's 1924 article, Freud explicitly contrasted the work of art and the dream for the first time. Repeating a number of his prior metaphors, Freud recalled the papers of 1908 to 1917 in this final summary statement of his views on artists and art:

> The artist, like the neurotic, had withdrawn from an unsatisfying reality into [the] world of imagination but unlike the neurotic, he knew how to find a way back from it and once more get a firm foothold in reality. His creations, works of art, were the imaginary gratifications of unconscious wishes, just as dreams are; and like them they were in the nature of compromises, since they too were forced to avoid any open conflict with the force of repression (pp. 64–65).

Fantasies, dreams, and neurotic symptoms were all seen by Freud as compromise-formations that come about as a result of the conflict between unavoidable and unassuageable unconscious impulses (erotic or aggressive) that as of 1923 Freud assigned to the Id (the Nietzschean *Es*), and a repressive, censoring agency that Freud now called the *Über-Ich* or superego. Within the individual this is the introjected voice of parental or societal norm; within the artist, here we hear that tradition and convention speak. Therefore even in dreams there can be no purely private circuit of impulse and repression, yet Freud sharply distinguished between works of art and the other products of unconscious compromise. Works of art, then,

> differed from the asocial, narcissistic products of dreaming in that they were calculated to arouse interest in other people and were able to evoke and to gratify the same unconscious wishes in them too (p. 65).

In this passage Freud backed away from assigning art to the narcissistic omnipotence of thought of children, primitives, and neurotics as he had done in 1912–13, and redeemed narcissism for object-relations by stressing the sociality of the work of art in its human context of artist and audience. As though in an afterthought, Freud also recalled here the "incitement-premium" of formal beauty that harks back to his treatment of aesthetics in his 1905 book on jokes. The superego modification of the economics of drive-relief would appear in a later reconsideration of this subject in his paper "Humour" (1927b), at which point "the victorious assertion of the ego's invulnerability" would be called a "triumph of narcissism" (p. 162) and credited to the agency of the superego (Waelder, 1965).

Art is a manifestation of the artist's narcissism, but this solipsism is transcended by way of the artist's address to his or her audience. But the gratification of the audience is reciprocal to that of the artist and therefore we might expect Freud to have considered a regression to narcissistic fantasies of merger with the maternal environment as a phenomenon common to painter and beholder alike. Indeed, in *The Future of an Illusion* (1927a) Freud wrote that art also ministers to the "narcissistic satisfaction" of the viewer who identifies with the cultural ideals that are pictured in the work (p. 14). Freud thus gave us to understand that the fantasy of the artist which Monet's critics claim to discern in the work is none other than the shared cultural fantasy of the critics themselves.

One of these fantasies was Nirvana. According to a well-placed critic in 1927, Monet's friends habitually referred to Nirvana in order to sanction the artist's subjective vision (Levine, 1976, p. 411). The water lily or lotus was of course a sacred symbol in the East, and Monet's self-immersion and self-immolation in the world of limitless flux was undoubtedly consciously thought of in terms of Oriental philosophy rather than Freudian psychology. But the self-object symbiosis, fusion, and ego-obliteration of primary narcissism are parsimonious notions that give contemporary psychological body to these critics' religious and philosophical speculations.

Here is how Gillet imagined Monet on the banks of his pond, on the eve of his death:

> Everyday the master descended there and absorbed himself for several hours in a mute contemplation: liquid, immobile visage, where upside-down skies, reflections of clouds, dawns, and dusks floated, mirror of phenomena, image of the uncertain abyss of life, upon whose surface the flower of dreams blooms, the divine dream of the lotus (1927, p. 92).

Monet's repetitive reenactments of this pursuit of reflections became in the end a process of self-reflection:

> By force of returning there, by force of meditation, by force of seeing turn by turn reflected in the source the dawns and the evenings, this strange contemplator invents this domain of the impalpable and the imaginary, this singular theater of water, this world of pure extension, of atmosphere and tonality, this half-aquatic, half-aerial universe which belongs to no one but himself and in which is reflected the spectacle of the universe. Astonishing painting without design or borders, canticle without words, pictures in which the painter has no other subject but himself (pp. 109–110).

And all of this, for Gillet, was an effect of Nirvana, "that secret of oblivion in which our wretched individualities are lost and which moreover is one of the forms of adoration" (p. 114).

In *Civilization and Its Discontents* (1930) Freud entered into direct dialogue with the philosophical position embodied in the writings of Geffroy, Gillet, and their colleagues. The occasion was a letter to Freud from the French writer, Romain Rolland, who as it happens admired Monet more than all other contemporary artists (Geffroy, 1922). In a letter to Monet, Rolland praised the *Water Lilies* of 1909 and recalled a painting of ocean and rocks of more than 20 years before. Rolland's "oceanic" motif recurs in the later letter to Freud as well; there the Frenchman proffered it as the source of religious sentiment, "a sensation of 'eternity,' a feeling as of something limitless, unbounded—as it were, 'oceanic'" (1930). Freud curiously refused to acknowledge the primary nature of this "feeling of an indissoluble bond, of being one with the external world as a whole" (p. 65), and then proceeded to describe the obliteration of boundaries between self and other, the prototype of which is the infant at the breast in the position of primary narcissism:

> An infant at the breast does not as yet distinguish his ego from the external world as the source of the sensations flowing in upon him. . . (pp. 66–67). Or, to put it more correctly, originally the ego includes everything, later it separates off an external world from itself. . . . If we may assume that there are many people in whose mental life this primary ego-feeling has persisted to a greater or lesser degree, it would exist in them side by side with the narrower and more sharply demarcated ego-feeling of maturity, like a kind of counterpart to it. In that case, the ideational contents appropriate to it would be precisely those of limitlessness and a bond with the universe—the same ideas with which my friend elucidated the "oceanic" feeling (p. 68).

Freud's friend was Rolland, but it could equally have been Gillet or Monet. As Gillet wrote, in Monet's art "naturalism . . . attains, upon the leaf of the lotus, the *Tao,* the vision of profound rhythms and supreme laws of nature"; for Gillet and many other critics of this Freudian era of oceanic narcissism, Monet's enterprise was reducible to a "new manner of identifying oneself with the elements of the universe" (1924). As Monet was already quoted as saying, "I was able to identify myself with creation and absorb myself in her."

In a few years after Freud's 1930 observations on the fantasy of oceanic merger with the environing maternal matrix, Melanie Klein (1935), Jacques Lacan (1937), and W. R. D. Fairbairn (1937–38, 1938–39) would all make important metapsychological amplifications of primary narcissism with direct implications for the psychoanalytic theory of art. Lacan's famous mirror-stage of the Imaginary and Klein's fantasies of pre-Oedipal identification and fusion with idealized parental objects subsequently spawned a swarm of papers in aesthetics running from Segal (1952) and Stokes (1955) to Winnicott (1967), Ehrenzweig (1967), and Fuller (1980). This shift in psychoanalytic theory from Oedipus to Narcissus, from repressed conflict with the Father (or father) to fantasied merger with the Mother (or mother)—this paradigmatic shift which has recently been traced by Victoria Hamilton (1982) and Greenberg and Mitchell (1983) and is reflected in the contemporary turnings from a psychology based on drives to those based on the relations with one's inner and outer objects and on the resulting constellation and deformation of one's self—this is a story that far overruns my capacities here to narrate. But as with Freud and fantasy, it is a story that for me has given satisfying shape to my own fantasies of Monet's art.

References

Alexandre, A. (1909, May 8). La semaine artistique: Un paysagiste d'aujourd'hui et un portraitiste de jadis. *Comoedia*, p. 3.

Bettelheim, B. (1982). *Freud and man's soul.* New York: Alfred A. Knopf.

Clemenceau, G. (1928). *Claude Monet: Les Nymphéas.* Paris: Plon.

Ehrenzweig, A. (1967). *The hidden order of art: A study in the psychology of artistic imagination.* Berkeley & Los Angeles: University of California Press.

Ellenberger, H. F. (1970). *The discovery of the unconscious: The history and evolution of dynamic psychiatry.* New York: Basic Books.

Fairbairn, W. R. D. (1937–38). Prolegomena to a psychology of art. *British Journal of Psychology,* 28: 288–303.

_____ (1938–39). The ultimate basis of aesthetic experience. *British Journal of Psychology,* 29: 167–81.

Farrell, B. (1963). Introduction. In S. Freud, *Leonardo da Vinci and a memory of his childhood.* Harmondsworth, G. B.: Penguin Books.

Freud, S. (1900). The interpretation of dreams. *S.E.,* 5: 339–686.

_____ (1905a). Jokes and their relation to the unconscious. *S.E.,* 8: 9–238.

_____ (1905b). Three essays on the theory of sexuality. *S.E.,* 7: 130–243.

_____ (1908 [1907]). Creative writers and daydreaming. *S.E.,* 9: 143–153.

_____ (1910a [1909]). Five lectures on psychoanalysis. *S.E.,* 11: 9–55.

_____ (1910b). Leonardo da Vinci and a memory of his childhood. *S.E.,* 11: 63–137.

_____ (1911). Formulations on the two principles of mental functioning. *S.E.,* 12: 218–226.

_____ (1912–13). Totem and taboo. *S.E.,* 13: 1–161.

_____ (1913). The claims of psycho-analysis to scientific interest. *S.E.,* 13: 165–190.

_____ (1914a). The Moses of Michelangelo. *S.E.,* 13: 211–238.

_____ (1914b). On narcissism: An introduction. *S.E.,* 14: 73–102.

_____ (1914c). On the history of the psychoanalytic movement. *S.E.,* 14: 7–66.

_____ (1914d). Remembering, repeating and working-through (further recommendations on the technique of psycho-analysis). *S.E.,* 12: 147–156.

_____ (1916–17). Introductory lectures on psycho-analysis. *S.E.,* 15–16: 15–463.

———— (1917). A difficulty in the path of psycho-analysis. *S.E.*, 17: 137–144.

———— (1919). Preface to Reik's *Ritual: Psycho-analytic studies. S.E.*, 17: 259–263.

———— (1920). Beyond the pleasure principle. *S.E.*, 18: 7–64.

———— (1923). The ego and the id. *S.E.*, 19: 12–66.

———— (1924). The economic problem of masochism. *S.E.*, 19: 159–170.

———— (1925 [1924]). An autobiographical study. *S.E.*, 20: 7–74.

———— (1927a). The future of an illusion. *S.E.*, 21: 5–56.

———— (1927b). Humour. *S.E.*, 21: 161–166.

———— (1930). Civilization and its discontents. *S.E.*, 21: 64–145.

———— (1933). New introductory lectures on psycho-analysis. *S.E.*, 22: 5–182.

———— (1940). An outline of psycho-analysis. *S.E.*, 23: 144–207.

Fuller, P. (1980). *Art and psychoanalysis.* London: Writers and Readers.

Geffroy, G. (1895, May 10). Claude Monet. *Le Journal.* In *L'art moderne* (1895, May 26, p. 164).

———— (1922). *Claude Monet: Sa vie, son oeuvre.* Paris: G. Crès.

Gillet, L. (1909). L'epilogue de l'impressionnisme: Les "Nymphéas" de M. Claude Monet. *Revue Hebdomadaire,* 8, 397–415.

———— (1924). Après l'exposition Claude Monet: Le testament de l'impressionnisme. *La Revue des Deux Mondes,* 7th Ser., 19, 661–673.

———— (1927). *Trois variations sur Claude Monet.* Paris: Plon.

Greenberg, J. R., & Mitchell, S. A. (1983). *Object relations in psychoanalytic theory.* Cambridge, MA & London: Harvard University Press.

Hamilton, V. (1982). *Narcissus and Oedipus: The children of psychoanalysis.* London & Boston: Routledge & Kegan Paul.

Klein, M. (1929). Infantile anxiety-situations reflected in a work of art and in the creative impulse. In *Contributions to psycho-analysis 1921–1945* (pp. 227–235). London: Hogarth Press.

———— (1935). A contribution to the psychogenesis of manic-depressive states. In *Contributions to psycho-analysis 1921–1945* (pp. 282–310). London: Hogarth Press, 1948.

Kohut, H. (1980). Summarizing reflections. In A. Goldberg (Ed.), *Advances in self psychology* (pp. 473–554). New York: International Universities Press.

Kuhns, R. (1983). *Psychoanalytic theory of art: A philosophy of art on developmental principles.* New York: Columbia University Press.

Lacan, J. (1937). The looking-glass phase (rev. 1949). In *Ecrits: A selection* (pp. 1–7). New York & London: W. W. Norton, 1977.

Levine, S. Z. (1976). *Monet and his critics.* New York & London: Garland Publishing.

Monet, C. (1864, July 15). Letter to F. Bazille. In Wildenstein (1974, p. 420).

———— (1884, April 6). Letter to A. Hoschedé. In Wildenstein (1979a, p. 250).

———— (1896, March 31). Letter to A. Hoschedé. In Wildenstein (1979b, p. 291).

———— (1921, January 26). Personal communication. In M. Pays, un grand maître de l'impressionnisme. *Excelsior.*

———— (1922, June 25). Letter to G. Geffroy. In Wildenstein (1979b, p. 302).

Régis, E., & Hesnard, A. (1914). *La psychoanalyse des névroses et des psychoses.* Paris: Félix Alcan.

Ricoeur, P. (1970). *Freud and philosophy: An essay on interpretation.* New Haven & London: Yale University Press.

55   Segal, H. (1952). A psycho-analytic approach to aesthetics. *International Journal of Psycho-Analysis,* 33: 196–207.

Stokes, A. (1955). Form in art. In M. Klein, P. Heimann & R. E. Money-Kryle (Eds.), *New directions in psycho-analysis* (pp. 406–420). London: Tavistock.

Waelder, R. (1965). *Psychoanalytic avenues to art.* New York: International Universities Press.

Wildenstein, D. (1974). *Claude Monet: Biographie et catalogue raisonné.* Lausanne & Paris: La Bibliothèque des arts. Vol. 1; (1979a). Vol. 2; (1979b). Vol. 3.

Winnicott, D. W. (1967). The location of cultural experience. In *Playing and reality* (pp. 112–121). Harmondsworth, G. B.: Penguin Books, 1974.

Gilbert J.
Rose, M.D.

Remarks on "Monet, Fantasy, and Freud"
by Steven Z. Levine

As lucidly set forth in the foregoing essay by Professor Levine, in briefest summary Freud's views on art were as follows: art starts out as a form of escape from reality, like child's play; thanks to the artist's special gifts, however, it is also a mode of return and even of triumph; it taps sources of pleasure in the unconscious that make it possible for the most painful experiences to become enjoyable and mastered; in the process it may satisfy the highest personal and cultural ideals, and even lead to the discovery of new truths.

Leaving aside the matter of Freud's personal antipathy to nonrepresentational art, including music, there are two problems with Freudian aesthetic theory: first, within the closed system paradigm of the 19th century it over-dichotomized as, for example, in the matter of reality/fantasy; second, it carries an inevitable clinical-pathological bias centering on the concept of regression.

As Levine makes amply clear, Freud's views on art revolved largely around the issue of the relative roles of reality and fantasy. Essential as it is for a clinician to make this distinction, it is of questionable utility in art. Nevertheless, during Freud's time it was already traditional among writers on aesthetics to make a similar contrast—that between intellect and feeling. Hanslick (1885) pointed out that "the older writers on aesthetics" keep making a "dilemma" of the contrast between feeling and intellect in art, "quite oblivious of the fact that the main point at issue lies halfway between . . ." (p. 11).

The contrast between art and science seems to fall easily into the same either/or categories: art as a flight, if often playful and pleasurable, into emotional subjectivity; science exemplifying arduous and altruistic work towards objective, intellectual truth. It should be noted in passing that this dichotomy of art/science implicitly involves another one, namely, pleasure/reality principles. And with it comes another problem. When Freud established the pleasure and reality principles, affectivity was subsumed under the pleasure principle. Affectivity was viewed as essentially a secretory and vasomotor discharge into one's own body without reference to the external world. Perception, on the other hand, and secondary process thought and communication, came under the reality principle. Affectivity was isolated. Both art and clinical experience, however, show that there is much more merging of thought and feeling, and feeling with perception, than is suggested by psychoanalytic theorizing. I will return to this issue later.

One problem with this simplistic categorizing is that science itself has outgrown it. Science has evolved to the point where the logic of dichotomy, including the separateness of subject and object, seems to have given way to one that emphasizes permeability. The sharp separation between the I and the world is no longer possible. For example, in metamathematics limitative theorems have mixed up subject and object. In physics, quantum mechanics has taught us that the observer is necessarily a factor interfering with what is observed. The new world-view in physics is that the universe is a dynamic web of interrelated events. The structure of the entire web is determined not by some basic building blocks—not even particles—but the overall consistency of mutual inter-relations. All forms are fluid and ever-changing. Their properties are understandable only in terms of their interactions mutually and with the rest of the world with which, together, they make up an inseparable whole. In the context of this new view, the old basic distinctions seem less absolute, more fluid, than formerly.

Thus the debate about how much Monet's vision is reality and how much imagination might be a nonquestion in that it presupposes assumptions that may no longer be tenable. Imagination does not refer to the unreal, but the possible; just as perception refers not to the real but to the given (Dufrenne, 1953). Like all perception and thought, aesthetic or intellectual vision is a mixture of knowledge and imagination. The two are inseparable. There is no objective, "immaculate" perception without subjective interpretation.

More relevant questions might be: does Monet's vision help to open up the world or close it down. And how? Similar questions might be asked of psychoanalytic aesthetic theory. Does it tend to reduce art to child's play, symptoms and dreams, or does it help explicate the uniqueness of art?

My reading of Levine's essay is that the Freudian Oedipal theory offers little illumination when it comes to Monet's aesthetic form, but that post-Freudian, pre-Oedipal theory, namely narcissism, promises to do better. This brings us to the problem of regression in aesthetic theory. Levine suggests that Monet's lifelong attachment to the sea is reenacted in his paintings and bespeaks a maternal fixation, an oral-erotic fantasy not unlike what Freud imagined he saw in the smiles of Leonardo's figures. The author raises the possibility of an underlying nihilisitc, oceanic fantasy having to do with Nirvana, self-dissolution, and oblivion. In current terminology, regression to self-object symbiosis, fusion, primary narcissism.

Because all of us, psychoanalysts as well as art historians, have emerged from the same sea, the same "maternal maritime matrix," without painting *Water Lilies* as "living epitaph," it would be of great interest to know how Monet manages to represent these universal fantasies in his oeuvre. On this score Levine promises that elaboration and substantiation will be forthcoming in a new book. For now there is only the tantalizing hint that it has to do with "a preoccupation with the structures of reflection and repetition."

This is a plausible beginning but its development will depend on a demonstrable relationship to narcissism as a heuristic concept—not merely the superficial resemblance to the myth of Narcissus enthralled and drowning in the embrace of his own reflection. It will also depend on the role he assigns to regression. As Levine stated, "In spite of frequent disclaimers that the artist is not a neurotic, Freud's correlation of art and neurosis is nevertheless very close in both directions." What will it gain us if Hamlet regresses us back to Oedipus, and Monet only further back to Narcissus?

The theme of the sea was indeed important for Monet: "Water's power to take up the quality of the sky, the day, the weather and yet remain itself; its power to reflect, and thus offer up symmetry; its power to reflect even as it is itself in movement and thus to interpenetrate, to annex, to fragment, to disperse appearances while yet holding them within a larger, more inclusive order" (Gordon & Forge, 1983, p. 77).

The theme of the sea taught Monet much that he rediscovered in his frontal approaches to the landscape: the redistribution and spreading of focus, the open invitation to movement, reorientation, and fusion. In a traditionally composed landscape there is a concentration on certain central points of focus. The eye is led forward toward the horizon. The Varengeville landscapes of 1882–83, for example, have qualities like water. There are few invitations for the eye to enter and explore in a pointed, directional way. Instead, the pictures face us all at once and we are "in" them at once, needing to look everywhere on the canvas (Gordon & Forge, 1983, p. 150).

This immersion and simultaneity, this conflation of time and space, everything into everywhere and at once, finds its culmination in the Water-Lily Decorations. Monet conceived it as a completely integrated environment which would interlock the paintings' and the viewers' space. In the waters, lilies are in continuous interaction with the reversed reflections of unseen trees upside down. Within the water's surface trees, sky, and the light of day are found simultaneously condensed into all possible conjunctions. "The plane of the water brought everything, near and far, into a single pattern, combining the drive of perspective with the enveloping frontality of the sea" (Gordon & Forge, 1983, p. 276).

Frontality, the absence of point of entry or exit for the eye, the lack of focus, the abrogation of near/far, up/down discrimination, the condensation of real and reflected objects on the water's plane—all make for a sense of simultaneous envelopment and limitless expansion reminiscent of the luminosity and ambiguity of early childhood.

Has the disciplined eye and hand of a master specialist in color and light ushered us back to a state of narcissistic regression? There is, to be sure, the momentary sense of union with the painting so characteristic of the aesthetic experience. But instead of a constricted awareness and the dreaminess of a hypnotic trancelike state of regression, what follows is the sparkling quality of hyper-alertness and fresh recognition of sensuousness and affect. Moreover, the heightened sense of aliveness persists after we leave the painting and may even permanently alter the way we visually experience atmosphere and light, as well as the passage of time (Rose, 1980).

This is no regression to narcissism in the sense of fusion of subject and object. The more lasting effect is that of an intrapsychic reintegration: sensuousness has been restored to experience, thought and perception have been reinvested with affect, quickening our experience of the world with the freshness it once had in the beginning. The world has indeed been reunified not through symbiotic fusion but through the integration of heightened faculties. This is less a regression in the service of the ego than a progression with the aid of the id.

A work of art is true not in what it recounts but how. Its sensuousness awakens feelings which in turn illuminate the world. Both art and science in their different ways—through forms and concepts—illuminate the real. Monet did not discover light in either particles or waves. His paintings of sensuous form evoke feelings that reveal light anew.

References

Dufrenne, M. (1953). *The phenomenology of aesthetic experience.* Translated by E. S. Casey, A. A. Anderson, W. Domingo, L. Jacobson. Evanston: Northwestern University Press, 1973.

Gordon, R., & Forge, A. (1983). *Monet.* New York: Harry Abrams.

Hanslick, E. (1885). *The beautiful in music,* trans. G. Cohen. New York: Liberal Arts Press, 1957.

Rose, G. J. (1980). *The power of form: A psychoanalytic approach to aesthetic form.* New York: International Universities Press.

Donald B.
Kuspit,
D. Phil., Ph.D.

Chaos in Expressionism

At one very special point in his novel *The Secret Agent,* Joseph Conrad described Stevie, the retarded adolescent son-in-law of Mr. Verloc, the secret agent, at work,

> seated very good and quiet at a deal table, drawing circles, circles, circles; innumerable circles, concentric, eccentric; a coruscating whirl of circles that by their tangled multitude of repeated curves, uniformity of form, and confusion of inter-secting lines suggested a rendering of cosmic chaos, the symbolism of a mad art attempting the inconceivable (1907, p. 39).

One can't help but think of the "degenerate" Stevie—who is later literally exploded by his mishandling of an anarchist bomb—as a very advanced abstract artist, on the order of the hero of Balzac's short story *Le Chef-d'oeuvre inconnu,* illustrated by Picasso in 1927. One etching, entitled *Painter with a Model Knitting* (Geiser 126), shows a realistically drawn painter creating a picture of a real-istically drawn model in a highly abstract—one might say ex-pressionistically abstract—manner. The artist in the Balzac story spends—"wastes"—his mature career trying to capture the like-ness of a model—who in the Picasso etching is a rather motherly looking figure—but never does, creating only a chaos of lines and shapes. He refuses to show the picture to his colleagues, who after his death find the unsuccessful mess, successful only in its novelty. Picasso may, in fact, be metaphorically describing the intention behind the creation of Cubism, the artistically original results being in fact a psychological failure to capture the living likeness of an intimate subject matter, a significant other. As indicated by the portraits that are customarily regarded as the height of Analytic Cubism, the figure collapses into an aesthetically interesting but psychologically disturbing chaos, or rather, never really emerges from chaos. We might even say that the Analytic Cubist portraits are constituted by chaos. And we might note that an extraordinary amount of modern art is covertly as well as overtly, theoretically as well as in practice, concerned with and tantalized by chaos, often in the form of an interest in chance or "gesture," sometimes more loosely in the form of an obsession with force or the formless.

Nowhere is this temptation by chaos—coincident with a recognition of its inescapability, both as a starting point for the creative process and as, less expectedly (except unconsciously), its terminal "form"—more in evidence than in the German Expressionist art produced in the first two decades of this century, i.e., in the chaotic years of its beginning. Harold Rosenberg has argued that during these two decades, particularly during the pre-World War I decade, all the ingredients of the modern manner came into being. By 1914 the "formal repertory" of avant-garde was "in full bloom"; what remained was the "working-out of the variations" (Rosenberg, 1973). Describing the sensibility—the "renovated attitude"—of the avant-garde in this formative period, Rosenberg noted the emphasis on "the quality of ephemeralness," on the way "three-dimensional substance gives way to images cast upon the screen of time," and the avant-gardist sense that "what seems to the ordinary mind solid fact is . . . infiltrated with process" (1973, p. 77). Rosenberg noted that

> Modern art oscillates between the two poles of omnipotent identity and the selfless eye and brain. At the extremes, the enhancement of self and the elimination of self converge: "Expressionism" becomes abstract and impersonal, constructed art becomes "Expressionist." Speaking of the poet Mayakovsky, Trotsky said that his megalomania was so complete he became objective. Cézanne paints to "develop his personality," and his paintings become in time an impersonal filter of space (1973, p. 75).

In both Mayakovsky and Cézanne there is a kind of crystallized lack of cohesion, an almost "institutionalized" fragmentation: the impersonal, the selfless, is used to create what has been called a "holding environment" (J. Gedo, 1979) for the personally realized chaos of the awkwardly "affinitized" elements of the modern poem or picture. The "expressionism" comes in not subjectively but as objectively recognizable: it is not a matter of the artist's making public his introspective report of his feelings, his private fantasies about a desirable or undesirable reality—although the libidinous aspect of the work's appearance, the way it is "charged" by its fragmentation can be read as that—but of the observed difficulty of containing the elements of the picture or poem. The fragments become almost free-floating, increasingly "arbitrary" factors, wild cards in a game whose rules always seem about to change. The aura of freedom generated by their uncertainty of relationship is articulated in an energy that seems perpetually to be on the verge of bursting the boundaries of the work, totally disintegrating it.

This tendency towards the formless, towards chaos, is what might be called "the expressionist moment." It occurs and recurs in the best modern art, whatever its outward style, and it can be understood in narcissistic terms—as a disturbance in the narcissistic self-regulation of the work, in its sense of its fundamental identity. This is what makes it truly "modern," i.e., inwardly "relative"—entirely a matter of relations in which no clear hierarchy of aims can be established, no clearly determined priorities of aim exist. This is what creates the aura of "freshness, sketchiness, and ambiguity"—the sense of "bodylessness" and the effect of devaluation of the individual—that Rosenberg regarded as characteristic of essentially modern art (1973). It is inevitable that "individuality"—including the presumably radically unique individuality of the modern work of art—seem unimportant when the narcissism that is the necessary substructure of individuation cannot be sustained and appears permanently wounded. The "differentiations," interpreted as signs of individuality, which one sees in modern works of art are in fact the signs of an unsecured narcissism, a fundamental insecurity and uncertainty of value—of self-value—that reduces all the endlessly secondary elaborations which make up the work—so endless that one cannot determine what is "primary" about it—to one simple meaning: the work's difficulty in identifying itself, in articulating its own aims.

The common modern assertion that the artist does not so much finish a picture as abandon it and that the spectator "completes" it by his interpretation of its meaning to him—an interpretation that gives it its authentic, full presence—takes on a new meaning in the light of this narcissistic problem. Incompleteness, "interpretability" as completeness, are further signs of the chaotic situation of the work, indications of how its borderline internal chaos or lack of cohesiveness makes itself manifest in its relationship to the world for which it is made. Latent internal chaos becomes manifest external chaos, showing itself in extreme public uncertainty about the modern work's meaning and value, and its trying to borrow a meaningful and valuable identity from the critical viewers who are willing to "trust" it. Indeed, the potentially chaotic modern work necessarily must generate viewer identification with it—a partisan advocacy of it. For that is the only way that it can escape what seems inevitable: accusations alternately of profound obscurity and self-evident triviality, met by its own grandiose, exaggerated claims of transcendent clarity and heroic significance. Baudelaire's insistence upon a passionate, partisan criticism is necessary in the modern, uncertain situation—the "expressionist" situation—and is matched by the missionary, indeed messianic, attitudes of such important early modern masters as Kandinsky, Malevich, and Mondrian—masters painting, in the Balzacian sense, then "unknown" works of art, strange, new masterpieces in terms of a new sense of mastery, namely, mastery of chaos. Practical partisanship and the self-partisanship evident in the theoretical writings of the first truly modern artists create an artificial narcissism—on the model of Baudelaire's conception of the work of art as an "artificial existence"—that masks the narcissistic disturbances evident in their work, that puts the best public face on an inner fear of the possible facelessness—threat of loss of face—of their art.

Expressionism proper has always been associated with chaos, whether the work of art is understood as uncertainly emerging out of primal chaos, or equally anxiously, depicting and threatening literally to become chaos. Kandinsky's consciousness of his own work, for example, stated in his typical religion-derived, inflated language—whose grandiosity masks enormous anxiety—views it as arising "like the Cosmos, through catastrophes which end by creating a symphony, called the music of the spheres, out of the chaotic blaring of the instruments" (Sotriffer, 1972, p. 14). The sense that this "Cosmos" is in fact "a spectacle of complete chaos," an "'explosive' chaos" which might actually "detonate," (Schvey, 1982) is convincingly argued by critics of Kokoschka. The critic Paul Kornfeld asserted, in a remark that will be generally relevant to our psychoanalytic understanding of this expressionist chaos—an ambivalent sense of foreordained, temporarily remote chaos (the sense that both are "expected" is crucial to an understanding of the unconscious factors involved in this free-floating sense of chaos)—that in both his paintings and plays Kokoschka "confronts the chaos of the world as though he were the first man, and invents technique and form ingenuously, as though he were the first artist. The people of his dramas are as huge and simple as the colossus of a mountain, and as natural as a landscape" (Schvey, 1982, p. 7).

Repeatedly these dramas of conflict—usually sexual, but that has been interpreted as metaphorical for a fundamental split in the self—end in chaos (Schvey, 1982), reflect "cataclysm and discord," reveal "an overturned world," exploit "chaotic elements" (which is why they were the first plays produced by the Dadaists), and have been astutely called, by the critic Bernhard Diebold, "screaming images," in which "the word has become an accessory; screams, spectacle, and images predominate. . . . Archetypal figures do not converse in lucid discourse" but in "sentence fragments, exclamations, and screams" (Schvey, 1982), i.e., in an infantile way, as if they were just learning language. Only in expressionistic drama and painting—painted drama—they are unlearning it, enacting this unlearning, with its consequent return to a primitive, "first," infantile state of selfhood. This return masks a revelation of what was always the case in the "inner self" which Kokoschka talked about, a self that had the prophetic "second sight" which in fact was an intense awareness of the ever-present threat of death (Schvey, 1982). In sum, the authentically expressionist work was organized chaos, art carried to the brink of chaos—art at once as a means of tearing away the social mask that hid the "obsessions" of the unhappy self, and of revealing them, revealing especially the unhappy self's obsession with its own feeling of being fragmented, incomplete, finally of being deeply split or narcissistically unreconciled to itself.

The major component in the expressionist sense of chaos—or chaotic selfhood—seems to be a sense of impending doom, a catastrophe. The previously given Kandinsky quotation speaks of transcendence through catastrophe, as if it was inseparable from the creative process—as if the famous "accidental gestures" of his paintings (to which the name "Abstract Expressionism" was first applied) were in fact all along expected, inevitable. The sense of the apocalyptic—of the apocalyptic as the revelation of the chaotic—as the essence of the Expressionist moment is explicit in the Conrad quotation about Stevie's "rendering of cosmic chaos" with the circles symbolic of cosmic order, even of its necessity. This turning to negative use of shapes that are intended positively—the creating of an effect opposite from the "positively" intended effect—is typically Expressionist. Conrad almost seems to be describing, as if they were abstractions rather than naturalistic descriptions, Leonardo's late drawings of the deluge, with the abstract swirls of rapidly curving line having very material effect. Expressionism also showed nature torn apart "from top to bottom," as W. Michel said (Sotriffer, 1972), and such horrific man-made events as war were experienced as natural catastrophes. As Otto Conzelmann noted, Otto Dix experienced World War I as "a ruthless, unfeeling outburst of Nature, beyond good and evil: like a tidal wave or a typhoon—a shock that sent a shudder through the earth, down to its foundations" (Sotriffer, 1972, p. 16).

This sense of catastrophe—as the instrument of chaos—made itself felt in the excution of Expressionist art, came to determine—to underlie—the most original, exciting aspects of execution. Execution itself became chaotic, attempted to be catastrophic—subjected raw material to a "catastrophic" technique to bring out the "chaos" in the matter itself. As has been pointed out, Gauguin's precept about the fundamentality of catastrophic crudity—handling that went to the brink of chaos—became de rigueur for Expressionist artists. "Don't polish too much, the subsequent hunting out of endless refinements only impairs the first draft; that is the way to let the incandescent lava grow cold, to petrify your foaming blood" (Sotriffer, 1972, pp. 17–18). Munch, for example, used, in the words of Gustav Schiefler, "rough pinewood slats from packing-cases, working on them with a coarse knife and utilizing the grain and the saw-marks as welcome texture of the background" (Sotriffer, 1977, p. 18). Similarly, Kokoschka, who thought of Expressionism as "the forming of experience" (Schvey, 1982, p. 23), also sought a raw, dissonant effect, painting his famous "early 'black portraits,' as he himself called them, . . . 'with the scalpel,' in an attempt to liberate the inner self from the encumbrance of the fleshly surface" (Schvey, p. 26). Henry I. Schvey introduced his discussion of Kokoschka's violent or catastrophic—catastrophe-creating as well as violent in itself—technique with a generally pertinent epigraph from William Blake's *The Marriage of Heaven and Hell:* "this I shall do by printing in the infernal method, by corrosives, which in Hell are salutary and medicinal, melting apparent surfaces away, and displaying the infinite which was hid."

Kokoschka wrote: "Seeing a Polynesian mask with its incised tattooing, I understood at once, because I could feel my own facial nerves reacting to cold and hunger in the same way" (Schvey, 1982, p. 17). Corrosive, violent technique is used to get at the nerves, to create the nerves of the image, to make it all nerves, and became central to Kokoschka's "interior portraiture," especially to his polychrome clay bust *Self-Portrait as Warrior* (1908), executed when he was 21 but depicting a much older man.

> The face is distorted with bumps and hollows and the mouth is agape with an impassioned cry similar to the faces of the actors in his first play. With its sunken eyes, blue-veined cheeks, and hostile yet terrified expression, it conveys the same mixture of confusion, fear, and brutality as the Man (also a "Warrior") in *Murderer Hope of Women* (Schvey, pp. 42–43).

The self-portrait is an archetypal image of the corroded, chaotic, fragmenting self, revealed in a process of disintegration that is beyond any simplistic concept of the protean self, of the metamorphosis of possibilities in the name of the infinite self. Experience of inward chaos stands behind the romantically pleasurable sense of the self's infinite possibilities, endless ability to aim or direct itself. The chaotic self is the aimless narcissistic self that has even given up searching for a double to heal it by mirroring it. It is self whose despair has made it chaotic, and seemingly beyond remediation, i.e., unable to re-mediate itself in the world through an alter ego. It no longer even wants a mirror, for it does not want to see itself. A reflection can only make it more chaotic, and would finally destroy it.

To understand psychoanalytically this chaotic self and the catastrophic world in which it is mirrored—and I think the psychoanalytic mode of understanding is the only one adequate to this art about inadequacy—is to read it symptomatically in terms of the conception of the narcissistically disturbed self developed in the last decade and a half. The fragmentation inherent to the Expressionist work of art—a fragmentation that disrupts landscapes and bodies, and which Expressionist-oriented artists as different as Max Beckmann and Ludwig Meidner regarded as self-evident in the chaotic modern city (Sotriffer, 1972, p. 14)—is symptomatic (and symptoms are symbols) of a dissociational process. This process is itself indicative of discontent with civilization or socialization and, simultaneously with—dialectically reflective of—the well-known Expressionist discontent with repression, a sign of the failure of the self to cohere in the face of an unwelcome reality. This reality is first and foremost the reality of language, for it is language on which free if formless consciousness is crucified, taught to conform by becoming communicative.

Expressionist dissociation shows itself in the malaise of space in the visual works, a malaise that is constituted, paradoxically, by the asides—even extended digressions—of energy, the so-called lines of force, which are "released" by the self's lack of cohesion, or rather, are signs of the self's attempt to cohere, to force itself to cohere. The aura effect they create, leading to an effect of grandiosity—the so-called "archaic grandiosity" of the narcissistic self (Kohut, 1971, p. 114)—is in fact not that at all. That is, where the conventional aura connotes positive presence, the Expressionist unconventional, negative aura connotes absence— the absence of a solid self, of a self that has gotten itself "together." A work like Kandinsky's *Painting with White Border* (May 1913) is a demonstration not of a possible new coherence, but of the impossibility of any kind of cohesiveness—any kind of unified perspective or rationalizable, controlled set of relationships between discrepant parts of a scene. It is, as it were, a kind of "primal scene" of selfhood that is represented, or rather, more precisely, a picture of the impossibility of representation of a self that does not exist coherently and cogently. This Abstract Expressionist's renunciation of representation—that famous move towards nonobjective art—is really not a renunciation but a failure to achieve a new kind of representation, representation of the self not the world.

To renounce conventional representation is for the artist to renounce the conventional world that seems to hold together and claims to be the mirror of a self that holds together—a self which, like the original Democritan atom, was thought to be indivisible, a fundamental unit of psychological being. This renunciation is to deny this false, distorting mirror, this mirror that lies about the state of the (modern) self, and to begin a kind of infinite regress to the primitive state of the broken or wounded self, the fundamentally hurt, unstable, incoherent, uncertain self. It is to begin a regressive search for a new mode of representation—which is what abstract art at its best (i.e., not as pure style) is. It is a mode in which the true state of the self can be mirrored without being told to cohere. It is a mode in which primal chaos can be represented—disunity asserted as fundamental—without becoming absolute. It is a mode of representation in which catastrophic chaos can be "tasted," can momentarily take possession of one— the source of the sense of spontaneity epidemic in Expressionist art—to remind one of the true state of one's self, but not falsely insist that one get oneself together, and be reflected in the mirror of the world which pretends that one is the fairest—the most together—of them all.

The Expressionist picture is a representation of a dedifferentiating process, in which centrality becomes so derealized as to become inconceivable, which is a state perhaps not unlike, in John E. Gedo's words, "some analogue of the 'oceanic feelings' reported by mystics and other adults able to experience profound regressive states without personal disruption" (1979). In this pictorial infantile state of self-formation there is no sense of personal disruption in the modern critical viewer because it represents perfectly his own sense of his fragmented, incoherent self, an objectification of it which helps him to accept it. This representation has narcissistic value to him; one might even speak of it as a substitute narcissistic gratification. That is, if one cannot become a whole self, with just and proper self-esteem, one can have the pleasure of seeing one's incoherent, chaotic self symbolically represented. Standard representation is a defense against this expressionistic representation, tending towards abstraction, of the fundamentally incoherent, self-alienated self, the self with no ideological anchors or absolute beliefs to give it stable form. "Chaos" means the destruction—deconstruction—of the traditional mode of representation, which implies that the world mirrors the self to its satisfaction, and the construction of a modern mode of representation to articulate the modern, "groundless" state of the self. "Chaos" means the loss of trust in and disruption of finite appearances to reveal the aura of infinity—an effect of the energy—that is released by the "inconclusive," narcissistically dissatisfied self. It is forever in a Faustian search for a mirror image it is bound to debase because such an image is finite, unless, like Eurydice, it disappears by itself into the nothingness which the regressive turn to the underworld of chaos heralds and masks.

As has been noted, Kokoschka's plays have been called "screaming images," images in which both the verbal and the visual are at their most elemental. The scream is a direct, simple, basic expression, an ingenuous mode of articulation, a pure verbal presence that is fraught with indeterminate meaning. It is dramatic and natural, as Paul Kornfeld suggested in his analysis of Kokoschka's plays and paintings. It is the "language" of the "first man," or rather, the prelinguistic articulation of "first feelings," of archetypal experience, not only of the world but of the self. It is a sign of the self's elemental experience of itself, its numinous terror at its own being. More particularly, I want to contend that the Expressionist cry is the self's recognition of its own chaos, an act of recognition which is at the same time purgative. The cry is the chaotic self's self-recognition and simultaneously self-cathartic, a way of alienating itself from itself by recognizing its own monstrous character. At the same time, the cry is the abstract, authentic representation of the chaotic self. The cry shatters the mirror of the world in which this chaotic self is falsely represented as finite, cohesive, contained within boundaries not of its own making. The chaotic self's only defense is to declare its infinity—its infinite energy. Thus, the cry is a narcissistic act, the self-image—self-assertion—of what Heinz Kohut has described as "the crumbling, decomposing, fragmenting, enfeebled self" of the child in "the fragile, vulnerable, empty self of the adult" (1977, p. 286); more precisely, of the artist about to be adult, struggling to understand what it means to be adult, mature. In a peculiar way, the cry is the archaic self at its most grandiose, the most grandiose expression of wounded narcissism. In its chaos there is a strange cohesion, so that it is the archaic self's self-transcendence, as well as a strange tragic quality, which involves an inability to believe in the ideal, a disavowal of ambition in the face of the actual. The self is thus frozen in its own archaic character, permanently frustrated. The cry is the archaic self's expression of frustration at its inability to idealize, which means to accept its social condition—its "derivation" from the ideals of society, which alone "fill" it, give it the "final force" Paul Klee thought art lacked when it did not have "the people" (*Volk*) behind it. The cry shows that the self cannot even postulate a hierarchy of goals, for it refuses any single "principle" of self-organization.

The cry has been a major subject matter—as well as form—of Expressionist art, and has always been understood by Expressionists as the beginning of art, and even its end, i.e., the expression of the cry is its only, or at least major, goal. Thus Kokoschka, in his essay on Munch,

> defines two attributes of Expressionist art: its visionary quality, "a single moment appearing in the guise of eternity," and its intensity, "a silence broken by a cry." The "cry" alludes to Munch's masterpiece *The Scream* (1893), but a cry is also characteristic of Expressionist drama—from Kokoschka's own *Murderer Hope of Women* to Reinhard Goering's *Naval Battle* (1917), both of which begin with an anguished cry (Schvey, 1982, p. 23).

The two aspects of Expressionism are really one: the cry is "the single moment," "the guise of eternity" being its simplicity and directness. The cry is the eternal moment in the silent graveyard of time, the unconscious moment breaking the surface of complacent consciousness. The cry represents what is really unchanging, fundamental: the sense of self that narcissistically defies what it regards as the oblivion of assimilation, for it correctly sees time and consciousness as the enemies of its feeling of omnipotence. The cry is the self-consciousness of this archaic self that denies the world.

Barnett Newman, in a certain sense the last of the great Abstract Expressionists, has written that: "Man's first expression, like his first dream, was an aesthetic one. Speech was a poetic outcry rather than a demand for communication. Original man, shouting his consonants, did so in yells of awe and anger at his tragic state, at his own self-awareness, and at his own helplessness before the void" (Chipp, 1968, p. 551). Newman noted that "the aesthetic act always precedes the social one," and that the aesthetic act which the poetic outcry is indicates that "language is an animal power." "The human in language is literature, not communication. Man's first cry was a song. Man's first address to a neighbor was a cry of power and solemn weakness, not a request for a drink of water." Newman was describing the aesthetic act of the "tragic self" as Kohut has understood it (Kohut, 1977), the cry being the archaic aesthetic act of the narcissistically disturbed self, or rather, the primal self which experiences its own narcissism as a disturbance. For primitive narcissism involves the self's search for its image—its attempt to complete itself by representing or reflecting itself—in a world which withholds it, or rather, which imprints it with its own image. Thus the self experiences "helplessness before the void," "solemn weakness," ambiguously mingled with its own "cry of power" and "anger" at its own "tragic state." Newman's famous painted "zip" is a cry—at once an angry assertion of primordial power and a tattered expression of weakness and helplessness in the void of the painting's infinite field.

What Expressionist artists from Kokoschka to Newman make clear is that what psychoanalysts regard as "narcissistic injury" and "narcissistic vulnerability and regression propensity" (Kohut, 1971, p. 12), is not a pathological condition, but a "normal" phase of self-formation, in fact, the elementary form of the self, as it were. The tension between chaos and cohesion—the anguish of the experience of chaos, with its feelings of hurt and helplessness, vulnerability and threatening void (the nothingness or "death" that is pre-birth, pre-creation, pre-creativity), and the reluctance to accept cohesion, which for all its gains (social, communicative) is experienced as loss of the "aesthetic" (and so living death)—is an essential part of existence, as much as the cry is inseparable from the infant. That the Expressionist artist clings to it, insists upon his screamed images—his dream outcry and his outcry of the dream of himself—is not a symptom of his pathology, but of the depth of his experience of being, and of being a self, with all its dialectical tension with the real world, which does not "represent" it properly.

It is the recognition, most of all, that the cry that is the symbolic, most grandiose form of the archaic self—which issues as if in a dream, and is its dream of itself—is an ambiguous statement of autonomy, a recognition of its absurdity. For the autonomy of the self which the cry asserts shows it to be vulnerable in the world, to be appropriable by the world, while at the same time shows it to be a defiant, undialectical assertion of its absoluteness, and the absoluteness of its experience of itself. Expressionism articulates the discontented autonomy of the un-civilized yet no longer self-possessed self, the self that, like a kind of Burden's ass, is paralyzed and trapped between nature and society. Nonetheless, whether it is form or symptom, the Expressionist artist takes narcissistic pride in his chaos. His exhibitionistic grandiosity is his chaos made manifest as a narcissistic end in itself.

References

Chipp, H. B., Ed. (1968). *Theories of modern art.* Berkeley: University of California Press.

Conrad, J. (1907). *The secret agent.* Garden City, NY: Doubleday-Anchor Book, Doubleday & Co., 1951.

Gedo, J. E. (1979). *Beyond interpretation.* New York: International Universities Press.

Kohut, H. (1971). *The analysis of the self.* New York: International Universities Press.

_____(1977). *The restoration of the self.* New York: International Universities Press.

Rosenberg, H. (1973). *Discovering the present.* Chicago: University of Chicago Press.

Schvey, H. I. (1982). *Oscar Kokoschka, the painter as playwright.* Detroit: Wayne State University Press.

Sotriffer, K. (1972). *Expressionism and Fauvism.* New York: McGraw-Hill.

Section Two   Self-Portraiture

Mary Mathews
Gedo, Ph.D.

The Healing Power of Art: Goya as His Own Physician

Between 1777 and 1794, Francisco Goya suffered three major illnesses which profoundly affected his physical status and reverberated through his art. A study of his oeuvre during these years reveals the multiple ways in which he utilized his creativity to comprehend, integrate, and master the effects of these repeated traumas. Virtually without exception, leading Goya scholars have recognized that the last of these three episodes, the life-threatening disease of 1792–93 which left the artist permanently deaf, constituted *the* crucial turning point in his artistic development.[1] Many of these same specialists have addressed themselves to the diagnostic problem posed by this sickness, a conundrum that has also fascinated medical and psychological authorities.[2] Paradoxically, these same Goya experts have failed to address themselves with similar concentration to the style and content of the paintings that the artist produced immediately before and after this crisis. Their lack of critical interest in the iconography of the 14 little cabinet pictures that Goya painted during his convalescence from the illness seems especially amazing, because the artist himself emphasized their highly personal symbolism in a letter written to his friend Bernardo de Iriarte, on January 4, 1794. In that letter, he consigned 11 of these pictures to Iriarte's protection, imploring him to exhibit them at the Royal Academy of San Fernando in Madrid. Clearly, Goya intended to utilize these works as a sort of calling card, a painted demonstration to his colleagues at the academy that he at last felt strong enough to resume his active role in artistic circles. He explained the origin of the set as follows:

In order to occupy my imagination mortified by the contemplation of my sufferings, and in order to compensate in
part for the considerable expenses which they have caused
me, I devoted myself to painting a series of cabinet pictures
in which I have managed to make observations for which
there is normally no opportunity in commissioned works
which give no scope for fantasy and imagination [*el capricho y
la invención*].[3]

Thanks to X. D. Fitzgerald, Xavier de Salas, and others, we
now know the identity of these little cabinet paintings (the set
eventually included 14 panels), which were dispersed early in the
19th century, although Goya clearly intended that they always be
kept together.[4] They consist of eight paintings of the bullfight
(which no doubt earned the entire set its description in the
minutes of the academy as scenes of "national diversion"), two
pictures showing strolling entertainers, and four works dealing
with man-made or natural disasters.[5] These include a murderous
attack on a coach by a group of brigands, a fire at night, a
shipwreck, and a scene in an insane asylum. In another letter to
Iriarte, Goya described the last work as a depiction of a fight
between two inmates while the keeper beats them and other
patients dressed in sackcloth mill about. He noted that he had
witnessed this scene himself in Saragossa.[6] Pierre Gassier and
Juliet Wilson suggested that several other paintings in the series
probably also represent sights Goya had seen or heard about in
Saragossa, while the *fiesta dos toros* or bullfight pictures, the
earliest in the group, seem to refer to memories of Seville, to
which the artist had paid a surreptitious visit just before his illness
of 1792–93 struck.[7] Although Gassier and Wilson noted that in
these pictures Goya makes "the decisive move towards a private
art where violence and tragedy were to find such powerful
expression," and José Gudiol mentioned the emphasis on themes
of disaster common to the last four pictures in the group, none of
these authorities discussed the series in detail.

Convinced that these 14 panels teem with references to the
artist's illness and the permanent sequelae with which it left him—
the bilateral deafness and ringing in the ears that thereafter
constantly tormented him—I began this work to correct that
omission. But as I studied the pictures Goya had painted during
the periods of his two earlier illnesses, I realized that all three of
these incidents, and much of the art which he created in reaction
to them, constituted a single, seamless experience. Consequently,
I decided to broaden my focus to include some consideration of
these works in this essay, although I plan to deal with the entire
series (1777–94) in greater detail in a subsequent paper. I shall
begin, therefore, with a brief review of Goya's health history
between 1777 and 1794 and will then discuss the diagnostic
problem posed by his three illnesses.

Goya's Illness: A Brief Résumé

The numerous self-portraits that Goya painted throughout his long career attest to his appearance of great vitality (Fig. 1). His self-images reveal a man with a powerful but compact physique; his figure generates an impression of stamina and force reminiscent of the similar characteristics possessed by the young black bulls he also loved to paint. Goya's prodigious productivity and his rapid rise to a position of eminence and power in the artistic world of his era reinforce this impression of vitality, a vitality joined to a canny shrewdness and sure political sense which enabled him rapidly to maneuver his way successfully through the complexities of royal artistic politics and reach a position of prominence and financial security. Nor did Goya's severe breakdown of 1792–93 permanently vitiate his endurance; after his recovery, he continued to work at a furious pace, constantly experimenting with new media and modes of expression until the

Fig. 1. *Self-Portrait in the Studio,* c. 1790–95. Oil on canvas. Private collection, Madrid.

final days of his life. Just two weeks before his death (on April 16, 1828), the octogenarian artist felt so well that he boasted in a letter that he might endure long enough to match Titian's legendary 99-year life span (Sánchez-Cantón, n.d., p. 27).

Despite his apparent sturdiness, however, Goya suffered repeated physical disturbances of the utmost severity throughout his long life. I shall not concern myself here with the illnesses he experienced after 1792, but prior to that time he had suffered two other serious episodes, one in 1777 or 1778, the other in 1790.[8] He evidently recovered from both these crises without showing obvious sequelae, and we possess few factual details about either incident. Following his illness of 1777, the artist wrote his childhood friend Martín Zapater that he had "only just escaped alive" from this interlude, adding that he was now painting "with greater acceptance" (Gudiol, 1971, p. 38). Around the time of this illness, Goya temporarily abandoned work on the tapestry-cartoon commissions on which he had been engaged. Perhaps it was during this period that he produced his etchings after the paintings of Velázquez. At any rate, we know that these prints had not been commissioned; Goya apparently began them on his own initiative, conceivably because they did not require as much exertion as easel painting.[9]

A number of the paintings that Goya produced between 1777 and 1790 seem to me to refer quite directly to sensations that accompanied this sickness and which recurred during the interlude preceding his next health crisis. These symptoms again reached crisis proportions in 1790, when he experienced a second major illness. This episode left him quite debilitated. Subsequently, as Jeannine Baticle noted (1970, n.p., no. 12), Goya's career, which had progressed so brilliantly during the previous decade, suddenly slowed down markedly. Between 1790 and 1792, the artist frequently described himself as exhausted and overburdened with work. But, in fact, apart from executing seven tapestry cartoons (by no means a large production for him during a two-year interval), Goya actually produced little, while repeatedly requesting leaves of absence. Baticle and others (Baticle, 1970, no. 12; Gassier & Wilson, 1971, p. 68; Glendinning, 1977, pp. 175–197) have attributed this declining productivity to the artist's growing anxiety over the political changes then becoming apparent in Spain. No doubt, the increasing repressiveness of the Spanish regime deeply disturbed Goya, and it certainly adversely affected several of his principal friends and protectors. However, the subject matter of these seven cartoons—a loosely defined commission that allowed him considerable latitude—suggests that the principal reason for the artist's lowered productivity was that he continued to be dogged by the same physical symptoms that had flared into a major illness in 1790 and would culminate in the terrible attack of 1792.[10]

As indicated above, Goya suffered the attack of 1792–93 while absent without leave from his official position as court painter, to which he had been elevated after Charles IV assumed the throne in 1789. We do not know exactly why or when the artist left Madrid and initiated his secret journey to Andalusia. He evidently remained in Madrid at least until October 14, when he presented an important report on painting to his colleagues at the academy.[11] Perhaps he left soon afterwards, lingering in Seville long enough to attend the bullfights and to sketch the bullring and other monuments which appear in the *fiesta dos toros* subseries included in the cabinet paintings of 1793–94. Eventually, the artist made his way to Cádiz and the home of his friend Sebastián Martínez, a wealthy merchant and discerning art purchaser whose collection Goya undoubtedly wished to study at leisure.[12] While a guest in the Martínez mansion, he painted the handsome portrait (Fig. 2) of his host now in the collection of the Metropolitan Museum of Art, New York. Signed and dated 1792, the work must be the last major painting Goya completed before his sickness overtook him.

Fig. 2. *Sebastián Martínez,* 1792. Oil on canvas. New York, The Metropolitan Museum of Art.

He planned to return to Madrid via Seville, but while he was in the latter city or its environs, he suddenly became quite incapacitated. He succeeded in summoning a friend who conveyed him once again to the Martínez home, where the artist spent the next 5 or 6 months, much of it as a helpless invalid. To cover his unexcused absence from court (as an employee of the king, he needed official permission to go on leave), which could have resulted in loss of salary, among other difficulties, the artist arranged through Martínez to obtain two months' official sick-leave time. His brother-in-law, Francisco Bayeu, who had succeeded Anton Mengs as first court painter, adroitly negotiated this permission, claiming that Goya continued to suffer from the same severe "colic" that had kept him bedfast in Madrid—and invisible—for the past two months (de Sambricio, 1946, nos. 157, 160). Utilizing this same ruse once again, Goya also obtained an advance from his leading private patron, the Duke of Osuna, who arranged to have money waiting for the artist in Seville when he "arrived" there from "Madrid" (de Sambricio, 1946, no. 158). On March 19, Martínez petitioned the Lord Chamberlain's secretary in Madrid to extend Goya's sick leave (de Sambricio, no. 160).

Ten days later, the merchant provided a more personalized and accurate account of Goya's current status for his friend Zapater:

> The noises in his head and the deafness have not improved, but his vision is much better, and he is no longer suffering from the disorders which made him lose his balance. He can now go up and down stairs very well and at last does things which he couldn't do before (de Sambricio, no. 161).

Goya apparently returned to Madrid in May or June, 1793. By July 11, he felt well enough to attend a meeting of the academy, and during the next six months he gradually began painting again, perhaps working on a few portraits in addition to the little cabinet pictures.[13] Although he was now clearly on the mend, the artist's convalescence by no means proceeded smoothly, and he continued to complain of episodic irritability and susceptibility to fatigue as late as the spring of 1794.[14] In an official report dated April, 1794, Goya's two fellow court painters, F. Bayeu and M. S. Maella, wrote the following evaluation of his condition: "Although it is true that Don Francisco Goya has suffered a serious illness, it is equally true that he is partly recovered and is painting, albeit without the same firmness and constancy as before."[15]

During the months that followed, Goya's strength and skill gradually returned in full force, and he painted a series of brilliant portraits, such as the imposing representation (Fig. 3) of the actress known as *La Tirana*. Although aging, puffy, and overweight, she glances out at us with all the imperiousness of a queen among actresses. By 1796 and 1797, the artist had evidently fully recovered from all the debilitating effects of his sickness except his deafness and the ringing in his ears. Around this time, he felt energetic enough to embark on his love affair with the Duchess of

Fig. 3. *La Tirana* (Maria del Rosario Fernandez), 1794. Oil on canvas. Madrid, Private collection.

Alba, surely a difficult and demanding partner, as well as to initiate the series of drawings that eventuated in the *Caprichos* etchings.

The Diagnostic Problem

Many theories of Goya's diagnosis overlook his virtually unbroken record of high-level productivity, sustained throughout a long lifetime. Speculations that he suffered from tertiary syphilis, manic-depressive psychosis, or schizophrenia, although frequently made, are all equally incompatible with the facts.[16] William Niederland's lead-poisoning hypothesis (1972, pp. 413–18) appears to be just as implausible in view of Goya's continued use of lead-based pigments for at least another 20 years after his 1792–93 crisis.[17] Terrence Cawthorne (1962, p. 215) proposes the possibility of a Vogt-Kiyonagi Syndrome (which permanently destroys the victim's hearing and vestibular sense), but this diagnosis is inconsistent with Goya's rapid recovery of his sense of balance. As the artist's friend Martínez noted in the letter cited above, Goya soon recovered his equilibrium, and only four years later, he was able to fresco the cupola of the church of S. Antonio de la Florida in Madrid, a feat impossible for anyone with permanent vestibular damage.[18]

Goya's art from 1777, when he had his first mysterious attack, to 1792, contains a significant number of motifs alluding to sensations of dizziness or fear of losing balance. This fact suggests that he suffered from a chronic, recurrent syndrome affecting his sense of equilibrium, such as Menière's Disease. It is characteristic of Menière's Disease to wax and wane, and victims typically experience alternating cycles of relief and distress.

In his work prior to the end of 1792, Goya often utilized such motifs as the dance and children's games to depict his own inner sensations of dizziness and impending loss of balance.[19] Thus, he seems to have distanced himself from his subjective experiences in two ways: First, by utilizing gay young people or mischievous little boys as protagonists, instead of mature men; second, by portraying these sensations as deliberately induced and self-limiting. These devices seem therefore to represent the artist's defensive attempts to deny the implications and severity of his symptoms.

The recurring themes of the sensations of giddiness, loss of orientation in space, and feelings of precariousness that characterize many of Goya's paintings of 1777–92 argue against the view that his illness of 1792–93 was a sudden, isolated attack akin to that experienced by victims by the Vogt-Kiyonagi Syndrome. Rather, these motifs suggest that the artist must have suffered for several years from milder attacks of the type that became acute and malignant in 1792. Perhaps at that point he contracted a viral infection which struck his most vulnerable system, his vestibular and auditory apparatus, already the focus of previous disorders.[20]

Goya's Painted Caprichos of 1793–94

It surely cannot be a coincidence that Goya initiated his painted meditations on his illness of 1792–93 with a series of bullfight pictures. Throughout his long career, he repeatedly returned to the theme of bulls and bullfights (as would his artistic heir, Pablo Picasso), portraying aspects of this national sport in every medium at his command—paintings, drawings, etchings, and lithographs. The artist's intimate identification with this sport bore other permanent fruit: The costume worn by matadors for special ceremonies preceding a bullfight depends from a design by Goya.[21] Perhaps this costume grew out of the special regalia the artist allegedly donned whenever he attended the *corrida*. In view of his enthusiasm for the bull ritual, one can understand why he sometimes wrote his name as "Francisco de los toros" and apparently took to boasting as an elderly gentleman that he had killed bulls in his youth.[22]

The first of these little bullfight pictures (Fig. 4), of 1793–94 depicts a bull round-up. It takes place in a barren stretch of

Fig. 4. *The Bull Round-Up,* 1793. Oil on tinplate. Paris, private collection.

country, and bulls of varying sizes and colors spill out, filling the foreground space and commanding our attention.[23] Their captors approach on horseback and foot, stealthily fanning out to surround the beasts in a viselike grip. Although one trusting white animal lies stretched out on the ground, others seem more apprehensive. The black bull who occupies the center of the group seems particularly wary. Clearly the leading protagonist in the drama, this bull—or his double—reappears in subsequent scenes that detail his terrible fate.

In Goya's earliest bullfight painting, the 1779 tapestry cartoon, *The Amateur Bullfight* (Fig. 5), the artist identified himself with the matador, and he appears in this canvas as a youth playing the bull with his cape while turning to fix the spectator with a bold gaze. By contrast, it is primarily as his bull *Doppelgänger* that the artist appears in the bullfight pictures of the cabinet series. Architectural landmarks of Seville included in several of these panels suggest that the ranch where the bulls are captured lies just outside Seville. Like the black bull of the first painting, Goya was also seized in or around Seville. His captor, however, was not a

Fig. 5. *The Amateur Bullfight,* 1779–80. Oil on canvas. Madrid, The Prado.

human agent, but a more insidious foe: A debilitating disease, which not only exposed him to the threat of death, but to possible humiliation and dismissal from his position as court painter for violating the terms of his employment with the king and leaving Madrid without official permission.

The panel that Gassier and Wilson classify as the third of Goya's cabinet pictures seems to me more likely to have been painted second. For this picture (Fig. 6), like the first one, takes place in a rural setting, the bullring at a breeding ranch or in a small village. It again deals with the theme of amateur (or perhaps semiprofessional) bullfighting, which Goya had depicted with so much bravura in his 1779 cartoon. In this instance, too, young men play a *novillo,* or calf. But now the game has turned more deadly; no longer content to tease the animal with the cape, or to

Fig. 6. *Placing the Banderillas,* 1793. Oil on tinplate. Madrid, private collection.

crown him with a paper rose, as the youths do in *The Amateur Bullfight,* the young men seemingly now prepare to stage a genuine bullfight, which will terminate in the animal's death. The painting depicts the beginning of the ritual, as the young *aficionados* take turns thrusting their *banderillas* into the animal's withers. The bewildered beast calmly accepts its fate, making no attempt to defend itself; its lack of fire may explain why it has been selected for a village arena, rather than to appear in the major bullring of Seville. Condemned to die at the hands of amateur or inept matadors, the animal appears destined for an ignominious end. Once again, the bull seems to symbolize Goya himself, who narrowly escaped suffering a similar death alone and abandoned in the unfamiliar setting of Seville. Like the poor bull, he suffered dreadful torments, but, unlike the animal, Goya was rescued by friends and survived to triumph over destiny.

The panel (Fig. 7) that appears as the second in the Gassier-Wilson reconstruction, but which I believe the artist probably painted third, presents an alternative history for the black bull: He has been selected for death in the Maestranza, the arena of

Fig. 7. *Capture of a Bull,* 1793. Oil on tinplate. Madrid, private collection.

Seville. He makes his last stand for freedom in the circular plaza fronting the Torre del Oro, a structure that rises on the banks of the river Guadalquivir in Seville, very close to the Maestranza (Gassier & Wilson, 1971, pp. 159–60, no. 318). The picador and his assistants have loosed a pack of dogs to help corral the bull, and the enraged animal has killed one of the tormentors: The dog lies belly-up in the foreground. But his death will not save the bull, for the noose has already been fitted around his horns, and the cowboy and his assistants start to tug at the rope while additional dogs worry the bull's throat and hindquarters. From the safe distance of the plaza, an enthralled audience watches a different type of contest: Two adventuresome boys compete for a cache of game birds tied to the top of a tall greased sapling. (This submotif repeats a theme Goya painted several years earlier, *The Greasy Pole* of 1786.[24] This is one of the representations of dizzying—and in this case, dangerous—children's games which Goya favored between 1777 and 1792.) The contrast between the joyousness of the crowd and the sad plight of the bull seems especially poignant and surely represents the artist's own perception of the unthinking reaction of bystanders when he himself became so ill.

The next five scenes all take place within the Maestranza, beginning with a composition showing mounted officials on horseback driving spectators from the ring so that the bullfight may begin. The following panel shows part of the ritual preceding the real contest: An assistant plays the bull with a cape while the matador studies the way the animal moves and hooks with his horns. By the time the next episode unfolds (Fig. 8), the combat has turned quite deadly. For the moment—and it will be a brief moment—the bull is in the ascendancy. The maddened beast, stung by *banderillas,* taunted by the matador and his assistants, has suddenly unhorsed a picador. The latter's mount falls to the ground, and the bull tramples him underfoot while spearing the hapless rider with his horns. Other members of the *cuadrilla* rush to their fallen comrade's aid; the picadors attack the beast with their lances while other men, on foot, tug at his tail. The crowd gazes with seeming impassivity on this tangled drama. The suc-

Fig. 8. *Picador Caught by the Bull,* 1793. Oil on tinplate. New York, private collection.

ceeding panel (Fig. 9), depicts the inevitable dénouement: The bull's brief triumph has ended; weakened by repeated wounds from darts and lances, he lowers his head and the matador moves in for the kill. In the background, one glimpses two disemboweled, dying horses, previously dispatched by the bull, who now faces his own death. The remaining bullfight panel portrays the ignominious final exit of the bull as gaily decorated mules drag the animal's carcass from the field.

These pictures are not only the earliest of the set of 14: They also reflect the full force of the artist's depressive reaction to his malady and its sequelae. The doomed bull, tormented into a dizzying contest with a superior power, eventually weakens and succumbs. The fact that he conducts himself with all the bravery and dignity possible under the circumstances does not spare him humiliation, agony, and, eventually death. But through these grim visions, the artist succeeded in mastering memories of the terror, pain, and shame he himself had suffered. Like the young bull, he had seemed sturdy, powerful, invincible. Yet, like the bull, he had faced almost certain destruction. But the matadors, picadors and

Fig. 9. *Matador Killing the Bull,* 1793. Oil on tinplate. Madrid, private collection.

other assistants in these panels also represent aspects of the artist himself. His struggle, after all, had been internal. It occurred within the enclosure of his own skull, not in the bullring of Seville. As a group, these scenes of the *fiesta nacional,* along with the six paintings that followed, might be compared to external projections of the nightmares suffered by the victims of traumatic neuroses. After an overwhelming experience, the person often relives these events and reactions in repetitive anxiety dreams. But with each repetition, the dreamer's sense of helplessness decreases; gradually, through this means, he masters and integrates the trauma and resumes his normal life course. These early scenes of the bullfight reflect the trauma Goya had suffered with all its vividness and immediacy; but by painting these pictures and the scenes to follow, he, too, gradually mastered his feelings of apprehension, rage, and impotence.

After finishing the eight *fiesta dos toros* pictures, Goya temporarily abandoned his meditations on the most tragic aspects of his recent experiences. In two seemingly more lighthearted panels, he addressed himself, instead, to another painful aftereffect of his disease: his permanent deafness and the devices he needed to master to cope with this handicap and continue his social contacts with others—undoubtedly a factor of great importance to this gregarious man. The first of these paintings, *The Strolling Players* (Fig. 10), represents a motif dear to Watteau, that of a group of *Commedia dell'Arte* players performing. The little troupe has set up an improvised tent theater on a slight rise above a stream. The embankment separates the players from their audience, and we see only the upper figures of the latter as they press forward to watch the action. (The size and enthusiasm of the crowd also offer an indirect comment on the dull, routine quality of everyday rural life during this period.)

The stage has been defined by drawing two concentric circles in the bare earth. At the far left, a masked Harlequin juggles tenpins while Columbine and Pantaloon direct their attention—and ours—to the antics of a grotesque dwarf who scampers around the inner circle on little bowed legs, grasping a tenpin in one fist and a glass in the other, as though enacting the role of an ebullient imbiber of champagne (Fig. 11). Does he represent Pulcinella, the hunchbacked dwarf later absorbed into the English Punch-and-Judy shows? If so, he wears neither the mask (his hideous features appear to be his own) nor the loose clown costume that constitutes this character's more typical attire. Instead, he appears in natty 18th-century dress, complete with ribbon and cocked hat. A fifth member of the troupe stands near the curtain; a fashionably dressed, elderly gentleman wearing an ornate wig, he assumes a pose of sophisticated—and rather condescending—ease as he holds Columbine's hand and watches the antics of the little dwarf. He probably represents a corrupt version of the stock character Doctor Graziano, the ridiculous, dissolute old man of the *Commedia dell'Arte.*[25]

In this instance, Goya, like Watteau (and, later, Picasso), identifies himself with the band of rootless, strolling players, who live

Fig. 10. *The Strolling Players,* 1793. Oil on tinplate. Madrid, the Prado.

on the edge of want and desperation, but who must always maintain their public façades, their roles as entertainers for the masses. Harlequin, juggling his tenpins, surely represents one aspect of Goya himself, attempting to cope with his terrifying sensations of giddiness and spinning around in space—sensations that certainly tortured him during the acute phase of his illness and, intermittently, no doubt, for months—perhaps even years—afterward. But just as Harlequin keeps his pins spinning merrily, never missing a beat, so Goya resolutely returned to easel painting and other aspects of his artistic career. The little dwarf, completing his dizzying rounds of the circle, not only comprises another implicit reference to Goya's giddiness, but even more pronouncedly to his deafness—a condition that transformed him into an isolated freak, as this hideous little dwarf is isolated from his fellow men by his deformity and by the framing boundary line of his circle. Forced now to communicate with others by means of writing or signing (a skill he apparently mastered as soon as he felt strong enough), Goya must have felt that he cut a ridiculous figure before others, just as the dwarf does. But the remaining

Fig. 11. Detail of
Figure 10.

characters also symbolize another of Goya's traits: his ability to
step outside himself, gaining distance to judge his own situation
and reactions with cool objectivity. He surely realized that when
he appeared in public before his fellow academicians—the "professors" as he ironically referred to them—these gentlemen would
study his responses with the same underlying disdain and superiority as the bewigged figure in this painting.[26] Like the dwarf,
Goya evidently was prepared to enact his role without faltering or
revealing any of his underlying anguish over his altered physical
condition.

A companion panel, *The Marionette Seller* (Fig. 12), portrays
another aspect of theater art popular in the period, the puppet
show. In this painting, Goya brings us into much closer proximity
with the protagonists than in the previous works.[27] We look over
the marionette seller's shoulder right into the faces of the eager
children and gullible young women who excitedly cluster round
the puppeteer. The luminosity of the landscape setting here seems
very close to the treatment of the distant riverbank in *The
Strolling Players,* while the light, delicate touch Goya employed in

delineating the faces of the audience offers a dramatic contrast to the looming, simplified silhouette of the puppeteer himself. With his huge dark hat, unkempt hair, and ragged coat, the marionette manipulator seems simultaneously sinister and pathetic, a threadbare wizard. Perhaps this sensation of his evil, unnatural influence arises in part because his cloak seems to engulf the child standing next to him (also with his back to us). It seems unclear whether this boy actually belongs to the puppeteer's troupe or is simply a child from the audience whom the vendor has selected to help manipulate the dolls and reinforce his sales talk. In any case, it seems to be this child, not the marionette seller himself, who conducts the mesmerizing demonstration. To the puppeteer's right, we observe a seated older man who appears strangely divorced from the intense proceedings involving the other protagonists. He stares off meditatively, for all the world as though he were alone in the landscape. Does he represent a member of the puppeteer's entourage (perhaps the real owner of the merchandise, with the cloaked man acting as his shill?) who has heard all this a thousand times before, or is he simply a chaperone who has accompanied one of the members of the audience and now simply bides his time while waiting to fetch his charge home again? But the man's pose seems strangely familiar: It closely resembles the posture assumed by Martínez in the painting of the latter that Goya completed just before his illness struck. This clue suggests that, on another level, this cabinet picture may also represent the acute phase of Goya's illness, the period when both Martínez and Death (symbolized by the sinister aspect of the marionette seller) kept vigil at the artist's bedside.

Like the bullfight scenes and *The Strolling Players,* this panel contains a complex of references, depicting many aspects of Goya's reactions to his illness. Once again, the painting shows both involved and detached spectators, and both groups seem to represent aspects of the artist himself. The audience in *The Marionette Seller* surely refers to Goya's own public (including his fellow academicians) whom he imagines eagerly awaiting his reentry into the everyday world, much as they would watch a puppeteer's performance. Like the puppeteer, the artist possesses the magical ability to evoke life from the inanimate, to create the illusion that his painted beings possess a real soul and depict the dramas of real people. But Goya himself had now become the puppet, as well as the puppeteer. Because his illness deprived him of his ability to communicate freely and to respond verbally to the comments of others, he had to convey his wishes and feelings, instead, through a series of hand signals rather similar to those the puppeteer uses to control his marionettes. The detached older man in this scene may not only symbolize Martínez but also the artist's own objectivity, his ability to observe and record his struggles with his handicaps.

The theme of *The Assault on the Coach* (Fig. 13), which Goya depicted next, was one that especially interested the artist, who had painted two earlier representations of this motif (see Gassier & Wilson, Cat. I, nos. 152, 251; the latter formed part of the Osuna commission of 1786–87). But Goya's final version of the theme develops the composition in a much more powerful, ominous manner than in the two earlier renditions. Those earlier pictures represent the robbery taking place in the verdant countryside; this one occurs in a more desolate spot, along a road winding through a barren, mountainous region. Forbidding rocks loom up in the immediate background, shutting off the distant view, while a stone wall, running from the edge of the picture to the point where it is obscured by the coach, acts both to cut off the view and the passengers' escape route to the right, simultaneously forming a dramatic dark background for the action. The bandits have apparently halted the coach just as it started down an incline, and its enormous back wheels and rear loom up directly behind the sprawling victims, cutting off the perspective of the distant road and compelling us to concentrate on the drama being enacted in the foreground. This time, Goya also eschewed the sentimental touch of including women or children among the victims. The passengers are all men; four of them lie sprawled

Fig. 13. *The Assault on the Coach*, 1793–94. Oil on tinplate. Madrid, private collection.

across the road, dead or dying. One of the bandits kneels next to a man lying almost under the coach; the latter has already sustained what appears to be a mortal wound, but the assassin prepares to strike him again, while another robber simultaneously trains his rifle on the dying man. In the right foreground, the only remaining uninjured passenger kneels with clasped hands, desperately begging for his life (Fig. 14). He addresses his pleas to the brigand who perches atop the coach; this man looks away disinterestedly, as though the scene before him did not exist. His duty consists only in watching the distant road, and he sticks stolidly to his assignment. Meanwhile, unbeknownst to the pleading passenger, another robber half-hidden by the shadow of the coach raises his rifle, preparing to draw a bead on the man's head.

The motif of the coach robbery, always a highly valent one for Goya, evidently acquired new meaning for him as a result of his illness. Like these travelers, the artist had been rudely and unexpectedly assaulted while in transit from Cádiz. But his opponent had been unseen and untiring, his ordeal much more prolonged than that of the poor coach passengers. Many times during

Fig. 14.   Detail of
Figure 13.

the first months of his illness, Goya must have felt he faced
certain death as surely as this band of travelers. We have absolutely no evidence that he was particularly religious—indeed, it
seems unlikely. However, as a native of Roman Catholic Spain, he
had surely been drilled from early childhood on the efficacy of
prayer, and he may have tested out the validity of these teachings
many times during the prolonged invalidism that followed the
sudden onset of his illness.

The Madhouse Yard (Fig. 15), which Goya probably painted
next, takes place in the walled courtyard of an insane asylum, a
dank world where perpetual twilight reigns. The scene is set in a
corner where two walls abut. The nearer wall has a single arched
opening, closed by a heavy grate. Dim light filters through this
aperture, as well as from the overcast sky above; the grayish and
olive-green tones that prevail in this panel reinforce the picture's
cheerless quality. The stone wall appears to be covered with
lichen, and one can well imagine the bone-penetrating chill experienced by the inmates, all of them either nude or scantily clothed
in sackcloth shifts. In the center of the group, two struggling

Fig. 15. *The Madhouse Yard,* doc. 1794. Oil on tinplate. Dallas, The Meadows Museum.

inmates grapple, unaware—or heedless—of the whip their keeper wields above their heads. His face seems rather impassive; he obviously beats his charges so regularly that he does it routinely, without much emotion. The other patients respond—or fail to respond—to the fighting couple in a wide variety of ways. The conflict clearly offers a welcome respite from the boredom of their miserable existence for some of the men, while others react with distressed agitation. Still others, like the sackcloth-clad man who sits holding his knees as he rocks back and forth, seem too engrossed in their own delusional worlds to attend the drama being enacted before them. The inmate closest to the spectator stands near the left front corner of the picture facing us, his arms clasped, his legs spread wide, his mouth open in a soundless yowl of horror, a mute plea for help that resounds through the centuries.

This picture reflects the full flowering of Goya's empathic response to suffering humanity, a reaction he revealed in more embryonic form in certain earlier tapestry cartoons, such as *Winter and the Injured Mason.*[28] If my conjecture that Goya began to explore subject matter of that type because he himself was experiencing so much physical—and consequent emotional—distress is valid, it is not surprising that the crisis he suffered in 1792–93 would bring this aspect of his personality into full flower. His illness not only made him deaf: it left him a prey to a bizarre world of internal noises which only he could hear. Technically, such sensations, always the result of nerve deafness, are known as tinnitus. When he first experienced these strange sensations, Goya must have feared that he was going mad, and that his fate would be similar to that suffered by the poor devils he portrays so vividly in this painting. With characteristic detachment, the artist visualizes the past, present, and future of these patients, abandoned to a fate literally worse than death. Long after he had adjusted to the torments of his tinnitus, Goya remained acutely interested in, and sympathetic to, the plight of the insane. Throughout the rest of his career, he frequently portrayed madmen, particularly in his more intimate sketches. He devoted one of his last series of drawings, executed in Bordeaux between 1824 and 1828, entirely to the depiction of different types of psychotic individuals. It was precisely Goya's lively curiosity and continuing interest in his fellow men that helped him ward off the extreme withdrawal and depression to which his sudden deafness made him a potential prey.

The remaining two panels depict horrifying disasters, but in both cases the artist softens the tragic implications of his compositions by focusing on the survival ability of the victims and their efforts to help one another. *The Shipwreck* or *The Flood* (Fig. 16), portrays a sodden band of survivors emerging from the boiling sea and crawling onto a rocky beach.[29] The harsh character of the seashore makes the cause of the tragedy all too plain; treacherous outcroppings of rock dot the water; undoubtedly, the ship has foundered on one of them. An especially awesome boulder dominates the left half of the painting. Its form seems almost zoomorphic, suggesting a gigantic sea monster with an open maw. But the poor drenched survivors—if not their boat—have eluded its fierce bite; they gain the beach, most of them more dead than alive. One stalwart fellow still retains enough strength to help a weaker comrade gain a foothold on shore. Another sturdy figure appears at the heart of the painting—a beautiful but distraught young woman, the only fully erect form in the painting. Although her soaked, torn blouse exposes her breasts, she has lost none of her dignity. She flings both arms towards heaven, invoking divine help. Other men and women, emerging from the sea, join her in prayer. The young woman's striking placement and pose make her the focal point of the composition, and Goya further underlines her almost allegorical symbolism by clothing her in warm creams and yellows, colors of light and hope that contrast vividly with the cold gray of the seas raging behind her. Goya's brushwork throughout this painting seems especially dashing and impetuous, underlying the dramatic movement of the narrative. Here and there, the artist's brush has touched the cold stones and sea with warm golden touches. The sky, painted with vivid beauty, echoes

Fig. 16. *The Ship-wreck* or *The Flood*, 1793–94. Oil on tin-plate. Madrid, private collection.

this optimistic note. The storm appears to be breaking; the ominous dark clouds, dissipating, expose the light of the approaching dawn. The artist's message seems evident: a new day begins, heralding the hope of survival and a fresh start to the battered survivors of *The Shipwreck.*

Most Goya scholars believe that the remaining painting from the cabinet series, *Fire at Night* (Fig. 17), represents "a far-off reflection" of the conflagration that destroyed the Teatro Principal in Saragossa in 1778, claiming many lives (Gassier & Wilson, 1971, Cat. II, no. 329). Gudiol calls attention to the impetuous drawing and convulsive character of this composition, "a marvelous expression of the impulses that move this group of human beings to huddle together as if seeking in one another their common salvation" (1971, pp. 93–94). Recoiling from the intense heat and brilliance of the burning structure, the tangled knot of victims and rescuers meld together in an intense synthesis, almost as though fused by the very heat of the flames which constantly threaten to engulf them, while casting flashing lights over their twilit forms and faces. Despite the terrible dangers to which they

Fig. 17. *The Fire at Night,* 1793–94. Oil on tinplate. San Sebastian, private collection.

expose themselves, the rescuers never falter in their attempts to aid the suffering. Like a unifying leitmotif, the repeated shape of prone bodies being lifted above the crowd echoes throughout the painting, as the stricken are removed and transported to a place of comfort and safety (Fig. 18).

Thus, Goya ended his little series on a note as dramatic as the climax of a great Verdi opera. The theme of these final "arias" consists of the reiteration of the artist's belief in man's triumph over the malign forces of human existence, a conquest that also constitutes a triumph of human selflessness. Like these victims of sea and fire, Goya emerged from his own ordeal with renewed faith in his fellow man and an increased concern for human suffering. Like these victims, Goya had been rescued by close friends, who provided him with shelter, care, and protection from potential enemies who might have utilized the opportunity to wreck his career. But Goya provided his own spiritual renewal, a cure effected through his art, for the creation of these 14 little panels permitted him to comprehend and conquer the terrible physical and emotional sequelae of his illness. Goya began the

Fig. 18. Detail of Figure 17.

series by equating himself—now effectively rendered mute—with a poor dumb beast, destined for destruction. But he concluded the set with a grand trumpeting of his faith in man's humanity to man. It seems especially appropriate that he terminated this group with a scene representing a conflagration. Like the phoenix, miraculously renewed by the flames, Goya had emerged from his searing experience reborn, transformed from a painter of pretty Rococo pictures into an artist of dark expressionist powers.

Acknowledgments   I owe thanks to several medical specialists consulted during the preparation of this essay, especially Stanton A. Friedberg, Professor Emeritus of Otolaryngology at Rush Medical School. Thanks, too, to Timothy Lennon, conservator at The Art Institute of Chicago, for discussing Goya's painting technique with me and supplying valuable bibliography. Professor Robert Rosenblum of the Department of Fine Arts, New York University, made a number of valuable observations when he discussed my ideas following a lecture I gave for the Art Therapy Series at NYU on December 18, 1983. As usual, too, I benefited from the opportunity to share my ideas with my artist friend, Regina Rosenzweig.

Notes

Illustrations of works in private collections have been reproduced from Gassier and Wilson, 1971.

1 To cite only a few examples, see: F. Licht (1979, p. 11), P. Gassier and J. Wilson (1971, pp. 112–113; see also the prefatory note to Cat. II, p. 169). See also, J. Gudiol (n.d., p. 29) and F. J. Sánchez-Cantón (1964, p. 52).

2 N. Glendinning (1977, pp. 165–177) devoted an entire chapter to a review of this question. See also Gudiol (1971, I, pp. 87–89), X. de Salas (1978, pp. 64–70) and Gassier and Wilson (1971, pp. 105–106). It should be emphasized that most of the art historians who have written about this problem merely review the history of Goya's illness and the related medical literature without committing themselves to a diagnosis. The medical and psychological specialists have been bolder about proposing diagnoses. Although I refer specifically to a number of these specialists, the interested reader should consult the more complete bibliography offered by A. Rothenberg and B. Greenberg (1974, p. 40).

3 Bernardo Iriarte was then vice-protector of the Academy; Goya addressed him with almost obsequious politeness in three letters dated January 4, 7, and 9, 1794. The original versions of these letters are in the Department of Manuscripts of the British Museum, but Gassier and Wilson reproduced the letters (1971, App. IV, p. 382; see also p. 108 for a translation of the first letter).

4 X. D. Fitzgerald (1967, pp. 252–255) identified the only painting from the series that Goya described in detail in the second of his letters to Irarte. Fitzgerald demonstrated that this picture must be *The Madhouse Yard* now in the collection of the Meadows Museum, Southern Methodist University, Dallas. The fact that this painting is executed on a tin plate (a ground Goya seldom used) of a distinctive small size, led to the rediscovery of the remaining cabinet paintings, executed on similar tin plates. Although Goya assured Iriarte in the January 7, 1794 letter that he could keep the pictures as long as he wished, two days later the artist requested their transfer to the home of a potential buyer. By around 1805, they formed part of the collection of the court goldsmith, Leonard Chopinot. The inventory of his collection, drawn up after his death, revealed that he owned "fourteen sketches by Goya which show different scenes of the bullfight, a shipwreck, an assault of bandits, a fire in the night, etc." Using this list, de Salas rediscovered the other paintings (1968–69, pp. 29–33, esp. p. 30).

5 Gassier and Wilson (1971, pp. 109–12, 159) concur with de Salas's identification of 13 of the 14 pictures. Gudiol (1971, I, pp. 31–34) accepted *The Strolling Players, Fire at Night, The Shipwreck, The Assault on the Coach,* and *The Madhouse Yard,* but rejected the eight bullfight pictures as earlier works. He proposed a number of additional candidates for the series, none of them painted on tin. Gassier and Wilson convincingly dated all the latter works much later. Most Goya scholars accept the Gassier-Wilson catalogues raisonnés of Goya's oeuvre as more accurate and reliable than the comparable catalogues provided by Gudiol, and I have also followed this practice. All dates and references to works by Goya in this paper, then, come from the Gassier-Wilson 1971 complete catalogue of the artist's works.

6 See the letter dated January 7, 1794 in Gassier and Wilson (1971, App.

IV, p. 382). In their notes to catalogue II (p. 161), they commented: "If the fourteen pictures were painted as a group, and if the twelfth [i.e., *The Madhouse Yard*] was described by Goya as the last of the series sent to the Academy via Iriarte, it seems likely that he would have added [*The Shipwreck*] and [*Fire at Night*] as afterthoughts, since they are the most advanced in style and subject matter." This reconstruction not only seems eminently logical, it also makes the best sense iconographically, providing the progression of subject matter that I discuss below.

7 Goya's successful career in Spain began around 1771, when he returned from a period of study in Italy. Just before he left Italy, he entered an art competition sponsored by the Parma Academy and was runner up. Soon after he returned to Saragossa, he received the first of many important commissions which would come his way, to paint a ceiling fresco for the small choir in the cathedral of El Pilar. He moved to Madrid in 1773, perhaps encouraged by his compatriot Francisco Bayeu, whose pupil he may have been. That same year, he married Bayeu's sister, Josefa. In 1775, the artist received his first commissions to execute tapestry cartoons from the Royal Tapestry factory (a boon he owed to A. R. Mengs, then First Court Painter), and executed his first portraits of the king and queen. During these years he also received numerous commissions to paint altarpieces, portraits, and other pictures for various powerful patrons. For a more detailed summary, see Glendinning (1977, pp. 22–30). Gassier and Wilson (1971, p. 28) provide a useful chronological table covering the period from the artist's birth through 1792.

8 There is some confusion about the date of Goya's first major illness, which occurred either in the spring of 1777 or 1778. Gassier and Wilson favor the earlier date (1971, p. 48 and Cat. I, p. 75, nos. 88–117).

9 The same confusion concerning the chronology of Goya's illness applies to that of the etchings. Sánchez-Cantón (1951) dates the illness to 1778 and suggests that Goya may have executed the etchings during his convalescence. He notes that the artist sent a complete set of the prints to his childhood friend Martín Zapater, in December 1778. Most Goya scholars emphasize the importance of this close study of Velázquez for the artist's future development.

10 The seven cartoons include multiple references to balance and equilibrium. There are scenes of young girls carrying water jugs on their heads, of youths stilt-walking, boys see-sawing, climbing on one another's backs to steal fruit from a tree, and riding on one another's shoulders. *The Straw Mannikin,* the most famous cartoon of the set, depicts young girls tossing a life-size male dummy on a blanket. The remaining cartoon, *The Wedding,* does not directly refer to equilibrium, but the wedding party is depicted as it spills down an incline under a viaduct, a strange setting that lends a note of instability to this enigmatic painting.

11 Glendinning (1977, pp. 44–46) reproduces a translation of this report in its entirety.

12 Gassier and Wilson (1971, p. 106) suggested that, apart from his illness, Goya's six-months' stay with Martínez must have been very important to his artistic development. Martínez allegedly owned over three hundred paintings and several thousand engravings, including works by Piranesi. Gassier and Wilson noted that "one can imagine Goya, still ill or semi-convalescent, racked by pain and a prey to darkest thoughts being deeply impressed by a series like the *Carceri* [Prisons], whose influence is clearly apparent in some of the *Caprichos* prints."

13 Gassier and Wilson (1971, Cat. II, p. 170) assigned ten portraits (nos. 333–345), including that of Martínez, executed just before Goya fell ill,

to the late 1792–early 1793 through 1794 period. Apart from the portrait of Martínez, only two of these pictures bear a date, that of 1794 in both cases (339, 340). It seems to me improbable that Goya would have essayed any major canvases before painting the little cabinet series. The small size of the latter pictures suggests that they could have been executed from a seated or semireclining position, an arrangement that might have facilitated their completion by the still-weak artist. Sánchez-Cantón (1964, p. 53) suggested that two of these portraits, that of *Don Francisco de Paula Caveda y Solares* and "the fine portrait" of *General Don Antonio Ricardos* must be dated in the last weeks of 1793 or the first few months of 1794. Gassier and Wilson do not include the former portrait in their catalogue, presumably because they do not consider it autograph. They assign the portrait of the general (who died in March 1794) to the same period as Sánchez-Cantón.

14 For example, on April 23, 1794, the artist wrote Zapater, "I am about the same as regards my health. At times I am so irritable (*rabiando*) that I can't bear myself. At other times I am calmer than he who has now taken pen in hand to write to you. But I am tired already; I will only just tell you, that on Monday, God willing, I shall go to the bullfights and I wish you could go with me" (in A. L. Mayer, 1924, pp. 15–16).

15 Quoted in de Salas (1978, p. 70). On the same page, he cited other virtually contemporary reports that suggest that Goya was still totally unable to paint, an assertion which the existence of the little cabinet pictures certainly disproves. Gudiol (1971, I, p. 89), proposed that these contradictory reports indicate that Goya may have exaggerated his attacks a bit to prolong his convalescence and avoid resumption of his official duties.

16 As just one example of the diagnoses of functional psychoses, see R. W. Pickford (1967, pp. 282–293), who concluded that Goya suffered from schizophrenia, paranoia, and manic-depressive psychoses, but that his illness of 1792–93 resulted from physical causes! S. L. Shapiro (1966, pp. 89–91) is one of the authorities who argued for tertiary syphilis. Shapiro maintained that Goya's 1792–93 illness must have been a case of meningitic lues, although no trace of the classic organic signs is ever present in the artist's drawings and paintings, not even those of his very old age. Glendinning (1978, pp. 166–172) cited several other authorities who proposed combined diagnoses, including one who suggested that the artist was both schizophrenic and syphilitic. See also Rothenberg and Greenberg (1974, p. 40) for additional references to various diagnoses of psychoses and syphilis.

17 Martin Wyld (1981, p. 38) noted that we possess very little technical information concerning Goya's painting practices. He reported, however, that a cross section of Goya's portrait of *The Duke of Wellington, 1812–14*, one of few such studies carried out to date, showed "a thick layer of red and white lead pigments." For additional information about Goya's techniques, data based on observations, rather than chemical analyses, see F. Schmid (1942).

18 The artist worked from scaffolding to paint this beautiful ensemble, whose autograph character has never been questioned.

19 The interested reader should consult Gassier and Wilson (1971, Cat. I) for numerous examples of this type. As I studied Goya's oeuvre during these years, I became more and more impressed with the unstable poses in which he frequently depicted figures.

20 In my correspondence with Friedberg, I mentioned the fact that several sources indicate that Goya suffered from ear trouble in childhood. (I did not cite any of these sources in this paper, because none of them

provides verification for this assertion, and none of the most renowned Goya scholars mentions it.) In his response (personal communication, March 31, 1982), Friedberg wrote that *if* this story of childhood ear trouble is accurate, one might hypothesize that Goya suffered from "chronic otitis media with invasion of the inner ear (deafness), loss of balance (labrynthitis) and, tho' remote, a localizing meningitis in 1792–93 which very nearly killed him." Although Friedberg emphasized the completely speculative nature of this reconstruction, it certainly fits the description of Goya's 1792–93 illness better than any other alternative.

21 *The Encyclopedia Britannica* (1979, Macrovol. 3, p. 476) noted: "At the height of his fame the artist Francisco de Goya designed a distinctive professional uniform worn only on commemorative occasions in Goya-style *corridas* or *corridas goyescas.*"

22 Goya allegedly made the boast about bullfighting during his youth to the dramatist L. F. de Moratín, who knew the aged artist during his last years in Bordeaux (in Glendinning, 1977, pp. 88–89). Glendinning believed that the legend that Goya fought the bulls is part of the romanticization which colored 19th-century views of the artist (see pp. 69–102). Gassier and Wilson (1971, p. 42) suggested that Goya probably never belonged to a professional *cuadrilla*—or company: "in Spain youths have always played at bullfighting with *novillos* or *becerros* (one- or two-year-old calves) without killing them."

23 Goya had depicted a bull round-up once before, as part of a series of paintings executed for the country estate of the Duke and Duchess of Osuna (Gassier & Wilson, 1971, Cat. I, no. 254). That earlier depiction seems less graphic and dramatic than the round-up portrayed in the cabinet paintings. In the earlier canvas, the bulls are placed much further from the spectator, and the horizontal format of the painting generally makes it less gripping than the second version.

24 Another of the paintings executed for the Osunas' country estate (Gassier & Wilson, 1971, Cat. I, no. 248), called *The Greasy Pole,* shows two little boys attempting to climb a tall, swaying sapling. The fact that several themes of the paintings for the Osunas recur in the cabinet series suggests that the artist enjoyed a great deal of latitude in carrying out the former commission and used the opportunity to paint highly personalized motifs.

25 See J. S. Kennard (1935) for information concerning typical costumes and characters featured in the *Commedia dell'Arte.* He noted that actors who participated in the late, corrupt versions of this artform often adopted enormous powdered wigs and lace shirts similar to those worn here by the Doctor Graziano character. The Prado Museum's official description of this work (1969) identified the characters as Harlequin, Columbine, Pantaloon, the Doctor, and the Dwarf. They also identified the descrition on the scroll in the foreground as *Alegorica menandrea,* used by the *Commedia dell'Arte* in homage to the Greek actor Menander. They suggested that the scene represents memories of Goya's stay in Italy.

26 In his first letter to Iriarte, January 4, 1794, Goya referred to his colleagues in the Academy as "the professors" in a context that suggests that he expected invidious judgments on their part. See Gassier and Wilson (1971, App. IV, p. 382).

27 De Salas (1978, p. 70), pointing to this feature, argued that *The Marionette Seller* does not belong in the 1793–94 series. He proposed substituting *The Prison,* another small painting on tin plate. However, I accept the Gassier-Wilson reconstruction, which seems to me more convincing in every way, especially iconographically.

28 In 1786–87, the artist painted a series of tapestry cartoons that reveal a new interest in the plight of the Spanish peasantry. Thus, *Winter* shows a group of poorly protected peasants struggling through a snowy landscape, while a companion piece depicts a ragged mother and her two frozen children at a public fountain. A third picture from this series, *The Injured Mason,* shows two workmen carrying their fellow mason, who has evidently fallen from scaffolding visible in the background. See Gassier and Wilson (Cat. I, nos. 265–67). Initially, Goya portrayed the mason as drunk, rather than injured. F. Licht (1979, p. 38) suggested that this alteration demonstrates a profound change in Goya, who here transforms a genre theme into a piece of social realism. Without disputing this point, I would like to note that it also represents another example of Goya's use of distancing; initially, he handled the (for him) anxiety-laden theme of a workman's fall from a scaffolding by transforming it into a visual joke; his detachment provided him with the objectivity to revise the theme, revealing its tragic implications.

29 De Salas (1968, p. 5, n. 9) argued that this painting represents a terrible flood in Aragón, when the rivers Ebro and Aragón overflowed their banks in September 1787. The event was much publicized, and he believed that Goya probably read about it in the commemorative journal published in Madrid. However, most authorities consider this scene to be a shipwreck, an identification that I find more convincing.

References

Baticle, J. (1970). *Goya* (rev. Eng. ed.). The Hague: Royal Gallery of Paintings, Mauritshuis.

Cawthorne, T. (1962). Goya's illness. *Proceedings of the Royal Society of Medicine,* 55: 215.

Fitzgerald, X. D. (1967). Una obra maestra desconocida. *Goya,* 76: 252–255.

Gassier, P., & Wilson, J. (1971). *The life and complete work of Francisco Goya* (F. Lachenal, Ed.; C. Hauch & J. Wilson, Trans.). New York: Reynal & Co.

Glendinning, N. (1977). *Goya and his critics.* New Haven and London: Yale University Press.

Gudiol, J. (c. 1941). *Goya.* New York: The Hyperion Press.

——— (c. 1971). *Goya: 1746–1828, biography, analytical study and catalogue of his paintings* (4 vols.; K. Lyons, Trans). Barcelona: Ediciones Poligrafica.

Kennard, J. S. (1935). *Masks and marionettes.* New York: Macmillan & Co.

Licht, F. (1979). *Goya: The origins of the modern temper in art.* New York: Universe Books.

Mayer, A. L. (1924). *Franciso de Goya* (R. West, Trans.). London and Toronto: J. M. Dent & Sons.

Niederland, W. G. (1972). Goya's illness: A case of lead encephalopathy? *New York State Journal of Medicine,* 72: 413–418.

Pickford, R. W. (1967). *Studies in psychiatric art.* Springfield, IL: Thomas, pp. 282–293.

106

Principales acquisiciones de los últimos diez años (1958–1968). (1969). Madrid: Prado.

Rothenberg, A., & Greenberg, B. (1974). *The index of scientific writings on creativity: Creative men and women.* Hamden, CT: Shoestring Press, Inc.

Salas, X. de (1968). Precisiones sobre pinturas de Goya: *El Entierro de la Sardina,* la serie de obras de gabinette de 1793–1794 y otras notas. *Archivo Español de Arte,* xli, 161: 1–16.

———(1968–1969). Inventario. Pinturas elegidas para el Príncipe de la Paz, entre les dejadas por la viuda Chopinot. *Arte Español,* xxvi, fasc. 1: 29–33.

——— (1978). *Goya* (G. T. Culverwell, Trans.). London: Studio Vista.

Sambricio, V. de (1946). *Tapices de Goya.* Madrid: Patrimonio Nacional Archivo General de Palacio.

Sánchez-Cantón, F. G. (1951). *Vida y obras de Goya.* Madrid: Editorial Penninsular.

——— (1964). *The life and works of Goya* (P. Burns, Trans.). Madrid: Editorial Penninsular.

Schmid, F. (1942). *The technique of Goya: A lecture for artists held at the Art Institute of Chicago.* Basel: Hirzen.

Shapiro, S. L. (1966). The fateful illness of Francisco Goya. *The Eye, Ear, Nose and Throat Monthly,* 45: 89–91.

The New Encyclopedia Britannica in 30 Volumes. (1979). Chicago: Encyclopedia Britannica. Macrovolume 3: 475.

Wyld, M. (1981). Goya's re-use of a canvas for Doña Isabel. *National Gallery Technical Bulletin,* Vol. 5.

Jack J. Spector,
Ph.D.

An Interpretation of Delacroix's
Michelangelo in His Studio

Throughout his career Eugène Delacroix felt drawn to certain great personalities of the past and present, and he represented them in real or imaginary portraits. In particular he portrayed admired personalities from the fine arts: Michelangelo and Raphael; Chopin and Paganini; Goethe, Milton, Montaigne, Rabelais, Tasso, and Virgil. Delacroix valued portraiture and apparently realized the significance of his portraits as self-expression. The artist, whose talent had usually been linked to dramatic historical subjects and combats of men and/or animals, wrote in 1840: "The greatest portraitists are the greatest painters" (Joubin, 1927).[1] He believed that the portrait (like all art) could reflect its author, and he quoted with approval Mme. Cavé's remark, "In painting, and above all in the portrait . . . mind speaks to mind," adding that painting is essentially "a bridge between the mind of the painter and that of the spectator" (J.: Jan. 25, 1857; also see O.L.: I, p. 17).[2] Théophile Silvestre, speaking of Delacroix's art in general, observed that "all his figures have his pensive and suffering air" (S: p. 45); but some of the figures, especially in his portraits, demonstrably meant more to him than others. None held more personal or intimate meaning for him than his *Michelangelo in His Studio* (Fig. 1).[3] This painting belongs in the popular 19th-century genre of scenes from the lives of great artists, and has been justly called "the masterpiece of the genre."[4] The object of this essay is to interpret the significance and meaning of the painting to the artist.

Michelangelo looms large from the very beginnings of Delacroix's art, both directly as a model and indirectly through his

Fig. 1. *Michelangelo in His Studio,* 1850. Oil on canvas. Musée Fabré. Photo: Giraudon/Art Resource, New York.

influence on masters whose art Delacroix studied, such as Raphael, Rubens, Gross, and Géricault. As Silvestre put it, "Michelangelo was always alive and present to Delacroix, who said: 'I am, by rights of posterity, the contemporary of the most remote souls . . . and I have taken as my own, with Michelangelo constantly in mind, Tasso's motto: *with wisdom and skill*'" (Silvestre, 1876, p. 306). This remark is interesting for its indication of Delacroix's feeling of contemporaneity with great past artists like Michelangelo, for showing that Delacroix linked Michelangelo and Tasso, especially through Tasso's motto, and for suggesting that Delacroix identified with both great figures.[5]

The primacy of the sculptor/painter Michelangelo for the painter Delacroix is not accidental. At least one of his contemporaries, probably the sculptor Préault, said of Delacroix: "But he is more a sculptor than a painter," and his childhood friend Rodrigues recounted that at the age of seven Delacroix recited a poem about a sculptor in an immensely impressive manner: "'A block of marble was so beautiful/ that a sculptor bought it./ What will my chisel make of it? Will it be God, table or bowl?/ It will be a god; I even want it/ to have a thunderbolt in his hand./ Tremble, humans . . . .'" According to Rodrigues, the last words were pronounced with especially great energy and a terrifying accent (in R.: I, p. xv).[6]

Delacroix's fascination with Michelangelo extended far beyond the technical and stylistic achievements of the master, and encompassed a curiosity about his biography, the anecdotes concerning his personality and work habits, and his poetry. We find evidence of his enduring involvement with Michelangelo in his *Journal, Correspondence,* and above all in two essays he published, one on Michelangelo's whole career (1830) and another on the Sistine *Last Judgment* (1837). In keeping with his belief that an artist's work bears his cachet, the impress of its author's personality, Delacroix incorporated some of Michelangelo's work into his portrait. But even more interesting, he fashioned his image of the artist in part—the pose of hand to head—after one of his works, the somberly meditative sculpture *Il Pensieroso* (Lorenzo de Medici) which he found characteristic of the master's temperament (O.L.: II, pp. 42–43).[7]

The hand-to-head pose of Delacroix's Michelangelo was current in the early 19th century. We find the pose among Romantics like Géricault (*Artist in His Studio,* 1818/19), with whom Delacroix sympathized, and those of a different tendency like Ingres and Girodet, a great admirer of Michelangelo.[8] In his essay on Prudhon (1846) Delacroix singled out the portrait of Empress Josephine (1805) whose subject sits hand to head, and observed: "Her melancholy expression portends her misfortunes" (O.L.: II, p. 144). One should note Delacroix's unusual placement of the hand in relation to the head's position. In the paintings of his contemporaries the chin is usually supported by the open palm, or the index finger points to the temple. Géricault's *Artist in His Studio* comes closest to Delacroix's, but the head, set somewhat statically at right angles to the hand, looks out at us with a meditative expression devoid of Michelangelo's intensity.

Surveying previous examples of the meditative pose one comes to suspect that Delacroix's *Michelangelo* may be a synthetic creation out of previous elements.[9] Delacroix fuses into his figure pensive melancholy, tormented genius, *terribilità,* and impatience (motive for the *non-finito*).[10] No other painting I know unites in the melancholy seated figure a cupped hand directed like a vector along the face, a dramatic tension of the body, and the suffering intensity registered on the face. Delacroix has resolved the problem of using the meditative pose to signify inactivity and moroseness while at the same time exhibiting Michelangelo's torment and frustration through the facial expression and the left hand gripping the cloak. To represent the complex mood of the artist Delacroix has, as it were, blended aspects of the four temperaments: the sanguine (the accents of white in the accessories framing the head, the red cloak starting behind the face, the vigorous massive hands); the choleric (the angry face, the flash of red cloak); the phlegmatic (the inactivity symbolized by the fallen chisel); and the melancholic (the pose).[11] It seems that Delacroix's Michelangelo conveys the mood of struggle with the earthly prison of the body encountered in the Renaissance master's *Slaves,* his only major sculptures in France. A remark of Panofsky's on Michelangelo's sculpture in general sums it all up: "His figures symbolize the fight waged by the soul to escape from the bondage of matter" (Panofsky, 1939, p. 181).[12]

Delacroix's feelings for Michelangelo went deeper than emulation or appreciation, and involved a spirit of rivalry that often inspired critical remarks about the latter's work. In 1854 he insisted that the Sistine *Last Judgment* that had excited him as a youth no longer had anything to say to him, and declared that "Titian, there's a man who was made to be relished by persons growing old" (J.: n.d., II, p. 282). Delacroix often thought of the relationships among the arts and—like a latter-day Leonardo—imagined his own *"paragone,"* and the painter/sculptor Michelangelo must have seemed central to this comparison.[13] Although he obviously regarded Michelangelo essentially as a sculptor, he faulted him once for being "more painter than sculptor" (in a preliminary sketch for the painting he placed a brush rather than a chisel at Michelangelo's feet)—meaning that unlike the ancients he proceeded not by "masses" but as though he "traced an ideal contour," offering one major plane like a painting. Delacroix especially criticized him for "disproportion" and for allowing the hasty inspiration of his genius to overwhelm him instead of controlling it, as he himself struggled increasingly to do as he matured.[14] Compared to the proportioned sculpture of Antiquity Michelangelo's seemed to him *gigantesque,* and he quoted with approval his cousin Léon Riesener's observation about the "giganticism," "turgidity," and "monotony" of Michelangelo's works that have inspired an "excessive enthusiasm."[15]

Delacroix often associated the large scale of a painting with the issue of greatness, which for him above all meant the masters of the Renaissance.[16] Small paintings allowed intimacy, personal expression, and pleasure, a relief from the competition with the grandeur of the past. On April 9, 1824, in the period of both his large *Scio* and his small *Tasso* and *Don Quixote,* he wrote in his *Journal:* "I have the desire, instead of doing another painting of rather large proportion, to paint several small ones done with enjoyment." In a letter of October 5, 1850 to Constant Dutilleux on *Woman Combing Herself,* a small painting worked on in 1849 and later (i.e., painted at the same time as the first plans for the the big paintings of Saint-Sulpice and as the *Michelangelo*), Delacroix wrote: "I often paint small pictures when I have nothing more important in hand. I am not at all encouraged to do so because the art collectors value them less than the large works. As for myself, I paint both with equal pleasure, and I believe strongly that one can give as much interest to a smaller work as to an entire large monument."[17] But in a different mood in 1857 he found interest and pleasure inadequate before the grandeur of the Renaissance, particularly Titian: "We are stunned by the force, productivity and universality of these men of the 16th century. Our wretched little paintings are made for our wretched homes . . . . Already, less than 100 years after the 16th century Renaissance, Poussin paints only little pictures" (J.: January 1, 1857). Early in 1853—probably about the time he was finishing *Michelangelo*—he expressed in a letter to P. Andrieu, his assistant on mural paintings, his view of the relation between small paintings and those of monumental size: "I am up to my neck in small pictures. Having gone some time without working I have been seized with a furious urge to paint, which I'm venting on small canvases: this keeps me occupied and at the same time relaxes me after my major tasks. I still feel rather resentful against large-scale painting, to which I owe my last disappointment" (J.: III, 134/6; Jan. 6, 1853).

The question of Michelangelo's artistic giganticism evoked a mixed compliment from Delacroix in his essay on Poussin, published in June 1853 but written earlier, probably about the time he was finishing his portrait of Michelangelo. After praising Poussin for not having imitated Michelangelo, Delacroix called the Renaissance master "that Goliath of painting, who had been so harsh an initiator for the artists of his time" (O.L.: II, p. 94). He certainly associated Michelangelo the decorator of the Sistine Chapel with large mural painting—he projected a *Michelangelo and His Genius* for the Palais Bourbon murals, and he started his *Michelangelo in His Studio* in the late 1840s, just as he was developing his ideas for the monumental decorations in Saint-Sulpice. Delacroix and his contemporaries perceived these great murals as a confrontation with Italian Renaissance masters. In the course of its elaboration he turned more than ever from the static linearity he saw in Michelangelo's art to a more dynamic line and to the richly textured color of the Venetian masters.[18]

Delacroix's complaint about the gigantic scale of Michelangelo's painting and sculpture takes on a paradoxical aspect when we consider the small size of *Michelangelo in His Studio*—24 by 16 inches! But perhaps we can understand the seeming inappropriateness of containing in this small format Michelangelo, whose personality and creative energy Delacroix considered so "gigantic," together with two of his monumental sculptures, in

112 terms of the ironic comments on the overestimation of Michelangelo noted above. Delacroix, speaking almost with the voice of French classicism, seems to suggest that physical size and swollen form have less to do with true grandeur than does force of imagination. Indeed he regarded the sculptures in the portrait of Michelangelo as "huge"; on a sketch for the painting he wrote: "the marbles gigantic—Michelangelo's figure relatively small." (Fig. 2). The intentional diminution of Michelangelo's figure compared to the sculptures suggests that Delacroix had in mind a rather complex interpretation of Michelangelo's "greatness."

Whatever antipathies Delacroix felt toward Michelangelo's art, he felt a deep affinity for the man. He could in fact identify with certain reported features of Michelangelo's personality, in particular the unexplained interruption in his productivity, accompanied by a mood of frustration and melancholy.

Fig. 2. Study for *Michelangelo in His Studio*. Pencil. Fitzwilliam Museum, Cambridge, England.

In his essay of 1830 on Michelangelo, Delacroix singled out the famous episode of arrested productivity and discouragement that essentially provided the basis of his painted image of Michelangelo: "Already having achieved a great reputation, and at the height of his powers, suddenly his creativity came to a standstill. This is a very rare occurrence. For three or four years Michelangelo no longer put his hand to chisel, brush or pencil. . . . How else can we regard this but as a mental illness *(maladie à l'esprit)*, a peculiar crisis of his talent? He was between 26 and 30 years old. Some historians attribute so sudden a discouragement to a momentary break in his commissions for work, for which he had hardly wanted up to that point. That is possible." (Delacroix may have been thinking here of his own case, in the years just before the exhibition of his *Sardanapalus* in 1827/28). "There is in the greatest minds a correspondingly great indolence. To work, to sharpen one's pen or pencil is not always enjoyable . . . more often it is a hell. . . . But, by a strange contradiction, he who lives with a genius that inspires him, often fears to wake the genius from sleep. . . . Michelangelo, unemployed, having no requests for his works, stops working. Boredom overcomes him; perhaps he exaggerated this boredom and disgust. . . ."[19]

In his essay on Gros (1848), Delacroix again alluded to the episode: "Gros was 30 years old. . . . We find in the life of Michelangelo a similar phenomenon, if we can believe his historians. For about the same length of time, this great innovator remained completely inactive; and, what's more astonishing, this idleness seems quite groundless. The Florentine artist had not been, like Gros, displaced from his customary behavior as an artist by events beyond his control" (O.L.: II, p. 172).

In a number of his paintings Delacroix presented the theme of the creative personality at work, always in an appropriate setting, with suitable tools: Chopin plays the piano, Paganini the violin; Milton dictates to his daughter; Archimedes inscribes mathematical symbols. The *Michelangelo* illustrates the reverse: the solitary artist at a noncreative moment with his implements fallen or thrown from his hands, one of which holds not a tool but his cloak, a poignant detail expressing Delacroix's insight that Michelangelo's self-involvement has resulted in his nonproductivity. The question of the hand is especially interesting, since Delacroix evidently understood its expressive potential in the portrait. In his painted self-portraits Delacroix never, so far as I know, included his hands, as though, convinced of the hand's power to reveal the inner person (he often showed them in portraits of others), he feared to expose his troubled intensity; but in a sheet of drawings for a self-portrait associated with his portrait of Michelangelo (and thus corroborating the identification of Delacroix with Michelangelo) Delacroix sketched several positions of his hands, including one with his left hand holding his scarf.[20] The conjunction of the Madonna and Child group and the

Fig. 3. Detail of Figure 1.

isolated, inactive Michelangelo suggests an antithesis between a moment of creativity (hovering genius) and one of paralysis (absence of genius). This frustrated creativity belongs with the traditional notion of Michelangelo's *non-finito* and presumably reflects a disturbance of the imagination. As De Tolnay first pointed out, Delacroix suggested the *non-finito* in his modification of the bases of the sculptures: "Delacroix has deliberately modified them by transforming the rectangular blocks serving as seats to the statues into irregular forms, thereby indicating that they are still unfinished" (De Tolnay, 1962, p. 45).

In another important way Delacroix's painting has modified reality in favor of an imaginative reconstruction of Michelangelo's biography: he has perpetrated an anachronism on the statues which in their unfinished state were not known ever to have been together in one place (see the discussion below). This willingness to tamper subtly with fact in favor of imaginative effect constitutes a difference between his subjective *Michelangelo* and Géricault's *Artist in His Studio* (1818/19): though both show artists accompanied by their unused tools, Géricault presented the type of the pensive artist analogous to the case histories illustrated in his famous series from the early 1820s of the mentally deranged, whereas Delacroix imagined a concrete historical personality, a great artist identified by his sculpture, at a particular moment of his career and exhibiting intense emotions. Delacroix's image unites the melancholy of the Romantic "superior man" with a portrait mode that evolved out of the 18th-century protoromantic model of the "imaginary portrait"—a construct composed by the artist from the life of an historical personage with objective details that provide an analogy to the mind of the subject.[21] Important examples of such imaginative portraits occurred in 18th-century France (e.g., Fragonard created a well-known series).[22] Like many of his fellow Romantics (but more like Balzac than the fantastic Gaspard de la Nuit) Delacroix was willing to read an emotional life into the features of a portrait that interested him. As an example, we find in his (1829) essay on Thomas Lawrence's *Portrait of Pius VII* a remarkably personal analysis in which he treated the thoughts of the Pope as though he could read them in the portrait.[23]

The grouping of the sculptures about Michelangelo in his studio is, as already indicated, an invention of Delacroix's. As De Tolnay observed, the *Moses* was sculptured in Rome in 1515/16 and the *Virgin and Child* in Florence from 1521 to 1532, so their juxtaposition as unfinished works runs counter to their histories: "This contradiction did not trouble Delacroix, because the two statues were evidently in his eyes representatives of the entire work of the master" (De Tolnay, 1962, p. 51, n. 8).[24] De Tolnay's explanation for the grouping—that it constitutes a selection intended to stand for the whole oeuvre of Michelangelo—seems plausible enough. However, it does not take into account Delacroix's identification with Michelangelo and overlooks the possibility that he intended these particular sculptures to relate to each other through their generic qualities. This means that the stone figures might not only illustrate their well-known subjects but—in a sense I will later elaborate—might represent a group of man, woman, and child connected to Michelangelo (and by implication Delacroix himself) psychologically or biographically.

The integration of sculptures into a composition as quasi-human participants in the action occurs frequently in the art of Rubens and throughout the 18th-century French Rococo. Thus, the garden Cupids and Venuses of Watteau, Fragonard, and Boucher often share in the light-hearted erotic escapades of the living heroes and heroines.[25] Delacroix was alert to the aesthetic problems engendered by the relation of statuary (in painting or sculpture) to "reality." While he did not comment on the playful impertinence of Rococo figures in paintings he did express dissatisfaction with the blatant realism of sculptures that intruded into real space: in 1850 he criticized the arrangement of sculpture in Brussels Park for the low pedestals that brought the sculpture to the level of everyday reality: "We could have a conversation with these heroes and demigods" (J.: Jul. 6, 1850). Delacroix admired Michelangelo's ability to give life to his sculptures, and wrote of him: "Happy man! He has shaped marble and animated canvas, etc. . . . But what does it matter, after all, if nature has given you the ability in any genre whatever, to animate, to bring to life. . . . What happiness to render life, soul!" (J.: n.d., II, pp. 378–379).

In his portrait of the artist Delacroix has, I believe, both animated his sculpture and suggested a parallel between the artist and one of his sculptures. The pose of Michelangelo has affinities with the *Pensieroso,* as already mentioned, a sculpture that Delacroix praised and which he knew belonged with the *Virgin and Child* of the Medici Chapel. In his essay on Michelangelo, Delacroix mistakenly placed Michelangelo's tomb in the same church as Lorenzo de Medici's, "beside his immortal masterpieces," thus associating the master and his *Pensieroso.*[26]

Delacroix's identification with Michelangelo is clearest in the way he presents the artist: the scarf about his neck indicates that the figure practically constitutes a symbolic self-portrait (we have already referred to the self-portrait drawings with hands holding his scarf). Maxime du Camp reported that at the time of their acquaintance (about 1848) the artist "enveloped his neck with a huge scarf, because he had a larynx susceptible to infection."[27] The red cloak may also have had personal associations. In his essay on Prud'hon (1946) Delacroix, as we have seen, praised the portrait of the Empress Josephine; but he found fault with the red shawl as having "perhaps a little dryness." In the red cloak of his Michelangelo the artist seems to have resolved the inadequacy he found in Prud'hon by creating an accessory charged with energy. But the brilliant red of the cloak expressed other aspects of Delacroix's empathy with the figure—an allusion to his incapacitating fever. Delacroix suffered periodically from a fever which more than once caused an interruption of his work—as during his laryngitis of 1842, and later when he was forced to interrupt his work on the murals of the Palais Bourbon and at Saint-Sulpice.[28] Evidently the degree of his illness dictated whether the fever would prevent his working or not only not prevent work but on occasion stimulate him; thus, the bout he suffered late in 1820 perhaps helped inspire the hellish milieu and burning reds of the *Bark of Dante.*[29] Perhaps the experience of melancholy and illness lies behind the somberness of Michelangelo's studio, for he once spoke of the equation of studio and hell.[30] The red cloak poignantly condenses into one detail personal references to the expansiveness of his creative energy, to the blush of angry frustration, and to the morbid inflammation of Delacroix's fever.

That Delacroix projected his ideas and sentiments onto the composition as well as on these details emerges when we take into account, along with the figure of Michelangelo, the group of

Fig. 4.   Detail of
Figure 1.

attendant sculptures. All the figures taken together constitute, I
believe, a "family constellation," a construction that Delacroix put
on certain biographical details known to him. The sculpture of
mother and child beside Michelangelo is in itself an incomplete
family group, and corresponds to the story attributed to
Michelangelo himself about his having been nursed by the wife of
a stonemason. Delacroix did not recount this story of the artist's
"vocation" in his essay of 1830 on the sculptor, where he
reported the antipathy of the artist's father to his child's wish to
devote himself to art (an idea represented in the painting perhaps
in the turning of the mother and child away from the "father"
Moses); rather he reported it in his essay on the great French
sculptor Puget (where he repeated the point about the repugnance
on the part of Michelangelo's father to his son's vocation): "He
[Puget] had this in common with Michelangelo who had a wetnurse whose husband was a poor sculptor, which caused him to

Fig. 5.   Detail of
Figure 1.

say that he had suckled sculpture with his milk" (O.L.: II, p. 105).
Delacroix presented without a skeptical comment this claim of
vocational influence through a nurse's milk; and I suspect that he
had himself been exposed to this idea as a child in the middle-
class family in late-18th-century France.[31] Is it far-fetched to
suppose that Delacroix intended the Virgin and Child group to
symbolize the wetnurse's influence: the stone child turns to the
stone mother's breast, and both figures are sculpture.[32]

The potential for highly complex grouping of the figures in this
"family constellation" permits several interpretations of Delacroix's composition. In presenting the bewildering profusion of
possibilities that follows I have wished to avoid reducing the
interpretation to a single all-encompassing one. I have instead
tried to reflect the complexity of Delacroix's mind and to indicate
how laden with "overdetermined" meaning is Delacroix's portrait
of a personality with whom he had for so long been intimately

involved. We can reduce the family to its essential members of father, mother, and son, but what meaning can we assign or, better, how can we know what meaning Delacroix assigned to the figures? On a literal level Delacroix has placed Michelangelo the grown-up "son" between his "father" (Moses) and his "mother" (Mary). Who, then, in this construction, is the infant Christ? Presumably the infant Michelangelo, present as a spiritual pre-figuration, a device well-known to Delacroix from older iconogra-phy (the Crucifixion prefigured at the Annunciation). In the simultaneous existence of infant and mature man Delacroix seems to imply the martyrdom of the suffering artist/Christ, and that the mature artist carries with him the experience of his past. (In this context Delacroix's attraction during the 1850s to the figure of Christ assumes a particular significance.) Metaphorically, in the figure of Michelangelo Delacroix could have signified himself, as we have already shown. In either case (Michelangelo as himself or as Delacroix) the Christ Child would signify the type of the artist as infant, happily nurtured and protected on its mother's lap. This scene of mother and child seems analogous to an image conjured up in an early undated notebook: "Happy he who, enamored of the powerful muses, reclining in their lap and disdaining unavoid-able fate, in congenial conversation forgets melancholy things."[33]

With the child Delacroix may also have wished to project onto Michelangelo a memory-scene of infancy if he had in mind the wetnurse, the only important reference to Michelangelo's infancy he makes, in which the infant suckles at the breast of the wetnurse, not the mother. Assuming the equation of Michelangelo the infant and the Christ Child, Mary could then equally well signify the mother and the wetnurse (or, more vaguely, the muse). This ambiguity is matched by the obscurity of the figure of Moses, which could have had either of two distinct meanings for De-lacroix: as the father of Michelangelo, himself a powerful paternal paradigm whom Delacroix considered the father of modern art (in this Delacroix followed, apparently, Reynolds) or—a logical con-sequence of equating Michelangelo to himself—as his own father Charles Delacroix.[34] Each of these interpretations of the Moses is consistent with the identification of Christ as Delacroix: In the first case Delacroix the child would be the last in the line of descent from Michelangelo's early Renaissance sources to Michelangelo the founder of modernism to Delacroix Michelangelo's artistic scion. In the second case Eugène De-lacroix/Michelangelo serves as a mediate term between the face-less quartered figure of Charles Delacroix/Moses and his infant son Eugène, with Eugène thus doubly present. The isolation of mother and child from the father and the absence of all but a fragment of the father's body, of which only the lower leg and foot are not blurred (ironically, *Moses* is one of Michelangelo's few completed sculptures), weakens the force of the father.[35] One might conclude that the truly potent being is the complete Eugène/Michelangelo, and that although he is not stony, hence in this respect not "consanguineous" with the Virgin and Child, he

Fig. 6.   Detail of
Figure 1.

rather than the quartered Moses was the father of the Infant. This
would imply that Eugène/Michelangelo was his own father, an
idea less farfetched than it sounds, since after her husband's death
in 1805 and up to her death in 1814—from Delacroix's ages of
seven to sixteen—Delacroix's mother was the sole parental authority. As to Mary, in the first case she would probably signify
one of the muse/nurses who cared for Delacroix in his infancy (a
parallel to Michelangelo's infancy), with perhaps an allusion to the
"virginity" of the nursing woman who is not his mother, and in
the second case she would signify his mother.

Delacroix appears to have emphasized in Moses the lawgiver
and the genius destined like Christ to solitude and incomprehen-
sion by the masses.[36] Delacroix's Moses shares with Socrates and

Christ the quality of genius isolated from and victim of the vulgar crowd.[37] The importance of Michelangelo's *Moses* was doubtless brought home to Delacroix by his friend Chenavard, with whom he held heated arguments about Michelangelo from the later 1840s through the 1850s. Chenavard reported how he himself once drew a life-size copy of *Moses* and stated that he "never worked with such passion (*feu*)" (S.: p. 265). We may assume that Delacroix accepted the then-popular view that Moses was about to drop the Tablets of the Law in anger, although by quartering the figure he omitted among other things hand and tablets.[38] Delacroix may have intended a displacement of the tablets from Moses to Michelangelo: Michelangelo has thrown down his chisel in vexation, and just behind his left knee is a portfolio, probably corresponding to Delacroix's note on a drawing for the painting, "architectural drawings/sketches."[39] The figure of the paternal Moses poses interesting and difficult questions: Why did Delacroix both make him a powerful and larger-than-life figure (compared to the scale of the others) and at the same time truncate his body, cutting off everything above the shoulders and passing a vertical through his genitals? Why did he show Michelangelo turning his back on the faceless Moses while placing Moses's foot so close to Michelangelo's wrist that it suggests contact? Probably we touch here on rooted Oedipal feelings of Delacroix toward his father.

Let us return to the Virgin, about whom De Tolnay observed that she "expresses a maternal anguish more pronounced than the original," and that compared to the sculpture she "leans more over the Child" (De Tolnay, 1962, p. 45). These changes in the Virgin that add to the intensity of the maternal anguish and intimacy are particularly interesting in the light of Delacroix's view that Michelangelo was incapable of expressing tenderness: "The painting of tender feelings has never been within the scope of Michelangelo's genius" (O.L.: II, p. 50). Delacroix, I believe, has transformed the sculptures into statements about both Michelangelo and himself. And by making the Virgin more emotionally involved he implicitly criticized Michelangelo, whose taste for the "terrible" rendered him unable to paint tender sentiments.[40]

The closeness of the mother and child contrasts with the distance between Moses the "husband" and Mary the "wife" in the family constellation I have posited. I believe that by separating the couple in this way Delacroix in effect gave the maternal priority over the conjugal aspect of the male/female relationship in Michelangelo's life. Delacroix himself abandoned the hope of achieving a satisfactory marriage and sealed his lifelong celibacy in the mid-1840s when he decided not to marry Mme. de Forget, with whom he had maintained his longest-lasting relationship. During these years he again and again expressed his disillusion with physical love, and in his essay on Michelangelo he maintained that the artist's slight interest in earthly love helped his art, and speculated concerning the "continual lapses in his work. . . . are we to attribute nothing to that mad passion that intoxicates us in our youth?" (O.L.: II, p. 52–53). During the later 1840s when he painted *Michelangelo* Delacroix illustrated this disillusioned view of women in engrossing paintings such as *Ariadne Abandoned* and the scene of the suicidal Ophelia. But more pointedly he developed concurrently (1847–50) with *Michelangelo* the theme of the *Woman Combing Herself,* which concerns the vanity of a woman who stands combing her hair before a mirror behind which crouches a leering demon.[41] Delacroix associated the theme with Eve (the demon had been Death in an earlier version), the woman who, seduced by flattery and curiosity, in turn seduces her mate.[42] Delacroix worked on the same days on *Woman Combing Herself* and the portrait of Michelangelo, and the paintings treat different versions of the theme of nonproductivity—the creative artist's inactivity causes his suffering, the woman's trivially self-indulgent occupation leads to her death or damnation. One might consider the women of the two paintings as moral antitheses in the Christian tradition that opposed Eve and the Madonna: in the one the egoistic temptress, in the other the devoted mother with son.

Delacroix puzzled in his writings over Michelangelo's periodic lapses of creativity without reaching an explanation that satisfied him; but in the portrait he seems to have implied that the burden of the idleness belongs on the shoulders of the artist, seated between his unfinished works *Moses* and *Madonna and Child;* i.e., that his incompleteness as a man may have caused and is surely reflected in the incompleteness of his creations. This idea is suggested by a detail of the painting: Michelangelo supports his back and arm by a tripod, an implement on which the sculptor places his unfinished pieces for further work.[43] Like his sculptures Michelangelo requires an agency outside himself, a higher being, to complete or finish him, an idea he expressed in a poem: "Though my rough hammer in hard stone describes/ Human appearances, this then the other,/ It starts its move in tracks it has taken over/ From a governor who watches, holds and guides.// Wherefore with me, unfinished, all is lost/ Unless the divine workshops proffer help/ To make it, for on earth this was alone" (Holt, 1958: II, p. 22).

The absence of a complete father image and the presence of the Virgin Mother and Son corroborate my hypothesis of Delacroix's preoccupation in the *Michelangelo* with the idea of the artist's self-begetting (self-realization) or what I would call his "autopygmalianism." In this self-centered concern the mother becomes the essential parent, but almost as an appendage of the artist, a supernurse (or muse, as in the youthful Latin poem cited above) necessary for the regulation of his moods and for overcoming his solitude. As Delacroix wrote concerning Gros: "He complains at the same time of his spiritual solitude. He would like to live close to his mother. 'If my mother were near to me,' he writes, 'she would regulate my life, something I'm incapable of doing for myself. Yes, at the bottom of my heart I feel that my illness is being alone.' To regulate your life, poor artist! Yes, doubtless that

Fig. 7.   Study for
*Michelangelo in His
Studio.* Pencil Fitz-
william Museum,
Cambridge, England.

is the secret unknown by men dominated by their imagination"
(O.L.: II, p. 171).

Delacroix had years before associated with Michelangelo the
themes of the solitude of the artist and the need to regulate the
artist's life. In 1824 he wrote: "Think of the great Michelangelo.
Nourish yourself with great and severe beauties that nourish the
soul. I am always turned from their study by foolish distractions.
Seek solitude. If your life is regulated, your health will not suffer
from your retirement" (J.: I, pp. 42–43, Jan. 4, 1824). He then
quoted Michelangelo's poem that we have in part already cited
from his essay of 1830—"Carried on a fragile boat . . ."—which
continues: "Thoughts of love, vain and sweet imaginings, what will
become of you, now that I approach two deaths, one which is
certain, the other which threatens me. No, sculpture and painting
cannot alone calm my soul which is turned toward divine love and
which is lit by the sacred fire."[44]

Intermittently throughout his life Delacroix suffered from the solitude that he felt plagued all great individuals. In May 1850, a month when he worked on *Michelangelo,* he was troubled continually by thoughts about the suffering of genius: "the greatest in talent, boldness, persistence, is usually not only the most persecuted, but is himself fatigued and tortured by this burden of talent and imagination" (J.: May 1, 1850). He grappled again and again during 1850 with this thought from Constant's *Adolphe:* "The consequence of independence is isolation" (J.: May 4, 13, 14; Aug. 1, 1850). Delacroix seems to have felt usually that, while doomed to solitude, the genius has the capacity to overcome the worst effects of that condition.[45] On one occasion he extolled privacy as an opportunity to enjoy one's mind: "Only in solitude can one truly enjoy one's self" (O.L.: I, p. 120). Again, while he often complained about the pain of solitude, in August 1850 he quoted this excerpt from Balzac: "Solitude is the void, and moral nature abhors it as much as physical nature. Solitude is habitable only by either the man of genius who fills it with his ideas, daughters of the mental world, or by the contemplator of the divine creations who finds solitude illuminated by heaven's light, animated by the breath and voice of God. Except for these two men, so close to paradise. . . ." (J.: Aug. 1, 1850).[46]

Delacroix saw two paths to a desired tranquility or overcoming of loneliness: creative art and fervent religious faith. What may have fascinated him most in Michelangelo in his own later years was probably the complex interplay of these alternatives in the aging Renaissance master. His identification with Michelangelo diminished steadily as he approached a solution to his life's problems through a deepened faith in the value of creativity.[47] Delacroix never shared Michelangelo's disillusion with art as he confronted ultimate questions, expressed in the second half of the sonnet on the "fragile boat." For his portrait of Michelangelo, Delacroix chose a moment when the artist's self-control lapsed, when the disturbance of the "regulated life" caused creative paralysis and melancholy. Delacroix noted that the aging Michelangelo, discouraged but compelled by his nature to work ceaselessly, came to regard "as vain and regrettable all the moments he did not devote to heaven" (O.L.: II, p. 51). Perhaps an anxiety not unlike Michelangelo's about the value of art and of artistic immortality touched Delacroix as he himself aged, and as he worked on his last great project, a religious mural of Jacob wrestling with the Angel. In moments of self-doubt he may well have compared himself to Michelangelo. In fact, one can find a parallel between the figure of his *Jacob,* often considered a symbolic self-portrait, and his *Michelangelo:* Both are isolated from society (the angel not constituting another person, but an alter ego of Jacob); both have thrown down their tools (spear and shield; chisel); both have red pieces of clothing (Jacob a mantle cast aside, Michelangelo a scarf); and both are engaged in mental wrestling (Jacob with a spiritual adversary, Michelangelo within himself).[48] But in his image of *Jacob* Delacroix has turned radically away from the dark path of artistic abnegation of the Renaissance master—he not only has chosen a scene in which the adversary physically engages the hero, but he has placed the whole scene in a magnificent landscape with its triumph of color and light. In drawing his figures he has chosen for his line a middle course between the violent and strained contours he found in Michelangelo and the graceful line he admired in Raphael, but more important, in the landscape he has made touch and, above all, color, dominant—the voluptuous color of the Venetians (already evolving in his *Apollo* ceiling) that made him call painting a "feast for the eye" and that points at once toward the color expression of a van Gogh and the luminous landscapes of the Impressionists (J.: June 22, 1863).

Probably the work at Saint-Sulpice helped stimulate the exultant self-confidence that he conveyed to Silvestre in the mid-1850s: "Whence does it come, Delacroix said to me one day, that at the present time I am not bored for a single moment when I have my brush in hand? . . . Today I hesitate no longer! My maturity is complete; my imagination is as fresh and active as ever, and freed from foolish passions . . . let us play at work for the sake of the work itself and for the delicious hours following it" (S.: pp. 7–8).[49] Does not this expression of joy in work for its own sake, without any rationalization—religious or sentimental— suggest that Delacroix was addressing the melancholy Michelangelo of his painting, trapped in his ambivalence between art and religion? In a similar mood he thrust aside his doubts in an entry to the *Journal* on October 12, 1862, and the Voltairean skeptic enunciated the enthusiastic credo of the virtuous individual and the artistic creator capable at moments of self-regulation and self-consolation—"God is within us." Those favored with a simpler, less passionate sense of divinity than Michelangelo's would have the privilege described by Voltaire of combining reason and enthusiasm: "Reasonable enthusiasm is the lot of the great poets. This reasonable enthusiasm is the perfection of their art. It is what once induced the belief that they were inspired by the gods" (J.: n.d., III, p. 339).

In summary, I have tried to show in this paper that in his *Michelangelo in His Studio* Delacroix addressed his recurrent problems or anxieties about artistic sterility, illness, solitude, and fear of dependence. His persistent need for a woman to fulfill the roles of mistress, guiding muse, and consoling companion conflicted with his equally strong need for independence, time for his art, and freedom from the constraints of sexual temptation or marriage. By the time he painted his *Michelangelo* he had relinquished the hope of finding one woman who could satisfy his needs. Instead he returned to the ideal women of his childhood— his mother and/or nurses who were caretaker, muse, guide, and loving companion. The deep congruence between his own problems, above all his occasional crises of nonproductivity, and Michelangelo's, is displayed in the painting *Michelangelo*. The crux of his problems is projected here in the tension between

Michelangelo's potency in displacing the father (Moses) and having the mother to himself, and his impotence and frustration as an artist owing to his failure to integrate the mother and achieve independence. The confrontation of this central problem, or at least its visualization, appears to have liberated Delacroix to some extent from it and from the Michelangelo who personified it. Even as he painted the red of Michelangelo's scarf as emblem of frustrated creativity and illness, he was evolving a more objective use of red in the color harmonies of his murals (the very act of painting *Michelangelo* was both creative and cathartic). His concept of reasonable enthusiasm shows that he was on the way toward fuller self-reliance and the integration within himself of the guiding mother. The triumph of his constantly evolving genius over his self-doubts is displayed nowhere more impressively than in the passage from the *Michelangelo in His Studio* to the *Jacob*, with its glowing landscape that reveals him "more painter than sculptor." In this passage he demonstrated the will to cut loose from his identification with the model of the melancholy Michelangelo of his portrait of 1850/53 and an ability to transcend his emotional problems and loneliness through his art, his "bridge" (as he called it) to an ideal spectator.[50]

Notes

Research for this paper was supported by a grant from the Rutgers Research Council

1 For a valuable discussion of the general critical attitude to portraiture as inferior and unimaginative, see Hauptman (1975, p. 320) and also Finke (1976, pp. 30, 67, and 85).

2 Arguing for the portrait by artists against that of the daguerreotype, Delacroix adduced the elusive nature of physiognomy.

3 Joubin noted, "This composition seems like a reflection of Delacroix upon himself, and this meditative Michelangelo, neck swathed in a muffler, strongly resembles Delacroix" (J.: I, p. 307, n. 1).

4 See Haskell (1971). Hauptman (1975, p. 369) perceptively discussed this painting. See also Honour (1979, ch. 7) for illustrations of 19th-century portraits, including the *Michelangelo*.

5 Delacroix considered painting a Tasso in the madhouse as early as 1822 (J.: Sept. 3, 1822) and actually painted several versions in the 1820s and one in 1839, all showing Tasso seated with hand to head in a pose similar to that of the *Michelangelo*. See Johnson (1981, cat. no. 106).

6 (In R.: I, p. xv.) The comparison of the artist or poet to a sculptor abounds in the 1850s and later. See Shroder (1961, p. 145).

7 We sometimes find the hand-to-chin pose assigned to artists other than Michelangelo. Gautier (1838) described Raphael, hand to head, agonizing over his imperfection. Delacroix himself painted a *Raphael Meditating in His Studio*. Louise Colet, who visited the atelier of the sculptor Jacques

(James) Pradier, wrote a poem in 1843 or later which she titled, with adjusted gender, "Penserosa." On the *Melancholia I* of Dürer and 19th-century art, see Hauptman (1979, p. 10).

8 De Tolnay (1962) drew attention to the Dürer. For Delacroix's comparison of Géricault and Michelangelo, see J.: Mar. 8, 1852.

9 For parallel examples in poetry to Delacroix's treatment of the themes of melancholy and death, see Fischer (1963).

10 See Rothstein (1976), who discusses the imaginative expansion of works of art and literature during the 18th century, while ignoring Michelangelo.

11 The incorporation of the four temperaments in a single person agrees with the old theory of the temperaments; but in contrast to practice of that theory, Delacroix had no thought of characterizing Michelangelo's personality deterministically in terms of a balance or imbalance of fluids. Rather, the hints of the four temperaments would have signified indefinite impulses of a psychological nature (O.L.: I, pp. 24–25, 27). See also Charpentier (1880).

12 Delacroix was doubtless aware of this aspect of Michelangelo's thought; in the spring of 1830, while preparing his essay on Michelangelo, Delacroix wrote to an unidentified person asking for a translation of the sonnet "Scarco d'una importuna e grave salma . . . " (C.: I, pp. 252–253).

13 Cf. Mras (1966) for an interpretation of Delacroix's "Paragone." For example, Mras quoted from J. (Sept. 23, 1854) on the superiority of nonverbal arts of painting and sculpture. For a distinction between sculpture, which renders "an object as it is," and painting, which renders it "as it seems (appears)," see O. L.: I, pp. 14–15.

14 For disproportion, a quality attached to the "sublime" rather than to the "beautiful," see J.: II, pp. 40–42; III, p. 37. For hasty genius making work "impossible to complete," see J.: II, pp. 42–43, 455–456.

15 For the comparison to the ancients, see J.: I, p. 216 with regard to painting. For Riesener, see J.: I, p. 216.

16 Eighteenth-century aesthetics, especially in Germany, often grounded feeling of the sublime on the awe experienced before great magnitude, perhaps following Burke. Such ideas could have reached Delacroix through Mme. de Stael's writings, which he admired.

17 In his essay on Gros of 1848, Delacroix praised the artist's small paintings for having the "expansiveness of large painting" (O.L.: II, p. 170).

18 Delacroix quoted lines from Dolce's "Aretino" about the supremacy of Titian over Raphael and Michelangelo (in Roskill, 1968).

19 I believe that Clark (1975, p. 138) referred to the wrong episode, a later one that appears in O.L.

20 See Joubin (1939, pp. 314–318, esp. 316–317). In unrealized projects of the early to mid-1840s for a pendentive of "Michelangelo and His Genius" in the Palais Bourbon, Delacroix showed the seated sculptor facing out with mallet in hand and legs in the same position as in the painting (as well as reversed), with a bust beside the legs. Michelangelo wears no hat; instead, a winged female genius hovers overhead. The position of her head over his bears a striking similarity to that of the Virgin over Christ's in *Michelangelo in His Studio*.

21 Cf. Wasserman (1964, p. 19), who cites Akenside's poem in which "man beholds 'in lifeless things/ the inexpressive semblance of himself/ of thought and passion.'" Cf. also Abrams (1965).

22 For the Fragonards, see Sterling (1964): " . . . all the sitters appear to be

possessed by an interior force which obliges them to turn their heads, cast a far-off look as if pursuing a thought or a dream: they are obeying the imperious command of their personal genius." Cf. also Voltaire (1765, "Fantasie").

23 See Delacroix (O.L.: II, p. 158). Delacroix committed errors in his description of the painting, in making the Pope older and sicker than he actually was or was depicted by others.

24 Trapp (1971, p. 267) has well observed that Delacroix was not "deeply committed to scholarly consistency."

25 A precursor appeared in the statues of Venus and Cupid in F. Colonna, *Hypnerotomachia Polifili;* and for a popular type in the 18th century see the engraving of Moreau le jeune, *Delights of Motherhood* (1777), in which the poses of the statues of Venus and Cupid match those of a mother and child beneath them.

26 Michelangelo was buried in Santa Croce, not in San Lorenzo, as Delacroix asserted in his essay on the artist (O.L.: II, p. 56) and in the editor's note. Possibly his confusion resulted from a dim recollection that the obsequies occurred in San Lorenzo before the burial in Santa Croce.

27 See du Camp (1883); also Jaubert (1881).

28 Cf. the letter to his brother Charles (C.: May 16, 1842): "An interruption of five months in my work [on the Palais Bourbon murals] has left large gaps. . . ." He had just had a *crise de laryngite,* as the editor noted.

29 Referring to the first idea for the painting, he wrote his sister (C.: Mar. 11, 1822): "The subject . . . comes from Dante. It's the one of which I made the drawing while I had my fever in the forest." Delacroix identified with Dante and once attended a costume party dressed as Dante.

30 In a letter to Rivet (C.: May 18, 1830), Delacroix wrote: "Mr. Gérard, with whom I conversed the other day on the dark side of life, told me that what he preferred *was Hell and the studio.* I find that very right. . . ." (Delacroix's italics). In this same letter Delacroix discussed Dante, Michelangelo, and Raphael, and the essay on Michelangelo he was then readying for publication.

31 For Michelangelo's time, see Ross (1974) and Liebert (1983) and my review of Liebert's book (1983). On the wetnurse in 17th-century France, see Marvick (1974).

32 Delacroix could have found this idea in one of Michelangelo's verses. (See Gilbert & Linscott, 1963, pp. 46–67). "With him a huge lazy and slow old woman/ Upon her milk nurses the ghastly creature . . ./ Her heart is of stone. . . ." Images of the breast and nursing recur in Michelangelo's poetry. I have not referred here to the popular hypothesis that Talleyrand begot Eugène, because the research of Paul Loppin has made this hypothesis untenable. Loppin, in articles and books (especially his *Delacroix, Père et fils*), has gathered evidence including the previously unpublished correspondence between Delacroix's parents before and after his birth showing their common concern for Eugène's well-being, and current opinions of French medical experts who agree that, assuming conception occurred on the last sure date that the couple was together, Eugène's birth after a six and one-half months or seven months pregnancy would have been premature but possible.

33 See Joubin (1927, p. 162). The original poem is in Latin. My colleague S. Palmer Bovie of Classics helped me with the translation. The happiness of the infant Christ in His mother's arms contrasts with the life of strife and torment of the mature Christ with whom Delacroix usually identified, as noted by Trapp (1971, p. 238).

34 The question of artistic "paternity" may have provoked Delacroix in his essay on Gros to omit from his source, from which he otherwise borrowed extensively, all references to David's "paternal influence" (O.L.: II). After all, it was precisely David, the bad and possessive father figure, who induced Gros to turn from his vigorously painterly style to the bland classicism of his later work, a phenomenon noted and deplored by Delacroix.

35 On the completeness of the *Moses,* see Rosenthal (1964).

36 See the unexecuted project for the Palais Bourbon (R.: nos. 816–817), "Moses giving the law to the people." Cf. also Delacroix (J.: May 31, 1849) for other Moses projects.

37 "The truth is revealed only by the genius, and the genius is always alone. What does one see in history? On one side, Moses, Socrates, Jesus; on the other the Hebrews, Greece, and the universe. On one side the people who persecute and kill; on the other the isolated victim who enlightens them" (O.L.: I, pp. 119–120). See Hauptmann (1975) for Delacroix's identification with Moses and Christ as lonely *hommes supérieurs* as well as victims.

38 See Panofsky (1939, p. 193): " . . . the still popular conception that Moses, after having sat down for unaccountable reasons, was angered by the dance around the Golden Calf, and was just on the verge of jumping and shattering the tablets. . . ." Freud (1914) wrote an essay developing this conception with great ingenuity.

39 For the drawing, see R.: pp. 1793–1794. Nineteenth-century portraits of Michelangelo sometimes showed him as an architect with plans of St. Peter's.

40 See Delacroix (O.L.: II, p. 50) referring especially to Michelangelo's image of Christ in the Sistine *Last Judgment.*

41 See Delacroix (J.: Sept. 16, 1849; May 18, 1850). In an undated passage, he quoted Byron to the effect that if you give women candies and a mirror they will be happy. See also Delacroix (O.L.: I, p. 124).

42 For Adam and Eve and Death, see Delacroix (J.: I, p. 222) and inscriptions on a drawing in R. (p. 1796). He worked on the parallel theme of Samson and Delilah according to the *Journal* (J.: May 7, 1850). See also the undated journal entry c. 1844 (J.: III, p. 440).

43 See the sketch (R.: pp. 1793–1794), and Delacroix (J.: I, p. 337).

44 The later version differs in several significant phrases, especially "divine love . . . fire" becomes "you, oh my God! and which the fire of your love ignites!" (J.: Jan. 4, 1824). Perhaps the acceptance of this change of wording bears on the subtle interplay between Delacroix's faith in his art and his pondering of larger existential questions associated with religion. This interplay evolved gradually. While Delacroix never committed himself to institutional Christianity, he did apparently identify with the isolation and suffering of Christ, as evidenced by his numerous paintings of Christ on the Sea of Galilee of 1853 and later.

45 See Delacroix (J.: May 1, 1850) for the opposite view; cf. also J. (May 13, 1850).

46 The association of solitude, creative idleness, and *vide* or emptiness bears on our painting. The space over Michelangelo's head, which resembles in effectiveness that over David's *Marat* (exhibited in Paris in 1845), takes on a poignant significance when compared to the earlier project for *Michelangelo and His Genius* previously mentioned, in which the space above Michelangelo is filled with a winged genius.

47 Perhaps Raphael played a role in this development. See Lichtenstein (1979, p. 129).

48 For the still life of Jacob as Delacroix's "epitaph," see Prideaux (1966, p. 185). Cf. also Delacroix (O.L.: I, p. 75): "Just by the sight of his palette, like the warrior seeing his arms, the painter draws confidence and boldness."

49 See also C.: Mar. 23, 1850.

50 Delacroix did not hold on to this highly personalized painting but sold it in 1853 to the great collector, Alfred Bruyas, whose sensitive appreciation of the work the artist must have welcomed. Bruyas then commissioned his own portrait, painted in April/May, 1853.

References

Abbreviations used:

C.   Joubin, A. (Ed.) (1935/38) *Correspondance générale d'Eugène Delacroix.*
J.   _____ (Ed.) (1950). *Journal d'Eugène Delacroix,* new ed.; 3 vols. Paris:

O. L.   Faure, E. (Ed.) (1923). *Oeuvres littéraires d'Eugène Delacroix.* 3 vols. Paris: Crès.
R.   Chesneau, E., & Robaut, A. (Eds.) (1885). *L'Oeuvre complet d'Eugène Delacroix: peintures, dessins, gravures, lithographies.* Paris: Charavay Frères.
S.   Silvestre, T. (1855). *Histoire des artistes vivants,* I. Paris: Blanchard.

Note: All dated *Journal* entries are cited in the text by J, followed by the date. Volume and page notations are given for undated entries. Correspondence is also noted by date, except in the case of unedited correspondence, published separately and noted under Dupont, 1954. Unillustrated works by Delacroix are referred to by their number in the Robaut catalogue raisonné.

Abrams, M. (1965). Structure and style in the greater romantic lyric. In F. Hilles & H. Bloom (Eds.), *From sensibility to romanticism. Essays presented to F. A. Pottle.* New York: Oxford University Press.
Camp, M. du. (1882–83). *Souvenirs littéraires.* 2 vols. Paris: Hachette.
Charpentier, P. L. H. (1880). *Une maladie morale: Le mal du siècle.* Paris: Didier.
Clark, T. J. (1973). *The absolute bourgeois.* New York: The Graphic Society.
Dupont, A. (Ed.). (1954). *Lettres intimes. Correspondance inédite.* Paris: Gallimard.
Finke, U. (1976). Dürer's "Melancholie" in der französischen und englischen Literatur und Kunst des 19. Jahrhunderts. *Z. dt. Verein für Kunstwiss. 30:* 67–85.
Fischer, U. (1963). *Das literarische Bild im Werk Delacroix.* Unpublished doctoral dissertation, Reinsche Fr. Wilhelms Universität, Bonn.
Freud, S. (1914). The Moses of Michelangelo. *S. E., 13:* 211–238.
Gautier, T. (1838). *Comedy of Death.*
Gilbert, C., & Linscott, R. N. (1963). *Complete poems and selected letters of Michelangelo.* New York: Random House.
Haskell, F. (1971). Old masters in 19th century painting. *Art Quarterly, 34:* 55–85.

131   Hauptman, W. (1975). *The persistence of melancholy in 19th century art.* Unpublished doctoral dissertation, Pennsylvania State University.

Holt, E. G. (1958). *A documentary history of art,* II. New York: Doubleday/Anchor Books.

Honour, H. (1979). *Romanticism.* New York: Harper & Row.

Johnson, L. (1981). *The paintings of E. Delacroix, 1816–31.* 2 vols. New York: Oxford University Press.

Joubin, A. (Ed.). (1927). Etudes sur E. Delacroix, II. *Gazette des Beaux-Arts.* Ser. 5, *15:* 159–182.

———— (1939). Delacroix par lui-même. *Gazette des Beaux-Arts,* Ser. 6, *21:* 305–318.

Lichtenstein, S. (1979). *Delacroix and Raphael.* New York: Garland Publishing.

Liebert, R. (1983). *Michelangelo: A psychoanalytic study of his life and images.* New Haven & London: Yale University Press.

Loppin, P. (n. d.; after 1964). *Delacroix, père et fils.* 2nd ed. Paris: Bearn.

Marvick, E. W. (1974). Nature vs. nurture. In L. de Mause (Ed.), *History of childhood.* New York: Psychohistory Press.

Mras, G. P. (1966). *Delacroix's theory of art.* Princeton, NJ: Princeton University Press.

Panofsky, E. (1939). *Studies in iconology.* New York: Harper & Row, 1962.

Prideaux, T. (1966). *The world of Delacroix.* New York: Time, Inc.

Rosenthal, E. (1964). Michelangelo's *Moses,* dal di sotto in su. *Art Bulletin, 46*(4): 544–550.

Roskill, M. (1968). *Dolce's "Aretino" and Venetian art theory of the Cinquecento.* New York: New York University Press.

Ross, J. B. (1974). The middle-class child in urban Italy, 14th to early 16th century. In L. de Mause (Ed.), *History of childhood.* New York: Psychohistory Press.

Rothstein, E. (1976). "Ideal presence" and "non finito" in 18th century aesthetics. *18th Century Studies, 9:* 307–333.

Shroder, M. S. (1961). *Icarus: The image of the artist in French Romanticism.* Cambridge, MA: Harvard University Press.

Silvestre, T. (1953). Michel-Ange dans son atelier. In *La Galerie Bruyas, 1876.* Paris: J. Calye.

Spector, J. J. (1983). A review of R. S. Liebert, *Michelangelo. Italian Quarterly* XXIV, no. 94, 113–19.

Sterling, C. (1964). An unknown masterpiece by Fragonard: *"Portrait of a Man" ("The Warrior").*

Tolnay, C. De (1962). "Michel-Ange dans son atelier" par Delacroix. *Gazette des Beaux-Arts,* Ser. 6, *59:* 43–52.

Trapp, F. (1971). *The attainment of Delacroix.* Baltimore: Johns Hopkins University Press.

Voltaire, F. M. (1765). *Dictionnaire philosophique,* s. v. "Fantasie."

Wasserman, E. (1964). The English Romantics, the grounds of knowledge. *Essays in Romanticism, 4* (Autumn, 1964): 19.

Michele Vishny, Ph.D.	**Paul Klee's Self-Images**

During the summer of 1905, when Paul Klee was 25 years old, he wrote in his diary: "If I had to paint a completely truthful self-portrait, I would show a peculiar shell. And inside—it would have to be made clear to everyone—I sit, like a kernel in a nut. An allegory of incrustation, this work might also be called." (F. Klee, 1957, no. 675; my translation; further references to Paul Klee's *Diaries* will be given as *D.* followed by the numbered passage).

Perhaps when Klee wrote these words, he was thinking about several of his etched *Inventions,* three of which he subtitled *Comedian,* executed in 1903 and 1904, and one just recently completed called *The Threatening Head.* Though none were entitled self-portrait, scholars have noted certain physical resemblances to Klee as well as symbols within the works showing his close identification with what he was portraying (see, for example, Haxthausen, 1981, pp. 125–126; Glaesemer, 1976b; Comini, 1977). In the years to follow there would be numerous works that can be proven by biographical data to be disguised self-portraits. This article, by no means exhaustive, discusses both acknowledged self-portraiture and disguised or symbolic self-images, in chronological sequence, beginning with a relatively objective student drawing of 1899 and terminating with the very moving allegorical painting *Death and Fire,* made in 1940, the year Klee died.

The Early Period: 1899–1919	The first of the acknowledged self-images which Klee documented in his oeuvre catalogue (begun 1911) is *Self-Portrait with White Cap* (1899/1), a small pencil drawing, signed "Selbst."[1] Its interest

lies primarily in the *Jugendstil* rhythms demonstrated by the arcing line that shapes the brow, swoops downward to form the cheek, and ends in the pointed chin, giving a somewhat heartlike contour to the face. The concavity of the facial planes is countered by the soft fullness of the peaked sport cap. Klee's wide, staring pupils are directed off to the side, undoubtedly fixed in this position by the use of a mirror to capture his image. What the portrait conveys is a tabula rasa, so blank and expressionless are the features. At this time the unformed 20-year-old artist was a student at Knirr's school, in Munich, and not at all sure of what his future would be. He expressed his predicament in a verse:

> Music, for me, is a love bewitched
> Fame as a painter?
> Writer, modern poet? Bad joke
> So I have no calling, and loaf (*D.*, no. 67).

More positive feelings toward becoming an artist were soon to be manifested. Klee meanwhile saw his immediate problem as a lack of sexual experience and felt this had to be resolved first: "In short, I had first of all to become a man: art would then follow inevitably" (*D.*, no. 66; see also nos. 83, 90).

Klee's sexual initiation was easily settled by several affairs beginning in 1900, but the development of his art required substantially more of his time and energy. Classes with Knirr were followed by studies with Franz Stuck at the Academy (in Munich) and a trip to Italy, where classical art both overwhelmed and alienated him, heightening the dilemma of this young modern artist searching for original expression. While in Italy (1901) he wrote: "I cannot find any artistic connection with our own times. And to want to create something outside of one's own age strikes me as suspect" (*D.*, no. 294). The following year he reiterated this idea: "The thought of having to live in an epigonic age is almost unbearable" (*D.*, no. 430). Had Klee noted the more advanced tendencies in art (Impressionism) exhibited at the 1899 Munich Secession, he might have felt more optimistic toward developing a modern style, but he mentioned only the romantics Puvis de Chavannes and Eugène Carrière enthusiastically. Klee's progress was slow; although he mastered line, color was beyond his reach and studies in Munich did not help him. At times he was so overcome by discouragement and depression that he thought about suicide.[2] But despite these dark moments, he remained steadfast toward achieving his goal: "I am starting to learn all over again: I begin to execute forms as if I knew nothing about painting. For I have discovered a very small, undisputed, personal possession: a particular sort of three-dimensional representation on the flat surface" (*D.*, no. 425).

Color, he realized, still presented problems. "But painting with its failures cries out for the relief of minor successes. Nowadays I am a very tired painter, but in other respects a persistently potent printmaker" (*D.*, no. 512, my translation). Klee had experimented with etching in 1901 and returned to this medium two years later to create a series of 11 grotesque, satirical prints called *Inventions*. A number of these etchings have been analyzed in terms of their iconographic and stylistic sources, and have been interpreted individually by various scholars, but they have not been examined as a series. That Klee numbered the prints (though not in chronological order) suggests some thematic development that remains unexplained (see Franciscono, 1974, pp. 54–64; Glaesemer in *The Graphic Legacy of Paul Klee,* 1983, pp. 69–81). These satires, serving a psychological function (part of which is catharsis), attack social conventions, sexual constraints and various human illusions. Our interest in the *Inventions,* however, is restricted to the three versions of *Comedian* and *The Threatening Head,* his "allegories of incrustation." These four works are symbolic self-portraits.

The first version of *Comedian* (1903/3) portrays a profile view of a mask which partially covers a man's profile. Both mask and man share the same cap. In contrast to the buoyant and somewhat mischievous expression of the mask, whose eye pops with delight and mouth turns up in a smile, the man's heavy-lidded eye and downturned mouth convey deep depression. Like the other plates in the series, the image is etched in an austere, hard-edged style, with the plate worked in such detail as to express tremendous surface tension. Almost unnoticeable in the left-hand margin of the sheet are tiny scribbled drawings known as remarques, made to test the etching process and usually removed after early proofs have been printed. On six of the *Inventions* plates, Klee drew near his initials a small clover, a punning reference to his surname (*Klee* is the German word for clover), but in the *Comedian* it takes on special significance, for a second clover appears in that part of the cap covering the man's head. It is the only etching to include a clover as part of the self-image and, as such, shows Klee's obvious identification with the man from the very inception of the *Comedian* series. In his diary (August 1903) he wrote of this first version: "Grotesque mask on a grave, moral head. Accompanying the reading of Aristophanes' comedies. . . . The mask as work of art; behind it, the man" (Klee, no. 517).

A second version of the *Comedian* (1904/10) (Fig. 1), like the first, portrays profiles of the head and mask, but differs in the style of the cap and the mask's lack of a chin and changed facial expression. Instead of a pleasant, rather benign smile, this mask's mouth has a wide, snarling grin, baring large clenched teeth which give a menacing character to the mask. The man behind it remains passive and depressed, little changed from the first version, but this mask is all energy and aggression—"getting out the anger," so to speak—and, as such, represents a healthier mental state. Klee's self-awareness, as expressed in this second *Comedian,* is revealed in a December 1903 letter to his fiancée, Lily Stumpf: "The contrast is now coming out better than in the older *Invention:* Head serious, mask grotesque-humorous. Its expression flowed from my deepest soul, so that for the indeterminate future I

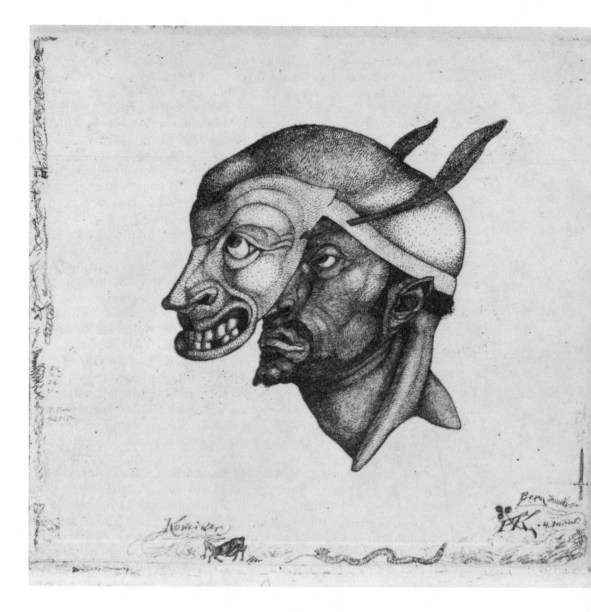

Fig. 1. Paul Klee,
Comedian. 1904 (10).
Etching, 5¾ × 6¼".
Courtesy Paul Klee-
Stiftung, Kunst-
museum Bern, ©
1984 by COS-
MOPRESS, Geneva,
and ADAGP, Paris.

believe myself to be healed. This *Comedian* is my most personal
work up to now" (F. Klee, 1979, p. 370). Though Klee saw the
mask as partially humorous, it is difficult to see it as anything but
menacing. As in the first plate there are remarques on the left
side; however, in two other margins there are a tiny frog, snake
and dagger, which because they are so carefully drawn, might have
been retained had there been a final edition of the print. While
the frog might be a conscious reference to Aristophanes' comedy
The Frogs, the other imagery may simply arise out of the artist's
unconscious, the visual equivalent of verbal free-association, which
cannot be definitively explained, although it is tempting to link
the dagger with Klee's fleeting suicidal moods.[3]

The last *Comedian* (1904/14), while still portraying profile
images of mask and man, differs in several respects from the two
earlier versions. Klee now placed the image on a dark ground,

eliminated his remarques and, most important, suggested an independent existence for the man. The mask, in the process of peeling off of the man, no longer caps the latter's head, which is now covered with its own headgear, a plumed helmet. A major change appears in the mask as well: it has been given a long beard, lending it a more human character. While the man depicted in the first two *Comedians* looks like Klee and both are unquestionably symbolic self-portraits, the third *Comedian,* although bearing no physical resemblance to the artist, is also Klee in its statement of his growing independence and maturity. The bearded mask shares some traits with Klee's father, Hans, who with his long, flowing beard, makes a formidable impression even today when we look at his photographs. In this etching the mask has been excised, the man behind it seems to be emerging. Thus, in employing the allegory of the theater (the mask), Klee analyzed and presented his own life situation: the struggle to free himself from the dominating father and what he symbolized—the outworn values of the waning 19th century.[4]

When Klee completed the three prints, he repeated an idea expressed earlier: "One more thing may be said about 'The Comedian': the mask represents art, and behind it hides man. The lines of the mask are roads to the analysis of the work of art. The duality of the world of art and that of man is organic, as in one of Johann Sebastian's compositions. It is quite delightful to elaborate such considerations in retrospect" (*D.,* no. 618). While, at the *Comedians'* inception, Klee's thinking indicates he viewed the mask and man as separate but equally important entities, when the series was completed, his comments accorded greater importance to the mask (art): he seems to say that man is concealed within the work, it is the work that is to be analyzed, but the two worlds are really inseparable. It is not surprising that Klee gave emphasis to the art, shifting it away from the artist. Will Grohmann, who worked very closely with Klee documenting his life and work, noted that the personality of the painter as revealed in interviews, diaries, and letters, overshadowed that of the man; Klee's extreme reserve discouraged others from trespassing upon his private world (Grohmann, 1954, p. 25). He can truly be described as the man behind the mask.

The final print of the *Inventions* series, *The Threatening Head* (1905/37) (Fig. 2), was described by Klee as "a gloomy conclusion to this set of etchings. A thought more destructive than action. Pure negation as demon. The physiognomy for the most part resigned" (*D.,* no. 610; my translation). That he still suffered from depression at this time is evident from a letter written to Lily while he was working on this print: *"Ich schaffe pour ne pas pleurer, das ist der letzte und erste Grund"* ("I create in order not to cry, that is the last and first reason") (F. Klee, 1979, p. 492).

Although the composition of *The Threatening Head* may well have been inspired by Aubrey Beardsley's work, which Klee saw in the Munich Print Room in October 1904, its dramatic intensity—its overwhelming sense of foreboding as expressed by the hard lines of the frowning brow, hypnotic stare, and downturned

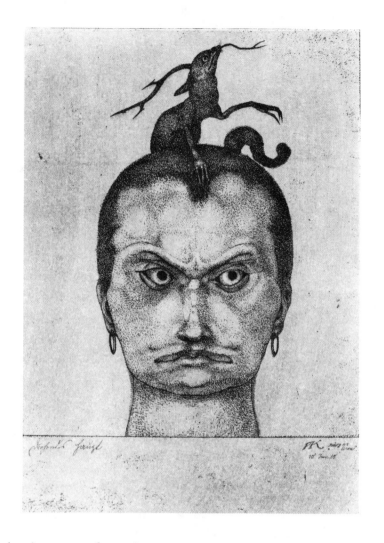

mouth—is remote from the art nouveau spirit of Beardsley. There is no doubt that this etching is a self-portrait; the physical resemblance is striking when compared to a photograph of Klee (Fig. 3). What better way to conclude two years of labor on his most important body of work to date than with this frontal self-image, the *Invention* which shows his strongest likeness? Through these bitter satirical etchings, he was able to "exorcise his demons," to move toward becoming the unique artist whom we know. Klee was well aware of having worked through his inner conflicts and was now ready to begin a new chapter in his art, despite the somewhat tentative way he expressed it: "I am almost inclined to believe that this [*The Threatening Head*] will be the last print in the strict style and that something entirely new will follow. I turn my eyes toward Spain where Goyas grow" (*D.,* no. 602; also see F. Klee, 1962, p. 10 for a reference to Goya).

Klee's next extant self-images do not appear until 1908. In the two years that elapsed, he struggled with new means of expression, still working in a satirical way but in a freer style, creating an art that was more closely based upon nature rather than the mannered deformations of the *Inventions*. A trip to Paris

Fig. 3. Photograph of Paul Klee, 1911, Munich. Photo by Alexander Eliasberg.

in the late spring of 1905 brought Klee in contact, finally, with late 19th-century French art. Manet (whom he mentioned a few times in his diary during his visit) made a strong impression, for after his return to Bern he wrote: "Manet elegantly brings out with the brush the pictorial values corresponding to the play of light" (*D., no. 664*). The French artist was to influence his development beginning in 1907 (when he saw the *Absinthe Drinker*) in his efforts with tonality (*D., no. 785*). Late in 1907, Klee began reading van Gogh's letters and early in 1908 saw exhibitions of his work (in Munich), which also affected his style (*D., nos. 804, 816*).

Six self-portraits were done in 1908, one of which, a dark watercolor, he cancelled with a light X mark and wrote *ungültig* (void), and two of which are now lost.[5] The three remaining works—all drawings—differ from each other stylistically; one is a caricature (and not called a self-portrait), while the other two are influenced by Manet and van Gogh respectively.

To understand the caricature entitled *The Father: Two Nudes* (1908/21), it is helpful to know a few biographical facts and some of Klee's attitudes as expressed over several years in his diaries.

Klee and Lily were finally married in October 1906, after a six-year engagement. They lived in Munich, her native city, where she supported them by giving piano lessons, while Klee kept house and continued to develop his art. Within six months, Lily, who was three years older than her husband, was pregnant. The father-to-be's response was hardly enthusiastic: "Apropos *papa*—that's just the way it goes. I can't call it a joy, but it certainly is better now than later, since Lily is thirty years old" (*D.,* no. 786). During the pregnancy Klee made a few portraits of Lily that are quite unflattering, partly because of the caricatural style he was then practicing, but possibly also, one suspects, because of earlier negative attitudes toward pregnant women which may have persisted.[6] While Felix's birth dispelled Klee's ambivalence toward fatherhood, how pleasurable could it have been to be awakened by the infant's cries during the night when Klee "had to resurrect from a deathlike state, heat some water, add some milk, press the bottle against my eye, and then shove it into the open gateway!" (*D.,* no. 802). Klee's response to his new role is captured in the grotesque drawing *The Father: Two Nudes* (Fig. 4). Portrayed as clinging to one another, the nudity of father and son seems to draw them even closer together and emphasizes the helpless state of each. There are androgynous aspects to the drawing in that Klee depicts himself with long hair and a swollen belly, which strongly resembles pregnancy. Klee, who was the household's "chief cook and baby bottle washer" and, as such, fulfilled the traditional female role, apparently added pregnancy to his burdens. The line circumscribing the figures, which Klee used in many of his 1907–1908 drawings, in this work suggests the late 19th-century oval format of portrait photography. The stiff poses and formal dress of the latter are satirized by Klee's candid-cameralike sketch of active nudes.

The two remaining 1908 self-portraits, while not of special psychological interest, show further developments in Klee's style. Though they differ in their debt to separate artists, both are fairly naturalistic. The *Sketch for a Self-Portrait* (1908/68), a charcoal drawing, was Klee's second attempt at doing a sketch of himself, having rejected his first draft, a dark watercolor (see note 5). In two letters he wrote to Lily from Bern, he mentioned working on self-portraits, one of which might have been this sketch, which he described as done from nature and pictorial (*Malerische*) (F. Klee, 1979, pp. 683, 687). In its simplification of form, emphasis on shapes (hairline, forehead, beard), and strong contrasts of light and shadow, the influence of Manet is apparent. The final self-portrayal, *Young Man with Goatee, Leaning on His Hand: Self-Portrait* (1908/42), expresses some moodiness because of its meditative gesture. Over delicate lines which model the forms are rows of thick lines that create the tonal values, achieved by holding the lead pencil sideways. These strokes show Klee's absorption of van Gogh's brushwork in that he too presents lines that have no basis in nature. It is possible that this composition was based upon van Gogh's *Self-Portrait* (1888), which is re-

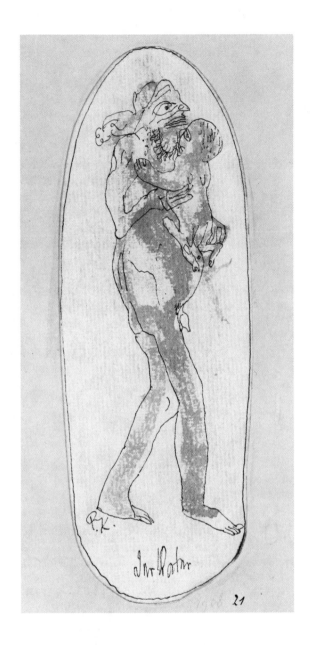

Fig. 4. *The Father: Two Nudes.* 1908 (21). Ink and wash on Ingres paper mounted on board, 6⅜ × 2¼". Courtesy The Blue Four Galka Scheyer Collection, Norton Simon Museum, Pasadena, Ca.

produced in Meier-Graefe's *Impressionisten,* a book Klee received as a birthday gift from Lily in 1908 (Haxthausen, 1981, p. 269).

For the next two years, Klee continued to work from nature, avoiding the satirical and concentrating on the plastic aspects of his art. At this time he had no awareness of 20th-century modernist developments in Paris, and living as he did in Munich, he was not exposed to the more avant-garde galleries found in Berlin. But Klee also failed to see the two major exhibitions of the Neue Künstlervereinigung (New Artists' Association) in Munich, held between 1909 and 1911. Even more surprising is the fact that Wassily Kandinsky, one of the founders and a principal officer of the Association, was his neighbor for three years before they met!

These circumstances suggest that Klee kept somewhat aloof from other artists who were also seeking new means of expression (see Vishny, 1978, for observations on Klee's great reserve and emotional distancing). Klee's self-portraits during this period are strictly external renderings which contain almost no clues to personality. Three remain from 1909, one of which, *Self-Portrait, Full Face, Head Resting on His Hand* (42), he gave to Lily. This dark watercolor is perhaps the closest Klee ever came to an objective rendering of his outer self. Most compelling are the wide-set, deep, staring eyes, his most prominent facial feature and the one which would always be given special emphasis in later portraiture. Another picture of the same year, *Self—Drawing for a Woodcut* (39), also draws attention to Klee's eyes, for he seems to be holding a monocle in front of his right eye to study more closely his image in an easel-backed mirror, thus presenting himself as though in the process of doing a self-portrait.[7] This work, flatter and without the tonal gradations of *Self-Portrait, Full Face . . .* , is executed in such a way as to suggest the boldness of an actual woodcut.

The third self-portrait of 1909 is *The Draughtsman at the Window* (70), a dark watercolor and colored-chalk drawing that portrays Klee seated in a high-backed chair before a dotted curtained window, with his drawing board on his lap. The locale is his kitchen, where he did much of his painting. Although the dark interior scene suggests Klee may have been influenced by Bonnard and Vuillard, whose works he saw in the 1908 spring Secession (*D.,* no. 816), there is an expressionistic feeling conveyed by the brooding features of the artist as he leans forward over his work. Despite the light flowing through the window, the dark-brown colors create a gloomy atmosphere. Possibly this self-portrait was executed at some time during the two-month period of Felix's grave illness, when Klee was totally responsible for his care (Haxthausen, 1981, p. 295).[8] An interesting question has been raised as to why the artist showed himself painting with his right hand, when in fact he was left-handed and did not become ambidextrous until later. Haxthausen (1981, p. 296) suggested that Klee used a mirror and carried the reversed image exactly into his picture. Grohmann, however, who could have discussed this portrait with Klee, flatly stated that the work was done "from memory" (Grohmann, 1967, p. 70). It is not possible to resolve the hand problem, but it can be noted that in three later self-portraits Klee also depicted himself using his right hand; since they are caricatures, it is probable no mirror was used.

Most of the self-images of the years 1910–15 continue to be of interest not because they reveal the inner person but because they show stylistic development. The first of these, *Youthful Self-Portrait* (1910/76), is relatively straightforward and, in its presentation of simple planes and washes of color, shows the influence of Cézanne, whom Klee discovered the previous year. In his diary he wrote, "in my eyes he is the teacher *par excellence,* much more of a teacher than van Gogh" (*D.,* no. 857). Nevertheless, it was to van Gogh that Klee paid homage in the wonderfully pensive self-portrait *Young Man Resting* (1911/42). It was in that year, we recall, that Klee began his oeuvre catalogue, about which he self-mockingly said: "I have become a bureaucrat . . . by compiling a large, precise catalogue of all my artistic productions ever since my childhood" (*D.*, no. 895).[9] That Klee connected *Young Man Resting* with the 1908 pencil sketch also inspired by van Gogh is apparent from his assigning both the same number, "42," in his oeuvre catalogue. He described *Young Man Resting* (and some other works) as an attempt "at mediation with the outer world" (*D.*, no. 897), meaning natural appearances were of major importance and would be fused with subjective feelings in these works. But objective rendering diminished in 1915 when he did the watercolor *An Artist with His Wife Under a Lamp* (194), in which broad washes of dark color efface his features, creating deep shadows across the eyes and exaggerating the mustache and beard area. The figures, painted in a flattened style, are in a somewhat ambiguous spatial setting, indicated by large, Cubist-inspired planes.

Cubism, which affected Klee's work in 1912 (after a visit that year to Paris), is clearly evident in the interesting 1915 self-image, *Poet-Draughtsman* (195). This pencil drawing, whose title is similar to the lost 1908 watercolor *The Artist (Poet-Painter)* (see note 5), unites Klee's dual creative activities and reminds us of a 1911 diary passage: "All things an artist must be: poet, explorer of nature, philosopher!" (*D.*, no. 895). Klee showed himself seated next to a table, with his left elbow propped on it, his hand supporting his head. His right hand, holding a pencil, is engaged in writing poetry (or drawing) on a scroll-like sheet of paper which rests on his lap. A vase of flowers sits on the table, not noticed by the artist, whose gaze is distant, his mind totally absorbed with his work. It is the inner vision which is primary to the poet or painter. Klee later expressed this in the often quoted phrase from his essay *Creative Credo:* "Art does not render the visible; rather, it makes visible" (Grohmann, 1954, p. 97).

Klee's next self-portrait was a satirical pen drawing, *When I Was a Recruit* (1916/81), made the year he was drafted by the German army for service in World War I. Depicting himself among a group of conscripts, Klee is easily distinguishable by his wide-set eyes beneath the visorless cap. His forehead, drawn into a frown, and bared, gnashing teeth convey his "grin-and-bear-it" attitude. Klee's vexation is understandable from the diaries, in which he wrote of the drills, long hikes, and uncomfortable boots, calling the latter "bottomless abysses." He thought his uniform made him look like a convict, and Lily certainly agreed, exclaiming when she saw him wearing it for the first time, "Why, you look just like a criminal!" (F. Klee, 1962, p. 143).

Despite his two and one-half years in the army, Klee was able to produce over 400 works. Even during the war his pictures were exhibited—at Der Sturm Gallery in Berlin, the New Munich Secession, the Galerie Dada in Zurich, and the Kunsthalle in

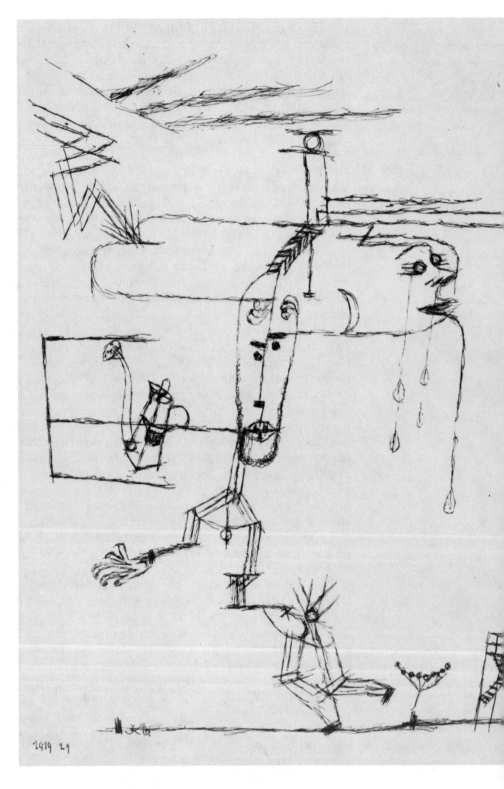

Fig. 5. *The Sultry Garden.* 1919 (29). Pen and ink on paper, 11⅜ × 8⅝". Courtesy Paul Klee-Stiftung, Kunstmuseum Bern, © 1984 by COSMOPRESS, Geneva, and ADAGP, Paris.

Bern. Sales were made and numerous articles and reproductions of his pictures were published. A monograph by Wilhelm Hausenstein, *Kairuan oder eine Geschichte vom Maler Klee und von der Kunst dieses Zeitalters,* although not published until 1921, was planned in July 1918. Thus, when the war ended, Klee emerged as a fully mature, recognized artist. It is significant that the diaries chronicling his long period of development ended in December 1918. Henceforth, Klee would express his thoughts in essays, lectures, pedagogical notes and copious letters, mostly addressed to Lily. And finally, after years of working in small quarters and surreptitiously in the army offices, Klee had his first adequate studio in 1919, a large room in a dilapidated house called "Suresnes Castle" on Werneckstrasse in Munich. Felix recalled that here, "wrapped up in a world all his own, Klee lived only for his art, serving it from the earliest hours in the morning until midnight" (*D.,* p. 415). In that year, his most productive to date, Klee created his greatest number of self-images, eight in all. None was formally entitled self-portrait, though each shows his features. For the titles of several, he preferred the more universal term "artist," which was germane to ideas he was expressing: *Thinking Artist, Sensitive Artist, Artist Pondering, Artist Forming,* and *Portrait of an Artist.* The remaining three of 1919 were the drawing and lithograph, both called *Lost in Thought,* and *The Sultry Garden,* which contains a disguised self-portrait (Glaesemer, 1973, p. 258).

Assuming that Klee's oeuvre catalogue numbers for 1919 might list the works in the order produced, *The Sultry Garden* (1919/29) (Fig. 5) would be the first to consider. Also, it will be demonstrated below that the later 1919 oeuvre catalogue numbers 71–75 showing portraits of the artist were seen as a series, and their numbering order reflects the development of a theme.

One of the significant aspects of the drawing *The Sultry Garden* is that it is the first of the covert self-portraits (there would be several in 1922) in which the artist included details in the setting which, when interpreted give the meaning of the picture, thus conveying Klee's attitudes on various subjects. In *The Sultry Garden,* a mustached and bearded figure, with his head in a cloud, stumbles along the ground, perhaps uncertain of his way. The cloud, one of Klee's ingenious inventions, has been personified and weeps enormous raindrop tears which fall earthward on the right side of the picture; to the left, lightning shoots out of the cloud's buttocks to join other streaks of lightning across the sky. Hanging in midair and aligned with the artist's head is a watering can. This picture, with its charged atmosphere, could be a portrayal of the expressionistic artistic atmosphere in Germany, which Klee was clearly a part of, as evidenced by the emotionally exaggerated style of his recently completed illustrations for Curt Corrinth's book, *Potsdamer Platz.*[10] In this drawing he gave visual form to his connection with Expressionism by showing his open head intersecting with the cloud. As the cloud moves off to the right, the artist takes steps in the opposite direction, perhaps to retrieve his watering can. The can brings to mind a phrase from Voltaire's *Candide,* for which Klee made numerous illustrations in 1911–12: "*Il faut cultiver notre jardin.*" This phrase became a guiding principle for Klee; it was central to his way of life to remain aloof from emotionally entangling situations, politics, artistic movements, etc., in other words, to cultivate his own garden. Although the term "expressionist" was to be used in two future self-portraits, Klee was adamant about not letting himself or his work be characterized by "-isms" or "-ists." In 1924, this attitude would be expressed in a letter to Emmy Scheyer, a dealer and dear friend, who showed the art of Klee and other artists in America: "It is perhaps quite good to mark the works . . . with some sort of collective word indicating that they belong together. . . . We are not certain about this name. Under no circumstance may it end in -ism or -ist. Instead, concerning the names of Jawlensky, Feininger, Kandinsky and Klee it should at most credit the founding character, the intellectual leadership and what is in fact even more beautiful, the friendship between them" (Galka Scheyer Blue Four Archive, Jan. 10, 1924). The name eventually given to the group was "The Blue Four."

In a series of five self-images that followed *The Sultry Garden,* Klee analyzed the stages of creation of a work of art and the role of the artist. As several of the titles of these drawings show, emphasis is given to the mental processes involved: *Thinking Artist* (1919/71; a now lost work), *Sensitive Artist* (1919/72), *Artist Pondering* (1919/73), *Artist Forming* (1919/74), and *Lost in Thought* (1919/75). In *Sensitive Artist,* he is shown seated at a work table, his head leaning on his right hand, looking outward, as though absorbing sensations, while his left hand holds a pencil over one of two empty sheets before him, ready to transcribe his sensations. In *Artist Pondering* Klee exaggerated the size of his hand, increasing its scale nearly to that of the head, perhaps to indicate that in creation, mind and hand are equally important. The artist carefully weighs his thoughts before building up his picture. What is now given visual form in these self-images, Klee stated verbally the previous year in his first version of the *Creative Credo,* a treatise on graphic art that contains his philosophy:

> Art is a parable of Creation; it is an example, as the terrestrial is an example of the cosmos. . . . The release of the elements, the grouping of them in subdivisions composed of parts, the articulation of the whole by building up several aspects simultaneously, pictorial polyphony, the achievement of equilibrium between the various movements, all higher and still higher questions of form, are vital factors in artistic communication; but they do not in themselves produce art of the highest level. For at that level, mystery begins and the intellect counts for nothing. At the highest level, imagination is guided by instinctual stimuli, and illusions are created which buoy us up and stir us more than do the familiar things of earth. In that realm are born the symbols which comfort the mind, which perceives that it need not be chained to the potentialities of terrestrial things (in F. Klee, 1962, p. 155).

Of these self-exploratory images, the fourth, *Artist Forming,* bears the strongest likeness to Klee and furnishes the most details of the setting. While the face is caricatured, as in the other drawings, the features are more carefully indicated. The artist makes eye contact with the viewer as he sits at his table puffing on a long-stemmed pipe, whose bowl he holds in his left hand. His right hand, holding a pencil (or brush), seems to be in the act of drawing on the sheet. Klee's head is framed by a window in the background and, to either side, pictures are hanging on the wall.

In complete contrast to this somewhat fussy, extroverted image, is the final drawing in this series, the powerful *Lost in Thought* (Fig. 6).[11] Though bearing a faint resemblance to the artist, it is a totally symbolic portrait. In its frontality it shows a striking likeness to *The Threatening Head* of 1905 (Fig. 2). The elements of the head that show his distinctive characteristics are the hairline, the wide shape of the eyes, and the beard. But the human head, a point of departure for this semi-abstract image, is transformed into an oblong, tabletlike monument, in which Klee inscribed his features as symbols. He eliminated the ears (for they would distract attention from the face), and in this concentration on essentials, created an effect that is mesmerizing.

Fig. 6. *Lost in Thought.* 1919 (75). Pencil on paper mounted on board, 10¾ × 7⅝". Courtesy The Blue Four Galka Scheyer Collection, Norton Simon Museum, Pasadena, Ca.

Although known simply as *Lost in Thought* (*Versunkenheit,* which can also mean "trance"), the picture has been given additional titles in the lithograph version: *Self-Portrait—Portrait of an Expressionist—Portrait* (in Kornfeld, no. 73). The use of the word "expressionist" should be understood in terms of Klee's philosophical outlook, not as a sign of adherence to a specific artistic movement that demonstrated a common style. It is perhaps a strange word to describe a picture that shows him in monklike retreat rather than emotionally involved with wordly events. The year of this portrait was one of political upheaval in Munich, where a Communist republic was established. That Klee wholly sympathized with this short-lived regime, overthrown at the end of April 1919, is evident from a letter he wrote to the artist Alfred Kubin (in Glaesemer, 1976, pp. 134–135). One of the revolution's leaders, the expressionist poet Ernst Toller, was hidden for three weeks behind a concealed door at "Suresnes Castle," where Klee had his studio, although it is not certain whether the aloof Klee was even aware of his presence (in Glaesemer, 1976, p. 135; also *D.,* p. 415). Thus, while one of the work's titles, *Portrait of an Expressionist,* suggests identification with the expressionist poets and painters, this image shows the very opposite, withdrawal into the self, meditation rather than activity. The duality and polarity of title and image are wholly consistent with Klee's idea of the duality of concepts joining to form a unity. It is expressed on the formal plane as well as theorized. In the portrait, the horizontality of the eyes, mouth, and shoulders finds vertical balance in the head, trunklike neck, and nose. In the case of the lithograph, there exists one colored example (Collection Felix Klee) that displays the complementary contrasts of yellow and violet. In his *Creative Credo,* Klee said: "Every energy calls for its complement, for art is always seeking the equilibrium that arises out of the play of forces, a state in which abstract forms can become meaningful objects, or else pure symbols as constant as numbers and letters of the alphabet. Taken all together, these may become symbols of the cosmos; that is to say, they become a form of religious expression" (in F. Klee, 1962, p. 154).

Another element of spiritual expression in *Lost in Thought* is the erotic imagery Klee used to represent his features. The eyes and mouth resemble pudenda and the nose is phallic (see Gohr, 1979, p. 84). In his depiction of the genital organs in the head, which symbolizes the ego, Klee called attention to the act of creation taking place within the artist. It is the artist who "creates a work, or participates in the creation of works, that are the image of God's work" (see P. Klee in Spiller, 1961, p. 67). The sex organs are thus used as metaphors for creation. Many other works of this period also contain sexual imagery in the heads: to mention a few, *Portrait of an Artist* (1919/260) (discussed below), *The Drawing for the Barbarians' Venus* (1920/212), *The Wild Man* (1922/43), and *Strange Garden* (1923/160), which indeed contains some strange erotic mutations! The last is perhaps Klee's richest work in terms of its physiognomic transpositions. In addition to portraying genitalia in the face, Klee frequently reversed the imagery, giving a face to the body. This appears in his drawings as early as 1906 (see reproductions in Glaesemer, 1973) and is also expressed in *Barbarians' Venus* (1921/132), *Women's Devil* (1921/147), and *A Face Also of the Body* (1939/HI19), in which breasts become eyes, and pudenda, the mouth. In his diary, Klee noted an early childhood fantasy that has a bearing on these works: "I imagined face and genitals to be the corresponding poles of the female sex, when girls wept I thought of pudenda weeping in unison" (*D.,* no. 35). That so many of Klee's pictures contain these biological references demonstrates a personal view of eros that is central to the meaning of his work (see Gohr, 1979).

Immediately following the series of five self-portraits (1919/71–75), are two very similar drawings, both entitled *Mask* (1919/76 and 77). The latter has been published as a self-portrait (see *The Morton G. Neumann Family Collection,* 1980, I, p. 71), and both pictures possibly are, even if they are not so identified in the oeuvre catalogue.[12] Both bear some resemblance to Klee in their portrayal of the beard and emphasis on huge, staring eyes. Unlike the early masks in the *Comedian* series, these do not have complex allegorical meaning.

The final self-image of 1919, the watercolor *Portrait of an Artist,* is executed in a caricatural style, showing Klee drawing with a brush in his right hand while his left arm is raised, the hand resting on a high-domed forehead. This feature, together with the slanting eyes, gives an Oriental cast to the face, suggesting a Chinese philosopher. The work also contains the sexual symbols discussed above, the eyes and the mouth resembling pudenda. Paramount, however, is the prominent role of the raised left arm; its position and importance are reminiscent of Dürer's famous drawing, *Self-Portrait with Head Resting on One Hand* (c. 1492; Erlangen, Graphic Collection of the University), which Klee undoubtedly knew. Both artists emphasize art as a union of hand and mind. Klee's self-image shows an intense concentration upon his work, recalling a 1918 diary passage: "Everything vanishes around me, and works are born as if out of the void. . . . My hand has become the obedient instrument of a remote will" (*D.,* no. 1104). *Portrait of an Artist,* the last work to show Klee absorbed in the making of art, occupies a position in his oeuvre that parallels the diary entries: just as his self-analysis in the diaries ended in 1918, so his self-portrayal as a producing artist found its final affirmation in this 1919 work.

The Middle Period: 1920–33

In 1920 Klee was still living in Munich. It was a year which must have brought him great satisfaction, following one which could only have been disappointing. Oskar Schlemmer, an active advanced art student at the Stuttgart Academy, had attempted to have Klee appointed to the faculty. The Academy unanimously rejected him, however, on the grounds that so dreamy and ethereal an artist could not be a teacher and that his "work as a whole reveals a playful character, in any case not the powerful impetus towards structure and composition that the new movement rightly demands" (in Spiller, 1961, p. 27). Therefore, the large retrospective exhibition featuring 362 of Klee's works at Hans Goltz's gallery in Munich, the publication of both the *Candide* and *Potsdamer Platz* illustrations, and the appearance of the first two monographs on Klee (by H. von Wedderkop and Leopold Zahn) were especially rewarding. In October 1920, an opportunity to teach presented itself once again, this time at the newly founded Weimar Bauhaus. Klee's first classes began in Janaury 1921; he was to remain at the Bauhaus (from mid-1925, located in Dessau) until his resignation in 1931, when he accepted a professorship at the Düsseldorf Academy of Art, where he taught until his dismissal by the Nazis in the spring of 1933.

Klee's best-known and perhaps most universally loved works were created in this middle period. Though the self-portraits are not as numerous as in the preceding decades, they are nevertheless informative, revealing how Klee viewed himself, his attitudes toward women and aspects of marriage, and finally, how he reacted to being ousted from Düsseldorf when Hitler came to power.

In his self-images of the early 1920s, Klee took on many disguises. He appears as a magician, alchemist, pseudo-scientist, mechanized ghost, expressionist artist, puppet, musician, and even as his own pipe! Strong physical resemblance is not necessarily the criterion for identifying many of his pictures as self-portraits, because many of Klee's works in this period are abstract constructions. We recognize Klee, rather, through what we know of his life and from descriptions by his contemporaries when he depicts himself in various roles. Many years earlier he had said: "My self . . . is a dramatic ensemble" (*D.,* no. 638).

The drawing *Magical Experiment* (1920/54), depicting a capped, wide-eyed, bearded figure standing in his laboratory surrounded by various kinds of apparatus, is a disguised portrait of Klee. Grohmann (1954, p. 49) noted that the cluttered appearance of Klee's apartment suggested a witch's kitchen rather than an average dwelling and that Klee himself tended to dress more like an alchemist than a Munich bourgeois.[13] And a Bauhaus colleague, the stage designer Lothar Schreyer, described Klee's studio in Weimar as a "wizard's kitchen . . . the place where the real magic potions were brewed" (see L. Schreyer in F. Klee, 1962, pp. 180–181). Klee portrayed himself again as a magician in the popeyed, bearded figure of the drawing *Black Magic* (1920/70) who is in the act of conjuring amid strange paraphernalia.

The most delightful treatment of this magic and pseudo-scientific theme, however, is in the superb watercolor *Analysis of Diverse Perversities* (1922/70). That the work was prized by Klee himself is evident from the letters he wrote on the sheet, *S Cl* (*Sonderclasse,* "special class"), which meant the work could be sold only after his oral or written agreement (Grohmann, 1967, p. 94).

In the style of its background—delicate, semitransparent colored planes in mauve, pink, and blue—one detects the influence of Klee's Bauhaus teaching, both in the stained-glass workshop and in his painting classes, where he often did color studies stressing tonal gradations.[14] The little mustached and bearded fellow in the right foreground with mechanical apparatuslike arms which connect with other contraptions, is Klee presenting himself as a wizard-scientist conducting an experiment. Arrows spiral and point upward, moving off into space without pointing to conclusions and pulleys rotate. An insect buzzes in the center of the picture and a fish swims along the bottom. In the upper left, an animated bird on a perch twitters away at the gadgetry, while its droppings fall into a basket. Stretched out on a table before the wizard is a half-mechanical female figure, who appears to be one of the subjects of the analyst's spurious study. The placement and size of the figure suggest that woman is the prime perversity. Possibly Klee is saying that there can be no understanding or real communication between the sexes. Even an understanding of nature, as represented by the fish, insect, and bird, seems beyond this "scientist." Because many of Klee's works contain elements of self-mockery, it is not surprising that he presented "diverse perversities" which were beyond his analysis, and allowed the bird to make a scatological comment summarizing the scene.

The mechanical imagery in this watercolor also appears in numerous other works of this period (e.g., *Plan of a Group of Machines* [1920/163], *Small Experimental Machine* [1921/11], *Twittering Machine* [1922/151]) and undoubtedly bears some connection to Dada, one of the artistic expressions found at the Bauhaus in the early 1920s.[15] Three versions exist of *Specter of a Genius* (1922/10, 1922/192, and 1923/38), an amusing self-portrait in which Klee used wheellike mechanisms to indicate his facial features and to attach his neck to his body. They are frontal self-images in which an overly large head with a somewhat sheepish facial expression tilts slightly to the right, directly confronting the viewer. Possibly these pictures were Klee's self-mocking comment on his teaching. He took extraordinary care in the preparation of his lessons, analyzing the elements of his art and formulating rules for his students. Altogether, Klee left over 3300 pages of teaching notebooks, consisting of memoranda, teaching projects, constructive drawings, and sketches for pictures. These extensive theoretical writings[16] show Klee to be one of the greatest artistic minds of the 20th century, certainly a genius, although his attitude was undoubtedly tongue-in-cheek when he created these pictures.

Another self-image appears in the pencil drawing *Portrait of an Expressionist* (1922/240) (Fig. 7). Although this title (among others) appeared on the 1919 *Lost in Thought,* the connotations differ somewhat in the context of the present work. The first phase of the Bauhaus, from the time of its foundation in 1919 until 1923, was known as its Expressionist period. Artists who represented this aspect of its character were Johannes Itten, who taught the

Fig. 7. *Portrait of an Expressionist.* 1922 (240). Pencil on paper, 12¼ × 8¾". Location unknown.

Preliminary Course, Klee, Kandinsky, and Feininger. In mid-1923 a change took place; the additions of Josef Albers and László Moholy-Nagy to the faculty and the growing influence of *De Stijl* theory and geometric abstraction brought about a Constructivist approach. Klee's 1922 portrait displays bristly forms suggesting expressionistic brushwork. There is an element of mild pathos to the features, possibly an allusion to expressionism's emotionalism, but there may be other reasons for it. By the time Klee did this portrait, late in the year according to its oeuvre catalogue number, *De Stijl* artist Theo van Doesburg had set up a rival course to those offered at the Bauhaus in Weimar and had also organized a Congress of Dadaists and Constructivists. In addition, two 1922 exhibitions, one of students', the second of Bauhaus Masters' works, were criticized—on the one hand, by Constructivist and *De Stijl* artists, on the other, by Weimar reactionaries. Although Klee distanced himself from nearly all issues, and for his reserve was jokingly called "the heavenly Father," perhaps *Portrait of an Expressionist* shows his sensitivities to the various difficulties the Bauhaus faced, and the growing dichotomy in viewpoints. The change in the orientation of the Bauhaus the following year might explain a 1924 self-portrait discussed below.

The Bauhaus was a unique institution in that it not only offered classes but held performances and festivals throughout the year. In connection with an early 1920s Midsummer-Night Festival, Felix (who at 14 was the youngest Bauhaus student) put on a puppet show. His father had begun to make puppets for him in 1916 (for his ninth birthday) and continued to do so until 1925. Among the 30 puppets is one of Paul Klee himself, made in 1922, in which he has on a coat and scarf and the same fur hat he is wearing in a photo taken with Emmy Scheyer in a Weimar park that year. Klee also made a puppet caricaturing Emmy, and at the festival, Felix showed Emmy trying to talk Klee into buying a work by Alexei Jawlensky. Felix recalled his puppet performance: "My father, however, doesn't want to, and Emmy breaks the Jawlensky on his head. The real Emmy and Klee arrived at the festival just as the performance was over, and the audience welcomed the originals, both unaware of the show, with applause" (see F. Klee, in Neumann, 1970, p. 41).[17] Christian Geelhaar (1973, p. 77) called the Klee puppet the last true self-representation. It would be more accurate, however, to say that this was the last work to be called a self-portrait, for Klee continued to depict himself in numerous works by portraying either his features or self-referential situations.

Two paintings of 1922 contain autobiographical elements. In each work the figures are abstract constructions, and though not bearing Klee's physical features, they are nevertheless self-images. The first of these works to be discussed, *Dance You Monster to My Soft Song!* (1922/54), a watercolor and oil transfer drawing, also rendered in pen only (1922/55), explores the marital relationship. Before analyzing this work, it is enlightening to read Klee's diaries and to examine an earlier work, not a self-portrait, but one that supports the interpretation of *Dance You Monster. . . !*

By 1915, Klee's diaries already show the lifelong path he chose to follow: preserving himself for his art by remaining steadfast to one person. He had observed how his childhood friend Hermann Haller had dissipated himself and aged prematurely in "the hunt for shattering emotional experiences. The effects on his artistic activity could only be negative. . . . In contrast to him, I thus had become a kind of monk, a monk with a broad, natural basis where all the natural functions found a place. I regarded marriage as a sexual cure. I fed my romantic tendencies with the sexual mystery. I found that mystery tied up with monogamy, and that was enough" (*D.*, no. 958). A retrospective diary entry again states Klee's position: "Later on, art absorbed all my morality, and, as a moral person, I was absolutely assured that I would end by being wholly absorbed by that world. Had I led a worldlier life, I probably could not have avoided painful conflicts" (*D.*, no. 101). Thus Klee chose monogamy, which allowed him to lead an ordered life, but at the same time, his ambivalence is apparent in a few works showing negative aspects of this domesticity.

Dance You Monster . . . and the two renditions of *Pandora's Box* (1920/155 and 1920/158) that preceded it, are obvious expressions of his hostility. Both works include a piano, which suggests the Klee household. In *Pandora's Box* an urn, decorated on the front with pudenda and containing thistlelike flowers, emit evil vapors which form a rectangular frame for the domestic scene portrayed above. Within this frame women and children are seated at a table in a room that in addition to the piano, is conspicuously furnished with pictures hanging on the wall.[18] The meaning of the work is explicit: sex leading to marriage and family life is a plague, as in the Pandora myth. Significantly, in Klee's second treatment of the theme, *Pandora's Box as Still Life,* he depersonalized it by omitting the household, portraying only the urn with its vapors terminating in the upper part of the picture in the word "Pandora." While Klee universalized the meaning in this second rendition, the picture is also self-concealing and, perhaps, self-censoring.[19]

Klee's negativism, however, reasserted itself in *Dance You Monster . . .* (Fig. 8). The picture depicts a male marionette, suspended in midair, with huge staring eyes, a nose resembling an erect penis, a kitelike mouth, and little beard. Its sexuality is emphasized both by its nose and the bell-shaped form between its legs. Below, a tiny figure of a lady holds a wedding band in her left hand and winds up a pianolike music box with her right, subtly controlling with her "soft song" the marionette-monster looming overhead.

Despite these occasional expressions of Klee's negative view of marriage, from what his biographers have written and, more important, the letters he wrote to Lily from 1900 until a month before his death in 1940 (these letters run over 1000 pages; see F Klee, 1979), they enjoyed an exceptionally fine relationship. Among other things, the Klees shared a deep love of music, and many family friends recalled hearing concerts in the Klee home on numerous occasions. Felix wrote: "My parents would spend their evenings playing sonatas by Bach, Handel, Mozart, Beethoven, Brahms and Reger—as a sort of rehearsal when they were alone, and as finished concerts when we had visitors, as we so frequently did" (F. Klee, 1962, p. 33). Klee's highly inventive oil and watercolor drawing *Contact of Two Musicians* (1922/93), which uses abstract forms to create the figures and instruments, depicts him holding a violin. A linear arabesque links his figure to Lily's, accompanying him at the piano. They are shown as though onstage, with curtains parted for their musical performance. (Klee was to present many of his compositions, even still lifes, as dramas, which he suggested by including stage curtains, as in this work.)

Another self-image appears in the ironic *Pipe Bowl and Overturned Antique: Sketch for a Still Life* (1924/32) (Fig. 9). In this drawing Klee might be commenting on recent changes in the ideology and program of the Bauhaus. During the summer of 1923, in connection with its first major exhibition, Bauhaus director Walter Gropius gave a lecture entitled "Art and Technics,

Fig. 8. *Dance You Monster to My Soft Song!* 1922 (54). Watercolor
and oil transfer drawing on plaster-grounded gauze, 17⅝ × 12⅞″.
Courtesy Solomon R. Guggenheim Museum, New York. Photo:
Robert E. Mates.

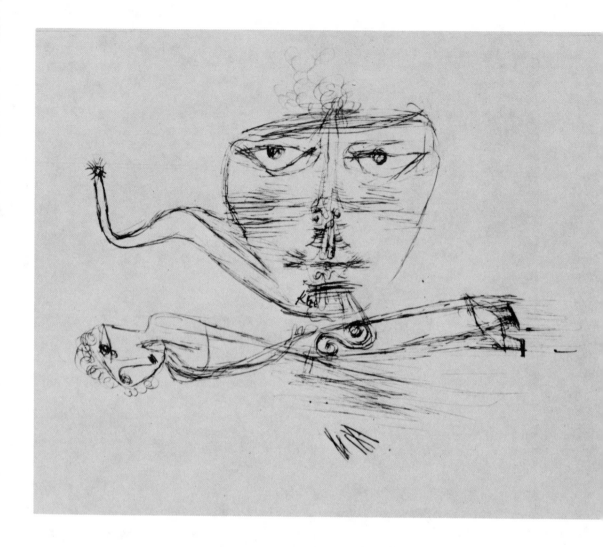

Fig. 9. *Pipe Bowl and Overturned Antique: Sketch for a Still Life.* 1924 (32). Pen and ink on paper, 7¼ × 8⅞". Courtesy Paul Klee-Stiftung, Kunstmuseum Bern, © 1984 by COSMOPRESS, Geneva and ADAGP, Paris.

A New Unity." He also published an essay that year, *Idee und Aufbau des Staatlichen Bauhauses Weimar* in which he stated that "contact with industry is consciously sought. . . . The old craft workshops will develop into industrial laboratories: from their experimentation will evolve standards for industrial production. . . . The teaching of a craft is meant to prepare for designing for mass production" (in Naylor, 1968, p. 93). Some of the Bauhaus Masters were upset with this new orientation, rejecting Gropius's motto and ideals. Feininger, who directed the graphic workshop, said: "This misconception of art is a symptom of our time. The demand to couple the two movements is nonsense in every respect. A real technician will rightly reject every artistic interference, and, on the other hand, even the greatest technical perfection can never replace the divine spark of art" (in Hess, 1961, p. 105). Schlemmer, who at the Weimar Bauhaus was director of the stone masonry and metal workshops, also was concerned and stated the following in his diary:

One thing is certain, and that is that the application of scientific principles to art is now widespread. Basic forms, laws, numerical configurations. Anything connected with the psyche has become suspect. When applied to the human figure, this scientific approach would yield what one might expect to see at a hygiene exhibit: a portrayal of the blood circulation in action, the movements of the soul portrayed in such a way as to "raise the level of self-awareness." One can see the contrast to Greek statuary, also a version of perfection (Schlemmer, 1972, p. 147, entry Dec. 29, 1923).

Klee, whom we know was aligned with Kandinsky and Feininger, generally remained quiet at Bauhaus meetings of the Masters' Council and did not involve himself in controversies; however, in *Pipe Bowl . . .* he seems to have been portraying the polemical situation. The horizontal antique statuette could represent classical principles and the spiritual side of art, now overturned by the new technological approach. Above the figurine rests Klee's pipe, his passive features drawn on the bowl and his signature appearing across the bearded chin.

Pipe Bowl . . . was the last of Klee's bearded self-images for a very good reason. In the spring of 1925, Klee shaved off his beard and mustache, never to grow them again. Possibly the watercolor (stencil spray technique) *Monsieur Perlenschwein* (Mr. Pearly-Pig) (1925/223), in which Klee presented himself in the guise of a harlequin with a bare, rosy complexion, shows how he felt without his beard.[20] Curiously, it was probably around this time that at one of the Bauhaus festivals in Dessau, Klee wore a mask with a turned up snout, which suggests identification with a pig or some other animal (see Schawinsky in Neumann, 1970, p. 150).

During the latter part of the 1920s, Klee and some of the other painters found the atmosphere at the Bauhaus disturbing. He no longer looked forward to teaching his classes. Gropius had resigned, and Hannes Meyer, his successor who served as director from 1928 to 1930, initiated the scientific, or rational, phase which stressed functionalism. A Marxist who felt that aesthetics played no role, not even in architecture, Meyer actually banned every activity connected with painting. Schlemmer, who left to teach in Breslau in 1929, had predicted the year before that "the Bauhaus will reorient itself in the direction of architecture, industrial production and the intellectual aspect of technology. The painters are merely tolerated as a necessary evil now" (Schlemmer, 1972, p. 221). As a result, Klee left the Bauhaus in 1931 to teach at the Academy of Art in Düsseldorf, where he continued to lecture on the elements of art. Relieved of teaching theory, he now devoted himself mostly to correcting the work of his painting class students. Frequently, meetings were held informally at his studio, where Klee and the students discussed and analyzed both his and their pictures.

Although the teaching atmosphere was more relaxed than at the Bauhaus, political tensions mounted with gains made by the Nazis in the elections of 1932 and their coming to power at the end of January 1933. In March, the Academy flew the swastika flag. Klee was dismissed in April with the explanation that it was necessary to restore the indigenous character of the art schools; from then on he never entered his Academy studio. The Nazis also demanded that all art displaying cosmopolitan or Bolshevist tendencies must be thrown out of German museums and collections and ultimately burned. In a self-image entitled *Struck from the List* (1933/G4) (Fig. 10), Klee showed his reaction to his dismissal from the Academy: lowered eyelids and turned-down mouth portray his dejection in this oil painting. A large, dark *X* is superimposed upon the back of his head, perhaps signifying that not only is the artist banned from teaching and exhibiting his work, but the creative mind is also to be expunged.

Klee spent much of the remainder of 1933 working as though obsessed in the cramped quarters of the studio in his home in Düsseldorf, creating the greatest number of works done in any one year to date. October was spent traveling: to Bern, southern France, Paris, and back to Düsseldorf. But living there became increasingly difficult, and Klee finally resigned himself to moving to the only place Lily deemed safe—Switzerland. On December 23, he left for Bern, never to return to Germany.

Fig. 10. *Struck from the List*. 1933 (G4). Oil applied with palette knife on transparent wax paper, 12⅜ × 9½". Courtesy Felix Klee, © 1984, by COSMOPRESS, Geneva, and ADAGP, Paris.

There is no question that Klee suffered from depression when he returned to Switzerland. It is reported that his family received them coolly, and Lily even believed she saw a glint of triumph in her father-in-law's eyes (F. Klee, 1962, p. 71). Klee did not have the stature in his native city that he had in Germany, or even other places such as Paris and the United States where he had exhibited his work. He had always felt Bern was provincial, and after the rich cultural life of Munich and the productive atmosphere of the Bauhaus, returning required a period of acclimation. Finally, he lost whatever money he had saved in German banks.

The Klees had to move three times that year, staying first with father Hans, then moving to a furnished apartment, and finally to a modern but small three-room apartment. Klee's studio was once again situated in his home, as it was in Munich during the first few years of his marriage. Four months passed before he felt like painting again, which began haltingly, or, as he described it in a letter to Grohmann, "with a very reduced orchestra" (Grohmann, 1954, p. 90). Lily wrote to Emmy Scheyer that, despite the tiny furnished apartment they occupied until June 1, Klee had a strong creative period which resulted in beautiful work (Galka Scheyer Blue Four Archive, Jun. 24, 1934). Still, his oeuvre catalogue showed a marked decrease in his production for 1934, only 219 works as compared with nearly 500 the preceding year, when, immersed in difficulties, he had buried himself in his art.

Among Klee's paintings is a small watercolor, *Broken Mask* (1934/S16), that could well be a self-image expressing the trauma of the events that led to his removal to Switzerland and his first trying months there. Although Klee had created dozens of works which included the word "mask" in the title, none seems as personal as this mask, which looks as though it had been dropped rather than placed where it rests, falling forward as it does on an angle. An upper quarter is missing, just above the widely spaced dots indicating the eyes. The mask's color is a ghostly white, except for a light spray of red across the crudely drawn nose and mouth. As simple as the imagery is, it nevertheless indicates great suffering.

Once having adjusted to Bern, Klee's life returned to normal, but only for a little over a year. During this time he created hundreds of pictures, played his violin with two string quartets, held exhibitions of his work in London and Paris, and was given a major retrospective in the Bern Kunsthalle in February-March 1935. At the end of the summer, however, Klee became ill, first with bronchitis, then a lung inflammation which also affected his heart, then a serious case of the measles, glandular disturbances, and scleroderma. (It was heart complications resulting from scleroderma that ultimately caused his death five years later.) That he produced so few works during the first year of his illness cannot be attributed primarily to depression (as stated by San Lazzaro, 1967, p. 256) but rather to the seriousness of his physical condition, which required months of bed rest followed by treatment in sanatoriums. Klee began to work a little in August 1936 but required another "rest-cure" that fall. Although he was far from recovered, Lily described Klee in a November 3 letter to Emmy as "active, cheerful again and even venturesome" (Galka Scheyer Blue Four Archive). At this time Klee's thoughts were not on death, for there was no reason to doubt that his good health eventually would be restored. Furthermore, his works of 1937 do not strike a tragic chord. Rather, in one painting—which could be a self-image relating to his illness—*Clown in Bed* (1937/W14), there is an element of humor.[21] Although Klee employed heavy black strokes for outlines, facial features and parts of the body, the red and yellow colors enliven the picture. Clearly not at ease in his reclining position—the clown's head barely touches the pillow—he gives the impression that this posture was forced upon him. It is the wide-set eyes once again that suggest Klee (and the nose is similar to that in *Broken Mask*) as well as the subject matter, with its source in his illness.

During the last few years of his life, however, Klee was fully aware that his days were numbered. He showed himself literally as "half out of the picture" in *Wedding Anniversary* (1939/E17) (Fig. 11). Only half of Klee's face is visible and it looks skeletal. The

Fig. 11. *Wedding Anniversary*. 1939 (E17). Watercolor and pencil on paper, 11⅝ × 8¼". Courtesy Felix Klee, © 1984, by COSMOPRESS, Geneva, and ADAGP, Paris.

eye is indicated by a hollow circle. Admittedly, this watercolor drawing is exaggerated, but photographs of Klee at this time do reveal marked physical changes caused by scleroderma.

This disease also affected his esophagus. Felix noted that Klee "often had difficulty eating; his esophagus had lost its elasticity and would no longer move solid food down to his stomach" (F. Klee, 1962, p. 71).[22] Carola Giedion-Welcker, who visited Klee a month before he died, said that in the course of their conversation, Klee was continually running in and out of the kitchen, preparing his special diet of liquid food, watching carefully for the desire and opportunity to eat (in San Lazzaro, 1967, pp. 209–211). In his last letter to Lily, written May 11, 1940 from Victoria Sanatorium in Orselina-Locarno, Klee mentioned his difficulty swallowing and his hope that the special diet would help him (F. Klee, 1979, p. 1289).

Klee's esophageal dysfunction suggests that the painting *Voice from the Higher Spheres: "And You Will Eat Your Fill"* (1939/GH8) might have a level of interpretation beyond the political one it has been accorded.[23] The quotation in the title, adapted by Klee, may have been extracted from Leviticus 25:19 or Deuteronomy 11:15. Portrayed is a head with large, hollow eyes and a salivating mouth supported by a structure that resembles a spinal column or inner organs, rather than a neck. To the left there is an elongated tubelike form with vertical striations which might be the esophagus. The paint, applied to this form and to an adjacent area with a palette knife, is laid on in sections, suggesting Klee has given visual shape to the mechanism of swallowing and the movement of food. It makes little difference whether this picture alludes to political propaganda or food, because the process of digestion is the subject, and, in this sense, its imagery is self-referential.

Creating art took precedence over everything during Klee's final two and one-half years, and there was a tremendous upsurge in the number of works he made—some 2000! Just as he had investigated many aspects of life in his pictures, he now explored death and the realm beyond. Some drawings, although lacking facial details, are nevertheless self-images: *A Sick Man Making Plans* (1939/FF11) and *A Sick Man in a Boat* (1940/W6). The latter, of course, refers to the rivers of the Underworld as does the painting *Dark Voyage* (1940/F5).

Most remarkable is how Klee bore his five-year illness. According to his family and friends, he never complained. In two letters to Emmy, Lily wrote that Klee had adjusted to his illness and, typical of his personality, accepted it tranquilly. She further described him as a long-suffering patient with "never a word of complaint" (Galka Scheyer Blue Four Archive, letters of March 8 and June 28, 1936). Felix echoed this, adding that although the condition had its ups and downs, his father must have suffered unspeakably the entire time (F. Klee, 1962, p. 71). Giedion-Welcker said Klee did not devote any particular attention to his illness, certainly did not discuss it, for he was "a man of great

162

silences" (in San Lazzaro, 1967, p. 211). One of Klee's last drawings, the self-image *Perseverance!* (1940/G17) (Fig. 12), portrays his attitude as death approached. Its title characterizes the path he chose in his final years: to continue creating, to endure, despite the illness, to the very end. Withdrawal into the self and silent suffering have never been more poignantly expressed than in this face, with its wide, woe-filled eyes but sealed lips.

The same face appears, this time as a smiling ghost, in *Death and Fire* (1940/G12) (Fig. 13); it is his final self-portrait. The painting's enigmatic symbols and incandescent color have inspired many interpretations. Perhaps the work is best elucidated through considering Klee's philosophy of death, formulated during various periods of his life, rather than attempting to explain specifically each sign, image, and color.

One of Klee's students at the Düsseldorf Academy recorded his having said: "Death is not evil. I long ago reconciled myself to it. Do we know what is more important, our present life or what comes after? Perhaps the other life is more significant. . . . I die willingly if I have created a few more good works" (in Petitpierre, 1957, p. 65). These thoughts on death were expressed in the 1930s, when the artist was middle-aged. But even in his youth (1901) similar attitudes were stated in his diaries: "I philosophize

Fig. 12. *Perseverance!* 1940 (G17). Black pastel on paper, 11⅝ × 8¼". Courtesy Paul Klee-Stiftung, Kunstmuseum Bern, © 1984, by COS-MOPRESS, Geneva, and ADAGP, Paris.

about death that perfects what could not be completed in life. The longing for death, not as destruction, but as striving toward perfection" (*D.,* no. 143). Possibly the golden circle poised aloft in the ghost's hand represents perfection.

Klee viewed himself as "an observer above the world" (*D.,* no. 713/14) whose "fire is more like that of the dead or of the unborn" (*D.,* no. 1008). *Death and Fire,* which shows a glowing skeletal head against a fiery-red background, is also reminiscent of a poem he wrote in his diaries in 1914:

> I stand in full armour,
> I am not here,
> I stand in the depths,
> I stand far. . .
> I stand very far. . .
> I glow with the dead
> (*D.,* no. 931; see translation by Hollo, 1962, p. 25).

One would expect a discussion of dozens of Klee's self-images to give a more or less coherent picture of his inner self, particularly since this was the artist's stated intention. At the age of 21 he

Fig. 13. *Death and Fire.* 1940 (G12). Oil on jute, 18⅛ × 17¼". Courtesy Paul Klee-Stiftung, Kunstmuseum Bern, © 1984 by COS-MOPRESS, Geneva and ADAGP, Paris.

wrote the following in his diaries: "Thoughts about the art of portraiture. Some will not recognize the truthfulness of my mirror. Let them remember that I am not here to reflect the surface (this can be done by the photographic plate), but must penetrate inside. My mirror probes down to the heart. . . . My human faces are truer than the real ones" (*D.,* no. 136). Certainly Klee did not reflect the surface nor care about external realism. Furthermore, only a very few of the titles he gave to his self-images contain the word *self.* But did he succeed in conveying inner truth? In spite of sporadic glimpses into himself (such as those pictures which reveal his depression, his attitude toward marriage and his reflections on himself as the creative artist), our analysis of the body of his self-portraits discloses a personality that is basically inaccessible. An invisible wall or shell seems to have existed between himself and others. Klee showed us the "peculiar shell" but not the "kernel." Perhaps the inner self was inaccessible to him as well, and the self-portraits in fact conceal more than they reveal.

Acknowledgment

I wish to thank Dr. Jürgen Glaesemer, Curator of the Paul Klee-Stiftung, Kunstmuseum Bern, and his staff for allowing me to do research in the archives and for their helpful assistance.

Notes

1 The title of the work given here and elsewhere is followed by the year and oeuvre catalogue number. We cannot be certain that this work was in fact Klee's first self-portrait; rather, it may have been the first he deemed worthy of preserving and listing in his oeuvre catalogue. That he was not satisfied with many of his student year creations and probably destroyed numerous early works is borne out by his including only three from the years 1892–1901, though over 200 works are extant. He said he was not cataloging "school drawings, studies of nudes, etc., because they lack creative self-sufficiency" (see *D.,* no. 895).

2 See *D.,* no. 469: "The feeling of responsibility toward my fiancée and parents and unsuccessful attempts to paint often brew a kind of suicidal mood" (my translation). See also *D.,* no. 505, my translation: "Zola's *L'Oeuvre*—what a gloomy book! It has a bearing on ourselves! How horrible to experience this book while oneself is at the verge of ghastly possibilities." Klee was referring to the painter Claude's suicide, occurring in the last pages of the novel.

3 Comini (1977) identified the dagger as a "sword," and suggested its source could be in the Bernese artist Niklaus Manuel Deutsch (1484–1530), who added a short dagger to his monogram, thus inspiring Klee to do so. This idea does not seem very convincing.

4 Jürgen Glaesemer pointed out the resemblance of the mask to Klee's father (1976b). He also noted that "even Klee's tragic end can be said to

have fallen under the sign of the mask, a mysterious symbol of the man's personality; for the fatal illness against which Klee struggled for years was a rare skin disease, scleroderma, which causes the skin to harden completely."

5 The cancelled watercolor, *Sketch for a Self-Portrait* (1908/53), appears on the back of another work, *Asters on the Window.* A photo of it is in the Paul Klee-Stiftung, Kunstmuseum Bern. Perhaps Klee was dissatisfied with its weakness in the lower part of the face. One lost work is *Self-Portrait* (1908/26), an ink drawing behind glass, which was documented by Klee, though no photo of it exists nor is there other information on it in the Stiftung. The second lost work, entitled *The Artist (Poet-Painter)* (1908/72), a dark watercolor, was sold to the well-known avant-garde Chicago collector, Arthur Jerome Eddy in 1914, who may have been the first American to acquire Klee's work. It is not surprising to see Klee referring to himself as a poet, for this was a major creative outlet from 1898 to 1901. Much of his poetry is in the *Diaries,* but it also has been separately published. See, for example, F. Klee, 1960.

6 Klee's negativism toward pregnant women is apparent as early as 1900, when his mistress informed him of her pregnancy—one would think distressing news—and his reaction was to go on and enjoy the day; see *D.,* no. 98. His dissociation from the whole episode is clear later: "Now I had achieved quite a good deal. I was a poet, I was a playboy, I was a satirist, an artist, a violinist. One thing only I was no longer: a father. My mistress's child had proved unfit for life" (see *D.,* no. 124). Two years later when Klee vented his disgust with Bern and its poor people, who depressed him on his Sunday afternoon walks, among his criticisms were: "The overloaded baby carriage, what a miserable sight! The pregnant mother, pale, cross and tough!" (see *D.,* no. 493, my translation). It should be understood that Klee's diaries are not direct, spontaneous records of his feelings. Rather, he revised them and thought of them as autobiography, keeping a reading public in mind. Therefore, the insensitive response to his mistress's pregnancy that Klee recorded was how he wished the public to view him. But his real response was evidenced in an unpublished letter to his close friend Hans Bloesch, in which he expressed his heartache over the pregnancy. The male infant lived for about three weeks. This information was presented by Dr. Christian Geelhaar in a lecture, *The autobiographical rewriting of Klee's diaries,* at the symposium "Paul Klee and the political radicalization of expressionism," Nov. 1–2, 1984, at Northwestern University, Evanston, Ill.

7 This self-portrait was never made as a woodcut, nor was the woodcut for which another 1908 drawing, *View from the Window . . .* was planned, ever realized. Four different woodcuts, however, were made in 1912 (though Klee's oeuvre catalogue lists just three), these being his only known works in that medium.

8 Klee recorded Felix's temperature three times daily on a fever chart during his long illness, also noting his condition, treatment, and medication given. In addition, for the first two years of his son's life, Klee kept careful records of his weight, behavior, speech, activities, etc., much the way a mother would keep a "baby book," except in greater detail. This remarkable document, known as the "Felix Calendar," is published in an abridged version in *D.,* pp. 420–424.

9 One wonders what inner needs of Klee's were served by his initiating an oeuvre catalogue, since at this early date he had neither produced nor sold enough works to keep such a careful accounting. Is it possible that he felt a need to justify to himself and ultimately to his critical father, who sometimes belittled even his mature productions, his activity as an

artist by keeping this record of his achievements? Hans Klee said of the adult Paul: "I am not saying that he has no talent, but he doesn't take enough care over what he does" (see San Lazzaro, 1967, p. 192).

10 Klee did ten lithographic illustrations for the book *Potsdamer Platz oder die Nächte des neuen Messias: ekstatische Visionen* (Munich, Georg Müller, 1920).

11 The drawing is almost identical to the later lithograph except for the softer and more blurred effects of the pencil in showing the hairline and facial hair.

12 Regarding *Mask* (1919/77), Elisabeth Kornfeld, Secretary of the Paul Klee-Stiftung, wrote: "It is rather difficult to judge if the Klee drawing 1919/77 is a self-portrait. The title "Maske" belongs to a couple of artist-portraits he made in a series of 1919/73, 74, 75, 77" (personal communication, January 18, 1984).

13 Carola Giedion-Welcker (1952, p. 139) proposed that Klee appeared incognito in *Witch's Kitchen*, a 1921 watercolor suggesting magic or alchemy.

14 For the content of Klee's classes, as recalled by a former Bauhaus student, see Vishny, 1975, p. 18. The crystalline style of Lyonel Feininger, Klee's Bauhaus colleague and close friend, probably also inspired some of Klee's works in the early 1920s.

15 Klee also had contact with some of the Dadaists—Hans Arp, Hans Richter, and Tristan Tzara—whom he met in Zurich in June 1919.

16 Klee's pedagogical writings were incompletely published in two volumes by the late Jürg Spiller (1961, 1973). Klee had intended to publish a treatise from his notes, but unfortunately did not complete the task of ordering the sheets. Though Spiller's books are valuable, they are, nevertheless, confusing. It is hoped the pedagogical notes will be published in their totality in correct form. For a review of a partial exhibition of these writings, see Franciscono, 1977, pp. 370–371.

17 Emmy was deeply in love with Jawlensky, and even prior to the formation of The Blue Four, devoted herself to promoting his work.

18 In the summer of 1976, I questioned Felix Klee (in Bern) about his interpretation of the imagery in the upper part of *Pandora's Box*, and he replied: *"Peut être sa propre maison"* ("perhaps his own [Klee's] house"). For a similar view, see Quintavalle, 1972, p. 153.

19 Using the domestic scene he eliminated from his second version of *Pandora. . . ,* Klee created another work, *Bad Musical Band* (1920/159). By giving each of the figures musical instruments, he transformed the meaning of *Pandora's Box*.

20 Marianne L. Teuber (1979, pp. 261–296) also identified *Monsieur Perlenschwein* as a self-portrait and pointed out that some of its formal aspects were influenced by the physicist Ernst Mach's *Analysis of Sensations*, published in 1886.

21 The tradition of artists identifying themselves or family members with clowns hardly needs to be demonstrated. Klee portrayed himself as a harlequin in the above noted *Monsieur Perlenschwein*, and his son as Pierrot (*Head of a Young Pierrot* [1912/99]). Picasso was later to do likewise in portraits of his son Paul (e.g., *Pierrot*, 1925).

22 Strictly speaking, "elasticity" is not the correct term to describe the esophagus; what is meant is muscle tone.

23 See C. M. Kaufmann, 1966, pp. 71–74. Kaufmann's relating this work to the Nazis and the outbreak of World War II was deduced from Klee's entry in his oeuvre catalogue; in addition to the title, Klee added the phrase "Head listening to propaganda." Glaesemer concurred with the political interpretation (Glaesemer, 1979, p. 44, n. 87).

References

Comini, A. (1977). All roads lead (reluctantly) to Bern: style and source in Paul Klee's early "sour" prints. *Arts Magazine, 52*(1), 105–111.

Franciscono, M. (1974). Paul Klee's Italian journey and the classical tradition. *Pantheon, 32*(1), 54–64.

———. (1977). Bern Kunstmuseum exhibition: Paul Klees "Pädagogischer Nachlass," zur Diskussion gestellt June 6 to August 28, 1977. *Pantheon, 35*(4), 370–371.

The Galka Scheyer Blue Four Archive, letters. Norton Simon Museum of Art, Pasadena. Quoted by permission of the KLEE Estate. (On microfilm, Archives of American Art.)

Geelhaar, C. (1973). *Paul Klee and the Bauhaus.* New York: New York Graphic Society.

Giedion-Welcker, C. (1952). *Paul Klee* (A. Gode, Trans.). New York: The Viking Press.

Glaesemer, J. (Ed.). (1973). *Paul Klee, Handzeichnungen I, Kindheit bis 1920.* Bern: Kunstmuseum Bern.

———. (1976a). *Paul Klee, die farbigen Werke im Kunstmuseum Bern.* Bern: Verlag Kornfeld u. Cie.

———. (1976b, November). *The art of Paul Klee: Between nature and abstraction.* Lecture delivered to the Print and Drawing Club, Art Institute of Chicago.

———. (1979). *Paul Klee, Handzeichnungen III, 1937–1940.* Bern: Kunstmuseum Bern.

Gohr, S. (1979) "Symbolische Grundlagen der Kunst Paul Klees," in *Paul Klee, das Werk der Jahre 1919–33.* Cologne: Museen der Stadt Köln.

The graphic legacy of Paul Klee. (1983). Annandale-on-Hudson, NY: Bard College.

Grohmann, W. (1954). *Paul Klee.* New York: Harry N. Abrams.

———. (1967). *Paul Klee* (N. Guterman, Trans.). New York: Harry N. Abrams.

Haxthausen, C. W. (1981). *Paul Klee: The formative years.* New York: Garland Publishing.

Hess, H. (1961). *Lyonel Feininger.* New York: Harry N. Abrams.

Hollo, A. (Ed. and Trans.). (1962). *Some poems by Paul Klee.* Lowestoft Suffolk: Scorpion Press.

Kaufmann, C. M. (1966). An allegory of propaganda by Paul Klee. *Victoria and Albert Museum Bulletin, 2*(2), 71–74.

Klee, F. (Ed.). (1957). *Tagebücher von Paul Klee 1898–1918.* Cologne: DuMont Schauberg. [*The diaries of Paul Klee, 1898–1918,* R. Y. Zachary & M. Knight, Trans., Berkeley & Los Angeles: University of California Press.]

———. (1960). *Gedichte.* Zurich: Die Arche.

———. (1962). *Paul Klee* (R. & C. Winston, Trans.). New York: George Braziller.

———. (1979). *Paul Klee, Briefe an die Familie: 1893–1940.* 2 Vols. Cologne: DuMont Buchverlag.

Kornfeld, E. W. (1963). *Verzeichnis des graphischen Werkes von Paul Klee.* Bern: Verlag Kornfeld und Klipstein.

The Morton G. Neumann family collection. (1980). 2 Vols. Washington, DC: National Gallery of Art.

168   Naylor, G. (1968). *The Bauhaus.* London: Studio Vista.

Neumann, E. (Ed.). (1970). *Bauhaus and Bauhaus people* (E. Richter & A. Lorman, Trans.). New York: Van Nostrand Reinhold.

Petitpierre, P. (1957). *Aus der Malklasse von Paul Klee.* Bern: Benteli Verlag.

Quintavalle, A. C. (Ed.). (1972). *Klee: fino al Bauhaus.* Parma: Parma Universita Instituto di Storia dell' Arte, Vol. 16.

San Lazzaro, G. di. (1967). *Klee: A study of his life and work* (S. Hood, Trans.). New York: Frederick A. Praeger.

Schlemmer, T. (Ed.). (1972). *The letters and diaries of Oskar Schlemmer* (K. Winston, Trans.). Middletown, CT: Wesleyan University Press.

Spiller, J. (Ed.). (1961). *Paul Klee notebooks, volume I, the thinking eye* (R. Manheim, Trans.). London: Lund Humphries.

_____. (1973). *Paul Klee notebooks, volume II, the nature of nature* (H. Norden, Trans.). London: Lund Humphries.

Teuber, M. L. (1979). Zwei frühe Quellen zu Paul Klees Theorie der Form. In *Paul Klee das Frühwerk, 1883–1922.* Munich: Städtische Galerie im Lenbachhaus.

Vishny, M. (1975). *Mordecai Ardon.* New York: Harry N. Abrams.

_____. (1978). Paul Klee and war: a stance of aloofness. *Gazette des Beaux-Arts,* ser. 6, 92, 233–243.

Francis V.
O'Connor,
Ph.D.

The Psychodynamics of the Frontal Self-Portrait

I. The Configuration and Its Prefigurement

Mediocre spirits demand of science a kind of certainty which it cannot give, a sort of religious satisfaction. Only the real, rare, true scientific minds, can endure doubt, which is attached to all our knowledge. I always envy the physicists and mathematicians who can stand on firm ground. I hover, so to speak, in the air. Mental events seem to be immeasurable and probably always will be so. (Freud to Marie Bonaparte; quoted in Ernest Jones, *The Life and Work of Sigmund Freud,* II, p. 419.)

It is as impossible to know directly the contents of the unconscious—one's own or another's—as it is to see one's face without a mirror. Artists have gazed into the catalyst of a mirror to depict their outer, and image their inner, selves ever since, toward the end of the Middle Ages, they came to sense their genius as separate from that of their community. Because an artist's medium of self-awareness is nonverbal configuration, laypersons "reading" self-portraits psychologically have tended to "see" what custom supposed about the "ages of man," and to be otherwise blind to what the image declared about its creator. While the style and iconography of a self-portrait may describe the outer artist's historical persona and era, it is the underlying configuration of the portrait that reveals inner states. As this essay will show, a portrait's configuration reveals the unconscious self, and we must learn to discriminate this deeper unconscious mirroring from what the glass superficially reflected.

While the literature about self-portraits has noticed in passing the artist's options concerning pose: profile, three-quarter view, or

frontal; head-and-shoulders, half-, or full-length; situated in a natural setting or isolated by an artificial light or space—it virtually has ignored the psychodynamic implications of the artist's choice among these formal possibilities. Occasionally, however, one configuration is pointed to as especially "dramatic," "powerful," "penetrating," or "forthright." And this is the frontal self-portrait in which the brow and shoulders of the artist are placed parallel to the picture plane with the eyes often gazing directly into those of the viewer. Yet, as often as this striking head-and-shoulders configuration is remarked, it is as swiftly passed over when it comes to interpretation. The reason for this lies partly in the fact that traditional art historians are committed to a humanistically stoic stance of object-oriented "verification" which precludes wide-ranging biographical speculation, and partly to their lack of any working theory of developmental psychology with which to inform their analysis of an artist's "stylistic" development from adolescence to extreme old age. Unlike their colleagues in literature and history, most art historians seem to have avoided the assimilation of the classical schools of psychology and psychiatry (except for theories of visual perception), with the consequence that most art historical writing demonstrates a psychological illiteracy that would be unacceptable in any other humanistic discipline.[1]

There is no such thing as an "exact" science—especially in the humanities. And just as Freud would no longer have cause to envy the "firm ground" of modern theoretical physics or mathematics, art historians cannot reasonably claim their enterprise to be merely a garnering of verified certitudes. We must risk the same doubts as the artist (and the scientist) when confronted with the creative process and turn to those methods best suited to reveal the genesis and meaning of its manifestations. And, above all, we scholars must not deny the creative process in ourselves. For science, like art, is as much personal intuition, hypothesis, and speculation, as it is measurement of nature's increasingly elusuve phenomena. For the similarly elusive phenomena of visual creativity, we need a more subtle art of knowing as well as a science of facts.

True, the first duty of scholarship is to establish rigorously *what* can be known; its second and equally important obligation, however, is to invent methods of interpretation which encompass *all* that is known. Too often the latter obligation is edited down to fit an all too narrow construal of the former duty. And what always seems lost in this reductive process is the adventurousness of the engendering intuition—with its possibly autobiographical etiology. And that energy denied in the name of scholarly "dispassion," the work is dimmed accordingly.

Because it is the argument of this essay that the frontal self-portrait is specifically autobiographical, marking points of transition and crisis in the life course of its creator which engender especially powerful compensatory images of centricity, I shall begin with a personal note about the circumstances which first

Fig. 1. (*Opposite*). Albrecht Dürer. Self-Portrait. c. 1506. Panel, 26¼ × 19¼ in. (66.7 × 48.9 cms.). Alte Pinakothek, Munich.

prompted these speculations.

It has been my good fortune as an art historian to have been born with some talent for visual expression and an Irishman's sense of language. The former has resulted in a lifelong private practice of painting and drawing; the latter in formal training in the writing of poetry. Before I ever studied the history of art I understood, through my own experience, the dynamics of both images and words in the creative process. I have therefore avoided that personal ignorance of making art so often encountered in my profession. Consequently, I have always selected art historical subjects informed and motivated by mysteries revealed in my own experience of creativity—and the subject of the frontal self-portrait is no exception to this proclivity.

One day, when I had just started graduate work in the history of art at The Johns Hopkins University (after taking an M.A. in poetry in its Writing Seminars), I quite spontaneously painted a frontal self-portrait. It took all of an afternoon to trace my face from a mirror, square up the developed drawing on the canvas, and lay in the colors. That evening I wrote the following in my diary:

> Off—raining all day. Did some studying in early morning. . . . Dropped everything to paint a self-portrait. Couldn't resist urge to create. Painted myself full-face. . . . Everything seemed to come out of the unconscious. Much has to be touched up but basic idea is down. . . . Felt greatly elated—full of power—when I walked over to supper. A strange sensation—as if I could do anything. . . . There seems to be looming a threshold to be crossed. . . (Wednesday, February 22, 1961).

It was just eight days after my 24th birthday and I had just made a whole series of decisions as a graduate student which determined the course of my life and professional career. One of them, two days previous, was to select Jackson Pollock, the future topic of my doctoral dissertation and two subsequent books, as the subject of a seminar report.

It would take a while, of course, before I could make the connections between the portrait and the overdetermined life events which surrounded it. For I could not then understand the implications of what I had also written that day about the looming threshold: "I am passing through a narrow street toward an open plaza. . . the act of gestation and birth has its analogies in life." Now, of course, I can see clearly that this portrait was a factor in my personal and professional initiation. It somehow summed up symbolically what was going on unconsciously. It was confirming and centering; after it was painted I knew what I had to do.

Later, after graduate work and psychoanalysis, the latent memory of this self-portrait was often with me when visiting museums and churches. I noted the many anonymous frontal faces hung in back corners (and often labeled with curatorial uncertainty "portrait of unknown man" or "possible self-portrait") and the looming pantocrators and saints posed with hieratic frontality to overawe the faithful. I was, nevertheless, more interested in unraveling Pollock's aesthetic and iconic intricacies, and trying to reconcile his determined solipsism with the social consciousness of the decade out of which he emerged. But deep down, I was intrigued by the many frontal self-portraits I began to collect in a special file—all linked to the memory of making my own.

It was not until about 10 years later, having finished and published the first stages of my Pollock research, as well as three books on his generation of WPA-era artists, that I found the opportunity to investigate systematically the etiology of the frontal self-portrait. As a senior research associate at the Smithsonian's National Collection of Fine Arts, I undertook to survey the membership of the National Society of Mural Painters and the National Academy of Design, along with a small number of other artists of my acquaintance from the same generation, concerning the circumstances surrounding the painting of frontal self-por-traits. I chose these older and rather conservative artists because I knew they would all be of an age and skill to have painted themselves, and would be possessed of sufficient experience to see such work in the perspective of evolved lives.

I sent detailed questionnaires to about 350 artists. Their pur-pose was purely descriptive. My only "scientific" ambition was to weigh tendencies and the distribution and interrelationship of events by inducing a review of motivations. Fortunately, the rate of response was such as to give the resulting numbers some claim to statistical significance, for I received back nearly 150, for a respectable 43% return.

Of these, 91 artists, or 60%, admitted creating one or more frontal self-portraits. Nearly one-half created such works between the ages of 21 and 30, with the next heaviest distribution falling between the ages of 41 and 50—life periods characterized by accomodation to adulthood and what is called the "mid-life crisis." (As we shall see, these periods correspond to the fourth and seventh cycles of the life-course model to be discussed in the next section of this essay.)

Of the artists who created frontal self-portraits, 57% related such works to outstanding changes or events in their lives. These occurrences were distributed between (1) interpersonal rela-tionships such as sexual affiliations, childbirth, or the death of loved ones; (2) extrapersonal relationships such as changes in geographical location, employment, professional status, or the impact of some jarring historical event; (3) noticeable changes in artistic style or technique (which could, of course, be the result of inter- or extrapersonal events, but which artists tend to see as events in themselves); and (4) personal traumata such as surgery, being drafted into the army, or even in one case the post-partem depression induced by completing the Ph.D.!

In reply to questions concerning the technical characteristics of their frontal self-portraits, the responding artists indicated that over 75% of the works were relatively small or under 36 inches at their greatest dimension. They nearly always depicted just the head and shoulders, with a sizable number also showing the hands. In general, the figure was depicted in an interior setting or with a dark background. Only a small percentage of the frontal portraits described were full-length or contained still-life elements, animals, or other persons. There was also a very large consensus that it is not more difficult technically to make a frontal view of oneself than to make an oblique or profile view, and thus "imagining" or "fantasizing" oneself is not a significant factor in making such portraits.[2]

These results confirmed that my own experience painting such a portrait was not unique, and that making a head-on self-image was motivated differently than making a nonfrontal one. The question remained, however, as to just why this should be so.

The common-sense explanation would seem to be that this is just the way artists face up to themselves at a turning point in the life course. It is a means of reestablishing or confirming identity. Many of the artists who answered my questionnaire admitted as much, and some of their remarks are worth citing here. (I shall, out of deference for the privacy of my living respondents, withhold their names even when they chose to sign the questionnaires.)

A female member of the Academy, who first thought my questions "awfully silly," nevertheless discovered she had made a head-on portrait of herself as a young girl and, over her parents' objections, submitted it to the Academy's annual show. It was rejected, but in retrospect, she now sees it—a view of herself in pajamas and curlers—as "an example of juvenile rebellion" and a "self-evident validation" of the idea that such portraits relate to points of self-realization.

A male Academician, active in the New York art world since the 1930s, noted that "most people have a 'crisis' age," and went on to comment:

> Mine was at the age of 30. Despite several one-man shows, many group showings and good reviews I achieved no unusual acclaim as an artist. So I looked into myself, did about six introspective self-portraits, and came to the consoling conclusion some artists never attain: namely, that the artist paints solely for himself. I felt very contented and peaceful with my work thereafter. . . . Maybe at 30 I did a self-analysis through the portraits. It seemed to work well for me.

Another male artist with a similar background recalled that in 1930 while at Yaddo he made a frontal portrait of himself.

> My studio was in the middle of Lake George. . . . The view was beautiful. . . . All in all, I don't think I ever had anything as nice before or since. One day. . . I looked into the mirror. . . . I liked the pose and the pattern of lights and darks. And so I made a drawing and when I returned to New York I made a lithograph of it. I never connected the drawing with any important event in my life, certainly noth-

ing "critical." However after receiving your letter I recall having absented myself from the island for a few days to visit a camp near by where I met a young lady whom I had known for some years. We were married in 1931 and we are still married. This is a simple statement of fact; I draw no conclusions.

Obviously, conclusions are unnecessary. Life parallels and informs art however artists perceive their work as they make it. Some are more immediately sensitive than others to the psychodynamics of creativity; others, like the previous witness (and the author) saw the connections only in retrospect.

Connections can also be made in the literature of art, where such portraits are often found in contiguity with some important event in the life of their creators. The data just reported confirm what is often mentioned in passing.[3] But explanations are most often avoided, or else offered in terms of cultural conventions. Thus, one of the first and greatest frontal self-portraits, Albrecht Dürer's (Fig. 1), was commented on by Erwin Panofsky (1955a) as follows:

> The Munich Self-Portrait marks that crucial point in Dürer's career when the craving for "insight" began to be so all-absorbing that he turned from an intuitive to an intellectual approach to art, and tried to penetrate into the rational principles of nature. At this stage of his development his concept of the "Christ-like" artist seemed to be best pre-figured in the impersonal clarity and calm of a hieratic image such as the *Salvator Mundi* (p. 43).

This explains the look of the painting in terms of Dürer's cultural situation. I shall return to a fuller discussion of it later. But right now I must point out that the reasons Panofsky gave do not explain why so many subsequent artists (especially from the 18th century on) have selected exactly the same calm, hieratic, self-configuration at similar points of personal transition. This is the crucial question that remains to be answered in terms of the psychodynamic development of the artist.

II. A Model of the Life Course

Spinning Song

There are seven that pull the thread.
One lives under the waves,
And one where the winds are wove,
And one in the old gray house
Where the dew is made before dawn;
One lives in the house of the sun
And one in the house of the moon,
And one lives under the boughs
Of the golden apple tree;
And one spinner is lost.
Holiest, holiest seven,

Put all your power on the thread
I have spun in the house this night!

(W. B. Yeats. A previously unpublished poem included in Richard
J. Finneran, ed., *The poems: A new edition,* New York: Macmillan,
1984. With the permission of Anne Yeats.)

The question posed in the previous section can only be answered when the historian of art has a working model of the life-
course with which to analyze an artist's stylistic and iconographic
development. Only with such a tool can the pattern of recurrence
of frontal self-portraits within an artist's oeuvre be given a meaningful interpretive context.

As a historian of recent American art, I have had the opportunity to observe an entire generation of artists who were born in
the first decade of our century, who were employed at a crucial
point in their development on the New Deal art projects of the
1930s, and who today are entering into the last era of their life-
course. By means of surveys and countless personal interviews
around the country, I have seen how their art developed in terms
of their lives, how they survived in an environment not always
open to their talents or vision, and how they have coped with
encroaching age in their art and living (O'Connor 1969, 1972).
Parallel to these observations, I have also studied in depth the life
and creations of one of the most influential artists of this generation—the painter Jackson Pollock, who died old at 44, as well as a
member of an earlier generation—the painter Albert Berne, who
died young at 96 (O'Connor 1978, 1979). What follows, then, is a
summary of theoretical considerations concerning the human life-
course based on observation, intuition, and personal knowledge of
the image-making process. Although speculative, I think they have
a certain heuristic utility when applied to concrete situations.

While theories of developmental psychology abound from
Freud, Jung, and Erikson to the "Passages" crowd, few get very
much beyond the so-called "mid-life crisis," and none do much
justice to life after 65. Textbooks such as those by Lidz (1968)
and Sze (1975) slight the second half of life, with Lidz getting to
the "Middle Years" on page 457 of a 558-page book. Parker
(1960) projects "seven ages of women" but falters at the sixth,
"Age of Menopause," admits the seventh "has never been accu-
rately named," and suggests the rather lame "Age of Serenity" for
life over 50! The most recent attempt is Levinson (1978), which
manages to get matters to age 65 and offers a sequence of age-
defined phases for life from birth to retirement.

None of these approaches to the human life-course succeeds in
integrating old age into life, and the most recent studies such as
Sheehy (1976) and Levinson depend on data derived from specialized urban populations whose life experience is hardly typical
of artists in general or humankind over history. Life phases
consequently get keyed to popularly perceived traumata such as
"turning 30" or the "mid-life crisis" of the 40s. These exercises in

psychosociology are seriously tainted by journalistic acquiesence to the current concerns of middle-class mid-lifers, and are hardly useful in analyzing the development of strong artists past and present—developments which often exceed by half the chronological scope of these studies.

I would like to propose, therefore, that we might fashion a useful heuristic tool for psychobiographical research in the humanities by projecting a systematic vision of the life-course in terms of the traditional symbolism of the seven-year cycle articulated by Western and Eastern visions of the four eras of individual evolution.

I realize to theorize about cycles is not popular. Cycles threaten our linear view of progress and imply natural processes beyond our will to control. For this reason cyclic views of history, such as those of Vico, Spengler, or Toynbee, are rejected because of the whiff of determinism clinging about them. They seem a priori and dangerously unscientific. Yet we have only to contemplate our individual genetic inheritance and its indifference to our ideal of physiological perfection, or the ever-widening sphere (now planetary in scope) within which humankind has managed over history to repeat the same territorial and psychological blunders, to accept both determinism and cycles as inbred characteristics of human existence beyond the defenses of any relativizing science or wishful idealism.

If the selection of a seven-year cycle seems arbitrary, consider those self-evident changes in intellectual capacity, sexuality and socialization which occur around ages 7, 14, and 21, and the more various changes which mark the vicinity of ages 28, 35, and 42. These provide the basis for the notion of the "seven-year itch," the imperatives of which pervade both folklore and common law, and which can reasonably be projected through the rest of a human being's life-course—if only to provide a working structure, based on traditional thinking and observation, where no structure at all now exists.[4]

One often sees this seven-year period explained in terms of a theory of cellular renovation whereby the actual substance of the body is claimed to change completely every six to eight years. The physiology of this would seem chronologically inconsistent; nerve cells, for instance, are immutable, and other cells change at different rates. But while no psychosomatic mechanism for these seven-year cycles is here adduced, the empirical and traditional evidence for the congruence of the septenary with universal experience is strong. So this would seem yet another medical/mental mystery to be plumbed than a myth to be rejected outright. And, as we shall see, its heuristic utility remains an argument in favor of its further investigation.[5]

The life-course model here projected can further be articulated and humanistically enriched by dividing it into four eras. Campbell (1968) pointed out that in India, for instance, life is divided into two parts, each in turn divided into periods of preparation and actualization. Thus the first is studenthood, in which one learns the skills and duties of one's caste. The second is marriage and family, which fulfill one's caste's duties. The third, at mid-life, is meditation, for which one retires to the forest. The fourth is achievement of release from the will to live and a final stage of wandering as a mendicant until the body finally "drops off." The Western tradition, which Campbell finds summarized in Dante's *Convito,* also provides for four periods. The first is adolescence, whose virtues are obedience, sweetness, sensitivity and comeliness, and which extends to 25. The second, from 25 to 45, is a manhood of achievement whose virtues are temperance, courage, love, courtesy, and loyalty. The third age, from 45 to 70, is a time of usefulness to and bestowal upon the community out of a fullness of prudence, justice, generosity, and affability. Finally one attains decrepitude, to be met with piety and resignation in the bosom of the family and community.

The Eastern ideal is thus a phased development from a thoroughly acculturated persona to a thoroughly fulfilled spirituality. The Western ideal is, in contrast, a progressive development of the persona to a peak of social productivity followed by a meek retirement—with fulfillment postponed until after death. Obviously, the Western ideal has become a shabby, rote, corrupt, and potentially enslaving remnant of its communal origins. What is needed is a composite concept of the life-course offering a union of the necessary life ideals of social contribution and spiritual fulfillment.

I would propose, therefore, that the human life-course be seen as consisting of two great phases of 49 years each, and that the total be divided into four eras. I shall diagram all this for clarity, and briefly summarize what can be said about each era in terms of the evolution of the visual artist.

The Eras and Cycles of the Life-Course

Era I

Development of Primitive Individuality through Childhood and Adolescence: Ages birth/zero to 20, divided into three 7-year cycles, or 21 years.
Cycle 1: Ages 0–6
Cycle 2: Ages 7–13
Cycle 3: Ages 14–20

This era of the life-course is by far the best studied, and needs no introduction to students of Freud, Erikson, and Piaget. For the artist it could well be called the era of influence, when the specifics of nature and nurture induce fixation at the aural, visual, or verbal level; when skills of expression are acquired; and the stylistic and iconographic achievements of dominant cultural figures are assimilated. As Kellogg (1969) has shown for the visual artist, the image of the round coalesces out of infantile markings during the first cycle, and frontal self-portraits are frequent during the second cycle.[6] As I shall show later, the first artistically developed frontal self-portraits usually appear in the third cycle toward the turn of the second era, when the young artist begins to reject influences and to present a personal, self-centered vision to the world.

Era II

Development of the Persona through Early Middle Age:
Ages 21 to 48, divided into four 7-year cycles, or 28 years.
Cycle 4: Ages 21–27
Cycle 5: Ages 28–34
Cycle 6: Ages 35–41
Cycle 7: Ages 42–48

This is the era in which the artist (or the critics) discover whether youthful image-making can sustain its psychodynamic motivations through the self-renewals of maturity, or whether those early efforts at expression are to be abandoned, or else repeated with increasing sterility unto death. Education and influences give way to a recognizably individual, or else a derivative, style. The psychological pressure prompting artistic activity forces even more personally meaningful solutions to artistic "problems." If this fails, the person can become a "sociological" artist acting out the role as a teacher or celebrity in an orgy of self-emulation. The alternative is the abandonment of the artistic persona for a more fulfilling enterprise. Rimbaud, for instance, seems to have given up writing for vagabondage at 21; Duchamp painting for chess at 36. The ultimate alternative, of course, is death: Pollock's accident, for instance, at 44. The "mid-life crisis" for artists is perhaps more pressing than for those whose livelihood affords a renewable regimen and socially perceivable culmination. The reinvention of expression must come out of its own need, unbuttressed by situational imperatives. For the artist after 35 generally must find the psychological motivation to transcend the successes of past styles or, if necessary, to ignore (as did one of the artists quoted above) superficial failures to create and sustain a more centered sense of self.

Era III

Fulfillment of the Persona through Late Middle Age:
Ages 49 to 69, divided into three 7-year cycles, or 21 years.
Cycle 8: Ages 49–55
Cycle 9: Ages 56–62
Cycle 10: Ages 63–69

This is the era of self-patronage. It sees the reestablishment of persona goals on a more individualized basis, happily, but not necessarily, reinforced by public recognition. The artist is now free to do as he or she will. This can be a period of sustained creativity, the realization of a certain cultural authority, and the

180

obligations of mentorship. It can also witness, alas, the bitter alliance of failures to berate the young and proclaim received values against innovations. (How many Social Realist artists emerged from the 1930s to damn Abstract Expressionism for "eclipsing" them!) But the strong artist, secure in his persona and not having to retire at 65 (unless, of course, he or she teaches) can now proceed to lose the acculturated mask for the unfettered adventure of re-creating both self and art under the even more versatile disguise of old age.

Era IV

Fulfillment of Individuality in Old Age: 70 to 97, divided into a possible four 7-year cycles, or 28 years.
Cycle 11: Ages 70–76
Cycle 12: Ages 77–83
Cycle 13: Ages 84–90
Cycle 14: Ages 91–97+

If the first era of the artist's life course is best characterized by the influences assimilated, the second by recognition achieved, and the third by a capacity for self-patronage, the fourth is notable for its dedication to abstraction. From the Latin *abstrahere,* to "take away," abstraction is used here to describe both the physical and social—as well as the stylistic—reduction experienced by the aging artist.

It is commonplace to note that the aging are repetitive, slow, and vague about detail. For strong artists in the last era of their lives, these can be virtues, not defects. It is unlikely that an aging artist will engender an entirely new imagery; rather, what has served the past will be reexplored and simplified. In this there is, I think, something of an unconscious reenactment of the psycho-sexual and psycho-social moratoria on the level of accumulated life experience. The physical and social isolation of the elderly induces a process of free-association with the old images of the life-course that is naturally therapeutic in the face of death.

Kenneth Clark, in his essay "The Artist Grows Old," which concludes his *Moments of Vision* (1981), noted that along with this creative isolation, the art of the aging shows "a retreat from realism, an impatience with established technique and a craving for complete unity . . . as if the picture were an organism in which every member shared in the life of the whole" (p. 174). These phenomena are the result of the inevitable physiological slowing down of the elderly—that desire to economize movement to utilize available energy. There is a greater simplicity of design and facture; just what is needed and no more. But the other side of this simplicity is that visual wisdom the abstractive process of time has accumulated. On the level of both subject and style one finds a certain symbolic transformation in which the archetypal transcends topical significance, and the whole becomes all. For an artist who has been seeing people and things analytically for 80 years they become more and more generalized. The aging artist becomes an abstract artist by reason of longevity—and it is this essentialism that constitutes his or her greatest gift to the precise, the swift, and the certain.

This heuristic schema of the ideal life-course is, needless to say, just that: a conceptualization hopefully capable of organizing insight. Life itself is not as neat—which is why we tame its variables with such diagrams. But based as it is on a symbolic rather than a statistical module, and incorporating the potential for spiritual growth as well as productive achievement, it can serve to structure thinking about artists' development outside the rather bleak, productivity-oriented pattern implicit in Erikson's famous rubrics—or Jaques's theatrical iambics.[7] For these celebrate essentially personal ideals based on the Western model of the working man's life. There is little room for inner growth except perhaps in perception and manipulation of failure to induce socially accepted behavior. Most strong artists, of course, ignore socially (and artistically) acceptable behavior and produce according to their own vision-oriented cycles. Artists, more than lay persons, grow to have a sense of their periodicity—possibly because they can actually look back over their image-making, see the changes, and relate the changes to events. Most of us who do not systematically record our lives in images feel life as rather flat. We leave behind no monuments to experience. We may sense movement and connection—and we most certainly can see our past cycles vividly recycled by others. One of the great gifts artists can provide us is the depiction of how they have reinvented themselves in such a way that we, if we respond to their work as kindred spirits, can see where we also have been—and can be.

It would be useful at this point to make a distinction that both summarizes what has been said so far, and anticipates what will be developed in the next two sections of this essay.

First, my survey of living artists provides strong evidence that full-face self-portraits occur at points of what I shall call *situational transition* during the life-course.

Second, my model of the life-course provides a way, when there are a sufficient number of such portraits to study over a long period of time (as we shall see later with Rembrandt) to observe how they also, but not necessarily, tend to constellate around points of what I shall call *natural transition* in the life-course.

Not surprisingly, it will be found that usually, but not always, the points of situational transition and natural transition coincide. But I think it is safe to say that whenever a frontal self-portrait appears in an artist's chronology, that point will be most often found to mark a crucial event the historian/biographer must take as seriously as the artist.

The question remains, however—perhaps now more forcefully than earlier: why do artists select this particularly calm, hieratic self-configuration at points of transition? I shall now turn to answering this question, and then conclude with a number of "case studies" of the frontal self-portraits of some old and recent masters.

III. The Centricity of the Frontal Self-Portrait

Finally, one day, I produced, almost without knowing it, a face to which I responded more strongly than I had to any of the others. . . . It was somewhat stiff. . . but impressive and full of a secret life of its own. . . . It resembled a kind of image of God or a holy mask, half male, half female, ageless. . . . For a time this portrait haunted my thoughts and shared my life. . . . It seemed to know who I was, like a mother, as if its eyes had been fixed on me since the beginning of time. . . . I began to sense that this was neither Beatrice nor Demian but myself. . . . One of the aphorisms [of Novalis] occurred to me. . . and I wrote it under the picture: "Fate and temperament are two words for one and the same concept" (Hermann Hesse, *Demian,* 1919, chap. 4).

Let us begin by considering the visual impact of a small exhibition of frontal self-portraits. It would be, without doubt, rather tedious: the same composition seriatim around the room, staring straight out. A squint induced by a yawn would reduce each static face upon shoulders to its constituent gestalt. And that would be a round over a horizontal. Indeed, it is hard to think of any other artistic motif (except perhaps certain styles of landscape) that would present such an effect. Even a room full of head-and-shoulders portraits of artists' sitters from various periods would appear more dynamic. So it is useful to speculate a bit about the nature and import of this persistent consistency.

It is a main point of this essay that the informing symbolic complex beneath the stylistic and physiognomic variables of the frontal self-portrait derives from our generalized experience of the round over the horizontal, microcosmically in our primal vision of the reassuring, nurturing head over the cradle; macrocosmically in the universal perception of the sun or moon over the horizon and the confrontational symbolism of authority figures during early development. This iconic configuration thus takes its power from positive, nurturing, awe-inspiring life situations that are common to all human beings, and it is the placing of the self-image in the context of such a vital icon that explains its integrative role in the lives of those artists impelled to identify with it in a self-portrait.

Let us consider the three main elements of this proposal in some detail: first, the relationship of this iconic configuration to early childhood perceptions; second, its embodiment of "cosmic" images; and third, its integrative function.

The Primal Vision

As Bullowa (1979) pointed out, one of the basic findings resulting from experimental psychology's recent interest in infant-watching has been that infants watch us! Beginning with Fantz (1961) it has become increasingly clear that neonates can recognize and are interested in the frontal human face and are not interested in rounds displaying distorted faces, bright colors, or print patterns to anywhere approaching the same degree. It has also been shown by Meltzoff and Moore (1977) that neonates can perceive and imitate facial expressions as early as 12 days after birth. These primal encounters with another human face—most often, of course, with that of a parent—initiate a series of reinforcing signals which become the basis for interpersonal communication.

Kagan (1968, 1978), Trevarthen (1979), and Brazelton (1979) all provide substantial evidence for this. Brazelton summed up the research—and the human situation—as follows:

> The old model of thinking of the newborn as helpless and ready to be shaped by his environment prevented us from seeing his power as a communicant in the early mother—father—infant interaction. To see the neonate as chaotic or insensitive provided us with the capacity to see ourselves as acting "on" rather than "with" him (p. 79).

He further described the situation of the "primal vision" which imprints the icon deep into the psyche of the future artist:

> If [a neonate] is presented with a human face, he will act "hungry" as he follows the human face laterally and vertically. When the infant begins to register his preference for human stimuli, it is impossible for an adult interactant not to become "hooked" to him. . . as he. . . maintains an intense period of eye-to-eye and face-to-face communication (p. 82).

It is just this primordial linkage to the great round of the nurturing, reacting, loving human face perceived frontally—eye-to-eye—at the earliest and most impressionable age, which provides the prefigurement for the later recurrence of this overwhelmingly positive gestalt at those moments of human transition when the artist must endow himself with an image of salvific stability.[8]

The Cosmic Vision

I would further suggest that this primal vision of frontality is reinforced by the developing child's perceptions of awe-inspiring natural phenomena, such as the sun and moon in the heavens, and positive encounters with the colorful and ever-various faces of flowers, pets, and dolls, not to mention soap bubbles, balloons, and Pacman. But these are superficial stimuli compared to those first pleasurable visual communications with the frontal visage of the nurturing parent.

More potent stimuli in the growing child's cosmos are the various ways the frontal face is utilized as a sign of authority by the propagandists of the world. I have already alluded to the use of frontality in religious iconography: the faces of God, Zeus, Christ, Buddha, and scores of lesser deities and saints are almost always shown frontally. The great Jungian scholar Erich Neumann stated that "the frontal position of a figure almost always indicates the numinous. . . ." (1963, p. 117) and it is not hard to understand why God the Father and Mother Church should instinctively select an image so sure to affect the deepest recollections of the faithful.[9]

Needless to say, the frontal image and its potent gestalt have not gone unnoticed by television anchormen (who must induce patriarchal associations of trust), political candidates (who would look "presidential" even if running for dogcatcher), and the designers of recruiting posters (who often add foreshortened forefingers). They all know the "hard sell" potential of the motif. And for those who would enslave the world, it also has its uses, as Orwell intimated on the first page of *1984:*

> The hallway smelt of boiled cabbage and old rag mats. At one end of it a colored poster, too large for indoor display, had been tacked to the wall. It depicted simply an enormous face, more than a meter wide: the face of a man about forty-five, with a heavy black moustache and ruggedly handsome features. Winston made for the stairs. . . . On each landing, opposite the lift shaft, the poster with the enormous face gazed from the wall. It was one of those pictures which are so contrived that the eyes follow you about when you move. BIG BROTHER IS WATCHING YOU, the caption beneath it ran.

Whatever the exploitability of its underlying gestalt (and who would not be greedy to exploit something naturally associated with both cradle and cosmos), the frontal self-portrait remains, for the artist, a private centering of the self's authority in the face of those twin determinants: nurture and nature, and the circumstances that flow from both. So I would conclude this section with some further comments on this potent image and the idea of centricity.

The Centric Vision

Jung, as is well known, has pointed out the centering, healing, and integrative properties of the spontaneously produced mandala in the rituals of primitive societies, the diagrams of the alchemists, and the drawings of his patients. He discussed the therapeutic nature of its spontaneous occurrence in the image-making of modern individuals as follows:

> As a rule a mandala occurs in conditions of psychic dissociation or disorientation, for instance. . . in adults who, as the result of a neurosis and its treatment, are confronted with the problem of opposites in human nature and are consequently disoriented. . . . In such cases it is easy to see how the severe pattern imposed by a circular image of this kind compensates the disorder and confusion of the psychic state—namely,

through the construction of a central point to which everything is related, or by a concentric arrangement of the
disordered multiplicity and of contradictory and irreconcila-
ble elements. This is evidently an *attempt at self-healing* on
the part of Nature, which does not spring from conscious
reflection but from an instinctive impulse (1969, pp. 387–
388).

I would suggest, therefore, that the frontal self-portrait is a
variation on the mandala contextualized in the features of its
creator and that it serves a similar unconscious therapeutic purpose at moments when the artist must find a center at a time of
transition.

But it can well be argued that when the idea of the mandala is
applied to self-portraits, as here, then why can it not be applied to
all portraits, however the face is oriented, since the abstract gestalt
remains a round over a horizontal? To answer this, the specificity
of the image in the frontal self-portrait must be stressed, for that
image participates in the "power of the center" Rudolf Arnheim
analyzed so cogently in his most recent book (1982). In discussing
frontality, Arnheim stated that "Symmetry, in particular, creates
centricity, and therefore makes the center extend as far as the
symmetry reaches [as] a central face with its vertical axis and its
pair of eyes. . . ." He also noted that when anything is set at
"dead center"—"where spatial dynamics is at a minimum" (as on a
turning wheel)—the effect created is one of "timeless stability."
Further, he distinguished the face from the head, seeing it as a
relief surface on a sphere, whose "constellation of vectors" can
create a particularly dynamic configuration or—when viewed sym-
metrically and thus frontally—"an island of classical serenity, often
in contrast to a complex pattern of body and dress" (pp. 73, 126,
162–163).

In short, it is the artist's deliberate choice of the centered,
stable, classically serene module of his frontal visage dominating
his frontal body and his pictorial composition, that makes the
symmetrical, full-face self-portrait distinct from all other portraits
and endows its arresting visual aspect with mandalic power.

IV. Case Studies   It remains to demonstrate more fully the congruity of the frontal
self-portrait with points of transition in the lives of artists—and to
show the life-course model developed here to be the flexible
heuristic tool it is. In so doing we shall see the infinite variety
with which creative individuals utilize this centering iconography.
But before facing up to the masters, let me begin with two artists
from my survey who engendered the inherent icon in the frontal
self-portrait with more than usual explicitness.

A male artist who recalled painting eight or ten frontal self-
portraits over his 74 years, noted that such works no longer
appealed to him because "they are too intimate—self-revealing,
autobiographical; there is an element of narcissism." But he went

Fig. 2. Anonymous
Male Artist. Self-Por-
trait with Images.
c. 1972. Embroidery
(detail). Collection of
the artist.

Fig. 3. Anonymous
Male Photographer.
Self-Portrait in Mir-
ror. 1972. Pho-
tograph, 5¾ × 4⅜
in. (14.6 × 11.1
cms.). Collection of
the artist.

on to note that he had nevertheless just recently made one while hospitalized. This work (Fig. 2) was a large embroidery in which the artist's frontal self-portrait is surmounted in the overall design by the image of half an apple, thus combining the portrait with its gestalt.

A more literal example is to be found in the self-portrait of a male photographer who was not part of the original survey. When he heard that I was doing this research, he told me that he had just retired after a long and successful career as a film-maker and had taken up creative photography. One day, after making a portrait of his first grandchild, he noticed in his son's back yard a "confused but interesting arrangement of discarded material. Then I saw myself in the piece of broken mirror. The portrait was a spontaneous result" (Fig. 3). What is of interest here, of course is that all that can be seen of the photographer is the circle of his camera lens situated over his belt-buckle: the very configuration of our iconic motif. Even more to the point is a simple statement he composed in an attempt to articulate what this self-portrait meant to him. His wife pointed this out to me tacked beneath the photograph on his studio wall. It read: "From the confusion of reality, Man's search is for Primal Form."

It is the life function of strong artists to reveal to themselves and, by extension, to their culture and posterity, those "primal forms" that prefigure and, in retrospect, certify, human experience. The artist's role is thus to nurture, both in terms of his or her own cyclic rebirthings and the value provided by the tangible enactment of such renewals, those who seek stimulus in art for their own reinvention. This essay will conclude, therefore, by discussing the frontal self-portraits made by a selection of strong self creators since the Renaissance.[10]

Albrecht Dürer (b. 1471-78-85/-92-99-1506-13/-20-27; d. 1528)*

Dürer's last self-portrait (Fig. 1) was frontal, and Panofsky was quoted earlier about its appearance at an intellectual turning point in the artist's life when he sought to identify his sense of himself as a creator with the image of Christ as world savior—a not unreasonable assertion either iconographically, or, as we have seen, psychologically. The portrait is inscribed with the date

---

*As a reference tool to the life-course model here projected, I shall give a sequence of dates in terms of the artist's age at multiples of seven. Thus, at the fifth date after the birth date, i.e. 1506, Dürer was 35. Slashes indicate the succession of the four life eras which begin at birth and at ages 21, 49, and 70. When an artist died in the first year of a cycle, the date will be preceded by a hyphen; otherwise by a semicolon. When I note a frontal self-portrait is "at the turn of a cycle," I mean that it appears in *the vicinity* of the start of one of the cycles of seven years. As already discussed, that "turn" is often the period during which important events of natural transition take place. Its precise duration depends on an individual's personal life rhythm, though usually it can be said to comprise the years either before or after the birthday that marks the turn. By using this system it is hoped the life-course model will provide a means of seeing the essential structure of a life while giving its protagonist room in which to live it.

"1500," and this has been generally accepted. Panofsky, however, along with Pope-Hennessy (1966), pointed to the apocryphal nature of this inscription, and the latter attributed the work to 1506, when Dürer was in Venice for the second time. The later date appears plausible not only for historical but psychological reasons—which deserve discussion.

Of Dürer's three painted self-portraits, the first, of 1493 (Paris, Musée du Louvre), is a marriage portrait revealing a self-conscious, 22-year-old Germanic bumpkin holding an eryngium symbolizing "luck in love." This he did not have, and he left his new wife and went to Venice the year he married her: 1494. On his return, and for the next decade (i.e., 1495–1505), he established an international repute as one of the few northern painters and printmakers working in the spirit of the Italian Renaissance. His second self-portrait, of 1498 (Madrid, Museo del Prado), consequently flaunts a self-satisfied Venetian gentleman before a German society (and perhaps a shrewish wife) which had yet to so recognize a local craftsman. It is hard to believe, therefore, just on stylistic grounds, that his third—and frontal—self-portrait could have been painted just two years later. The change in self-image is just too radical. On the other hand, the date 1500 is not so far from the turn of the 29-year-old Dürer's fifth cycle as to suggest a sudden sense of transition—perhaps the turn of the 16th century itself, with all its promise and the leading role he could see for himself in it. Yet, when one considers Dürer's situation in 1506, that later date for the painting becomes far more plausible on all levels. Consider the chronology: in 1502 his father died; in 1503 he suffered a serious illness; in 1504 his mother moved into his house with his wife; in 1505 the plague broke out in Nuremburg (or so was his excuse) and he again fled south without his family. His reputation preceded him: he was lionized at Augsburg and given several major commissions in Venice. He stayed there until January 1507. Having mastered the techniques of his art and established his reputation with the Italian humanists over the last decade, he could now—at the age of 35, and precisely at the turn of his sixth cycle—find his psychological center in an environment totally open to his gifts, and face with self-confidence his grim personal and cultural life to the north. Panofsky described his life after his return in 1507:

> he bought a stately house, settled down to study languages and mathematics, made the first draft of a great treatise on the theory of art, the gradual elaboration of which was to occupy him up to his death, and in a touching attempt at real universality, he even tried to write verse. Thus he developed more and more into an "erudite" artist, capable of collaborating with scholars and scientists and fully participating in the intellectual movements of his period (1955a, p. 9).

And it is in terms of this experience of 1505–1507 that one must re-read Panofsky's earlier quoted comments on the "1500" self-portrait and agree with Pope-Hennessy that its objective relation to the traditional image of Christ is problematic. Pope-Hennessy noted that frontality was being experimented with by Venetian portraitists and Dürer would have been aware of them, as he would have been aware of Byzantine models. Indeed, a frontal caricature of one of the humanist Wilibald Perkheimer's paramours in a letter of September 8, 1506 (Conway, 1958, p. 55) so suggests. But whatever the influential motif that permitted the innovation, and just as the Byzantine/medieval iconographic tradition used frontality to overawe the faithful, Dürer—for the very first time in the history of art—used it to express an artist's inner awe at, and confidence in, the manifestation of his creative genius. For his second trip to Venice had centered, confirmed, and matured his personal sense of self-worth. What others thought no longer mattered. "How I shall freeze after this sun!" he had written on October 13, 1506 to Perkheimer (whom his wife detested); "Here I am a gentleman, at home only a parasite" (Conway 1958, p. 58).

Rembrandt van Rijn (b. 1606-13-20/- 27-34-41-48/ -55-62-d.1669)

Any discussion of frontal self-portraits must account for those produced by Rembrandt within the large corpus of his self-depictions. Of the 98 self-portraits accepted by Wright (1982, hereafter W plus number) 10 are centered, head-and-shoulders images and another five show frontal heads on full- or three-quarter-length frontal bodies. Of these, eight are oil paintings (W37,38,50,68,78,83,87,91), four etchings (W47,48,71,74), and three drawings (W53,75,85).[11]

Stylistically, Rembrandt's frontality is different from Dürer's absolute facial symmetry. The dramatic use of lights and darks in his famous chiaroscuro, his increasingly bravura brushwork, and his overall Baroque sense of pictorial dynamics give the illusion of a subtle torque to almost all his portraits. The chiaroscuro effects especially can make a frontal face seem to turn into its shadows (just as those cast by an oblique light on a straight picture frame can make it appear crooked). Consequently, almost all of the portraits to be considered here present a self-image that seems momentarily arrested in motion rather than rigidly fixed to a frontal plane. In identifying his frontal self-portraits, their overall centricity has, therefore, been considered as much a factor in their frontality as the absolute anatomical visibility of both sides of the face.

Rembrandt's favorite pose, found in 43 of his self-portraits, is turned and looking over his left shoulder.[12] It is obvious that he was most comfortable with the mirror to his left, and this configuration is evenly distributed through the 98 works from around 1629 to 1669. Of the remaining, nonfrontal works, 11 show him turned and looking over his right shoulder, seven reveal a turned head over a body turned in the opposite direction, four a turned head over a frontal body, and 18 a frontal face over a turned body. Thus, only 15 are frontal in the centered sense used here.[13] A correlation of these 15 centered self-portraits with events of Rembrandt's life-course reveals the following.

The two earliest (W37,38) date from 1631, the last year in Leyden before the artist moved to Amsterdam. These rather awkward, full-length self-depictions are the most striking, although certainly not the best, productions of Rembrandt's fourth cycle when, between the ages of 21 and 26 he created 45 self-portraits. These are roughly divided between paintings and graphics and all but six were done during the Leyden period of youthful experimentation.

Thereafter, of the remaining 13 frontal self-portraits, 11 fall within the fifth and eighth cycles which correspond to major high and low points in the artist's life. Thus, between 1634 and 1640—his fifth cycle which runs from his marriage to Saskia to the death of his mother—there are five frontal self-portraits, four of which cluster directly at the time of his marriage (W47,48,50,53). The fifth (W68), dated c.1639, corresponds to the year he bought his huge house in Amsterdam.

This unwise purchase marked the beginning of the first of several very difficult periods in Rembrandt's life. At the turn of his sixth cycle, his mother died, and the birth of his son Titus in 1641 was quickly overshadowed by the death of Saskia in 1642. During this sixth cycle, from ages 35 to 41 only two nonfrontal self-portraits were done. The first, an etching of 1642 (W70) shows a tight-lipped, harried figure looking distractedly away to the left; the second, of about 1646–48 (W72), a tense frontal face gazing intently over the left shoulder. These two works suggest this cycle was a period of psychological readjustment—perhaps depression—when to face the self, let alone admire it, was thwarted by life events.

In 1648, however, directly at the turn of his seventh cycle, Rembrandt did an etched frontal portrait of himself drawing at a window (W71). It is an introspective self-image, and one of the rare self-portraits that show him at his art. During this cycle, from 1648 to 1654, he did only one other frontal self-portrait, a minor image on an etched sheet of studies which dates from 1651 (W74).

His eighth cycle, from 1655 to 1661 (i.e., from ages 49 to 55), contains the remaining six of his frontal self-portraits. Two date from 1655 (W75,78) at the exact turn of the cycle. The year before his mistress, Hendrickje Stoffels, bore him a daughter. (She had entered his life about 1645 as a servant; he could not marry her lest he lose an inheritance from Saskia.) The next year, 1656, he went bankrupt and applied to the courts for relief. The next two frontal self-portraits clearly date to the years in which he was forced to auction his belongings: 1657 (W83) and 1658 (W87). The last two are both dated about 1660 (W85,91) and mark the end of his financial problems when Hendrickje and Titus arranged a partnership which preserved both his legacy from Saskia and current income, and provided a measure of security for his old age.

Of these last four frontal self-portraits, the two paintings, in the Frick Collection, New York, and at Kenwood House, London (W87,91), are certainly the best and most striking of his works of

Fig. 4. Rembrandt van Rijn. Self-Portrait. 1658. Oil on canvas, 52⅝ × 40⅞ in. (133.7 × 103.8 cms.). Copyright The Frick Collection, New York.

this kind and deserve special comment.

The Frick painting (Fig. 4) shows Rembrandt enthroned like an Oriental potentate and wearing an elaborate gold costume. His eyes look straight out, fixing the viewer (and originally himself) with a calm, authoritative gaze. The painting is dated 1658, the year the artist's house and furnishings, and his collection of graphic art, were sold in February and September respectively.

191

These sales realized only a fraction of their worth (Rosenberg, 1964, n. 15, p. 346). If any proof is needed as to the compensatory function of the frontal self-portrait, this powerful work provides it. As Wright pointed out "Only this once did Rembrandt permit such extravagance of color and brushwork" (1982, p. 32). Publicly humiliated and stripped of his most valued worldly possessions, the artist could now defiantly show himself to himself—in a way he could not after the death of Saskia—as still ruler of his studio and the powers of creation.

The undated frontal self-portrait at Kenwood House, sometimes given to the very last years of Rembrandt's life, is dated by Wright to "a little after 1660" (1982, p. 32), thus placing it at the turn of the artist's ninth cycle. This extraordinary work (Fig. 5), the very last of his full-face self-portraits, is unique in that it shows Rembrandt standing against a light background. And it is especially pertinent to this study, since that background is articulated with two large half-circles.

Wright suggested, in his usual dry way, that "These famous half-circles could well have been introduced for decorative reasons in order to enliven an unusually large expanse of plain background due to the painting being wider in proportion to its height than is usual with Rembrandt" (1982, p. 32). Others have been more erudite, suggesting that the circles are cabalistic signs of God's perfection, emblematic symbols of Theory and Practice between which the artist stands as creative spirit, and, more prosaically, the two hemispheres of a world map. (Bolten & Bolten-Rempt, 1977, p. 151 summarize these theories.) I would suggest that, whatever the formal or iconographic permissions for these extraordinary circles, the artist is here unconsciously acknowledging the icon that inheres in the frontal self-portrait itself. But in doing so, he is situating himself as its manifest embodiment breaking the round with the greater center of his visage.

Almost all of Rembrandt's self-portraits, frontal or otherwise, are placeless; the artist emerges out of a dark, ambiguous location, lit by an artificial light. Here Rembrandt situated himself in a real space—and even more emphatically—has consciously revised his mirrored reflection to show himself standing in that space as separate from himself and the viewer. The proof of this is found in the result of a recent inspection of this canvas by the Rembrandt Research Project (Levy, 1976). Pentimenti reveal that the palette and brushes the artist holds in his right hand (if the image were a reflection) were switched from the left hand. An artist would normally carry his palette on his left arm the better to paint with his right hand. In the mirror, his left would be to the left—but he chose to reverse this so as to appear actually standing behind the picture plane—his left to the viewer's right. He is thus separated from his reflection and isolated in the gulf between the two half rounds, which are forever denied a wholeness he himself now assumes. He has, in effect, created his own double.[14]

Whatever else this pattern of forms and events may mean, it lends to this last of Rembrandt's frontal self-portraits an air of unutterable sadness, irrevocability and dignity. It also demon-

Fig. 5. Rembrandt
van Rijn. Self-Por-
trait. c. 1660. Oil on
canvas, 41 × 37 in.
(114.3 × 94 cms.).
The Greater London
Council as Trustees
of the Iveagh Be-
quest, Kenwood.

strates the power of the strong artist in old age to engender the
archetypal from the particular. Perhaps the great Rembrandt
scholar Jakob Rosenberg's statement that "The self-portraits in
particular reveal that blend of the subjective with the universal
which characterizes Rembrandt's genius" (1948, p. 37) aptly sums
up this brief discussion of the import of frontality among them.

Having considered the first historical frontal self-portrait, that
of Dürer, and Rembrandt's extraordinary sequence, I want now to
leap, for brevity's sake, to recent times. But I cannot resist, if only

to make the point that writers as well as artists make centric portraits of themselves, pausing in the 19th century long enough to examine one the future Jesuit, Gerard Manley Hopkins, drew in a moment of youthful poetic epiphany.

Gerard Manley Hopkins (b.1844-51-58/-65-72-79-86; d.1889)

On August 14, 1864, the future poet and priest drew himself perched on a dock "reflected in a lake," as he inscribed the picture. The rather skillful work shows the artist's full face topped by a derby and framed by the soles of his shod feet (Fig. 6).

This frontal self-portrait is further framed by two significant life events. Hopkins had just celebrated his 20th birthday on July 28 and was precisely at the turn of his second era and fourth cycle. Also, on September 10 he wrote a long and now famous letter to his friend, A. W. M. Baillie, in which he stated that he had "begun to doubt Tennyson" (Gardner, 1953, p. 155). In this letter he conceptualized the poetic aesthetic he would develop later in life, and acknowledged (without, of course, knowing it) the role of the unconscious in the creative process. He posited three kinds of poetry. The first is that of "inspiration" engendered by "a mood of great, abnormal in fact, mental acuteness, either energetic or receptive, according as the thoughts which arise in it seem generated by a stress and action of the brain, or to strike into it unasked. . . . In a fine piece of inspiration every beauty takes you as it were by surprise" (Gardner, 1953, p. 156–57). He went on to call the second "Parnassian," which is the language of uninspired, yet true, poets. The third, "Castalian," is "merely the language of verse as distinct from that of prose."

Fig. 6. Gerard Manley Hopkins. Self-Portrait. 1864. Pencil on paper, 2¼ × 2¹³⁄₁₆ in. (5.7 × 7.2 cms.). From *The Journals and Papers of Gerard Manley Hopkins,* edited by Humphrey House and completed by Graham Storey. Published by Oxford University Press. © The Society of Jesus, 1959.

In making these discriminations Hopkins was clearly defining the territory he planned to inhabit as a poet—not the godly crags of Tennyson's popular versification, but the essentialist world of "inscape" where "lives the dearest freshness deep down things" which can only be explored and revealed by the truly inspired.

Hopkins would convert to Roman Catholicism two years later and abjure writing poetry from 1868 to 1874 while studying for the Jesuit priesthood. Most of his best poetry came in two bursts: in 1877, the year of his ordination at the turn of his sixth cycle; and in 1885, when he took up teaching at the University of Dublin at the turn of his seventh cycle. He died, unpublished and unknown as a poet, at age 45 in 1889. In the light of this history, we can see that the self-portrait of 25 years earlier—for which he chose the mirror of Narcissus—not only presaged Hopkins's initial unconscious insight into the necessary centricity of his poetry, but also his acceptance of the young god's fate.

Piet Mondrian (b. 1872-79-86/-93-1900-07-14/-21-28-35/-42; d.1944)

While best known for the "grid" paintings he began in earnest about 1920 at the turn of his third era, Mondrian spent the first seven cycles of his life creating representational works—including three frontal self-portraits (Seuphor, 1956, Classified Catalogue 1, 2,7).[15] These fall, not unsurprisingly, at three key points: the turn of his fifth cycle about 1900; in 1908, when he was deeply involved with Theosophy; and in 1918, a year of transition between his representational and geometric styles.

The most striking of these is that of around 1900 (Fig. 7). It was painted about a year after meeting his lifelong friend Albert Van den Briel, with whom he debated the merits of Theosophy during the winter of 1899–1900 (Seuphor, 1956, p. 53). Brought up a strict Calvinist under a domineering father, for Mondrian religion was a source of tension and inspiration in both life and art. Theosophy was a popular alternative to conventional Christianity at the time, and as Welch (1971) pointed out, would play a crucial role in Mondrian's aesthetic thinking and in the genesis of his abstract style. In 1900 he was just beginning to explore these ideas and to develop an inconography around them. Thus, about the same time, he created a watercolor of a single chrysanthemum (Guggenheim, 1971, pl. 7) which embodies the configuration of the transcendent round inherent in his frontal self-portrait.

This intense portrait is inscribed with an old Icelandic poem which translates: "So I take the risk of thrusting myself into the world—and I wait calmly—for the destiny which eternally pursues us lifts my desire to the point of complete self-confidence" (Seuphor, 1956, p. 63). While these sentiments were added to the canvas by Mondrian's friend Van den Briel four or five years after its completion, they describe the state of mind of the artist around 1900. Van den Briel said "The text is certainly dramatic and exaggerated. But Piet himself had not gone beyond that stage" (Seuphor, 1956, p. 63). Mondrian would quickly evolve; indeed, this portrait came into Van den Briel's possession when he

Fig. 7. Piet Mondrian. Self Portrait. c. 1900. Oil on canvas mounted on masonite, 19⅞ × 15½ in. (55 × 39.4 cms.). The Phillips Collection, Washington, D.C.

rescued it from Mondrian's impulse to use it as a target for pistol practice! Unintegrated manifestations of the unconscious are always a threat.

Mondrian's subsequent artistic development shows a systematic attempt to deal with this image of frontality—an attempt that can only be briefly outlined here.

About 1901, Mondrian combined the motifs of flower and frontality in another watercolor called *Passion Flower* (Guggenheim 12) which shows a frontal woman in deep meditation with heraldic blossoms over each shoulder.

The round of a flower is even more emphatically related to his frontal self-portrait of 1908, which was created the same year as the painting *Devotion* (Guggenheim 24). This again repeats the motif of a meditating female, this time in profile, contemplating the transcendent face of a flower. Indeed, single flowers are a recurring motif from about 1906 to 1911. In 1908 Mondrian was deeply immersed in Theosophic literature. He would join the Theosophical Society in 1909, and paint his major "theosophic" work, *Evolution* (Guggenheim 46), which depicts three hieratic women, in 1911.

As for Mondrian's relations with women, they consisted mostly of passionate encounters which came to nothing sexually. His paintings of this period suggest an unconscious process of idealizing the female and an identifying of her with the fragility of the flower. The rage induced by this self-imposed worship was vented more abstractly on nature, as Gay (1976) so brilliantly demonstrated. For it was just about this time that Mondrian launched on a series of reductive analyses of natural objects—first in terms of the motif of the tree from about 1909 to 1913, and later, just at the turn of his seventh cycle, in terms of the sea. These date from about 1913 to 1915 and are most often created within a horizontal ovoid which suggests the shape of the frontal human face—as do the vertical ovoids which contain his abstractions of a church tower.

Mondrian's third frontal self-portrait—a drawing—dates from 1918, a year in which he did only five works, two of which are self-portraits (Seuphor, 1956, p. 426). The last vestiges of recognizable subject matter vanished from his work about 1916, and by 1918 he was just beginning to experiment with grids (Seuphor, CC.294,297). This portrait thus marks the point when he abandoned nature entirely for a world of rigid abstract signs: the horizontal of the earth, the vertical of growth, and the primary colors.

There would be no further frontal self-portraits, since Mondrian had found his permanent center. He had taken his art into a realm of the most relentless pictorial denial. And there would be no further growth, just incremental stylistic changes. Whatever the philosophical reasons and aesthetic results, the psychodynamics are perhaps best summarized by Gay:

Mondrian's aesthetic choices emerged from his unconscious conflicts; as he translated these choices into his paintings, wielding his ruler and applying his brush, these conflicts guided his hand. He found sensuality so frightening that it was his dread of desire, rather than the desires themselves, that ultimately shaped his abstract designs. No sentiment, no curves, no touching—that is how he lived and that is what his paintings proclaim. . . . [They] offer impressive evidence just how much beauty the talented can wrest from fear. . . . Painting was, for Mondrian, the aesthetic correlative for his repressions, his way of coming to terms with himself—at once an expression of his problem and an embodiment of his solution (1976, pp. 225–226).

It is, of course, possible that Mondrian may have conceived one or more of his later grid paintings as self-portraits; once he told Van den Briel that a certain grid was his friend's portrait (Guggenheim, 1971, p. 33). But Mondrian, whatever his projections upon horizontals and verticals, had taken art out of the context of life. His work is the earliest and most influential embodiment of that dubious humanistic dissociation born of 20th-century "modernism," which would decontextualize traditional iconography, leaving geometric patterns invested with arbitrary verbal meanings. Such a reduction from symbol to sign denies the aesthetic a world other than itself, and relegates art's power to center to a mode of moral etiquette.[16]

Arnold Schoenberg (b. 1874-81-88/-95-1902-09-16/-23-30-37/-44-d.1951)

The influential Viennese composer Arnold Schoenberg, best known for his development of the twelve-tone system, was also one of his city's minor expressionist painters. Significantly, his favorite motif as an artist was the frontal face in general, and his own in particular (Fig. 8).

Schoenberg's visual works have been catalogued in the *Journal of the Arnold Schoenberg Institute* (1978; hereafter Catalogue with number) and discussed by Freitag (1973, 1978). Of the 250 sheets reproduced, 163 or (65%) depict frontal faces. Of these, 85 (or 52%) are self-portraits of which 70 (82%) are frontal. Unfortunately, only 13 of the full-face self-portraits are dated. It is, however, clear that the dated sheets are constellated at three chronological points. These are around 1910, where four are dated; in the period between 1918 and 1925, where there are another five; and from 1933 to 1936, where another four are found. Many of the undated frontal self-portraits can be related to these three periods on stylistic and physiognomic grounds.[17]

Also concentrated around 1910 (Freitag, 1973, dated several around 1908) are a number of symbolic self-portraits of violently expressive frontal faces. These *Gaze* and *Vision* paintings tend to focus on blazing eyes in heads exploding with unconstrained rage.

Schoenberg apparently began to paint about 1906 under the tutelage of the young Expressionist artist Richard Gerstl. By the following year the youth had started an affair with the composer's wife which led to her running off with her lover in 1908. She was soon persuaded to return to her two children, and the devastated Gerstl committed suicide late in 1908 at the age of 25.[18]

This traumatic situation was paralleled in time by a number of other factors in Schoenberg's life which made the period from 1908 to 1911, beginning with the turn of his sixth cycle at age 35, of more than circumstantial importance.

The composer was already something of a scandal in European musical circles. His first major work, the symphonic poem *Pelleas und Melisande* (1902–1903; Op.5) had provoked enormous hostility at its première, and his gradual rejection of the familiar conso-

Fig. 8. Arnold Schoenberg. *Blue Self Portrait*. 1910. Oil on wood, 12³/₁₆ × 8⅝ in. (31 × 22 cms.). Arnold Schoenberg Institute, University of Southern California, Los Angeles.

nances of traditional music for a disconcerting reliance on the dissonances of atonality, made him a controversial figure. His professional stature was also threatened by the latent antisemitism of his milieu. Since he made his money teaching, this increasing notoriety effected his livelihood. In 1910 he even sought portrait commissions to supplement his income (Stein, 1965, pp. 25–26).

These years also witnessed his musical breakthrough into the first phase of his rejection of traditional tonality. His *Three Pieces for Piano* (1909; Op.11) demonstrates a reliance on dissonance which further outraged the conservative music world of Vienna. The next year, 1910, he wrote a book about harmony which aimed at the "demythologization" of tonality (Stuckenschmidt, 1977, p. 136). During these same years he also completed the orchestration of his vast *Gurrelieder,* which he had completed a decade earlier just at the turn of his fifth cycle.

Parallel with all these events, he composed the monodrama *Erwartung* (1909; Op.17) and began *Die glückliche Hand* (1910–13; Op.18)—two short operatic works on the transparently autobiographical theme of violated love. And during the same period he lost the companionship and moral support of Gustav Mahler, who left for the United States in 1908 and returned to die in 1911—the latter event having a profound emotional effect on Schoenberg.[19]

Given these complex internal and external pressures, it is not surprising to find the composer in need of some device to center himself, and that he turned to the visual rather than aural image to contain and express his disappointments and anger. Thus, the frontal self-portrait would seem to have become for him the vehicle of the former need, while the *Gaze* and *Vision* paintings became the outlet for that "primal scream" even the uninhibited dissonances of his music could not adequately convey (Fig. 9).

Schoenberg's lack of success during the first half of his life induced a certain bitter reclusiveness during the second. In 1911, the composer painted a striking full-length self-portrait that depicted himself from the back walking away up a street (Catalogue 7). This was the psychological stance of his future persona, literally acted out at the première of the *Gurrelieder* in Vienna in 1913, when he refused to acknowledge the ovation that greeted his first success, and stalked in self-righteous fury from the hall, cursing the fickleness of his admirers.

His paintings were exhibited in Vienna in the fall of 1910. Later Kandinsky included the rear-view self-portrait and two *Visions* in the first Blaue Reiter exhibition in 1912, and published an essay by the composer in the *Blaue Reiter Almanac* of the same year. But Schoenberg's powers as a German Expressionist, despite Kandinsky's approbation, were modest and contributed to his life and music more acutely than to the history of art.[20]

It is easy to understand Schoenberg's need for psychological centering during the period just after the war. It was during this seventh cycle of his life—from ages 42 to 48—that he labored to systematize his earlier atonality into the twelve-tone method of composition. He began to write music based on his new system in 1922, at the exact turn of his third era. All during this cycle, and into the early part of the next, there is evidence of a more diffuse

Fig. 9. Arnold Schoenberg. *Gaze.* c. 1910. Oil on cardboard, 11 × 6¹¹⁄₁₆ in. (28 × 17 cms.). Arnold Schoenberg Institute, University of Southern California, Los Angeles.

distribution of frontal self-portraits, the final two dating to 1925 (see Fig. 10). These last may well relate not only to the formulation of his greatest musical innovation, but also to major changes in his personal situation during the first two years of his eighth cycle and third era. In 1923, when Schoenberg was 49, his first wife died; he remarried in 1924. By 1925 he had entered into a relatively tranquil period in his life which continued until the rise of Hitler in 1933.

The last concentration of frontal self-portraits occurred when Schoenberg defiantly asserted his Jewishness in the face of the threat of Nazism and, turning his back on a hostile Europe, fled to the United States. The first dated sheet (Catalogue 12) occurred in 1933, when the composer left Vienna for Paris, lost his academic position because of his religion, and, with the painter Marc Chagall standing witness, reconverted to the Jewish faith he had rejected in his youth. Later that year, unable to find suitable employment in Europe, he immigrated to America, where he taught for a year in Boston and New York. In 1935, the year of his next dated frontal self-portrait (Catalogue 16), he was in Hollywood, where he began to give private lessons and lecture at the University of Southern California. By 1936, the year of his last two dated frontal self-portraits (Catalogue 17,18), he had bought a house and been appointed professor of music at the University of California. These events occurred directly at the turn of his tenth cycle, and presaged the last fruitful 15 years of his life. He retired from the University of California at the turn of his 11th cycle and fourth era, and died in 1951 at the turn of his 12th cycle.

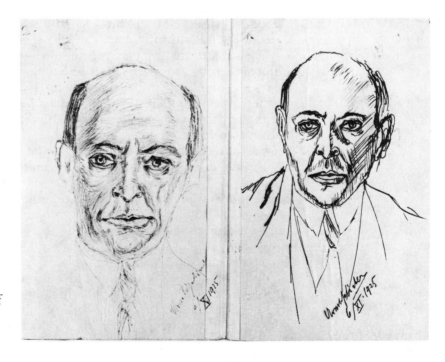

Fig. 10. Arnold Schoenberg. Self-Portraits. 1925. Pen and ink on cardboard, 5½ × 7½ in. (14 × 19 cms.). Arnold Schoenberg Institute, University of Southern California, Los Angeles.

Fig. 11. Arnold Schoenberg. Self-Portrait. 1936. Ink on tracing paper, $9^{7}/_{16} \times 7^{7}/_{8}$ in. (24 × 20 cms.). Arnold Schoenberg Institute, University of Southern California, Los Angeles.

Schoenberg's two 1936 frontal self-portraits (Fig. 11) show the 60-year-old composer staring severely from the canvas, in contrast to the rather blank, stunned look of the beset innovator found in the earlier self-images. By now, perhaps, humankind had justified his scowls.

But his recourse to the visual—that spatial rest center between the fleeting temporal worlds of the aural and the verbal—had served to preserve his creative daemon from an increasingly coruscating misanthropy. One can also speculate that the visual experience afforded by painting and drawing had an important influence on two formal aspects of Schoenberg's music. It can be said with some justice that to study his scores provides greater aesthetic pleasure than to listen to their performance—so elegant are they in the clarity and unity of the parts. The scores thus become works of visual art, comparable to those of Mondrian. One recalls also Einstein's dependence on visualization to project upon a tangible plane the pure abstractness of his thought. Further, the permutations of the tone rows ultimately favored by Schoenberg—their intricate inversions and retrogressions—raise some of the same enantiomorphic problems any self-portraitist must encounter while contemplating the paradoxes of a mirror. When Schoenberg stated that his painting meant the same to him as making music (*Journal of the Arnold Schoenberg Institute,* 1978, p. 179), he was not just expressing love for a hobby, but respect for a medium which may well have helped him see clear to reinvent traditional harmonic functions while stabilizing himself at three difficult points of transition in his life-course.

*Charles Burchfield
(b.1893-1900-07/-
14-21-28-35/-
42-49-56/-63;
d.1967)*

Charles Burchfield, one of America's great visionary artists, made two frontal self-portraits in 1916 at age 23. The first (Fig. 12), a watercolor, was created in January when he was a last-year student at the Cleveland School of Art; the second (Fig. 13) in late fall, just before he fled New York and a one-day stint at the National Academy of Design. The year between these two works saw his first love affair, a growing agnosticism and "pantheism" which expressed themselves in a fervent devotion to natural phenomena as opposed to sectarian doctrine, and a firm conviction that he needed no further formal schooling as an artist. Two days after his return to Ohio late in 1916, he went sketching in the country. Later in life he recalled the trip:

> One of the supremely happy moments of my whole life was when I stood in the woods and listened to the wind roaring in the tree tops. After New York it seemed to me the most wonderful music I ever heard. The result of that day's walk was six watercolors, done in the evenings of the following week (Baur, 1984, p. 57).[21]

Thus was established the pattern of working that Burchfield would pursue throughout 1917. This "golden year" of his artistic life (Baur, p. 58) saw the creation of nearly 200 paintings of extraordinary stylistic originality and synaesthetic sensibility. This outpouring continued until his induction into the army in July 1918. In these paintings Burchfield showed himself fascinated with the radiant aura of natural sounds as well as things and sought in every work to capture visually the interpenetrations and correspondences of these phenomena. Titles such as *The August North* and *The Insect Chorus* (Baur, pl. XI, XII) convey the scope of his artistic ambitions. (Only Arthur Garfield Dove was as daring, resourceful, and successful in his more modernist envisioning of nature.) And the painting *Bright Summer Sun* can stand not only as a literal example of his achievement at this time, but also as a splendid acknowledgment of the icon implicit in the frontal self-portraits that presaged his outpouring of visual insight during these 18 months of intense creativity (Baur, pl. VIII).

Burchfield's art changed after his discharge in 1919, and until 1943 he seemed to have been more attentive to the exterior practicalities of life and nature than to its inner aura. At the turn of his fifth cycle in 1921 he moved to Buffalo, New York from Salem, Ohio. His work became more urban in emphasis; his depictions of nature less poetic. In 1922 he married, engendered a child a year from 1923 to 1926, and worked in a wall-paper factory. By 1928, at the turn of his sixth cycle, he had developed chronic nervous indigestion and a profound hatred for his time-consuming and soul-destroying job. He did only 33 paintings during his fifth cycle: 1922 to 1928 (Baur, pp. 128,147). In 1929 he finally quit, and greeted the birth of the fifth child with a new life of freedom for himself and (miraculously during the Depres-

Fig. 12. Charles Burchfield. Self-Portrait. 1916. Pencil on paper, 11½ × 9 in. (29.2 × 22.8 cms.). Private Collection. Courtesy of Kennedy Galleries, Inc., N.Y.

sion) a modicum of financial security due to a relationship with a new dealer. Throughout most of the 1930s he practiced what might be called an art of urban regionalism and his nature paintings partook with rare exceptions of a similar objectivity. During these years, however, he harbored a secret yearning for the halcyon years of 1917 and 1918 and the visionary powers of his youth. In 1935, at age 42 and the turn of his seventh cycle, he dreamt that a voice said to him "You should go back to those old interpretations of nature moods again" (Baur, p. 192). But he resisted, his pantheism perhaps overwhelmed by his wife's campaign to convert him to Lutheranism, which he also resisted until 1944. By then, however, he had finally returned to his golden year. In 1943, just after the turn of his eighth cycle and third era, he began to rework some of his 1917 paintings. This led to a complete reexploration of his earlier vision in terms of his mature technique, and ultimately to his masterful expressionist paintings of the last two productive cycles of his life through around 1963. In these great works of his old age he came full circle to his

youthful visionary year—a year preceded by one of determined self-definition and marked by his two frontal self-portraits.

Frida Kahlo (b. 1910-17-24/-31-38-45-52;d.1954)

The determining fact of Mexican artist Frida Kahlo's life was the massive injury she suffered at the age of 15 when she was impaled through the pelvis in a bus accident. Her biographer, Hayden Herrera (1983), reported her stating in an 1944 interview that: "Three concerns impelled her to make art. . .: her vivid memory of her own blood flowing during her childhood accident; her thoughts about birth, death and the "conducting threads" of life; and her desire to be a mother" (p. 319). Given the intensity of the motivation, it is therefore of some interest to find among the nearly 40 self-portraits published by Herrera—which constitute well over half Kahlo's oeuvre—only six that are frontal. These are distributed at points of specific joy and anguish over her life course.

The first (Herrera, pl. II, hereafter H) was done in 1929, the

Fig. 14. Frida Kahlo. Self-Portrait. 1940. Oil on canvas, 24½ × 18¾ in. (62.2 × 47.6 cms.). Iconography Collection, Humanities Research Center, University of Texas at Austin.

year she began a tempestuous marriage with the famous Mexican muralist Diego Rivera. As if to emphasize the centering icon inherent in her pose, a round-faced clock appears over her right shoulder. The heavy jade pendant around her neck is incised with a circle with four arms which echoes the form of a small plane in the sky above her head whose propeller crowns the axis of her body.

The second, *Remembrance of an Open Wound* (H40) shows her seated frontally and lifting her skirt to display a gash on her right thigh. This 1938 work, created at the turn of her fifth cycle, is a defiant response to Rivera's affair with her sister and was painted at the time she herself had a brief liaison with Leon Trotsky, which renewed her self-confidence after repeated humiliations by

Fig. 15. Frida Kahlo. *Sun and Life.* 1947. Oil on masonite, 15¾ × 19½ in. (40 × 49.5 cms.). Lic. Manuel Perusquia, Mexico City.

her philandering husband. Herrera commented that it was at this point in her art that she began "to use physical wounds as symbols for psychic injury" (p. 188). One may also wonder, given the two politicians in her life (Rivera was a leading Communist who was harboring Trotsky), if she was not on some level also emulating Portia in Shakespeare's *Julius Caesar,* who wounds herself on the thigh to obtain her husband Brutus's attention and confidence concerning his conspiracies.

The next year, 1939, Kahlo had reason to conclude that she did indeed dwell in the suburbs of her husband's good pleasure, and the couple divorced. Alone through 1940, she painted that year the most powerful of her frontal self-portraits (Fig. 14). It reveals her surrounded by a monkey and a black cat and wearing a necklace of thorns which prick her flesh. From it hangs a dead hummingbird—a Mexican charm used to conjure luck in love.

The Riveras remarried late in 1940 and thereafter maintained an uneasy truce concerning affairs, the operating principle of which was reciprocity. Yet Kahlo retained her love for Rivera and her desire for his regard. This is evident in her next frontal self-portrait, of 1943 (HXXI). Dressed in the elaborate costume of a Tehuana, her slightly turned face is centered by the oval ruffle around her head as well as by a frontal portrait of Rivera painted in miniature on her forehead. This overall configuration of the work in effect embodies the vital, centering icon inherent in the frontal self-portrait—and reveals how explicitedly close to it she was getting in her art.

In 1945 Kahlo's fifth frontal self-portrait took the form of an image of herself holding an orange mask with purple hair in front of her face (Whitechapel, 1982, p. 78). Her tears run out the holes in its eyes. She was, at this time, at the turn of her sixth cycle and in grave physical and mental condition. The progressive deterioration of her spine required cruel orthopedic corsettes and agonizing surgery. Confined for almost a year in the hospital, she was also in despair at her indifferent husband's escapades. Herrera noted the "feeling of hysteria" (p. 368) conveyed by this work. And, indeed, the gallant persona Kahlo so long affected would seem to have collapsed—and must be held before her face to provide whatever centering it can still provide.

Kahlo made her last frontal self-portrait in 1947 (HXXIV), at the time of the miscarriage of a child by one of her lovers. This was accompanied the same year by a painting called *Sun and Life* (Fig. 15) in which the icon appears explicitly in the context of phallic plants as a mandala bearing a frontal face with a "third eye" on the forehead.

Hereafter her health declined relentlessly, and she painted only five more self-portraits, none frontal, up to her death at age 44 in 1954. Her last self-portrait, done the year of her death, is *Marxism Gives Health to the Sick* (H80). It is a weak work, pathetically and futilely grasping at ideology in the face of death. The more so since Kahlo was radicalized by her fate in a way her husband was never radicalized by Marxism. "Murdered by life" as she often said, she found in art the means to depict her pain and rage, and to gain that sympathy and attention her pride forbade her to solicit otherwise. Her radicalism was purely psychosomatic, manipulating the politics of love and hate and occasionally finding the centered loyalty of her own fierce face.

Jackson Pollock (b.1912-19-26/-33-40-47-54;d.1956)

Jackson Pollock's only frontal self-portrait (Fig. 16) is dated between the time he first came to New York from California in the fall of 1930, and 1933, the year his father died. It thus appeared at the turn of his fourth cycle, about the age of 21, when he was studying with Thomas Hart Benton at the Art Students League. This was a period of enormous excitement and breakthrough for Pollock. He had grown bored and unsettled studying art in California. In a letter dated January 31, 1930, he told his brother Charles in New York:

> the truth of it is i have never really gotten down to real work and finish a piece i usually get disgusted with it and lose

Fig. 16. Jackson Pollock. Self-Portrait. c. 1930–33. Oil on gesso on canvas mounted on composition board, 7¼ × 5¼ in. (18.4 × 13.3 cms.). Lee Krasner Pollock, New York.

interest. water color i like but have never worked with it much. altho i feel i will make an artist of some kind i have nver proven to myself nor any body else that i have it in me. This so called happy part of one's life youth to me is a bit of damnable hell if i could come to some conclusion about my self and life perhaps there i could see something to work for (O'Connor & Thaw, 1978, 4: D7, p. 209; Pollock's spelling and punctuation are retained).

In contrast, he could write the following to his father in California in February 1932:

I'm going to school every morning and have learned what is worth learning in the realm of art. It is just a matter of time and work now for me to have that knowledge apart of me. A good seventy years more and I think I'll make a good artist— being a artist is life its self—living it I mean. . . . Mural painting is forging to the front—by the time I get up there there out to be plenty of it—Sculptoring I think tho is my medium. I'll never be satisfied until I'm able to mould a mountain of stone, with the aid of a jack hammer, to fit my will (O'Connor & Thaw, 1978, 4: D12, p. 212).

And three months later, in May 1932, he told his mother:

I'm coming along I guess—painting and sculpturing is life it self (that is for those who practice it) and one advances as one grows and experiences life—it doesn't exceed ones experience. So it is a matter of years—a life. I have much to learn tecnequelly yet. I am interested and like it which is the main thing (O'Connor & Thaw, 1978, 4: D13, p. 213).

Pollock's adolescent confusion of early 1930 has resolved into a sense of a life's vocation: He could imagine the future evolution of his art parallel to his life. He could yearn to paint murals—a not unreasonable ambition for a kid in the early 1930s who already knew Benton and the Mexican José Clemente Orozco. And later he would do so, in his own way, revising our conception of large-scale painting in the process. He could also hope to move mountains as a sculptor—though here he would succeed only figuratively: moving the potential of painting itself beyond Picasso.

His tiny frontal self-portrait—it is 7¼ × 5¼ inches—shows only his head and neck emerging from a crudely painted dark ground. It certainly reflects, however, his new self-awareness and ambitions. It is painted in oil on gesso, with the white gesso forming an irregular edge around the image. The little work resembles a fresco sketch, something he would have seen Benton or Orozco making to test out colors and formal problems for their murals at the New School for Social Research during the winter of 1930–31.

But more striking than this indication of technical experimentation is its depiction of a boy much younger-looking than the nearly 21-year-old man who painted it. It is clear from his letters that Pollock was more than aware of time. He speaks of needing 70 years to "make a good artist." He would, of course, achieve his goal over the 23 that remained to him. The youth of the face in the portrait—which does not resemble the Pollock we know from contemporary photographs—seems to presage the half-life of the

Fig. 17. Jackson Pollock. *Portrait and a Dream.* 1953. Oil on canvas, 4′10⅛″ × 11′2½″ (147.6 × 341.6 cms.). Dallas Museum of Fine Arts, Texas; gift of Mr. & Mrs. Algur H. Meadows and the Meadows Foundation, Inc.

man while initiating him on the path to his achievements.

Fittingly, the other two recognized self-images of Pollock: a drawing in one of his sketchbooks, which can only be dated roughly between 1933 and 1938 (O'Connor & Thaw, 1978, 3: 410r), and the elaborate face to the right of the painting *Portrait and a Dream* (Fig. 17), which dates from 1953, his last fully productive year and just at the turn of his seventh cycle—only show the right half of the artist's face.

The drawing, a naturalistic rendering of the ruggedly handsome man Pollock was at the time, is situated to the bottom left on a page of sketches after El Greco. The painting shows a "Picassoid" divided face done in black, silver, red, and yellow, and is anatomically legible only to the right. Pollock claimed it was of him "when I am not sober" (O'Connor, 1980, p. 20). This image is to the right of another done in poured black paint on the same canvas which contains a portrait of his wife.

Both of these self-images are dominated by the round of a single eye—yet their bisection negates centricity. Only the small frontal self-portrait, done as a student, initiates a sense of centeredness and destiny.

Pablo Picasso (b.1881-88-95/-1902-09-16-23/-30-37-44/-51-58-65-72;d.1973)

Let me conclude this essay on the primal form inherent in the frontal self-portrait with one by Picasso that faces up to the last transition of all: death (Fig. 18). Dated June 30, 1972, at the turn of his 14th cycle and nine months before his death at the age of 91, it was first exhibited in Paris in December 1972 and published by the novelist, art critic, and close friend of Picasso, Pierre Daix (1973) as a self-portrait of the great master. It is executed in blue, green, brown, and black crayon with red-violet crayon in the hair and to the left of the face. It stands out dramatically among his final suites of drawings and prints in a group of frontal faces Picasso made between June 27 and July 13, 1972. This interlude is found in an almost continuous outpouring of flamboyant, explicitly exposed female nudes drawn between 1970 and the artist's death in April 1973. Daix stated he visited Picasso the day after this portrait was finished. Picasso showed it to him and said he thought he had "hit upon something new." In October 1972 Daix returned to Picasso's villa and found the drawing conspicuously displayed on the wall of the sitting room. Daix recalled that he was "struck by its autobiographical quality. . . . I had the impression that he was looking the image of his death in the face." This may well be—but with one eye on what remained of life.

Indeed, if one looks at the eyes in this self-portrait, one is immediately struck with how they differ from Picasso's usual treatment of his dark, penetrating orbs (as seen, for instance, in the constellation of frontal self-portraits Picasso made around 1900 to 1902 at the time of his gradual transferral from Barcelona to Paris at the turn of his third cycle). Here Picasso's right eye seems indrawn and dim while his left eye is larger and brighter. At the same time, the left side of the head seems to dissolve while

Fig. 18. Pablo Picasso. June 30, 1972. Pencil and colored crayons on paper, 25⅞ × 19⅞ in. (65.7 × 50.5 cms.). Private Collection, Japan. Courtesy of The Solomon R. Guggenheim Museum, N.Y.

the right is carefully delineated.[22]

Indeed, the left eye is emphasized in a number of extraordinary ways, surrounded as it is by a violet spiral, articulated diagonally into violet and black halves (as if partly covered by a reptile's nictitating membrane), while its socket is seemingly suspended from the crown of the head by a stark blue and violet line. It is an eye virtually unprecedented in Picasso's enormous oeuvre, fully justifying his statement that he had "hit upon something new," though one can find a similar motif in two 1900 frontal self-portraits in which a shadow or strand of hair connects the left eyebrow with the hairline (Rubin, 1980, p. 29).[23]

We can thus see in Picasso's last self-portrait an association of the two images we have dealt with in this essay: the frontal face of the artist, and the transcendent round of the inhering icon. Despite the cadaverous bone structure, the phosphorescent colors and the withered shoulders, the left eye blazes with a vitality of spirit alive in the wasted but centered physiognomy of our century's master of visual revelation.

This last work by Picasso demonstrates that the artistic process is essentially psychodynamic (however artists, critics, or historians may choose to explain it), that the making of a frontal self-portrait, while most often marking a natural or situational transition in life, can sustain an act of self-confrontation and self-renewal even in the face of death, and that the stuff of art remains those ageless visual archetypes that serve the perennial needs of spiritual celebration and survival.

Notes

1 Part of this problem lies in the tendency, first evident in literary studies, to reduce Freudian and Jungian interpretation of a text to a mode of cryptography. The extreme "bump and hollow" school of psychoanalytic criticism competed for a while with the "archetypal" Jungians, in an attempt to decode "symbols" at the expense of historical common sense and the overdetermined nature of the creative process. (A balanced view of this situation can be found in Hyman, 1948). Recently, a younger generation of art historians, noting the special relevance of Jung to visual exegesis, have repeated the same sins of literal-mindedness and insensitivity to creativity, failing to realize, in most cases, that unconscious phenomena can only be discussed by those who have had some experience of their own unconscious. Traditional art historians, observing all this from the fustian ramparts of a tried and true, object-oriented, Germanic scholarship (and forgetting, perhaps, the rich, freewheeling humanism of Abby Warburg and kindred founders of their profession) drew up the drawbridges and declared in unison "they'll never get in here!" There is some justification for such an attitude, though it ought not forever forbid a reappraisal of psychodynamic theory and a more eclectic, selective, and imaginative application of it to the visual arts—a process well begun by Gay (1976) and demonstrated here.

2 It should be noted here that the frontal portrait is not restricted to self-portraits. Asked if they had made a frontal portrait of someone other than themselves, 90% of my responding artists answered yes. Of the portraits painted, 60% were of loved ones or close friends; the rest of paying clients. While several artists pointed out that a frontal pose might be selected to flatter (and flatten) otherwise ungainly features, the element of self-projection and emotional encounter in such portraits is too strong to be dismissed entirely, as is the probable identification of those beloved with the power of the iconic motif inherent in the configuration.

3 Unfortunately, the literature on self-portraits is of little interpretive value when it comes to frontality. Goldscheider (1937) and Masciotta (1955) are essentially picture books with the former's introduction both dated and problematic in many respects. There are numerous exhibition catalogues about self-portraits, the most useful being those of the Metropolitan (1972), Wildenstein's (1976), Heckscher Museum (1979), and National Academy (1983). Michael Quick's essay in the latter, and the various texts in the Wildenstein catalogue are notable for their intelligence and insightfulness. The most imaginative treatment of the self-

portrait, that of Kinneir (1980), which traces the human life-course with self-portraits ranging from Dürer at age 12 to Hokusai at age 83—and of which a third are frontal—failed to provide any consistent documentation about the circumstances under which the works illustrated were created, and thus proved maddeningly useless for this study. Indeed, this book, and the others also, cry out for some theory of developmental psychology compatible with the study of an artist's creative evolution into old age.

4 I first presented my seven-year cycle model of the life course during a private conference at Chatham, Massachusetts in July 1980 and as a public lecture for a conference on "Metaphors of Self: Creativity and Reminiscence in Old Age" sponsored by the Institute on Humanities, Arts, & Aging of the Brookdale Center on Aging at Hunter College's School of Social Work on Feburary 27, 1981. About the number seven in general, the best discussion of its cultural ramifications is found in Varley (1976). Its wide-ranging folkloric manifestations are listed in Thompson (1955–58, pp. 688-9) and most thoroughly in terms of themes in Jobes (1961, pp. 1421–1426). The common law follows folk custom, with the result that seven units of time are often stipulated in juridical proceedings—such as the passing of seven years required before the missing can be declared legally dead.

5 Brevity requires that no attempt be made here to expound the psychodynamic structure of each seven-year cycle. Suffice it to say that each such cycle seems to contain three aspects of varying duration, sequence, and intensity: a period of purposeful calm, a period of crisis, and a period of reintegration. This "life-death-rebirth" cycle can be explicit in the iconography of an artist's work during such a cycle. For my thoughts on "death" imagery, see O'Connor (1979). The frontal self-portrait is clearly an aspect of rebirth symbolism.

6 Almost all children's art is frontal. For a striking international survey of children's frontal self-portraits, see International Jugendbibliothek (1952). The primal origins of this are discussed in Section III below.

7 But it is not all that incompatible with other life-course systems, as far as they go. The difference lies in a symbolic regularity as opposed to a statistically induced variability. In this respect, consider the comparison in the chart opposite with Levinson (1978). It should perhaps be noted here that Levinson's system, and most others also, are based on research with male populations; my system, being symbolic not statistical, is compatible with female experience as well.

8 In a more generalized context, Jaffe (1980, p. 10) showed that Leonard Baskin unconsciously incorporated into the two facial types found in his sculptures the distinct physiognomies of his parents.

9 See Panofsky's famous essay "The History of the Theory of Human Proportions as a Reflection of the History of Styles" for a discussion of the "three-circle scheme" of Byzantine art by which the head of Christ or a saint was designed within the proportions of three concentric circles—thus fusing the mandala with the iconic image (in 1955b, p. 79).

10 I should like to state for the record, and in anticipation of those who will suggest these "case histories" were carefully selected to prove my point, that they were chosen primarily because these artists had done frontal self-portraits (and it is surprising how many major artists do not depict themselves at all, let alone frontally). Also, it was necessary, given the deplorable state of art historical literature when it comes to biographical detail, to find artists for whom such detail was available at this writing. No artist has been rejected because of incompatibility with my system;

O'CONNOR: *The Human Life Course*	LEVINSON: *Development Periods for Men*
Era I—Development of Primitive Individuality through Childhood and Adolescence: Ages 0–20 Cycle 1 0–6 Cycle 2 7–13 Cycle 3 14–20	Childhood and Adolescence: Ages 0–22 0–17 Childhood and Adolescence 17–22 Early Adult Transition
Era II—Development of the Persona through Early Middle Age: Ages 21–48 Cycle 4 21–27 Cycle 5 28–34 Cycle 6 35–41 Cycle 7 42–48	Early Adulthood: Ages 17–45 22–28 Entering Adult World 28–33 Age 30 Transition 33–40 Settling Down 40–45 Mid-Life Transition
Era III—Fulfillment of the Persona through Late Middle Age: Ages 49–69 Cycle 8 49–55 Cycle 9 56–62 Cycle 10 63–69	Middle Adulthood: Ages 40–65 45–50 Entering Middle Adulthood 50–55 Age 50 transition 55–60 Culmination of Middle Adulthood 60–65 Late Adult Transition
Era IV—Fulfillment of Individuality in Old Age: Ages 70–97+ Cycle 11 70–76 Cycle 12 77–83 Cycle 13 84–90 Cycle 14 91–97+	Late Adulthood: Age 65+ (Levinson's system stops here; he recognizes but does not elaborate a stage after 80.) Late Late Adulthood: Age 80+

all studied have proved its general validity. In due course, I hope to expand this study into a book and deal with a larger population of artists who created frontal self-portraits.

11 There is only one other study of Rembrandt's self-portraits, that by Erpel (1967). It is a less discriminating selection, though its color plates are of higher quality than those in Wright.

12 In describing artists' self-portraits in directional terms, it is usually best to imagine yourself the artist and the portrait a mirror. Thus the right shoulder of the portrait image is to the right; the left to the left. For an artist's portrait of someone other than himself, of course, this is reversed: you face another person beyond the picture plane, not a mirrored image. Thus the right shoulder of the sitter is really to the left. If this is confusing, consider the awkward difference in shaking hands with your mirrored image as opposed to a real person standing before you. If this is still enantiomorphically confounding, refer to Needham (1973), M. C. Corballis and I. L. Beale (1976) and C. G. Gross and M. H. Bornstein (1978).

13 The following table shows the relationship of Rembrandt's 15 frontal self-portraits with his 83 other self-portraits as reproduced in Wright (1982). It should be noted that there is no meaningful correlation

between the centric portraits and the portraits having just frontal faces. More interesting is the fact that they do appear during cycles of intense self-portraiture, though the significance of this, in the absence of comparative data from equally prolific artists, is unclear.

Cycle	Dates	Age	Total Number of Self-Portraits	Number of Frontal Self-Portraits	Number of Frontal Heads on Turned Bodies	Number of Turned Heads on Frontal Bodies	Number of Turned Heads on Turned Bodies
4th	1627–33	21–27	45	2	13	3	27
5th	1634–40	28–34	23	5	3	1	14
6th	1641–47	35–41	2	0	0	0	2
7th	1648–54	42–48	5	2	1	0	2
8th	1655–61	49–55	18	6	1	0	11
9th	1662–68	56–62	2	0	0	0	2
10th	1669–	63	3	0	0	0	3
TOTALS			98	15	18	4	61

14 While Rank (1971) and Tymms (1949) discussed the concept of the "double" or "doppelgänger" mostly in terms of literary texts and anthropological data, Rank's elaboration of mirror images and his associations with shadows, guardian spirits, the soul, and an individual's narcissistic fear of death provide a rich context in which to contemplate the psychodynamics of artists' self-portraits. If such portraits are generally to be construed as protection against ego destruction, then frontal self-portraits, with their centric, eyeball-to-eyeball encounter with the viewer, and especially those adjusted, as here, to separate image from reflection, are to be seen in a special category which provides even more potent magic for ego perpetuation. See also Arnheim (1982, p. 78).

15 Mondrian's remaining seven self-portraits all show him with his body rigidly perpendicular to the picture plane and his head turned to gaze over his right shoulder. See Seuphor (1956, CC. 3–6,8,9). The best of these dates from 1918 and shows him standing at right angles to one of his transitional geometric paintings as well as the picture plane. It was painted as a favor to a friend, since the artist felt such portraits belonged to an earlier phase of his development (Seuphor, 1956, p. 192).

16 The total separation of the gestalt/archetype from its context in realtiy is one of the great aesthetic and ethical problems of "abstract" art. The frequent appearance of the round over the horizontal in the works of Max Ernst and especially Adolph Gottlieb (just as the constant repetition of the frontal face by Raphael Soyer and Chuck Close) distances it from any original psychodynamic cause. It thus becomes a personal convention—or, in the work of second-rate printmakers and graphic designers, an utterly exploitable motif. It also inhibits the personal and artistic growth of the artist—as the grid did for Mondrian—by becoming the only theme open to variation. It is so visually and iconically seductive that it stimies the exploration of other images. Mark Rothko's colored clouds are a similarly obsessive image from which he could not escape. This fixation on a particularly alluring image is unhealthy if it continues much after childhood. Jung (1969, p. 351) saw identifying with an

archetype as dangerous and ultimately unproductive. Constellating an archetype—as in the frontal self-portrait—is not, as we have seen, pathological; identifying with it to the exclusion of other iconic realities is—both for art and life.

17 While Freitag (1978, pp. 166–167) pointed to the difficulty of dating Schoenberg's self-portraits, and while I have not had access to the attempt he made in the catalog-appendix of his dissertation (which unfortunately is not published in Freitag 1973), I find that the frontal self-portraits can reasonably be organized for the present purpose into three groups around those that are dated. Thus the following (from which the visually problematic have been eliminated) can be constelled circa 1908–11: Catalogue numbers 1 (1908), 2 (1910), 3 (1910), 4 (1910), 5 (1910), 22–26,28,32,45–47,53–55,57,58,235,247; circa 1918–1925: 8 (1918), 9 (1919), 10 (1925–two portraits on same sheet), 37–40,49,59, 61,230 (1921), 241 (the epaulets suggest his military service c. 1916–1917); and circa 1933–1936: 12 (1933), 16 (1935), 17 (1936), 18 (1936—his last dated work), 29–31,36,41,48,50–52,60,65. In interpreting these works I have relied on Reich (1971), Stein (1965), and Stuckenschmidt (1978) for biographical information. For an excellent overview of Schoenberg and his Viennese circle, the members of which were much given to frontal self-portraiture, see Comini (1984).

18 Richard Gerstl made a number of frontal self-portraits during his short life, the last just 20 days before his suicide. See Kinneir (1980, pp. 86–87).

19 Schoenberg painted a frontal portrait of Mahler (Catalogue: 76) in 1910 and an undated *Burial of Gustave Mahler* (Catalogue: 237) after his friend's death in May 1911. For the relationship between the two composers, see Stuckenschmidt (1977, pp. 101–114).

20 For a discussion of Schoenberg's relation to the Blaue Reiter, see Breitenbach, 1977, who justly states that the renowned composer "does not have a place in the history of art, nor does he need one" (p. 38). Schoenberg's art is best seen as a means of insight into his total achievement—as, indeed, we can view the visual creations of Goethe, Hugo, Gautier and, as seen earlier, Hopkins.

21 I have relied exclusively on Baur (1984), which is the most thorough and thoughtful study of Burchfield. I have also adopted Baur's idea about the artist's "pantheism" from the masterful Chapter 14. I do feel, however, that such a term, along with "expressionism" and "fantasy," loaded as they are with historical freight, do a subtle injustice to so far-seeing an artist, even if he did use them himself. Burchfield's naturally penetrating vision requires a more imaginative historical and psychodynamic analysis. But that is for another time and essay.

22 I am presuming Picasso used a mirror to make this self-portrait; thus his left is to the left. One must wonder if this curious self-image, especially the dissolution of the left side of the face, adumbrates some visual defect or paralysis. Obviously, this self-portrait cannot be completely interpreted without access to Picasso's medical history in the last years of his life. Schiff (1968, p. 67 and pl. 47) publishes as a "symbolic self-portrait" Picasso's *Man with a Big Hat* of November 23, 1970, in which the eyes are treated in the same way—thought the frontal face does not otherwise resemble Picasso.

23 This motif occasionally results from the artist's familiar superimposition of profile and full face. See Galerie Louise Leiris (1972, pl. 36) which shows such a double head dated April 13, 1972. On the other hand, plate 103 in the same publication shows a frontal head of July 2, 1972

(done just two days after the work discussed here) which is a similar but less developed frontal self-portrait. Its most striking feature is a large notch in the upper left of the head which follows exactly the contours of the left socket and "suspending" line of the earlier self-portrait—as if Picasso was intrigued with the new motif and wished to explore it further. But, again, there is also the intimation of a somatic cause, and one is reminded of the typical deletion of useless body parts in the self-portraits of hemiplegic patients (see P. Bach, H. W. Tracy, and J. Huston, 1971).

(NOTE: After this essay was submitted for publication, it was brought to my attention that the idea of seven year cycles is popular among the members of Rudolf Steiner's Anthroposophical Society, and that awareness of the early seven-year periods of life forms a basic pedagogic strategy of his Waldorf Schools. His ideas about this are expressed in *The Education of the Child in the Light of Anthroposophy* (London: Rudolf Steiner Press, 1965) and have been developed by his followers—sometimes in dubious directions. For instance Beredine Jocelyn, in her *Citizens of the Cosmos: Life's Unfolding from Conception through Death to Rebirth* (New York: Continuum, 1981) builds on Steiner's modest educational theory to project an elaborate astrological system upon a human life course of seven year cycles through age 77, each dominated by a heavenly body. In general, such occult and astrological employment of seven year cycles and similar natural patterns tends to be rigidly dogmatic—and totally antithetical to the heuristic approach taken in this essay. Another follower of Steiner, the art historian Konrad Oberhuber, has lectured to the New York Anthroposophical Society on art and seven-year cycles, but at this writing I am not familiar with his precise views on the subject.)

References

Arnheim, Rudolf. (1982). *The power of the center: A study of composition in the visual arts.* Berkeley: University of California Press.

Bach, P., Tracy, H. W., & Huston, J. (1971). The use of the self-portrait method in the evaluation of hemiplegic patients. *Southern Medical Journal,* 64, 12, December, 1475–1480.

Baur, J. I. H. (1984). *The inlander: Life and work of Charles Burchfield, 1893–1967.* Newark: University of Delaware Press (An American Art Journal Book).

Bolten, J., & Bolten-Rempt, H. (1977). *The hidden Rembrandt.* Chicago: Rand McNally.

Brazelton, T. B. (1979). Evidence of communication during neonatal behavioral assessment, pp. 79–88. In Bullowa, 1979.

Breitenbach, E. (1977). Arnold Schoenberg and the Blaue Reiter. *The Quarterly Journal of the Library of Congress,* 34, 32–38.

Bullowa, M. (Ed.). (1979). *Before speech: The beginning of interpersonal communication.* Cambridge: Cambridge University Press.

Campbell, J. (1968). *The masks of God: Creative mythology.* New York: The Viking Press.

Clark, K. (1981). *Moments of vision.* New York: Harper & Row.

Comini, A. (1984). Through a Viennese looking-glass darkly: Images of Arnold Schönberg and his circle. *Arts,* May, 107–119.

Conway, W. M. (Ed.). (1958). *The writings of Albrecht Dürer.* New York: Philosophical Library.

Corballis, M. C., & Beale, I. L. (1976). *The psychology of left and right.* Hillsdale, NJ: Lawrence Erlbaum Associates.

Daix, P. (1973). Picasso—"Painters are never better than in the evening of their lives." *Art News,* September, 56–59.

Erpel, F. (1967). *Die selbstbildnisse Rembrandts.* Vienna: Langen-Müller.

Fantz, R. L. (1961). The origin of form perception. *Scientific American,* 204, May, 66–72.

Freitag, E. (1973). *Arnold Schönberg in selbstzengnissen und bilddokumenten.* Reinbek/Hamburg: Rowohlt Taschenbuch Verlag.

_____. (1978). Expressionism and Schoenberg's self-portraits, pp. 164–172. In *Journal of the Arnold Schoenberg Institute,* 2, 3, June.

Gardner, W. H. (1953). *Gerard Manley Hopkins: A selection of his poems and prose.* Baltimore: Penguin Books.

Gay, P. (1976). *Art and act: On causes in history—Manet, Gropius, Mondrian.* New York: Harper & Row (Icon Editions).

Goldscheider, L. (1937). *Five hundred self-portraits.* Vienna: Phaidon.

Gross, C. G., & Bornstein, M. H. (1978). Left and right in science and art. *Leonardo,* 2, 1, Winter, 29–38.

The Solomon R. Guggenheim Museum, New York. (1971). *Piet Mondrian 1872–1944* (centennial exhibition).

Heckscher Museum, Huntington, NY. (1979). *As we see ourselves: Artists' self-portraits.*

Herrera, H. (1983). *Frida: A biography of Frida Kahlo.* New York: Harper & Row.

Hyman, S. E. (1948). *The armed vision: A study in the methods of modern literary criticism.* New York: Alfred A. Knopf.

Jaffe, I. B. (1980). *The sculpture of Leonard Baskin.* New York: The Viking Press (A Studio Book).

Jobes, G. (1961). *Dictionary of mythology, folklore & symbols.* New York: The Scarecrow Press.

Internationale Jugendbibliothek, Munich. (1952). *Ich selbst, myself, moi-même: Kinderselbstportraits aus aller welt.*

Journal of the Arnold Schoenberg Institute. (1978). Issue title: Schoenberg as artist. Vol. 2, No. 3, June, 163–255. Catalogue of Schoenberg's works pp. 189–231.

Jung, C. G. (1969). *The archetypes of the collective unconscious.* Princeton, NJ: Princeton University Press (Bollingen Series XX:9.1).

Kagan, J. (1968). The many faces response. *Psychology Today,* 1, January, 22–27;60–61.

_____. (1978). *The growth of the child: Reflections on human development.* New York: Norton.

Kellogg, R. (1969). *Analyzing children's art.* Palo Alto, CA: Mayfield.

Kinneir, J. (Ed.). (1980). *The artist by himself: Self-portrait drawings from youth to old age.* New York: St. Martin's Press.

Galerie Louise Leiris, Paris. (1972). *Picasso: 172 dessins en noir et en couleurs.*

Levinson, D. J., et al. (1978). *The seasons of a man's life.* New York: Alfred A. Knopf.

220

Levy, A. (1976). The Rembrandt research project: Old myths, new methods. *Art News,* 75, September, 34–42.

Lidz, T. (1968). *The person: His development throughout the life cycle.* New York: Basic Books.

Masciotta, M. (1955). *Portraits d'artistes par eux-mêmes du XIVe au XXe siècle.* Milan: Electa Editrice.

Meltzoff, A. N., & Moore, M. K. (1977). Imitation of facial and manual gestures by human neonates. *Science,* 198, 75–78.

The Metropolitan Museum of Art, New York. (1972). *Portrait of the artist.*

National Academy of Design, New York. (1983). *Artists by themselves: Artists' portraits from the National Academy of Design.*

Needham, R. (Ed.). (1973). *Right and left: Essays on dual symbolic classification.* Chicago: University of Chicago Press.

Neumann, E. (1955). *The great mother: An analysis of the archetype.* Princeton, NJ: Princeton University Press (Bollingen Series XLVII).

O'Connor, F. V. (1969). *Federal support for the visual arts: The New Deal and now.* Greenwich, CT: The New York Graphic Society.

———— (Ed.). (1972). *The New Deal art projects: An anthology of memoirs.* Washington: Smithsonian Institution Press.

————. (1979) Albert Berne and the completion of being: Images of vitality and extinction in the last paintings of a ninety-six-year-old man, pp. 255–289. In Van Tassel, D. (Ed.), *Aging, death and the completion of being.* Philadelphia: University of Pennsylvania Press.

————. (1980). Jackson Pollock: The black pourings, pp. 1–25. In Institute of Contemporary Art, Boston. *Jackson Pollock: The black pourings—1951 to 1953*

O'Connor, F. V., & Thaw, E. V. (Eds.). (1978). *Jackson Pollock: A catalogue raisonné of paintings, drawings and other works.* 4 Vols. New Haven, CT: Yale University Press.

Panofsky, E. (1955a). *The life and art of Albrecht Dürer.* Princeton, NJ: Princeton University Press.

————. (1955b). *Meaning in the visual arts.* Garden City, NY: Doubleday (Anchor Books).

Parker, E. (1960). *The seven ages of woman.* Baltimore: The Johns Hopkins University Press.

Pope-Hennessy, J. (1966). *The portrait in the Renaissance.* New York: Pantheon Books (Bollingen Series XXXV:12).

Rank, O. (1971). *The double: A psychoanalytic study.* Chapel Hill: University of North Carolina Press.

Reich, W. (1971). *Schoenberg: A critical biography.* London: Longman Group Ltd.

Rubin, W. (1980). *Pablo Picasso: A retrospective.* New York: The Museum of Modern Art.

Rosenberg, J. (1948). *Rembrandt: Life and work.* Cambridge, MA: Harvard University Press.

Schiff, G. (1983). *Picasso: The last years, 1963–1973.* New York: George Braziller (in association with the Grey Art Gallery & Study Center, New York University).

Seuphor, M. (1956). *Piet Mondrian: Life and work.* New York: Harry N. Abrams.

Sheehy, G. (1976). *Passages: Predictable crises of adult life.* New York: E. P. Dutton.

Stein, E. (1965). *Arnold Schoenberg letters.* New York: St. Martin's Press.

221   Stuckenschmidt, H. H. (1978). *Arnold Schoenberg: His life, world, and work*. New York: Schirmer.

Sze, W. C. (1975). *Human life cycle*. New York: Jason Aronson.

Thompson, S. (1955–58). *Motif-index of folk literature: A classification of narrative elements*. . . . 6 Vols. Bloomington: Indiana University Press.

Trevarthen, C. (1979). Communication and cooperation in early infancy: A description of primary intersubjectivity, pp. 321–347. In Bullowa, 1979.

Tymms, R. (1949). *Doubles in literary psychology*. Cambridge: Cambridge University Press.

Varley, D. (1976). *Seven: The number of creation*. London: G. Bell & Sons.

Welsh, R. P. (1971). Mondrian and Theosophy, pp. 35–51. In *Piet Mondrian: 1872–1944*. New York: The Solomon R. Guggenheim Museum.

Whitechapel Art Gallery, London. (1982). *Frida Kahlo & Tina Modotti*.

Wildenstein's, New York. (1976). *Modern portraits: The self and others*.

Wright, C. (1982). *Rembrandt: Self-portraits*. New York: The Viking Press (A Studio Book).

Section Three   Sculpture

Laurie Wilson,
Ph.D.

Louise Nevelson, the Star and her Set; Vicissitudes of Identification

Louise Nevelson, the celebrated American sculptress, has achieved renown in the past 30 years for her large enigmatic structures built from various materials including wood, metal and plastic (see Fig. 1). Nevelson has always proclaimed that her work has no meaning, and she and her critics have asked the audience to accept it on purely formal grounds. I have argued elsewhere that Nevelson's work is rich in iconographic meaning (Wilson, 1981) and propose here to add to that argument. Traditionally in art historical studies an iconographic approach implied the search for meaning of particular works of art in the cultural, religious, and intellectual milieu of the artist. Thus a local preacher's or philosopher's text might be a key to the understanding of an otherwise obscure set of images. Or, seemingly mundane images of flora and fauna in the background of a religious painting might actually have as their principal purpose reference to specific saintly qualities. A well-known example is the emergence of young leaves and branches in barren landscapes or from dead tree stumps which is frequently found as a reference to faith in Christ's resurrection.

As the artist's world has changed, so have iconographic studies. It has always been true that individual artists working within historical and cultural contexts bring a personal psychological meaning to their work. However, as the cultural context for art has become both less homogeneous and less structured, artists have been enabled and forced to rely more on idiosyncratic sources to give meaning to their formal productions. It is therefore not surprising to find a burgeoning of psychological studies of artists in the past half century.

Fig. 1. Louise Nevelson, *Total Totality—All.* 1964. Painted wood. Photo Courtesy of the Pace Gallery, New York.

An artist's self-image is inextricably tied to the products he creates. I believe this factor has considerable significance for Nevelson, an artist with a reputation as a dramatic individual whose very life is a work of art. She has stated repeatedly that the viewer's reaction to her work is incidental and that she has created it for herself alone. We might understand this to mean that unlike most artists whose narcissistic needs are gratified by an audience's response to their work, Nevelson's gratification must be sought in the more immediate response to her actual person. Thus the sculptural walls serve as a backdrop or stage set for the artist who is at once performer and beautiful woman meriting adulation and applause.

Many, if not most, artists are considered self-centered and place more importance on their relationship to their work than to their family and friends. A number of psychoanalytic observers have explained this phenomenon by describing the intense perceptual sensibilities of the artist. This heightened sensitivity results in the very strong attraction that the perceptual world of objects can hold for the artist—rivaling the pull of relations with human beings who can so easily prove to be disappointing (Greenacre,

1957; Eissler, 1961). However much this may be true for Nevelson, there are additional features that mark her almost hermetic relationship to her work and the world she has created with it.

By exploring Nevelson's identification with her mother and with a series of women whose outstanding visual appearance marked them as different, we can learn something of Nevelson as an artist. An examination of Nevelson's interest and experience in the performing arts is also illuminating, particularly as related to her development as a visual artist.

Nevelson has often proclaimed her closeness to her mother and her identification with her. "If my mother told me to jump out of the window, I would jump. She was the closest thing in my life" (L. Nevelson, personal communication, July 19, 1977).

Nevelson's mother, Minna Berliawsky, was a poor farmer's daughter and grew up in a tiny village on the Dnieper River in Russia. According to her daughter Louise, she married Isaac Berliawsky with great reluctance at a very young age and was forced to leave her entire family when her husband sent for her to join him in America in 1904. During her two last years in Russia, while her husband was finding his way in the coastal town of Rockland, Maine, Mrs. Berliawsky lived with her young children in her parents' home, and the final separation from them seems to have been a trauma from which she never recovered. Arriving in America, she became chronically depressed and almost an invalid. She was frequently confined to bed with undiagnosable symptoms, and her children remember her crying for years about the mother she would never see again. No medical care seemed to affect her severe headaches and backaches (A. Berliawsky, personal communication, July 12, 1976).

Adding to her sense of isolation was the anti-Semitic atmosphere in Rockland. There were very few activities in which she could participate, because a woman's life outside the house in this New England town was centered in the church. Participation in Jewish communal life was made difficult by the location of the Berliawsky home at the opposite end of town from most of the Jewish families. She had no close friends and stayed mostly at home, tending house and caring for her children.

However, in the light of her very provincial background, she had several unusual characteristics. Most striking to her son and three daughters was her sense of style and fashion. Fastidious in her selection of clothes, she would buy the highest quality and often the most expensive dress and hat available in Rockland or Boston and then preserve it in perfect condition for many years. Preparing for her infrequent forays into the main part of Rockland, she would spend many hours dressing, and the final stunning effect earned for her a reputation as one of the most beautiful women in town.

Nevelson's devotion to her mother obscured an objective understanding of her, but had lasting effects on both her life and work. She recalled her mother's unhappiness and credited it to an inability to adjust to American life and her marriage to a man she did not love:

I adored my mother. She was a brilliant woman, and she was a most beautiful woman. When we were growing up in Rockland, she dressed like for New York. She used to rouge her face and everything when they didn't do it. She brought that from the Old World. She had a great flair. But I knew she was very unhappy. She was so ill-adjusted and was so beautiful that I never shed a tear when she passed away. I never felt that she was happy on earth. I never saw her happy. But I always felt so sympathetic to her that I was determined to open every front door. . . and to walk right through the door. I didn't care if I had to build the house myself (MacKown, 1976, pp. 10–13).

Minna Berliawsky's inability to adjust to America must have rendered her unavailable in many ways to her daughters and forced them to find adult models outside the house. In her earliest years in school Louise developed an attachment to her art teacher, Miss Cleveland, who became her staunchest supporter and ultimately her friend and ego ideal. Miss Cleveland encouraged Louise, telling her that she would be a great artist, and spurring her on to win competitions in the school art classes and frequently announcing to the class that Louise Berliawsky would make a name for herself as an artist. As Nevelson recalled in her autobiography:

So I loved this particular teacher. Her name was Miss Cleveland, and she came from Camden. I think she also went to Pratt. A woman about fifty-five. Never married. Conventionally she certainly wasn't beautiful, she was an old maid and behaved like it, yet she had something that no one around me had. She was gracious. And what appealed to me even then was, she had a beautiful purple hat and purple coat. For Rockland, that was something (MacKown, 1976, pp. 24–25).

In spite of her avowed intention throughout high school to go to New York and become an artist, Nevelson surprised her family after graduation at 18 years of age by deciding to marry Charles Nevelson, a wealthy and refined shipping merchant from New York.

Louise's father was an enterprising, highly ambitious, and moderately prosperous real estate contractor and lumber merchant who loved music and was sensitive to art. Both parents had great hopes for their children's advancement in America and provided their three daughters with whatever cultural opportunities were available in Rockland—piano, violin, and voice lessons. Louise, the shy, artistically inclined daughter, had been encouraged to attend art school in New York after high school in 1918. By marrying Charles Nevelson and moving with him to New York she had instead entered a life of ease and wealth.

Nevelson immediately began to study voice and soon added private painting lessons to her pursuits. However, Charles Nevelson's set standards of "correct" behavior weighed heavily upon his wife, who had grown up with considerable freedom of expression. Furthermore, the birth of a son, Michael, in 1922, severely restricted the young woman's opportunities for self-expression until the child reached school age.

Nevelson was ready to respond to an opportunity that offered some narcissistic gratification for her growing need. This opportunity came in the form of an excursion into the world of theater—an apt foray in view of Nevelson's long-standing outspoken interest in appearances and façade:

> I always had a flair for clothes and liked them because I have a whole feeling about appearance. Because I think you very carefully can identify a person by their appearance. It's important. It's not skin deep, it's much deeper.

> I'm a great believer in a person who presents themselves, not too consciously, but that they feel right about their appearance. . . But the point is, when I go to a party or I'm invited someplace, I project something. For me clothes and presentation of self is a projection of a total personality (MacKown, 1976, p. 187).

Conscious of her own strikingly handsome appearance, and never forgetting her mother's beauty, Nevelson continued to be fascinated by beautiful and dramatic women, with whom she identified. Such was the case with the Princess Norina Matchabelli whom she placed next to Greta Garbo as one of the two most beautiful women she'd ever seen (L. Nevelson, personal communication, January 8, 1976). Her admiration for these two women extended to their sense of fashion. Both were famous for wearing large hats, and Nevelson adopted and continued this characteristic until long after it was out of fashion. She was known by many people in the art world as "the Hat," and most recollections of her begin with a description of her large, floppy Garbo hats (A. Walinska, personal communication, June 25, 1976). We can see that Nevelson's identification with celebrated women offered her an ego ideal that not only fit her grandiose wishes and fantasies but also served to compensate for her disappointment with her mother.

Both Matchabelli and Garbo had earned their fame as actresses, and during the 1920s when for three years she studied acting with Princess Matchabelli, Nevelson seems to have contemplated such a career for herself. Matchabelli had originally achieved recognition in the part of the Madonna in Max Reinhardt's production of *The Miracle* in London. She later married Prince George Matchabelli, and came to the United States in 1924 to recreate the Madonna role in a revival of *The Miracle.* This venture ended in humiliation and she soon found herself stranded in New York with a husband whose fortunes had declined and whose resistance to her resumption of a theatrical career seemed to have been justified. It is easy to imagine Nevelson identifying with the older, more sophisticated princess, since her situation at this time was similar.

Feeling constrained by family life and both socially and culturally inferior to her husband's family and circle of friends, Nevelson responded eagerly to studying with Matchabelli and stayed with her for three years, although the only performances that resulted from these studies were the public productions put on by Matchabelli's class.

Soon Nevelson's strongest cultural interests came to be the theater and voice, and her sisters felt that had she been allowed freer rein by her husband, she would have had a career on the stage. Her husband's jealousy and somewhat rigid notions of wifely duties led him to discourage most of her attempts to pursue seriously any creative career (L. Mildwoff and A. Berliawsky, personal communication, July 13, 1976).

After Nevelson completed her period of study with Matchabelli, she started art classes at the Art Students League in 1929 at age 29 and began a serious pursuit of an artistic vocation. At the league she studied with Kenneth Hayes Miller and Kimon Nicolaides, from whom she heard about the German painter Hans Hofmann. She recalls learning that he was the only person who could explain and teach Cubism, Picasso, and Matisse (Glimcher, 1976).

Having determined to go to Munich in the fall of 1931, Nevelson first returned to Rockland with her nine-year-old son. Her family agreed to finance the trip and care for her son while she was away.

She began to attend the small, daily drawing classes at Hofmann's school in Munich. She recalls that Hofmann paid attention only to the students who could help him with his plans for immigration to the United States. Being ignored was discouraging enough, but Hofmann added a more devastating blow. He asked Nevelson to leave the class, telling her that she would not only never be a great artist, but that she would never be an artist (L. Mildwoff and A. Berliawsky, personal communication, July 13, 1976; L. Mildwoff, personal communication, July 14, 1976).

Evidently, after Hofmann's rebuff, Nevelson turned again to singing and acting. In Munich she had been spending her evenings in cafés and night clubs and was frequently invited to sing the then-popular American songs: spirituals, jazz, and ballads. Her talents were soon recognized and she was offered opportunities for a movie career by theater friends from the cafés. Seeing this as the means of earning her passage home, she played small parts in Munich in the winter of 1931–32. Her brief experience as an extra in German movies had not been satisfying for Nevelson because so much time was spent passively waiting for directions. She recalls that she would have preferred the role of creator-director (L. Nevelson, personal communication, July 19, 1977). However, that experience had restored her confidence and she traveled on to Italy and Paris, and then home.

Within a year Nevelson separated from her husband, sent her son to be raised by her parents in Maine, and set herself up in a studio, determined to achieve success as an artist.

It is interesting to note the oscillations that occurred in the early years of Nevelson's development as an artist. After devoting several years to theater and meeting obstacles there, she turned to the visual arts. Three years later, meeting frustration in Hofmann's class, she turned back to being a performer. Not satisfied with less than star billing, however, she returned again to making visible products—paintings and eventually sculpture.

We can see that when Nevelson was frustrated in her efforts to be a star and the center of attention through the presentation of her bodily self to the observer, she turned to a career of producing objects that could be exhibited and admired. When these representations of the artist's self were not appreciated, she again presented her bodily self to the audience. Following a second disappointment in that area, she made her decisive step toward life as an artist—leaving husband and family and embarking on a career that would eventually allow a resolution of the conflict represented in her alternating choice of self or self-representation to be exhibited to the world for approval.

Dance

Although Nevelson never again involved herself in any organized theatrical activity, she did embark on a 20-year study of dance and movement shortly after her return to New York. Her experience in dance as both participant and observer has had significant effect on her work.

In the late 1920s and early 1930s dance in America was undergoing a revolution. The pioneers of the modern movement had thrown off the fetters of both the balletic tradition and the exotic manner of Denishawn. Martha Graham, Doris Humphrey, Charles Weidman, Helen Tamiris, and Edwin Strawbridge were developing and presenting to a small but wildly enthusiastic audience their new vision of a dance with freedom to explore and express the "drives, desires and reactions of alive human beings," unencumbered by decorative conventions (Sorell, 1967). Some of the most ardent supporters of the new directions in dance were the visual artists, particularly those based in New York, who had the greatest opportunity to observe and participate in the new art forms.

The large number of exhibitions devoted to dance and theater at the Museum of Modern Art during the 1940s indicates the intense interest in this field. Eighteen shows between 1940 and 1948 illustrated, described, and generally educated the museum-going public about these two performing arts. Nevelson recalls in her autobiography:

And at that time dance was a vital force. It was like dance was carrying America at that time. Martha Graham, by the nature of her spirit, by the nature of her energy, by her presence and intensity, reflected our times. Graham was undoubtedly movement of the twentieth century. She was a pioneer (MacKown, 1976, p. 67).

Nevelson's enthusiasm for modern dance inspired her not only to attend dance concerts weekly, but also to take up the study of this new art form. It was not the mastery of technique that intrigued her, but rather the promise of freedom that modern dancers held out to their devotees. Fundamental to all modern dance is this concept of freedom which developed partly in reaction to the rigidly formal balletic tradition and partly in response to the individualistic philosophy inherent in the new form. "Modern dance in its strongest impulses looks within the individual whose expressive needs then determine the types of gesture that will emerge when the dancer starts to move" (McDonagh, 1976, p. 1).

It was no accident, then, that Graham was Nevelson's favorite among the pioneers, for she perceived this devoutly serious dancer as someone who, unlike herself, had never compromised in her pursuit of personal freedom and artistic achievement. In an interesting lapse of memory, Nevelson once stated: "It takes a Martha Graham who never married and never had children to control her body. . . ." In fact, Graham did marry at mid-career, the first man she included in her company—Erick Hawkins (McDonagh, 1975). Graham's total devotion to her work was legendary and had been noted by her colleagues and teachers at Denishawn. Her marriage to Hawkins enhanced rather than interrupted Graham's career. Hawkins proved to be an able teacher, administrator, and fund-raiser, and their liaison inspired some of her greatest pieces: *Deaths and Entrances, Appalachian Spring, Cave of the Heart,* and *Night Journey.*

However great was Nevelson's admiration for Graham, she selected for herself a very different sort of teacher—Ellen Kearns, a woman whom she met through Diego Rivera and John Flannagan in 1932. Kearns had studied and worked with Edwin Strawbridge, had also been trained in physical movement, and was a skillful masseuse. In her classes she taught students to relate body movement to expressive emotional content, attempting to free them both physically and psychologically (MacKown, 1976).

Kearns seems to have been a combination dance teacher, dance therapist, and spiritual advisor. Some of her ideas appear to have deeply impressed Nevelson, Kearns's student, assistant, and personal friend for 20 years. Much of Kearns's teaching came out of Eastern philosophy and concerned the dualism of flesh and spirit: "By way of the glorification and the spiritualization of the flesh, man may achieve oneness with the divinity within himself, and so with the divine life of the world. The body reflects the spirit." The aim of her method was to arouse or release the "flow of rhythm" that is contained within the body. "The mind must be trained to relax, renounce, and abandon itself to the pattern. Only then will the unscheduled, unplanned. . . come into being and use the body to express its own fulfillment, peace, poise, and joy" (Howard, 1974, pp. 15–16). These ideas would have appealed strongly to Nevelson, with her grandiose wishes. Mary Farkas, a fellow Kearns student during the late 1930s, described the classes and remembers Nevelson's participation as follows:

> Classes were small and the students frequently stayed for many years working both individually and with Ellen in groups. Louise was a serious student and benefited very much. She became much freer. She had an interesting body, rather like what we used to think of as modern sculpture at that time—very heavy—not fat—sort of an earthy quality. Many of the movements which were done were very deep to the ground and Louise was very good at that (M. Farkas, personal communication, August 17, 1976).

Nevelson also recalls the personal benefits that her study of dance seemed to provide:

> I became aware of every fiber, and it freed me, so that if I pick up a cup, or if I put on something—that livingness is all with the same kind of thinking that I put in my work. Now this was all new to me—modern dancing and the vitality. And I question whether I'd have had the energy I have without studying with her [and feel] that we can tap and regenerate our own energy. I think physical activity can be a great source of intelligence. Modern dance certainly makes you aware of movement and that moving from the center of the being is where we generate and create our own energy (MacKown, 1976, pp. 65–66).

Because Nevelson began her extended period of study with Kearns in 1933, while she, at 33, was floundering in both her personal and artistic life, it is likely that these studies had a profound and lasting effect on the development of her philosophy and upon the nature of her work. It is even possible that this intense concentration on her own body and its movements in space was an important factor in her decision to turn to sculpture, which might be seen as the concrete residue and tracing of the temporary positions taken by the body as it moves through space. Several of Nevelson's pieces done in the late 1930s or early 1940s are examples of this notion (see *Dancer,* c. 1944 [Fig. 2]). Mike Nevelson confirmed this hypothesis when he said that the sculpture his mother made in the 1930s and early 1940s was consciously derived from her studies with Kearns (M. Nevelson, personal communication, July 29, 1977).

The many years of study that Nevelson devoted to dance and dramatics were primarily dedicated to her own personal and spiritual growth rather than to the development of marketable skills. Thus, it was generally only in the privacy of her home that she performed, often with her assistant, Ted Hazeltine (L. Mild-

Fig. 2. *Dancer.* c. 1944. Plaster or bronze. Whereabouts unknown.

woff, personal communication, July 14, 1976). It is not difficult to see in retrospect that the spiritual goals inherent in the teachings of Matchabelli and Kearns found their way into Nevelson's sculpture and into her understanding of the creative process. Her conception that the glorification of self was the primary aim in life and art was an idea catalyzed by Kearns's exhortation that her students must get in touch with the divinity within themselves.

We have seen that when Nevelson's need for exhibitionistic display of her bodily self was frustrated, she turned to the creation of art work. Now we can better understand how she came to identify with the concrete products of her labors. A private exploration of her body in movement lasting over several decades can be linked to the simultaneous exploration occurring in her artistic development. Discoveries in one arena are made visible in another in part through the psychological mechanisms of displacement and projection.

In the 1940s European Surrealism, including the Surrealist penchant for self-dramatization, became a prominent influence in the New York art world. Nevelson's years of studying drama and dance encouraged her receptivity to the notion of the self-dramatizing artist. That aspect was evident in her first thematically titled show, "Circus: The Clown is the Center of His World," in 1943.

The placement of the clown (an arch-Surrealist subject in itself) as the central focus of the exhibit may be seen as a glorification of the performer who not only sets the stage, but is the principal presence within it. Nevelson, in seeing herself as the central figure of this circus, may also have been remembering Graham's very successful recent dance, *Every Soul is a Circus*. Making herself empress of the arena, Graham satirized the character of a silly woman who has difficulty choosing between two men. Both Nevelson and Graham included in these works figures who represent spectators as well as performers (McDonagh, 1975). In Nevelson's show the spectators are put together in a composite piece called *Audience Figure* (Fig. 3).

The next self-image that Nevelson placed at the center of an exhibit is *The Bride of the Black Moon* (Fig. 4), a piece in the show "Ancient Games, Ancient Places" in 1955. That she perceived herself to be *The Bride* is confirmed by the fact that she willingly accepted that appellation in letters from friends at the time (D. Smith, personal communication, June 21, 1977). In the instance of this exhibition, the titles of several pieces suggest the importance of dance (and Graham in particular) as influential for Nevelson. Nevelson's continuing discomfort about her personal life, and the difficulties and uncertainties of being above all other things a professional artist, stimulated in her a great curiosity about the personal and professional lives of prominent American women, particularly those in the arts. Her admiration for Graham was enormous and, having followed closely Graham's career from the 1920s, she would have been alert to any important developments, either personal or professional.

In 1940, after two years of collaboration, Graham began living with Hawkins, her partner in the many pieces she designed around their relationship. These works, which explore both the joy and pain inherent in the subject, include *Appalachian Spring* (1944), *Dark Meadow* (1946), *Cave of the Heart* (1946), and *Night Journey* (1947). In 1948 Hawkins and Graham were married, and by 1950 they had separated. For 10 years Graham had lived with Hawkins, a man 14 years her junior.

Although he had choreographed some dances while a member of the Graham company, Hawkins did not produce his first truly independent pieces until 1952 when he did a concert of three new dances at the Hunter Playhouse. The first of these was entitled *The Bridegroom of the Moon,* and the set was designed by Louise Bourgeois. Hawkins had been moved by Bourgeois's looming, vertical wood pieces which he had seen at her exhibtion in 1950 at the Peridot Gallery in New York. Nevelson, a good friend of Louise Bourgeois's since at least 1944, would have been likely to attend this dance program designed by the former husband of one

Fig. 3. *Audience Figure*. 1942–43. Wood and metal. Destroyed.

Fig. 4. *Bride of the Black Moon*. 1955. Wood, painted wood and fabric. Destroyed.

of the women she most admired. Surely the similarity of her titles—*The Bride of the Black Moon*—cannot be accidental. The unattainable moon serves equally as spouse for Hawkins and Nevelson.

The theme of Nevelson's next show at the Grand Central Moderns Gallery, *Royal Voyage* (Fig. 5), may also be related to a Martha Graham work. In 1947 Graham choreographed one of her most famous dances, *Night Journey*. The theme of this piece centers on Queen Jocasta's discovery of her true relationship to Oedipus and her consequent suicide. In 1953 Graham introduced a new work, *Voyage,* which was basically an erotic frolic with three men a great deal younger than she was.

Nevelson's *Royal Voyage* is ostensibly a trip to unknown lands by way of the sea. However, the presence of a king and queen suggests that the theme of the exhibition may not be so distant from that of Graham's dance. At the very least, Nevelson placed herself in a starring role in both this and the previous show and, as in Graham's work, the female characters carry more weight and substance than do the male. Nevelson's personification of herself as the queen was confirmed in a recent interview in which she

Fig. 5. *Royal Voyage.* 1956. Painted wood. (Grand Central Moderns Gallery installation, *Queen* in center.)

also related her childhood dreams of glory to placing herself at the center of her work (L. Nevelson, personal communication, July 19, 1977).

The exhibition in which Nevelson's interest in the performing arts was clearly revealed was *Moon Garden + One* (Fig. 6). Until this exhibition the evidence of such an interest was subtle or indirect, probably the result of its not being consciously perceived by the artist. But in *Moon Garden* these influences coalesced in such a way as to turn the installation into a theatrical setting.

For *Moon Garden + One* (1958), Nevelson covered an entire wall of the Grand Central Moderns Gallery with black boxes piled to the ceiling. Narrow vertical boxes of various sizes stood against adjacent gallery walls like ominous specters. Some pieces were positioned on decorated pedestals in the center of the room, but black-stained wood reliefs enclosed in boxes with and without lids made up the majority of the works in the show. Nevelson originally wished to use no lights at all, but the ingenious solution of the gallery's owner, Edwin Barrie, prevailed several hours before the opening. Sympathetic to the effect she was seeking, Barrie suggested colored light, and demonstrated by throwing a

Fig. 6. *Moon Garden + One.* 1958. Painted wood. (Grand Central Moderns Gallery installation.)

blue scarf over a lamp. Nevelson acceded and the installation was lit with a small number of blue lights.

This theatrical solution clearly suited the artist's intentions. Once the pieces had been set in their final arrangement and the lighting determined, the 58-year-old Nevelson and her assistant, Ted Hazeltine, proceeded to do what they did frequently at home at the end of a day's work—they danced. On this occasion, she removed her blouse and the two of them did what seemed like a ritual dance in front of the sculpture.

This exhibition represented a critical point in the artist's development. With this dramatic exhibition, Nevelson's style was finally established after 30 years of experimentation. Not only was it Nevelson's first use of sculptural walls, but it was the first exhibition that brought her celebrity as well as critical acclaim. Illustrated articles in *Life* and *Time* magazines brought her to the attention of a wide public.

And here we must address one of the most enigmatic aspects of Nevelson's psychology—her professed, and possibly actual, indifference to the audience's reaction. About *Moon Garden + One* she has said: "It was not really for an audience; it was really for my visual eye. It was a feast—for myself" (MacKown, 1976, p. 133). When asked about the pleasure her work gives to others she responds: "There's no room in my life for other people or to please anyone. Trying to find myself is a full time job" (L. Nevelson, personal communication, January 8, 1976).

It seems that the work itself is a mute witness to the artist's performance, both during its production and afterward as she dances or gestures before it in the darkness. What does this mean for Nevelson? Do the objects stand in for the world of human beings who could never sufficiently gratify the artist's needs, beginning with her chronically depressed mother, her unhappy marriage, and continuing throughout her life in her inability or unwillingness to establish lasting loving relationships? By producing her own objects, the artist gains control over the child's sense of helplessness in relation to people. May we not also see a condensation of motives in the production of sculptured walls which can be observed by an audience and simultaneously can serve as audience and setting for their producer—who can find her identity only in confrontation and proximity to her work? Nevelson's life and relationship to her work, as evidenced in her behavior and many statements, suggest an affirmative answer to all these questions.

References

Eissler, K. R. (1961). *Leonardo da Vinci: Psychoanalytic notes on the enigma.* New York: International Universities Press.

Glimcher, A. (1976). *Louise Nevelson.* New York: E. P. Dutton.

Greenacre, P. (1957). The childhood of the artist: Libidinal phase development and giftedness. *The Psychoanalytic Study of the Child,* 12: 47–72.

Howard, B. (1974). *Dance of the self: Movements for body, mind and spirit.* New York: Simon & Schuster.

MacKown, D. (1976). *Dawns and dusks: Louise Nevelson, taped conversations with Diana MacKown.* New York: Charles Scribner's Sons.

McDonagh, D. (1975). *Martha Graham: A biography.* New York: Praeger.

_____ (1976). *The complete guide to modern dance.* Garden City: Doubleday Co.

Sorrell, W. (1967). *The dance through the ages.* New York: Grosset & Dunlap.

Wilson, L. (1981). *Louise Nevelson: Iconography and sources.* New York: Garland Press.

Laurie
Schneider,
Ph.D.

The Theme of Mother and Child in the Art of Henry Moore

In Western art, many aspects of the mother-child relationship are evident in the iconography of the Madonna and Christ, including the conflation of majesty and infancy.[1] In the Middle Ages, artists typically presented the infant Christ as a majestic homunculus whose gestures and attitudes are aloof and imperious. He is babylike only in size and in location—on His mother's lap (Fig. 1). The Madonna, in such representations, becomes the literal throne of heaven and observes a similar royal distance from the spectator. With the dawn of Renaissance style, this emphasis changed and artists begin to call attention to Christ's humanity, as well as to His divinity, depicting Him as a winsome baby with normal bodily proportions and characteristics. Christ interacts with His mother as any human baby might, tugging at her veil, searching for her breast, even actively nursing. Almost invariably, however, these nursing Christ images turn to confront the spectator as they suckle. Although such imagery reflects the accurate observation of Renaissance artists, aware of the simultaneous curiosity and greediness of babies, the motif also serves another purpose. As Leo Steinberg (1983) pointed out, in this gesture, the Christ child calls our attention to the fact that, although divine, He shares our human nature and needs. Steinberg also noted that Renaissance artists often reinforced such references to Christ's divinity and to the symbolic nature of their imagery by portraying the Christ child engaged in activities too mature for His apparent chronological age—like eating grapes or slipping a ring on St. Catherine's finger.[2] In reality, a normal infant of this age could not eat grapes, nor would a conscientious mother permit him to

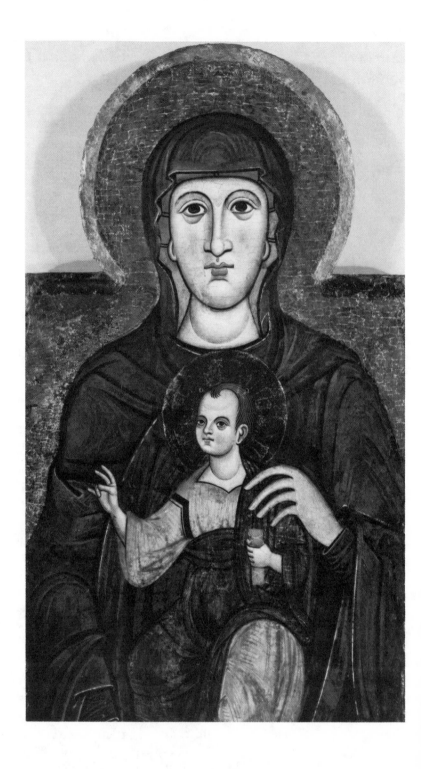

Fig. 1. Meliore Tuscano, *Madonna and Child Enthroned*. C. 1270. Tempera on panel. 32¼ by 18¾". The Art Institute of Chicago, Mr. and Mrs. Martin A. Ryerson collection. Photo: courtesy The Art Institute of Chicago.

do so. In an iconography such as this, the infant's activity combines normal orality with a symbolic reference to the Eucharist, uniting Christ's childhood with references to His eventual passion and death in a typical Christian condensation of time-reality differences and fusion of human-divine content.

This new Renaissance interest in physical reality mirrored a growing awareness of psychological implications, an awareness reflected in the greater formal and psychological freedom of the Madonna and the greater intimacy depicted between Madonna and Child. This development is evident, for example, in many paintings by Raphael and Titian. In Titian's *Madonna and Child* (London, National Gallery), Mary and the nursing Christ are portrayed as a single libidinal unit. Christ has lost the medieval qualities of kingship, assuming the physical and psychological character of a typical infant. Titian's painting also highlights the infant's dependence on the mother for food, support, and tactile stimulation.

But even these Renaissance achievements are often blurred by the simultaneous imposition of complex Christian symbolism, as in Masaccio's painting of the grape-eating Christ child. Often, too, Mary is depicted as a large, even voluminous form, a fact generally interpreted as a reference to her symbolic role as the Church.[3] From the psychological point of view, Mary's monumentality can also be seen as an unconscious projection of the infant's view of the mother as an imposing, powerful, magical figure. The architectural aspect of this symbolism has deep biological roots reflected in references to both Mary and the Church as "the House of God."

In the 19th century, the traditional representation of the Madonna-Child was supplanted by secularized images of the mother-child relationship from which all vestiges of symbolic references had been eradicated. Thus, Renoir's *Maternity* of 1885 (Paris, private collection) illustrates infantile oral dependence, as the baby nurses while simultaneously holding his toe. This gesture replaces the Renaissance symbolic allusions to Christ's assumption of the mortal coil with the more profane references to the infant's pleasure in eating and self-stimulation. Mary Cassatt's *Sleeping Baby* of 1890 (Dallas Museum of Fine Arts) portrays dependency in relation to the physical relaxation of sleep. In Christian art, on the other hand, the sleeping Christ child refers to the temporal condensation of His infancy and His death.

In summary, throughout the history of Western art, painters and sculptors have portrayed various aspects of infancy and childhood. Yet, the historical shift from regal aloofness and symbolic overlay towards greater emotional intimacy gathers momentum as the modern period approaches. The development of certain nonrepresentational styles in Europe and America in the early 20th century offered artists a new approach to the infant-mother relationship. Styles that minimize literary content provide an appropriate vehicle for dealing with the essentially preverbal quality of the early stages of infancy, and the very nature of abstraction permits the artist to free associate in a nondiscursive, rather than a verbal, way. The various nonobjective modern styles lend themselves more readily to depictions of inner psychological reality than those more representational styles whose conventions require formal boundary differentiations.

Henry Moore and Aspects of the Mother-Child Relationship

The coincidence of style and content in contemporary art is nowhere presented more convincingly than in the mother-child sculptures of Henry Moore. The fact that Moore's style typically expresses such characteristics as merging, flowing, and interrelationships of forms makes his work particularly suitable to such correlation. These sculptures suggest meanings that coincide with aspects of modern psychoanalytic researches and theories about the mother-child relationship, notably those of Winnicott (1965) and Mahler (1975).

The present discussion neither follows the chronology of the sculptures nor implies a connection between their chronology and the developmental stages implicit in them.[4] Nor does it suggest that Moore had any conscious intention of illustrating psychoanalytic theories or even possessed any knowledge of them. Rather, like many great geniuses, he demonstrates an astonishing perspicacity which enables him to portray fundamental emotional states and relationships with which we all resonate.

Moore himself is quite conscious of his passion for the mother-child motif, which he connects to his close attachment to his own mother. "From early on," he wrote, "I have had an obsession with the Mother-Child theme. It has been a universal theme from the beginning of time and some of the earliest sculptures we've found from the Neolithic Age are of a Mother and Child. I discovered, when drawing, I could turn every little scribble, blot or smudge into a Mother and Child. . . . I suppose it could be explained as a 'Mother complex'" (Moore & Hedgecoe, 1968, p. 61).

Moore's mother-child sculptures span his entire career, although he himself noted a revival of the theme following his daughter's birth in 1946. "A new experience," he said, "can bring to the surface something deep in one's mind" (Moore & Hedgecoe, 1968, p. 173). In the light of the sculptor's own statements, it does not seem too speculative to suggest that the new experience of fatherhood revived the artist's memories of his own parents and his early childhood experiences. Moore also connected the genesis of another sculpture, *the King and Queen* (Fig. 2) that he created in 1952–53 to his new paternal role. These royal figures, he explained, evolved from his habit of reading fairy tales peopled with kings and queens to his six-year-old daughter every night (Moore & Hedgecoe, 1968, p. 221). Does this work, like the artist's mother-child figures, revive aspects of his own childhood relationship with his parents, here presented as idealized, regal figures?

Moore portrays the normal symbiosis of infancy in various ways that illustrate his enormous capacity for creative identification. Symbiosis is represented literally in the *Mother and Child* of 1936 (Fig. 3). In this work, Moore implies the symbiotic relationship between mother and child by the smooth flow of planes between them. Just as the infant perceives himself as unindividuated from his mother, so, in this sculpture, mother and child are attached both through literal and formal lack of differentiation. Thus, the baby's arm and his mother's form a continuous, diagonally raised

surface; their bodies flow together as a concave indented plane, while below, the baby's legs repeat the form and movement of their arms.

Moore expresses a similar but more intense feeling of engulfment in a later work entitled *Internal–External Forms* (Fig. 4). Here, the embracelike enclosure of the external form is strongly suggestive of maternity. The artist consciously conceived this sculpture as a helmet or armored figure, although he also emphasized its metaphorical relationship with maternity. "These [i.e., *Internal–External Forms* and similar sculptures, such as the *Helmet* (Fig. 5)] are some of the helmets I did in 1939 in which the interior of the helmet is really a figure and the outside casing of it is like the armour by which it might be protected in battle" (Moore & Hedgecoe, 1968, p. 198).[5] But the physical and psychological protection of the helmet also reminded Moore of the mother-child relationship. "I suppose in my mind [the helmet] was also the Mother and Child idea and of birth and the child in the embryo. All these things are connected in this interior and external idea" (Moore & Hedgecoe, 1968, p. 198). The bird-like

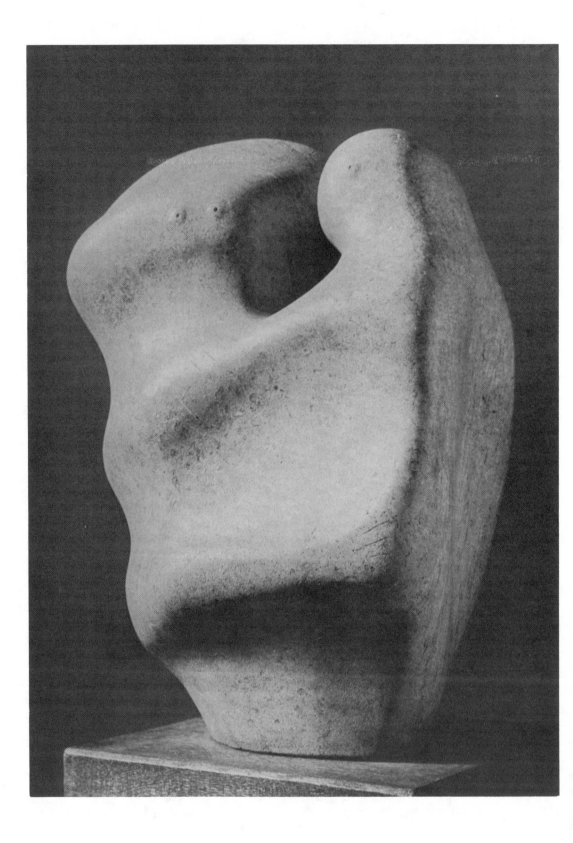

Fig. 4. *Internal–External Forms.* 1952–53. Bronze editions, 79″ high.

Fig. 3. *Mother and Child.* 1936. Ancaster stone, 20″ high. The British Council, London.

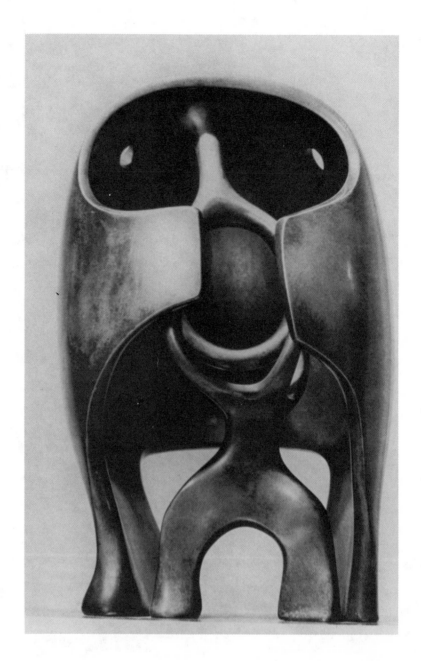

head and slight proportions of the enclosed figure in *Internal–External Forms* recall those of a developing fetus, while the upright poses and vertical planes of both figures simultaneously suggest those of a standing mother and child. The obvious metaphorical nature of this work permits a continuous interplay of associations on the mother-child theme. As such, it corresponds—on a more abstract level than Fig. 3—to the early symbiotic period in which the child still experiences himself as inseparable from the mother.[6]

249

In another variation on the infant-mother theme, Moore devoted a group of sculptures to representations of nursing, directly relating symbiosis to the breast. The *Suckling Child* of 1930 (Fig. 6) portrays the oral stage from the infant's point of view, when the baby's perception of the world depends on the efficiency of services rendered. As long as the service is satisfactory, according to Winnicott (1965), his "serene highness" barely notices his surroundings or, in Ferenczi's words (1956) his *entourage*. At this point, the child does not perceive his mother as separate from himself because he has not yet grasped the concept of personhood. Aware of the child's oral needs, Moore represents the mother as little more than a pair of breasts, positioned in a way that is convenient for his majesty's dinner. The child's lack of self-object boundaries is reflected both in his undifferentiated facial features and the sculptural merging of his form with the breast. The artist also depicts the determined concentration with which the hungry infant typically nurses as he leans over his mother's torso and grasps the breast between his hands.

Fig. 6. *Suckling Child.* 1930. Destroyed cast.

Similarly, in *Mother and Child on a Bench* (Fig. 7), the nursing infant focuses intently on the mother's breast, oblivious to all else Moore highlights the child's intense concentration in part through pose and gesture but mainly by contrast with the mother herself. While the child pulls down on one breast, the space that would normally be occupied by the other breast is hollowed out. The mother's right shoulder is exaggerated and seems to pull away toward the upper right. Her head echoes this movement as she turns away from the child, tilting her shoulder in the same direction. In this work, then, Moore humorously contrasts the mother's ambivalence toward the nursing situation with the child's single-minded absorption in it.

In an even more humorous variation on the same theme, Moore represents this distinction with open aggression in a unique sculpture of *Mother and Child* (Fig. 8). Though still symbiotically attached to his mother in the fusion of his legs with her thighs, the child attacks her breast and she withdraws, holding him off at the neck. But, at the same time, her head tilts toward the child and her breast stands erect as if in anticipation of the child's approach. The more aggressive mood of this sculpture, in contrast to the curvilinear softness of Fig. 6, is enhanced by the points and sharp edges with which Moore endowed it. The child's open, beaklike mouth, poised as if to snap at the expectant breast, is reminiscent of the early oral sadism attributed to infants by Melanie Klein.[7] This child, more than most in Moore's mother-child sculptures, exhibits aggressive qualities, not merely in the implied wish to eat but also in the formal design. The elongated neck, combined with the pointed head, suggests a hammer while much of the body (like that of the mother) is characterized by thin forms, sharpness and points. The mother's reaction combines ambivalence with anxiety, resulting in both psychological and artistic condensation. She echoes some of those very qualities which Klein (1960) attributed to the oral sadistic child whose character will be dominated by "sadism and ambivalence." By endowing the mother as well as the child with these qualities, Moore conflated the figures' forms with the emotions he has them portray.

Two mother-child sculptures of 1931 (Figs. 9 and 10) demonstrate the close relationship of baby to breast but without the sadism of Fig. 8. In Fig. 10, the child sits upright; his head replaces the mother's left breast and formally matches the right, so that her breast and the baby's head merge into a single, circular unit. In Fig. 9, on the other hand, the baby curls up in the

Fig. 7. *Mother and Child on a Bench* (detail). 1932. Green Hornton Stone, 35" high. Private collection, London.

Fig. 8. *Mother and Child.* 1953. Bronze editions, 8″ high.

Fig. 9. *Mother and Child.* 1931. Verde di prato stone, 8″ high. Private collection, Oxford, England.

mother's arms at about waist level so that his head and knee work as formal echoes of the mother's breasts. In both sculptures, the mother's embracing arms (cf. Mahler, 1975) position the baby in a comfortable and visually significant pose. The mother's entire upper torso assumes a nearly rectangular shape, enclosing the child and emphasizing his form. This framing device also focuses our attention on the psychological link between the child and the breast. In both these sculptures, the portions of the mother's body outside this enclosed rectangle seem relatively unimportant and undeveloped; in both, her lower limbs are absent altogether and her head seems disproportionately small. By these devices, Moore highlighted the interior of the rectangle as his primary focus, while simultaneously reaffirming the infant's perception of its mother as the primary source of oral satisfaction.[8]

In his sculptures, Moore often portrays the mother being differentiated along with her child. This becomes clear when one compares the *Mother and Child* shown in Figs. 11 and 12 with some of the sculptures discussed above. In Fig. 11, the child is still symbiotically attached to his mother, but their faces are

Fig. 11. *Mother and Child.* 1932. Carved concrete, 7″ high. Private collection, London.

differentiated and specific features are portrayed. The mother holds the child at shoulder level, relating his head to *her* head rather than to her breasts. In Fig. 12, too, even though the child is held at waist level and plays with his mother's breast, he is physically differentiated; his facial features, like his mother's, have been rendered individually.

Fig. 12. *Mother and Child*. 1930. Ham Hill stone, 31″ high. Private collection, New York.

Moore refers to the postsymbiotic mother-child attachment in three other sculptures in which the child assumes a vertical position but still functions formally and psychologically as an extension of the mother. In the *Mother and Child: Hollow* of 1959 (Fig. 13), the mother's torso—as in *Internal–External Forms* (Fig. 4)—is hollowed out in order to accommodate the child. She leans forward, her torso forming a slow curve against which the standing child leans his head. The vertical plane of the child's figure closes and visually concludes the mother's open form. Likewise, in a *Mother and Child* of 1938 (Fig. 14), the maternal form curves toward the standing child so that *his* vertical image stabilizes the sculpture. Here, the attachment is literal as the two figures are joined by a wedge. The wedge seems to penetrate to the other side of the child's body, forming a breastlike shape that implies fantasies of oral incorporation on his part.

The bronze sculpture, *Mother and Child Against an Open Wall* of 1956 (Fig. 15) presents an older, more individuated child, a fact reflected in the formal, physical differentiation of the child's body. Nevertheless, the artist referred to the child's continuing attach-

Fig. 13. *Mother and Child: Hollow.* 1959. Bronze editions, 12¼″ high.

ment to its mother in two ways—in the pose and gesture of each figure and in the background arrangement of bench and wall. Mother and child face one another with arms bent so that they share an intermediate space, indicating in a physical bond their psychological tie and its origin. Their spatial enclosure, in turn, is echoed by the curved planes of bench and wall.

Moore's use of an "open wall," an apparent contradiction in terms, is consistent with his predilection for employing forms moving in and out of unexpected spaces. It is also another example of the inside-outside theme characteristic of both the mother-child relationship and the creative process itself. The arrangement of the elements of the wall conforms to that of the mother and child; each figure is set against a circular opening and, at the same time, frames the solid part of the wall. Thus, in addition to its formal role, the "open wall" echoes the combined physical and psychological sense of transitional inside and outside found in the "good-enough" mother-child relationship.

Moore made a series of sculptures in the 1950s showing the mother and child indulging in active play. In these works, he represented the figures with long, thin, wiry proportions that reflect the activities in which they engage. One of these playful

Fig. 14.   *Mother and Child.* 1938. Elm-wood. Museum of Modern Art, New York.

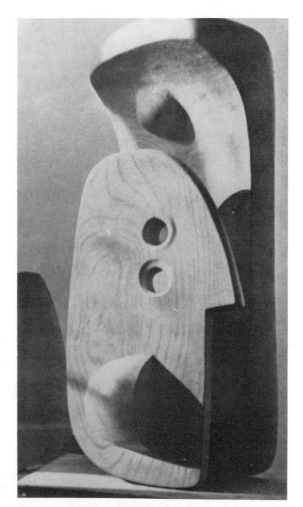

Fig. 15.   *Mother and Child against an Open Wall.* 1956–57. Bronze editions, 8″ high.

Fig. 16. *Rocking Chair #1.* 1950. Bronze editions, 5¾" high.

themes depicts a series of rocking mothers and babies. Moore began this series with *Rocking Chair #1* (Fig. 16) in which he fused the mother's body with the chair. Although formal problems dictated this solution, which counters and balances the active pose of the mother as she throws her head back and holds the child high in the air, Moore's treatment also recalls those traditional hieratic treatments of Madonna and Child in which the Virgin simultaneously serves as her Son's throne. Moore's rendition of the fused mother-chair also reflects his innate sensitivity to the stages of normal child development, including the imperious character of the infant, who seemingly regards his mother not only as his majesty's entourage, but also as his throne.

A Madonna and Child by Henry Moore

In traditional representations of the Madonna and Christ, Mary is often her Son's throne. This is most likely in early Christian, medieval, or Byzantine art, although even in the Renaissance and later the iconic nature of Mary and Christ may be retained.

In the 1940s Moore did a *Madonna and Child* for St. Matthew's Church in Northampton, England (Fig. 17). By his own assertion, this sculpture raised problems which he would not expect to encounter when making an anonymous mother and child. "The Northampton Madonna and Christ," he wrote, "was one of the most difficult and heart-searching sculptures that I ever tried to do. Possibly it is the only sculpture of mine that can be called a commission" (Moore & Hedgecoe, 1968, p. 159). Moore had to be pressured into doing a religious work, he went on, because even though the "Mother and Child theme is common to nearly half my work," he would not make an ordinary mother and child for a church and "call it a Madonna and Christ." He did many studies for the statue and showed them to various friends and critics to see if they were suitable. One of Moore's problems was the rendition of Christ "as an intellectual-looking child, that you could believe might have more of a future than just an ordinary baby."[9] This he has done, for, if one compares the head of Christ with the heads of Moore's other babies, it is obvious that Christ's

Fig. 17. *Madonna and Child*. 1943–44. Hornton stone, 59″ high. Church of St. Matthew, Northampton, England.

features are much more individuated. "The face of the Madonna," continues the artist, "has got a certain aloof mystery" (Moore & Hedgecoe, 1968, p. 160). Indeed, she stares off into an undefined space. In traditional Christian iconography, this attitude, as if looking into the future, is a standard reference to the Madonna's foreknowledge of the Crucifixion, an allusion Moore apparently also intended.

The relative differentiation of Moore's *Madonna and Child* makes the sculpture seem more old fashioned than those he did as many as 10 or 15 years earlier. Like the medieval homunculus, Christ is endowed with physiological development beyond his years. He sits upright and looks away from His mother onto the world, His kingdom. Furthermore, the spatial intimacy of mother and child that Moore usually expresses by having the two figures face each other is absent in this sculpture. As with a king, Christ's infancy belongs to the world rather than to his mother. The contrast between this sculpture and the anonymous mothers and children he produced highlights Moore's imaginative freedom when not working by commission. It is also possible that church patronage inhibited the artist's willingness to portray infantile sexuality. This effect is indicated by Moore's stated hesitation and need to consult others before deciding on the "suitability" of his work. As is true of traditional Christian art, Moore's *Madonna and Child* adds literary metaphor and symbol to the libidinal nature of the mother-child relationship.

As already noted, Moore has emphasized that his "obsession" with the mother-child theme determines much of his work. It is a theme to which he has continuously returned over the long span of his creative years. His ability to "turn every little scribble, blot or smudge into a Mother and Child" (Moore & Hedgecoe, 1968, p. 161) reflects the formal free association that is more characteristic of 20th century art than the art of the past. It is also more in tune with the preverbal essence of the mother-child relationship itself.

Moore recognized in himself the same associational ability in connection with the reclining figure, a theme (like that of mother and child) that can be traced back to the Neolithic era.

Moore also extended the interior-exterior theme which has often preoccupied him to the reclining figure where, either by separating the parts of the figure or by cutting holes out of it or both, he forces the viewer to look through the inside and out again onto the landscape. As in the mother-child theme, the reclining figures derive both from traditional iconographic convention and from Moore's personal proclivities. His intense observations of nature and organic form are well-documented; his particular fascination for the hole increases the three-dimensional quality of his work, and he has commented on his fascination with "the mystery of the hole," and "the mysterious fascination of caves in hillsides and cliffs."[10] The association of the reclining figure to earth and the mother is found in myth, religion, and literature as well as in art, and is literally represented in Moore's

Fig. 18. *Reclining Mother and Child.* 1960–61. Bronze editions, 86½" long.

outdoor reclining figures that blend into the real landscape. In describing a sculpture of a seated woman whose back view reminded him of his mother, Moore reminisced about rubbing his mother's back as a boy. "My mother's back meant a lot to me," he said (Moore & Hedgecoe, 1968, p. 328), echoing the role of the mother's body as the child's earliest landscape (Cf. Neumann, 1959).

In several sculptures, Moore extended the mother-child theme to include the reclining figure. "I have a particular liking for this *Reclining Mother and Child*" (1960–61, Fig. 18), he wrote. "This work combines several of my different obsessions in sculpture. There's the reclining figure idea; the mother and child idea; and the interior-exterior idea. So it is the amalgamation of many ideas in one sculpture" (Moore & Hedgecoe, 1968, p. 356).

Conclusion

The power of Moore's sculptures does not lie merely in his great skill in manipulating his materials to create awesome figurative configurations. While he offers such percepts, at the same time he presents us with a visual articulation of the laws of human nature—at least of a particular view of human nature. (For example, the idea of infantile oral sadism central to the theories of Melanie Klein, and which Moore's *Mother and Child,* Fig. 8, illustrates so beautifully, has by no means won universal acceptance among psychoanalysts.) Like other contemporary abstract figurationalists, Moore does not create a naturalistic world which mirrors the observer's actual perceptions. Rather, he portrays states of being, which he depicts with amazing psychological acuity. Although we do not possess detailed biographical information concerning Moore's childhood history, the artist himself insistently relates the various phases of his creativity to memories of his mother and their relationship. This suggests that she played a major role in stimulating his artistic development and honing his empathic abilities. In a metaphoric sense, then, she might be described as the throne upon which he has erected his majestic opus.

Notes

EDITOR'S NOTE: All photographs of works by Henry Moore reproduced with the permission of the Henry Moore Foundation.

1 In psychoanalysis, Freud (1914) articulated this identity by writing of "His Majesty, the baby." Several years later, D.W. Winnicott (1965) coined the phrase, the "good-enough mother" as a counterpart to the "royal" baby. Just as the parallels between majesty and baby are endless, so the "good-enough mother" is an entire royal household rolled into a single stock character. Who else but the "good-enough mother" keeps the royal bottom clean, changes the royal sheets, tends the royal wardrobe? Not to mention the royal troubadour who soothes the troubled brow and the court jester who keeps his majesty amused. At feeding time, who but king and baby has a resident food-taster and who else eats his fill, carelessly tossing scraps on the floor for the dogs and the "good-enough mother" to pick up?

Sandor Ferenczi's (1956) discussions of stages in the sense of reality development describe the child's growth from king to commoner. *The Period of Omnipotence by the Help of Magic Gestures* is that stage following the child's illusion of total omnipotence when he adds gestural language to the wish, thus maintaining his self-image as all-powerful (Ferenczi, 1956, p. 191). A little later, according to Ferenczi, "speech symbolism . . . gets substituted for gesture symbolism" (p. 195), still allowing the child his sense of omnipotence. Even at this stage, "the entourage," ever ready to serve, hastens to fulfill the child's "regal" demands as soon as possible. It is the task of the "good-enough mother" to ensure as smooth a transition as possible from infantile royal omnipotence to adult social reality.

2 Cf. Steinberg's figures 133 and 135 and the center panel of Masaccio's *Pisa Altarpiece*. Cf. also Ferenczi (1980, pp. 349–350), where he points to some typical instances of the conflation of childhood with advanced intelligence. Thus, at the age of 12, Christ astounded the doctors with

his wisdom. Ferenczi attributed this exaggerated childhood intelligence to a reversal of children's perception of the adult as superior. At the same time, however, Ferenczi noted that children *do* possess much sexual knowledge which is later repressed.

3 Panofsky (1953, p. 145):

> In order to lend artistic expression to this mysterious and many-leveled identity of Virgin and Mother, Mother and Daughter, Daughter and Bride, Queen of Heaven and Church on Earth, an image had been devised which can be described as 'the Virgin Mary in a Church and as The Church.' The figure of the Mother of God, who at the same time personifies the Church as a spiritual entity, was framed by an aedicula or tabernacle which, however much diminished in scale, conventionalized in form and abbreviated in structural detail was meant to suggest a complete ecclesiastical building.

Cf. also Bettelheim (1976), who discusses the child's perception of his parents as gigantic, a fact that is demonstrated by the parental role of giants in fairy tales and the mythological belief in a primeval race of titans.

4 In this paper, I purposely do not deal with the influence of primitive art on Henry Moore's development as I prefer to keep the discussion within the context of European Christian tradition. Nor do I discuss the Jungian archetypal interpretations of Moore's sculpture which Erich Neumann (1959) has thoroughly explored. Cf. also Digby (1955).

5 Cf. also Steinberg's discussion of Mary's hand over Christ's genitals as a "protection motif" in which the mother shields the "vulnerable humanity" of her Son (1983, p. 72).

6 The interplay of interior and exterior discussed by Winnicott and elaborated by Deri (1978, p. 49) may be related to Moore's work on at least two levels. On the one hand the content or subject of the sculpture depicts the interior-exterior theme as directly associated with mother and child. On the other hand, however, the broader issue of creativity from Winnicott's point of view also concerns the interior-exterior *idea*. This latter aspect has to do with the very nature of creativity itself as an interior-exterior process in which the pre-conscious (which Deri [1978, p. 57] says "becomes the internalized heir of the caring mother . . .") mediates between the unconscious store of memory, fantasy, and energy and the conscious work that transforms these ingredients into art. This relationship of inside and outside, characteristic of all artistic process, becomes a *subject* in the art of Henry Moore.

7 Klein (1960, p. 180):

> It would seem that the polarity between the life-instincts and the death instincts is already coming out in these phenomena of early infancy, for we may regard the force of the child's fixation at the oral-sucking level as an expression of the force of its libido, and, similarly, the early and powerful emergence of its oral sadism as a sign of the ascendancy of its destructive instinctual components.

8 At this point, I would like to digress for a moment and compare these works with an Italian Renaissance painting of 1490 by Carlo Crivelli (Victoria and Albert Museum, London). Without the benefit of modern abstraction, Crivelli has used a combination of formal repetition and literary symbolism to evoke associations like those found in Moore's work. Crivelli's Christ holds an apple, placed as a reference to Mary's breast as well as a formal repetition of the Child's own chubby face. The apple, of course, must be bitten into, rather than sucked, which suggests infantile oral sadism. But, unlike Moore's sculptures, the Crivelli is enriched with symbolic references to the apple as the instrument of man's fall. Mary, as the new Eve and Christ, the new Adam, have

typological (as well as incestuous) implications. (Steinberg, 1983, provides a thorough discussion of eroticized aspects of the Madonna's relationship with Christ as portrayed in Renaissance art.) The little tree at the bottom of the picture, together with the apple, confirms the traditional association of Christ as the Redeemer of Adam's sins by iconographic reference to the Garden of Eden.

9 In this statement (Moore and Hedgecoe, 1968, p. 160), Moore expresses the inverse of Renaissance Madonna-Child iconography as described by Steinberg. In the development of Christian art from the middle ages to the Renaissance, artists attended more and more to Christ's humanity, including his sexuality. Henry Moore seems to have had the opposite problem, namely how to *reduce* the libidinal aspects of his Madonna and Christ while *increasing* Christ's intellectual development.

10 Moore, 1944, p. xli. Cf. also Rudolf Arnheim (1948), for a discussion of the tangible nature of Moore's open spaces. Moore has repeatedly discussed his fascination for holes and for the interior-exterior protection theme, nearly always in regard to the universal mother-child relationship. During World War II, he did a series of shelter drawings, scenes of the London underground, and he found himself unexpectedly excited and fascinated by the subject of this work (Ghiselin, 1952, p. 212). He has said that it was in these drawings that the mother and child protection motif first appears (Clark, 1974, p. 249). There is, however, another facet to these themes that is of an earlier autobiographical nature, namely the relationship which Henry Moore had with his father. Moore's unique approach to open and closed spaces may derive in part from his father's occupation as a coal miner. Moore's relationship with his father and its impact on his art deserves further investigation.

References

Arnheim, R. (1948). The holes of Henry Moore. *Journal of Aesthetics and Art Criticism,* 7 (1):29–38.

Bettelheim, B. (1976). *The uses of enchantment.* New York: Knopf.

Clark, K. (1974). *Henry Moore drawing.* London: Harper & Row.

Deri, S. (1978). Vicissitudes of symbolization and creativity. In S. Grolnick & L. Barkin (Eds.), *Between reality and fantasy.* New York: Jason Aronson.

Digby, G. W. (1955). *Meaning and symbol in three modern artists.* London: Routledge and Kegan Paul.

Ferenczi, S. (1956). Stages in the development of reality. In *Sex and psychoanalysis.* New York: Dover.

——— (1980). The dream of the clever baby. In *Further contributions to the theory and technique of psychoanalysis.* New York: Brunner/Mazel.

Freud, S. (1914). On narcissism. *S.E.,* 14:73–102.

Ghiselin, B. (1952). *The creative process.* Los Angeles: UCLA Press.

James, P. (1966). *Henry Moore on sculpture.* London: MacDonald.

Klein, M. (1960). *The psychoanalysis of children.* New York: Grove Press.

Kris, E. (1952). *Psychoanalytic explorations in art.* New York: International Universities Press.

Mahler, M., et al. (1975). *The psychological birth of the human infant.* New York: Basic Books.

Meiss, M. (1976). Sleep in Venice: Ancient myths and Renaissance proclivities. In *The painter's choice.* New York: Harper & Row.

Melville, R. (1970). *Henry Moore.* New York: Abrams.

Moore, H. (1944). *Henry Moore.* London: Lund, Humphries.

Moore, H., & Hedgecoe, J. (1968). *Henry Moore.* New York: Simon and Schuster.

Neumann, E. (1959). *The archetypal world of Henry Moore.* New York: Pantheon Books.

Panofsky, E. (1953). *Early Netherlandish painting.* Cambridge: Harvard University Press.

Steinberg, L. (1983, Summer). The sexuality of Christ in Renaissance art and modern oblivion. *October,* 25.

Winnicott, D. W. (1965). *The maturational processes and the facilitating environment.* New York: International Universities Press.

Section Four	Book Reviews and Responses

Mourning, Perversion, and Apotheosis

I

Robert Liebert's *Michelangelo,* subtitled "A Psychoanalytic Study of His Life and Images," is the first book-length biography of an artist written by an analyst-clinician since the publication of Albert Lubin's life of van Gogh, *Stranger on the Earth,* over a decade ago. There could be no better way to launch *Psychoanalytic Perspectives on Art* than through in-depth, multidisciplinary reviews of Liebert's book. For *Michelangelo* is no ordinary psychobiography: true to the promise of his subtitle, Liebert has attempted to use the tools of psychoanalysis to illuminate not only the inner life and public behavior of his subject but also some covert meanings of his created products, principally with regard to iconography but with occasional forays even into the realm of formal innovation. Diverse psychological themes are correlated with Michelangelo's artistic images in a series of his most important works. Liebert chose not to deal with the possible psychological meaning of the artist's architectural projects, but he subjected much of Michelangelo's sculpted and painted oeuvre to psychological interpretation. His survey includes major components of the tomb of Julius II, of the Sistine ceiling and *Last Judgment,* and of the Medici Chapel. Altogether, more than 30 specific works or important segments of great ensembles are considered from a psychoanalytic point of view.

Liebert's interpretations of Michelangelo's art are invariably based on a coherent schema of his subject's personality, a psychoanalytic character diagnosis he developed through conscientious study of the biographical data—in this case, source materials of an unusually detailed sort. To be sure, as Liebert well knows, even this mass of information leaves innumerable gaps to be filled through the method of inference psychoanalysts call "reconstruction"—producing hypothetical statements which, in the clinical situation, are submitted for assessment to the analysand. Liebert is explicit about offering us, his readers, a speculative psychological portrait for similar consideration. Clearly, the primary task of the psychoanalyst-reviewer is the evaluation of Liebert's reconstructive work, for his specific conclusions about Michelangelo's art are merely logical reflections of this set of assumptions about the artist's inner life.

Before I attempt to respond to Liebert's interpretations as if I were a present-day Michelangelo "on the couch," I should point out that his basic methodology, albeit perfectly legitimate, is by no means the only one available to the "psycho-iconographer." To mention only one of the more obvious alternatives, it is possible to base psychological reconstructions primarily on the totality of an artist's imaginative productions—a strategy diametrically opposed to the biographical emphasis used by Liebert. This alternative approach would be most fruitful in studying artists whose work is securely autobiographical. Mary M. Gedo's *Picasso: Art as Autobiography* is probably the most ambitious effort cast in this particular mold. Wayne Andersen employed a third method altogether for his *Gauguin's Paradise Lost*: the historian detected a mythic theme running through a substantial portion of the artist's oeuvre, and it is this quasiliterary content that he has subjected to psychological interpretation and correlation with Gauguin's actual behavior. Other scholars will doubtless invent further avenues of approach specifically suited to the study of particular bodies of work and their creators.

Liebert himself alludes to his choice of method in a brief concluding chapter. He retraces the reconstructions of Michelangelo's psychological world in childhood he based on biographical data; he then reviews the inferences he made about the derivatives expectable in the artist's adulthood, putatively manifest in the latter's behavior or his creations, based in turn on this schema of early conflictual experiences. The crux of Liebert's hypothesis is that the loss of his natural mother as well as of his wetnurse before the age of six left the child Michelangelo filled with terror and preoccupied with death. Liebert further assumes that the child achieved emotional restitution by turning to powerful idealized males, a need echoed in the artist's later life both in his relations with certain patrons and in his love for beautiful young men. The vicissitudes of specific relationships of either type profoundly influenced both the content and the form of Michelangelo's art. Finally, Liebert believes that Michelangelo never lost hope for reconciliation with some maternal figure; therefore, "waves of yearning, pity, and rage" (p. 416) periodically erupted in his art in connection with the theme of mother-son relations.

This is a moving and compelling conception of Michelangelo's emotional development, and it certainly correlates well with numerous familiar aspects of the artist's life. Michelangelo was undoubtedly anxiety-prone—witness his repeated panicky flights when confronted with stressful circumstances. His obsessional concerns with death fill his surviving letters and poems. His entire oeuvre demonstrates pervasive preoccupation with Herculean male nudes commanded by some divine choreographer. Michelangelo was most productive when he could serve awesome personalities like Julius II or Paul III, and his love for Tommaso Cavalieri evoked some of his most beautiful works: "presentation drawings," as well as poems of stunning power. The artist's spiritual friendship in his seventh decade with Vittoria Colonna attests to his persisting need for reconciliation with women, and modern viewers generally find his depictions of mother and son in his series of Pietàs among the most stirring of his works.

Not only does Liebert's thesis possess *prima facie* credibility, it also has the virtue of "inter-rater reliability": similar conceptions of Michelangelo's personality development have been proposed by other psychoanalytic students of his life, most recently by Jerome Oremland (1978, 1980). Minor differences of opinion have revolved around the precise timing of Michelangelo's separation from his wetnurse: authors who accept de Tolnay's conjectures that Michelangelo did not return to the Buonarroti household until after his mother's death (e.g., Sterba & Sterba, 1956, 1978; Frank, 1966) naturally place more emphasis on the child's expectable sense of rejection by his natural mother. In his earlier papers on Michelangelo, Liebert (1977a, 1977b) did not comment on the timing of Michelangelo's return to his family. In the book, he has accepted the argument (see Spector, 1978) that Michelangelo's difficult and brittle personality in adulthood speaks for a derailment of emotional development relatively early in life; consequently, Liebert now assumes that the child was separated from his wetnurse at the time customary in his parents' social group, i.e., probably after weaning in the second year of life. Liebert's empathic reconstruction of the next several years of the child's life, punctuated by his mother's last three pregnancies and her death, postulates insufficient bonding between Michelangelo and his mother.

Liebert also adheres to the point of view that Michelangelo's later vulnerability can fruitfully be conceptualized on the basis of "pathological mourning" (p. 38; cf. Oremland, 1980). It is Liebert's understanding of such a condition that differs from that of previous authors, because, as I read him, he applies certain theories of object relations—in the version favored by Otto Kernberg (1975). Briefly, Liebert postulates that Michelangelo's intrapsychic representation of his own self as well as those of his maternal images were permanently split into polar opposites. Mothers became idealized Madonnas or filicidal Medea figures; their victim-sons were correspondingly divided among matricidal Orestes-types and sacrificial Christ figures. Liebert assumes that the matricidal and filicidal representations remained unconscious but led Michelangelo to choose certain prototypes for specific works that betray the underlying theme of murder. For instance, the source for the emotionally "detached" Madonna in Michelangelo's *Taddei Tondo* (p. 98) was a Medea sarcophagus portraying the futile effort of her children to flee her—an action mirrored in the panic of the infant Jesus in Michelangelo's relief. Similarly, the gesture of Adam in *The Expulsion from Paradise* (p. 102) on the Sistine ceiling echoes a figure on a Roman Orestes sarcophagus. It cannot be a coincidence that, as Liebert notes, the Deity Michelangelo depicts in *The Separation of Light from Darkness* (p. 143) is unmistakably bisexual, with prominent feminine breasts.

Liebert gives appropriate emphasis to the fact that Michelangelo dwelt in an exclusively masculine world from early childhood until the end of his sixth decade, when he befriended Vittoria Colonna. He points out that, although Michelangelo was ambivalent toward his father (whose relatively modest horizons he mocked in the account of his life he transmitted to Ascanio Condivi in old age), the artist's attachment to his surviving parent was "unbreakable" (p. 30). To prove the point, Liebert refers to that poignant detail of the Sistine *Deluge* (Fig. 1) wherein "an aged, powerful father bears his fully grown, dead son in his arms" (p. 31). He rightly points to the persistence of his attitude beyond the death of Lodovico Buonarroti; it is revealed in the identical message encoded in the Florence *Pietà* (Fig. 2). Here, however, roles have been reversed: it is not the dead Christ who has Michelangelo's features, but the person carrying Him, Nicodemus. At any rate, Liebert assumes that Michelangelo's lifelong preoccupation with family honor was an effort to please his father, a man unduly proud of his ancestry. He gives proper weight to the other side of Michelangelo's ambivalence, however; namely, to the artist's disappointment about his father's "shameful" inadequacies.

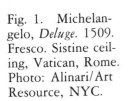

Fig. 1. Michelangelo, *Deluge*. 1509. Fresco. Sistine ceiling, Vatican, Rome. Photo: Alinari/Art Resource, NYC.

Fig. 2. *Pietà*. Before 1555. Marble. Florence Cathedral. Photo: Alinari/Art Resource, NYC.

This theme is implicit in the Sistine *Drunkenness of Noah* (Fig. 3): Liebert demonstrates that Michelangelo must have been in conflict about pointing the finger of blame at Lodovico (as Noah's son is doing in the fresco) for he has depicted the sons to be as naked as the inebriated father, thus negating the shameful impact of the entire scene. That disillusionment caused by parental imperfections was an important issue for Michelangelo is further shown in a drawing of 1533, *Children's Bacchanal* (Fig. 4). In the foreground of this work, one group of figures presents a reprise of *The Drunkenness of Noah:* several putti, exhibiting sadistic glee, here replace Noah's full-grown sons. The presence of a wizened satyress, indifferently giving suck to another putto in the left foreground, surely suggests that the artist was making reference to his personal history in this private work. According to Liebert the self-contained world of *Children's Bacchanal* alludes not only to Michelangelo's enraged response to his childhood disappointments, but also to his lifelong need to avoid emotional attach-

Fig. 3. *The Drunk-enness of Noah.* 1509. Fresco. Sistine ceiling, Vatican, Rome. Photo: Alinari/Art Resource, NYC.

ments through the use of his extraordinary powers to maintain self-sufficiency.

Liebert departs from the psychoanalytic consensus in taking a firm position opposed to the common view that the artist was overtly homosexual (see Kavka, 1980; Oremland, 1978, 1980). Liebert asserts that Michelangelo would have experienced orgasm as disorganizing and would therefore have remained continent. Although certain cases of frigidity are caused, in part, by anxieties of this kind (and K. R. Eissler [1961] applied the idea to the case of Leonardo da Vinci), I believe it is unwarranted to apply this formulation to homosexuality. In my clinical experience (see Gedo, 1983, chap. 6) male homosexuals are compelled to use frequent sexual contacts as home remedies for the manifold anxieties that beset them. For them, Michelangelo's words, in an unfinished sonnet, "He is like a corpse/ Who leads his life and keeps from [Love] secure" (Gilbert & Linscott, 1965, p. 23) are *literal* truth: without the vital experience of sexual release, these afflicted persons feel subjectively dead.

Liebert reviews the available evidence about Michelangelo's ambiguous relations with a series of beautiful young men. He comes to the conclusion in every instance that the case for overt homosexuality remains unproved. For an author who presents his readers with a frankly speculative book, Liebert here applies an odd double standard: surely the issue cannot be one of proof; it is a matter of plausibility. With the possible exception of the beloved Tommaso Cavalieri, I believe, on the evidence of the

274

Fig. 4. *Children's Bacchanal.* 1533. Red chalk drawing. Windsor, Windsor Castle.

very facts Liebert presents about these relationships, that all of Michelangelo's young men must have been sexual partners. Instead of summarizing the data offered by Liebert (pp. 269–311), let me acknowledge that my skepticism about his position is not really based on the historical "facts." I am convinced, of course, that neither is Liebert's contrary attitude. How can one explain our differing evaluations of a piece of "evidence" such as Michelangelo's line in a poem of 1544, ". . . attest for him how gracious I was in bed when he embraced" (Clements, 1968, p. 98)? Clearly, such differences originate in a priori conceptions of Michelangelo's character for which each of us merely seeks to collect supporting evidence in historical records.

It is barely possible that documents may be unearthed to resolve this question; it is much more likely, however, that it will forever remain unanswered. Each generation of scholars will have to make its own assumptions about it, based on its particular prejudices. In my judgment (cf. Gedo, 1983, chap. 1), a biography aspiring to be called "psychoanalytic" should show awareness, preferably explicitly, about the nature and sources of the author's personal bias toward his subject. As Moraitis (1985) has cogently observed, the biographical enterprise is invariably fraught with transferences: those of the biographer toward his subject! Before revealing my own affective responses toward Michelangelo I wish to comment on Liebert's decision to avoid making explicit reference to his own attitudes about that formidable man. Needless to say, it is a choice I regret, for it leaves us in doubt about the extent of Liebert's awareness concerning the motivations dictating his necessarily speculative conclusions.

To illustrate: Why does Liebert ignore the most notorious incident from Michelangelo's early life, the fracas that culminated in his nose being broken by his fellow-artist Torrigiani? The omission is not likely to be based on any lack of long-term psychological significance, for the injury left Michelangelo permanently disfigured—a matter that must have had enormous impact on a young man forever obsessed by the ideal of masculine beauty. Michelangelo provoked Torrigiani by mocking and depreciating his artistic efforts when they were working side-by-side, drawing Masaccio's frescoes in the Brancacci chapel. Liebert's reticence about his subjective reactions to Michelangelo's poisonous provocativeness toward direct competitors leaves me with the impression that he ignores this unpleasant quarrel because it throws such a damning light on the character of his subject. Michelangelo did not confine his denigrations to his contemporaries and/or artistic inferiors: he was reportedly equally abusive toward Leonardo da Vinci when they were working on their respective projects for the Great Hall of the Palazzo della Signoria in Florence (Clements, 1968, p. 4) and, later, toward Raphael in Rome (Fischel, 1948, p. 313). Liebert's discussion of these matters reduces them to intolerance for "alternative visions," based on infantile sibling rivalries (p. 193). Such a view of Michelangelo's behavior raises the possibility that the author needs to idealize him; perhaps Liebert's judgment that Michelangelo was not overtly homosexual is another consequence of such idealization: He attributes to the artist capacities for heroic self-control not to be expected of the vast majority of people.

Are there further examples of judgments based on this unacknowledged attitude on the part of Liebert? I believe so. For one thing, he tends to underplay Michelangelo's debt to his artistic predecessors. Even where Michelangelo quotes Masaccio in painting God for the Sistine *Creation of Eve* (p. 156), Liebert does not discuss the possibility that the artist, when he worked on his most ambitious cycle of paintings, might turn for support to his greatest Florentine predecessor in fresco. With respect to some of Michelangelo's younger collaborators, moreover, Liebert seems to espouse the contemptuous attitude adopted by Michelangelo toward men of great worth. His estimation of Sebastiano del Piombo, for example, is unduly harsh, despite Liebert's realization that Michelangelo quarreled with this loyal friend in a frankly paranoid manner. Liebert asserts that Sebastiano became unable to paint after Michelangelo broke with him; this claim is not sustained by some recent historical research.[1] In an analogous manner, Liebert attributes Jacopo da Pontormo's psychological illness to the power Michelangelo's art had over him; he assumes that Pontormo's persecutory anxieties were specifically caused by his hostility toward his mentor. Even if these conjectures are more or less correct, Liebert's way of stating his hypotheses about Pontormo's private thoughts attributes the latter's difficulties too narrowly to this single aspect of his life, as if he had been no more than a planet in a solar system centered on Michelangelo.[2]

Liebert's adoption of Michelangelo's attitudes toward other artists and his handling of the question of Michelangelo's probable homosexual activities are important because they are indicators of his underlying bias. Such a bias assumes significance only insofar as idealization might have led Liebert to formulate his understanding of the artist's *personality* in the most favorable guise consonant with the facts. In my experience, psychoanalytic clinicians tend often to fall into this error: as a group, we shy away from facing the depth of our patients' pathology. I do not mean to imply that Liebert's view of Michelangelo's integration is incorrect—only to point out that it is the most optimistic view conceivable. In the clinical situation, when we present patients with an unduly rosy picture of their inner life, they are likely to respond in one of two ways. Many will joyfully seize upon this relatively hopeful portrait and organize themselves around it, as if forming a benign *folie-à-deux* with us. I suspect that may be the way many admirers of Michelangelo will accept Liebert's formulation of his personality: he gives us a person with whom we can empathize, a genius tragically wounded by Nemesis early in life. The second response I have observed clinically is more interesting: some patients will refuse to accept the false comfort of our unwarranted optimism. They tell us, often with anger, that we fail to grasp the extent of their disorder. I shall try to react to Liebert's interpretations of Michelangelo's psychology in the spirit of their despairing protests.

Let me begin by challenging the author's repeated conjectures about the persisting influence of castration anxiety (i.e., of fears of retaliation for hostile oedipal wishes toward male rivals) on Michelangelo's art and life. He assumes that Michelangelo remained in conflict about having surpassed his father, and that his lifelong family loyalty expiated his unconscious guilt about success. Liebert views the artist's abstemious living habits as part of this expiatory effort. According to him, Michelangelo would have justified whatever competitive hostility he harbored against his father and brothers by allowing himself to be exploited by them (pp. 35–36). The father's death would only have exacerbated this chronic intrapsychic conflict; in Liebert's view, henceforward Michelangelo felt persecuted by the introjected reproaches of his father (p. 38). As a corollary of these assumptions, Liebert believes that Michelangelo "feared death and castration as the consequences of sexual love for a woman" (p. 283). Liebert finds echoes of these unconscious conflicts in Michelangelo's lost cartoon for *The Battle of Cascina* (p. 109), which he interprets as a depiction of the transition from passive gratifications to battle-readiness. Moreover, Liebert agrees with authors who view the central details of *The Last Judgment* (Fig. 5) as an expression of Michelangelo's feeling that he was deserving of damnation. Al-

Fig. 5. *The Last Judgment* (central detail). 1536–41. Fresco. Sistine ceiling, Vatican, Rome. Photo: Alinari/Art Resource, NYC.

though Liebert lists a number of potential sources for this profound guilt, he prominently includes patricidal impulses among them (pp. 359–360).

Although these speculations are not *prima facie* implausible, I think it is highly unlikely that the child Michelangelo formed a bond with his mother of sufficient significance to arouse an oedipal conflict of this kind. As the author himself states, Michelangelo's childhood was marked "by little experience with the continuity in attachments and the dependable and consistent environment that are necessary for the development of stable self and object representations" (p. 16). To the contrary, there is ample evidence pointing in another direction: the artist's entire career suggests that meaningful early childhood bonds developed only toward his father. Of course, Liebert is by no means unmindful of this crucial aspect of the artist's personality; he merely postulates additional, desirable developments in the direction of the "positive" oedipal constellation—experiences with normative connotations. Yet, if we accept Liebert's persuasive interpretation that the youthful sculptor's first major work, *The Madonna of the Stairs* (p. 17), alludes to the unsupportive attitude of his mother before her decease—maternal deprivation that underlay Michelangelo's legendary *terribilità*—there is every reason to doubt that the child could have achieved the level of emotional development Liebert assigns him.

As Liebert has correctly noted, the great artist's adult view of his father was by no means idealized. Retrospectively, the earliest mark of his disillusionment may be detected in the story the aged artist related to Condivi about having overcome Lodovico Buonarroti's strenuous opposition to embark on his apprenticeship. Liebert fails to question the veracity of this tale (p. 30); yet it has all the earmarks of a myth: on this earth every Hercules must labor to overcome paternal opposition. To be sure, Michelangelo's adolescence was soon to take on the qualities of myth in actuality: Lodovico Buonarroti was replaced in his son's pantheon by his first dazzling patron, Lorenzo the Magnificent. Nonetheless, when his father died, the 56-year-old artist expressed in a long, moving poem his longing to be eternally united with him (Gilbert & Linscott, 1965, p. 64).

As for Michelangelo's subsequent relations with a succession of patrons, Liebert rightly describes them in terms of the transference of childhood attitudes about the artist's father. This interpretation is strongly buttressed by the fact that the artist was scarcely able to discharge his obligations to previous patrons if they became unavailable to him in person. His abandonment of the commission for the Piccolomini Altar in Siena upon the death of Pius III foreshadowed his failure to persevere on the tomb of Julius II after the death of that Pope. As he did with Lodovico Buonarroti, so Michelangelo claimed he was exploited by the various patrons he agreed to "serve." This pattern was most conspicuous in relation to Julius II, a messianic figure easy to idealize. In the project for his tomb, artist and patron initially gave way to megalomania, for, as Liebert perceptively shows, the plan they devised was impossible to complete. While he was unconsciously merged with this awesome personage, Michelangelo's grandiosity knew no bounds: he fantasied carving a Colossus out of a mountainside at Carrara! Condivi reported Michelangelo's mythical story that the Pope had a drawbridge constructed in order to be able to visit the artist privately; Liebert rightly calls this fantasy a measure of Michelangelo's longing for paternal favor. The artist's paranoid reaction to his great rivals for della Rovere patronage, Bramante and Raphael, must have echoed his competition with his brothers for the love of their father.

The Pope soon came to his senses about the unrealistic nature of the plans for his tomb; his refusal to continue the project so wounded Michelangelo that he temporarily abandoned papal service. When their collaboration was resumed, the Pope shrewdly provided him with the external structure he needed to work productively, "forcing" him to cast Julius's portrait in bronze, then setting him the task of painting the Sistine ceiling. Liebert implies that *The Creation of Adam* (p. 157) gains its unique power because, in the context of this relationship with the empathic Pope, Michelangelo was able to convey the aura of our lost infantile innocence, one characterized by complete trust in an all-caring, omnipotent parent. Perhaps the depression the artist experienced when he completed the ceiling might best be understood as a reaction to the termination of this period of exceptional closeness to an ideal patron. Indeed, a few months later Pope Julius died.

The Medici Popes who followed him, with a brief *caesura,* for a span of two decades, had been Michelangelo's boyhood companions in Florence. Although the artist claimed that he was coerced into working for them, the actualities behind these fantasies of bondage were quite different. For instance, Michelangelo apparently had to engage in intrigue to obtain the commission from Leo X to design the façade of S. Lorenzo. Moreover, Leo was seemingly too uncomfortable with the artist's *terribilità* to employ him on projects in Rome. During the early years of his pontificate, the great papal commissions went to Raphael; in this interval, Michelangelo carved the two Louvre *Slaves* for the tomb of Julius. Liebert has recognized that the *Dying Slave* (Fig. 6) marks the first appearance of erotically charged imagery in Michelangelo's public work: it is a depiction of homosexual passion. In noting the formal resemblance between this sculpture, the *Laocoön,* and one of the female figures in the painted *Entombment* (p. 71; probably not entirely autograph but surely conceived by Michelangelo), Liebert comes close to interpreting the statue as an expression of the artist's feminine identification. I believe the interpretation of the *Dying Slave* (p. 166) can go further: in this work, Michelangelo seems to struggle with his loss of Julius II by depicting his bondage to the great Pope. If both *Slaves,* as well as the *Moses* intended for the tomb of Julius, were inspired by the *Laocoön,* we might think of these three related figures as symbols of Michelangelo's wish forever to be tied to this Holy Father (an idea I owe to Mary Gedo). In this sense, his refusal to finish the tomb, through a series of decisions that led him to complain, at the age of 67, that he had been "chained" to it, constitutes the live reenactment of the subject matter of the group as he devised it, in 1513–15, when he did most of the work on these three statues.[3]

Michelangelo's dissatisfaction with the patronage of Leo X presumably led to the emergence of poorly disguised fantasies of passive anal coitus in the *Dying Slave.* It is also likely that the loss of Julius and the disappointments with the Medici Popes resulted in a parallel regression into overt homosexuality on the part of Michelangelo, then in the fourth decade of his life. It should also be recalled that after he designed the S. Lorenzo façade, Michelangelo wasted himself in endless marble quarrying and produced very little art for a number of years. As Mary Gedo has found in the case of Picasso (1980), in artists with archaic symbiotic needs, such creative paralyses often follow the disruption of a vital relationship. Yet we may gain some understanding of Michelangelo's decision in 1517–19 to repeat his frustrating

Fig. 6. *The Dying Slave* (detail: upper half of statue). Before 1513. Marble. The Louvre, Paris. Photo: Alinari/Art Resource, NYC.

efforts of 1505, when he had quarried marble for the tomb of Julius, if we interpret his enigmatic statement—that in the marble quarries he was attempting to "raise the dead"—as a reference to Giulio della Rovere.[4]

During the pontificate of Clement VII, Michelangelo was commissioned to execute the Medici chapel. In spite of the regular salary granted by the Pope, the artist's letters convey a sense of chronic depression during these years in Florence. This mood is reflected in his contemporaneous poems, as well as in the funerary chapel, where, as Liebert puts it, Michelangelo conducted a "private inquiry into the nature of death" (p. 241). In the statue of *Day* (p. 245), Liebert perceives the sculptor's hidden self-portrait—once again, forced into submission, this time to the idealized figure of Giuliano de' Medici. The Giuliano effigy (p. 92) allegedly portrays a recently deceased princeling, but its noble features bear no resemblance to its putative subject. Clement VII was also born "Giuliano de' Medici"—hence I believe

Michelangelo was once again expressing, through this sculpture, his need to be "in bondage" to an idealized patron. The third figure in this sculptural group, *Night* (p. 250), has been interpreted on the basis of a sonnet Michelangelo wrote on the same theme. In the poem, Night, a "shadow of death," is called the "good healer" who overcomes "vexing anger" (Gilbert & Linscott, 1965, pp. 73–74). May we conclude that Michelangelo's rage had its origin in his disappointment with the Medici Pope?

The nature of the nocturnal remedy he used to soothe himself may be gleaned from closer scrutiny of the psychological meaning of *Night*. On the basis of the formal source of its motif in a relief of *Leda* (p. 251), Liebert concludes that this sculpture alludes to sexual surrender to an omnipotent male. Perhaps because he is convinced that Michelangelo did not indulge in homosexual activities, Liebert refrains from the logical conclusion that follows: in the absence of a satisfactory patron, Michelangelo's need for a relationship to an idealized male became erotized. Yet Liebert is well aware of the fact that the artist was unable to convert his male models into images of sexually convincing females, either in the case of *Night,* or in its counterpart, his painting of *Leda* (now lost, but known from early engravings). Liebert rightly calls attention to the phallic qualities of the nipples and braids of *Night* but does not make it explicit that the statue therefore constitutes

Fig. 7. Cornelius Bos, after Michelangelo. *Leda and the Swan.* Engraving. London, the British Museum.

Formosa Iure Leda est, cicinus fit Iuppiter illam
Cum ..., hic geminum quis credat parturit ouum,

Ex illo gemini pollux, cum castore fratres
Ex isto erumpens Helene pulcherrima prodit.

another self-portrait, an image of Michelangelo's fantasied erotic life. Liebert does state, however, that the *Leda* barely disguises the artist's fantasies of fellatio.[5]

My own conjecture is that there is a causal connection between the earliest reports we have about Michelangelo's erotic attachments to young men—his relationship to Gherardo Perini in 1520—and the worst disappointment of his artistic career, the cancellation of the S. Lorenzo project by Leo X. Ambiguous love affairs of that sort succeeded each other for the next 25 years. At the same time, Michelangelo's complex relations with Clement VII underwent all the vicissitudes of extreme ambivalence. Although he continued to draw a salary while working on the Medici Chapel and the Laurentian Library, Michelangelo joined the Florentine Republicans who expelled the Medici in 1527, at the nadir of Clement VII's political fortunes. He served the Republic as a military engineer; and thus, after the fall of Florence to the resurgent Medici in 1530, he had to go into hiding to escape Clement's vengeance. Within a few months all was forgiven: Michelangelo resumed his previous status in the Pope's service. But Clement's illegitimate son, Alessandro, the actual ruler of Florence, remained a bitter enemy. Hence, the artist's ultimate move to Rome in 1534 constituted an admission of the fact that he could expect no patronage in his own city under its current regime. Liebert postulates that the artist's self-exile from Florence echoed his displacement by a series of younger brothers in the Buonarroti household. I believe this formulation is valid; Michelangelo's sibling surrogates in the Florence of Alessandro de' Medici were younger sculptors like Bandinelli, who was given the commission for a statue of Hercules Michelangelo wanted to carve.

Michelangelo's arrival in Rome coincided with the death of Clement VII. Although a succession of subsequent Popes—notably Paul III, Julius III, and Paul IV—strove to favor Michelangelo with patronage, the focus of the artist's emotional life now seemed to shift to other issues and relationships. In all probability, this change had been in process for some years before 1534; it is very tempting to assume that it was initiated by the death of the artist's father in 1531. "Who is the man who would not cry/ for his dear father dead?" Michelangelo wrote afterward. He bid Lodovico Buonarroti adieu with the lines, "If the best of Love in Heaven increases/ between father and son, as all virtues grow. . ." (Gilbert & Linscott, 1965, pp. 62–64). We may share Liebert's opinion that, in his letters and poems, Michelangelo continually tried to minimize the negative aspects of his attitude toward his father, but the fact that he developed close human ties outside his family only after Lodovico died should persuade us that the bonds to his father were predominantly positive. Let us recall the letter Michelangelo sent his disturbed brother, Giovansimone, in June 1509, vehemently reproaching him for his misconduct toward Lodovico: "Now I know for certain you are not my brother, because if you were you would not threaten my father—no, you are an animal, and I shall treat you like an animal. Let me tell you that whosoever sees his father threatened or struck is obligated to interpose his own life . . ." (Gilbert & Linscott, 1965, pp. 202–203). I understand these words as literal expressions of the artist's deepest feelings.

The lasting, Platonic love affair with Tommaso Cavalieri that began almost immediately after Lodovico's death was, I assume, largely a result of Michelangelo's need to replace the bond to his father with another affectionate relationship. Liebert is surprised by the fact that the artist could pursue an affair with an "inappropriate" lower-class boy, Febo di Poggio, at the early stages of his lofty relationship with Tommaso, "the armed cavalier" whose prisoner he professed to be (Gilbert & Linscott, 1965, p. 71). This was a long-standing fantasy of Michelangelo's, articulated in several previous poems and immortalized in his *Victory* group (p. 248), in which his own features, barely disguised, are given to the captive. Such inconsistencies are characteristic of persons who suffer from perversions, whose sexual activities are not pleasure seeking, but essential adaptive measures that ward off emotional catastrophe.

Michelangelo commemorated his desperate need in a sonnet, as follows: "His feathers were my wings, his hill [*poggio*] my steps,/ Phoebus [*Febo*] lamp for my feet, and dying then/ for me less my safety than my marvel./ Dying without, no soul to Heaven leaps,/ Heart is not freshened by remembering them,/ for late, after the hurt, who will give counsel?" (Gilbert & Linscott, 1965, pp. 71–73). These lines clearly describe *The Rape of Ganymede* (p. 280), a drawing Michelangelo presented to Tommaso to begin their relationship. Liebert understands this work as an effort to spiritualize the homosexual act; in my judgment, it could have served equally well as a "calling card" through which Michelangelo made an effort to acquaint his beloved with his sexual history. This interpretation makes all the more sense if we recall that one of the other presentation drawings for Tommaso depicts *The Fall of Phaeton* (Fig. 8). Although Liebert comprehends that the imagery of this work amounts to a confession of Michelangelo's homosexual love for Febo (i.e., Phoebus Apollo, depicted triumphant at the top of the page), he does not account for its inclusion among the drawings given to Tommaso, presumably because of his assumptions about Michelangelo's sexuality. He is better able to interpret a third drawing from this group, *The Punishment of Tityus* (Fig. 9), in which divine vengeance for physical lust is portrayed as producing masochistic sexual gratification: in other words, Michelangelo seems to have understood that his own erotized sufferings safeguarded him from an even more cruel fate.[6]

II

Some years ago, in a lecture to the Chicago Psychoanalytic Society, Richard Sterba compared Michelangelo's love affair with Tommaso Cavalieri to a successful psychotherapeutic effort. The

Fig. 8. *The Fall of Phaeton.* 1533. Black chalk drawing. Windsor, Windsor Castle.

artist's fervent and open erotic feelings were tamed in the course of years of loyal friendship, without injury to his self-esteem or traumatic disillusionment with the beloved. After Tommaso's marriage in 1538, Michelangelo again fell in love with a young man, Cecchino de' Bracci, whose death in 1544 he commemorated in a cycle of poems. This was the boy about whose embraces Michelangelo wrote the sardonic confession I have already quoted (p. 275). By then, the artist was almost 70, and we have no record that his sexual passions were awakened thereafter. Liebert demonstrates the consideration and tact Tommaso used to soothe his vulnerable octogenarian friend by quoting a letter of 1561 (p. 276)—clearly, the relationship fulfilled a variety of Michelangelo's emotional needs to the end of his life. It was the early promise of this bounty that Michelangelo must have sensed when he confided

Fig. 9. *Punishment of Tityus*. 1532. Black chalk drawing. Windsor, Windsor Castle.

to Sebastiano del Piombo that if Tommaso "slipt [sic] out of my mind, I believe that I should suddenly fall dead" (Clements, 1968, p. 93). Michelangelo's late sonnet to Tommaso (Gilbert & Linscott, 1965, p. 145) rightly credits him with the artist's salvation: the relationship had more than lived up to Michelangelo's Platonic ideals.

Probably as a consequence of Tommaso's loyalty, in his old age Michelangelo's need for fantasied merger with an omnipotent other took new forms: at any rate, it was no longer played out with his patrons. Because he was spared the disappointments that characterized his relationship with his own father and with the Medici Popes, his need for an idealized male was never again erotized. Instead of seeing himself as a Ganymede ascending to Heaven in the embrace of Zeus, Michelangelo portrayed himself, in the sculpture intended for his own tomb, as Nicodemus, carrying the dead Christ. Liebert is properly aware of Michelangelo's "yearning to merge with Jesus" (p. 393). To demonstrate this yearning, he cites the artist's sonnet of 1554 in which Christ is described as "that holy Love/ that on the cross opened Its arms to take us" (Gilbert & Linscott, 1965, p. 159). It is therefore regrettable that Liebert uses this insight merely to explain Michelangelo's willingness to devote himself to the construction of St. Peter's Basilica, without pay, for the last 18 years of his life, for the theme of merger with Jesus illuminates many works of the aged artist.

We may note the beginnings of this new pietistic direction in Michelangelo's work in a drawing he made for Vittoria Colonna (Hartt, no. 408) in which the viewer confronts the crucified Christ, uttering his plaints of abandonment to His Father. Perhaps

286

this unique subject marks the transition between Michelangelo's previous preoccupation with his own sufferings and his later commitment to Vittoria's pietism. I do not share Liebert's conviction that in this and subsequent images of the Savior, Michelangelo is presenting symbolic self-portraits. For the aged artist, Jesus became that omnipotent Other he had been seeking for almost seven decades, I believe. He repeated this motif in a large number of devotional works drawn for his private use.[7] In several other drawings, the crucified Christ is flanked by the Virgin and St. John (Fig. 10).[8] I do not think it is far-fetched to assume that in these unbearably poignant works the bereaved stand for Michelangelo and Vittoria Colonna as well.

A parallel series of works on the theme of the Holy Family also began with a presentation drawing, *The Madonna of Silence* (Hartt, no. 437), most likely made for Vittoria Colonna. The Christ Child sleeping in the Virgin's lap is shown in a pose suggestive of a Pietà; the St. Joseph on the right foreshadows the Nicodemus of the later *Florence Pietà* (Fig. 2). Hence the iconography suggests that Vittoria's influence will lead Michelangelo to salvation

Fig. 10. *Crucifixion with the Virgin and St. John.* 1550–60 (?). Black chalk drawing, corrected in white. London, the British Museum.

288

through faith. The so-called *Pietà for Vittoria Colonna* (Fig. 11), which presents the Virgin and her dead Son frontally, might well be read as an avowal that Michelangelo had achieved identification with Vittoria's beliefs. The great cartoon for a *Holy Family with Saints* (Hartt, no. 440) and several drawings on related themes,[9] including the initial conceptions for the *Rondanini Pietà* (Hartt, no. 459) extend the range of Michelangelo's contemplation of Christ.

Liebert has reached the conclusion also espoused by Oremland (1978, 1980) that in his sculpted Pietàs Michelangelo expressed the unconscious wish for reunion with the mother(s) of his infancy. I do not believe that this assumption is valid. Clinical experience suggests that the early life of personalities similar to the artist as I see him is generally filled with frustration, pain, and anger. Generally, such individuals try to avoid the repetition of these subjective states, if necessary by staying aloof from intimate human contacts. It seems highly unlikely that Michelangelo's childhood memories could have included very much in the way of affectionate intimacy with maternal figures. As Liebert himself argues, if the *Doni Tondo* (Fig. 12) Holy Family contains the clearest allusion to the artist's earliest experiences with his foster

Fig. 11. *Pietà for Vittoria Colonna.* 1538–40. Black chalk drawing. Boston, the Isabella Stuart Gardner Museum.

Fig. 12. *The Holy Family (Doni Tondo)*. c. 1503. Oil on panel. Uffizi Gallery, Florence. Photo: Alinari/Art Resource, NYC.

parents in Settignano, the child Michelangelo is most probably represented in this scene in the guise of St. John, shown as the lonely outsider wandering in the wilderness. In other words, Liebert persuasively shows that Michelangelo's statements idealizing his infantile experience with his wetnurse must have been reaction formations masking his rage about being excluded from her family. At bottom, the elderly artist must have longed for a more perfect relationship than anything to be expected from reunion with a primary caretaker with whom he had had mostly pain and frustration. Contrary to prevailing views, I feel that the works of his old age in which Virgin and Christ are shown in intimate contact—two magnificent drawings of Mother and Child (Hartt, no. 439, and Fig. 13) and the *Rondanini Pietà* (p. 413)—should be understood as further examples of the long series of works in which Michelangelo attempted to merge with a divinity. In other words, it makes better sense to view the artist's self-representation in these works as that of the Virgin, instead of interpreting the Christ as a self-image.[10]

If we review some of Michelangelo's earlier works with this interpretation in mind, we may find tentative answers for some hitherto puzzling questions. As did Oremland (1978, 1980),

Liebert explains the unnatural youthfulness of the Virgin in the *St. Peter's Pietà* (p. 69) as a reminiscence of the youthful mother(s) Michelangelo lost in childhood. This interpretation overlooks the fact that the *Pietà* represents the young mother as a mourner, i.e., the actualities of the artist's past history are here portrayed with the roles reversed. If we recall that he carved this sculpture before he reached the age of 25, we may read the youthfulness of the Virgin as an early indication of Michelangelo's capacity to identify with her bereavement. To be sure, I would assume that as a very young man Michelangelo was less concerned with his childhood losses than about contemporaneous ones: the successive deaths of

Lorenzo the Magnificent in 1492, the disruption of the Medici regime in 1494, and the execution of the admired preacher Savonarola in 1497.

As for the series of images on the theme of Virgin and Child, I agree with the succession of observers who have commented on the unprecedented aloofness of Michelangelo's protagonists. This is the issue Liebert had connected to fantasies of filicide and matricide in his discussions of the *Madonna of the Stairs* (pp. 20–22) and the *Taddei Tondo* (pp. 96–99). He also found allusions to such fantasies in the formal source for mother and child in the *Doni Tondo,* a relief of the infant Dionysus supported by a satyr (p. 80). The estrangement between mother and child is perhaps most marked in the *Bruges Madonna,* a work Liebert has chosen not to discuss in detail. On the other hand, he has perceptively noted the precarious position of the Infant Jesus, clinging to His mother's leg, in the Sistine *Creation of Adam* (pp. 156–158). In Michelangelo's last major work on this theme, the *Medici Madonna* (p. 93), the Christ Child is actually suckling at the breast but the Virgin appears aloof—a version that echoes the relations between mother and infant in the earlier *Pitti Tondo* and is echoed, in turn, in a later drawing (Hartt, no. 438).[11]

I would conclude that Michelangelo's childhood experience had only prepared him to depict the tragic aspects of the relations between Virgin and Child. Insofar as he yearned to be merged in fantasy with a godlike male, the Christian myth could ill satisfy his desires when it presents the Deity as an infant. Hence in the five sculpted and two painted early versions of this theme, the tendency to identify with the Virgin is not yet in evidence. It should also be noted that, in other contexts—those which did not arouse Michelangelo's need for an omnipotent male—he was perfectly capable of depicting affectionate relations between mothers and children, as if from a *spectator's* vantage point. In this regard, the best known of his creations is the *Deluge* on the Sistine ceiling, in which the largest of the foreground figures is a heroically proportioned, almost entirely nude mother, cuddling an infant in her arms, while a child of about three clings to her, both arms encircling her thigh.[12] There are a number of other depictions of affectionate mother-child couples on the Sistine ceiling among the figures portraying Ancestors of Christ, such as Salathiel and his mother, Obed and Ruth, etc.[13]

Under the circumstances, Michelangelo's ability at the very end of his life to produce worshipful images of ecstatic intimacy between Virgin and Christ Child, as well as to carve a *Pietà* that shows mother and son "each consisting of parts carved out of the other," as Liebert felicitously put it (p. 412), constitutes a significant shift in his psychology. As a young man, he desired fusion with masculine power, preferably in the guise of an anthropomorphic deity; as an octogenarian, transformed by the spirituality acquired through identification with Vittoria Colonna, he could appreciate the Divine even in the guise of a newborn—or a corpse.[14]

To repeat, my reading of the visual evidence fails to confirm the prevalent opinion that Michelangelo's work betrays unconscious wishes for symbiotic reunion with a maternal figure. My skepticism is, in fact, supported by a number of cogent points Liebert himself introduces about iconographic clues concerning the artist's earliest years, those antedating his attachment to his father. I have already cited his convincing interpretation of the isolated St. John in the *Doni Tondo* as "the outsider," viewing family life in the stonemason's yard—from a distance. In another brilliant *aperçu,* Liebert notes that the only vegetation shown on the Sistine ceiling in the scenes dealing with Man's origins consists of dead trees—a finding he interprets as an indication of the barren and depressive atmosphere of Michelangelo's beginnings. Thirdly, Liebert understands Michelangelo's choice to give his own features to the flayed skin of St. Bartholomew (Fig. 14) in *The Last Judgment* as an avowal of guilt for matricidal impulses. I have reservations about interpreting this image as a confession of deserving damnation (v.i.) but I concur with Liebert's opinion that the idea of excoriation conveys the sense of an infantile atmosphere in which soothing was insufficiently available.[15]

We may draw essentially similar conclusions from the information available about Michelangelo's repeated panicky flights in adult life—a subject already cogently discussed by Sterba and Sterba (1956). It will be recalled that the first of these episodes occurred shortly before the overthrow of the Medici regime in 1494: Michelangelo rationalized his sudden departure for Venice on the basis of having been told a prophetic dream about the imminent doom of the Medici. Liebert correctly notes that the dream must have been the artist's own; I would add that it is equally likely that he simply formed a *delusion* about having been given such a message. Michelangelo attributed his second flight, from Bologna to Florence about a year later, to his fear of bodily harm at the hands of artistic rivals. He developed a similar paranoid delusion in connection with his flight from Rome in 1506, on the eve of ceremonies for laying the cornerstone of Bramante's St. Peter's. Michelangelo's temporary abandonment of his post as military engineer during the siege of Florence in 1529 was not even rationalized: he naively described that a stranger "arranged" his clandestine departure to avoid great danger. He called this helper either God or the devil, thereby indicating his realization that he was not assisted by a mere human (Gilbert & Linscott, 1965, pp. 250–251). Liebert ascribes this incredible tale to conscious fabrication; I think it is more plausible to view it as a delusional experience.

We have sufficient detail about the incidents of 1494, 1506, and 1529 to detect a common element in Michelangelo's situation in each instance: he experienced a threat to his integration that he concretized as mortal danger. In all three cases, Michelangelo felt threatened by his perception of imminent loss of a relationship to the authority upon whom he relied: the Medici rulers of Florence in 1494, Julius II in 1506, and the Florentine Republic in 1529. Each time he saw the crumbling of the protective influence of

Fig. 14. *The Last Judgment* (detail: the flayed skin of St. Bartholomew with the supposed self-portrait of Michelangelo). Fresco. Sistine ceiling, Vatican, Rome. Photo: Alinari/Art Resource, NYC.

masculine powers, Michelangelo had reason to fear regression to a psychotic state: this was the experience he concretized in a paranoid manner as "mortal danger." It is legitimate to assume that these temporary lapses into paranoia constituted repetition of infantile states of disorganization. As we know from clinical experience, individuals with such childhood histories tend to conceptualize their own subjectivity in the concretistic manner characteristic of childhood thinking: they view psychological disorder as an actual dissolution of the *bodily* self.

Liebert's best thoughts about formal aspects of Michelangelo's oeuvre refer to the artist's propensity to experience emotional stress in terms of fears of bodily harm. Presumably, the artist chose certain formal solutions in part in order to reassure himself about the integrity of the human body. Thus Liebert ascribes Michelangelo's invention of the style of High Renaissance sculpture to his solution of the problem of conveying emotional agitation by showing the human body both contorted and immobilized—an achievement first attained with the *St. Matthew* of 1506 (p. 134). In a general sense, he believes that Michelangelo's preoccupation with the idealization of male nudes as inviolable was an effort to buttress his deficient sense of bodily integrity; he finds the best example of this tendency in the cartoon for *The Battle of Cascina*. These splendid insights demonstrate that Michelangelo's deepest longings could not have concerned the reestablishment of a bond with his primary caretaker; his most pressing psychological need was to avoid any repetition of the terrifying consequences of such dependency: repetitive subjective experiences of bodily dissolution.

Liebert is well aware, of course, that Michelangelo's mental representation of mother-infant transactions must have been laden with aggression (see note, p. 22) but for the most part he assumes that the child must have been stimulated to experience murderous rage by the *loss* of his primary caretaker. Clinical work suggests that traumata of that kind often do lead to severe personality disorders but are not sufficient in themselves to produce either the chronic rage or the paranoid propensities that characterized Michelangelo.[16] Such qualities are most likely to develop in people whose earliest human bonds were in themselves confusing and unsatisfactory. In this regard, we should note Wohl's (1982) discussion of Liebert's thesis, in which he pointed out that the Infant Jesus of the *Taddei Tondo* is not seeking His mother's protection, as Liebert assumed; on the contrary, in His panic, He is leaping from her lap! If we are to read Michelangelo's early representations of Virgin and Child in autobiographical terms, this unique iconography can only be taken to mean that he never sought the maternal symbiosis so many analytic scholars claim he needed.

In terms of the usual psychoanalytic categories, Michelangelo's emotional development is therefore better understood if we focus on "narcissistic" issues, rather than on longings for love. Liebert periodically recognizes this, as in his discussion (pp. 115–116) of the possible restitutional function of creating powerful masculine images for Michelangelo's fragile sense of bodily integrity, or when he quotes the artist's statement (recorded by Gianotti in 1546) that he feared intimate relations with individuals he could admire because he experienced the loss of his own selfhood through total surrender to the other (p. 137). I wish to make this point even more explicit: only in unconscious fantasies could Michelangelo satisfy his need to merge even with omnipotent males; in the social sphere, he was compelled to withdraw from real intimacy until he began his relationships with Tommaso Cavalieri and Vittoria Colonna.

Despite occasional concessions to the view I espouse, Liebert generally adheres to the conclusion that Michelangelo had a positive symbiotic bond to his wetnurse, one that he would forever wish to recreate. I am in fundamental agreement with the proposition that man's basic need is to repeat the qualities of his earliest subjective experiences—in Michelangelo's case, however, I see the repetition compulsion producing an endless series of disappointments, if necessary through severe distortions in reality testing on his part. Witness his paranoid fears that he would lose the Sistine ceiling commission to Raphael, many years after Julius II began to *insist* on taking Michelangelo into his service! The issue is tersely summarized in the artist's *Madrigal*, written around 1544: "As in hard stone, a man at times will make/ Everyone else's image his own likeness, I make it pale with weakness/ Frequently, just as I am made by her/ . . . The stone where I portray her/ Resembles her . . . because it is so hard and sharp;/ Destroyed and mocked by her,/ I'd know/ Nothing but my own burdened limbs to sculpt" (Gilbert & Linscott, 1965, p. 135).

Liebert concurs with Sterba and Sterba (1978) who averred that Michelangelo restituted himself in sculpting or quarrying by venting his rage on the stone; he believes that such a "discharge" of aggression permits a fantasy of idealized reunion with the primary object. I disagree: without a change of circumstances, rage only feeds upon itself. If Michelangelo was restituted by these angry activities, we must find the explanation for this in the fact that the stability of our personality is guaranteed not by pleasure but by the possibility of actively bringing about whatever is most familiar to us. In Michelangelo's case, this was apparently the experience of suffering and rage.[17] In this connection, let us recall his sonnet about his work: "Whenever a master keeps a slave in prison/ Locked in strong fetters, and entirely hopeless,/ He grows so much accustomed to his anguish/ That he would hardly ask again for freedom/ Tiger and serpent too are checked by custom,/ And the fierce lion, born in the thick forest;/ And, toiling at his works, the raw artist/ By custom and sweat doubles exertion" (Gilbert & Linscott, 1965, p. 16).

To repeat, although Liebert postulates that Michelangelo's life-long rage must have originated in the reaction to his wetnurse's preference for her own family (i.e., her children?) and he acknowledges that the artist avoided true intimacy before his healing relationship with Cavalieri (p. 284), he nonetheless bases his hypotheses about Michelangelo's personality on the putative effects of the *loss* of the wetnurse. Oremland (1978, 1980) made the same choice in his work on Michelangelo: he explicitly placed the issue of mourning at the center of the artist's psychology. If one concentrates on the last three decades of Michelangelo's long life, Oremland's contention appears to be valid. Thus, when his friend and financial advisor Luigi del Riccio died in 1546, the grief of the 71-year-old artist impressed observers as if he had been stunned and abandoned himself to despair (see Liebert, p. 366). The death of Vittoria Colonna in 1547 so devastated him that Condivi (1553, p. 103) described him as "in despair and as if out of his mind." In a sonnet on the subject of her death, Michelangelo characterized his own reaction through the metaphor of being reduced to ashes (Gilbert & Linscott, 1965, p. 149). The death in 1555 of his faithful servant Urbino, who assisted him for 25 years, left the 80-year-old artist feeling lifeless: ". . . the greater part of me has gone with him and nothing is left me but an infinite sorrow," he wrote Vasari (Gilbert & Linscott, 1965, pp. 304–305). Yet Michelangelo went on working for close to another decade: Ackerman (1961) described his unexecuted design for S. Giovanni dei Fiorentini (completed in 1560) as work conveying resignation. Incidentally, this trenchant insight into one piece of Michelangelo's architecture makes one regret Liebert's decision to leave that body of work out of consideration in his study, for it demonstrates that this facet of Michelangelo's creativity is no less closely connected to his inner life than were his sculpture, paintings, drawings, and poetry.

Be that as it may, for an overview of Michelangelo's emotional development, we have to compare his mourning reactions in old age with his behavior in similar circumstances of loss earlier in his life. It is striking that we possess no evidence of grief reactions to the deaths of his great patrons; this circumstance suggests that these relationships had for the artist only narcissistic significance. He did react profoundly to the death of his father in 1531; Liebert notes (pp. 266–267) that Michelangelo plunged himself into a frenzy of work, so that his friends were concerned that he was endangering his own life. The fateful love affair with Tommaso Cavalieri followed. At the very least, we can conclude that, at the age of 56, Michelangelo was not yet capable of resignation. Many scholars date the Boboli *Slaves* (pp. 231–233) to the artist's last years in Florence; if this view is correct, the figures trapped in stone, as the sculptor left them, may well represent his continued inability to free himself of the need for symbiotic bonds to father surrogates.

It seems to me that we must assume that Michelangelo's personality underwent important changes when he was about 60 years of age. Whether these can be ascribed to the influence of Tommaso Cavalieri or, conversely, whether they made it possible for the artist for the first time to permit himself a meaningful relationship with a person of excellence is an unanswerable question. Similarly, the successful spiritual friendship with Vittoria Colonna opened new opportunities for Michelangelo's development and followed as a result of the changes he had already made. At any rate, both relationships promoted a shift in his religious feelings in the direction of growing humility and faith in Christian salvation. In psychoanalytic terms, we can describe this change as a diminution of personal grandiosity, in favor of fantasies of ecstatic participation in the greatness of a Divine Other. In this context, Michelangelo's human relationships also improved: he became kinder to his nephew and heir, Lionardo Buonarroti; he was able to mourn the deaths of Riccio, Vittoria Colonna, and Urbino, and he avoided the rancorous attitudes toward fellow artists that marked his earlier career.

This revolution in Michelangelo's inner being took place while he was painting his immense fresco, *The Last Judgment*. The presence of the artist's features on the flayed skin of St. Bartholomew (Fig. 14) near the center of the composition betrays the personal significance of this great public statement for its creator. Liebert postulates that these private meanings are confined to the figures at the core of the work: Christ as the impassive judge, His image echoing those of Apollo in Hellenic art; the Virgin at His side, almost melting into Him, and the artist as the alter ego of the excoriated saint. Although Liebert accepts the interpretation of Wind (1969) that the flayed artist confronting Apollo indicates Michelangelo's identification with Marsyas (i.e., one who achieves divine ecstasy through his art, although for this hubris he is subjected to great suffering), he gives equal weight to another view, first proposed by Sterba and Sterba (1978). These authors read the painting as a condemnation of Michelangelo-as-St. Bartholomew for his aggressive reproaches to the Virgin-Mother about the sufferings to which he has been subjected. Liebert adds the conjecture that the artist's sense of grievance was heightened in the late 1530s by his disappointment over Tommaso Cavalieri's marriage. In the context of the favorable changes in Michelangelo's personality during this period, I am more inclined to interpret this imagery as an avowal of Michelangelo's conversion—the dedication of his art to the greater glory of the Christian God. St. Bartholomew is his intercessor for divine mercy for his former presumption, the use of his genius for private or secular ends. Henceforth, by learning humility, Michelangelo would transcend Marsyas, challenger of the gods in pursuing his own glory.[18]

III

I trust that I have now presented a coherent psychological portrait of Michelangelo that can serve as an alternative to the one Liebert offers in his book. As I have already stated, the historical data always permit a number of equally plausible interpretations, and our preference among these will be determined by extraneous considerations. At the same time, our choice will decisively affect our understanding of the hidden psychological messages encoded in the artist's work. Thus, Liebert consistently reads Michelangelo's numerous representations of Christ as self-references; with almost equal consistency, I see them as images of an idealized other. Liebert assumes that the Virgin in Michelangelo's works stands for the perfect mother the artist always desired; I almost always interpret this theme as an expression of Michelangelo's unconscious feminine identification. I shall refrain from listing further examples of the divergent conclusions we have reached on the basis of espousing differing conceptions of the artist's personality—I think it is evident that these differences are almost as numerous as are instances of agreement between Liebert's understanding of Michelangelo's art and my own.

I hope I have also made it clear that I do not claim to have superior insight into the artist's inner life—the Michelangelo I have described is simply the one I have found within myself. I am reasonably confident that Liebert claims no more for *his* Michelangelo. Hostile critics often attempt to dismiss psychoanalytic efforts to penetrate the inner life of figures from the past by pointing out that the biographer does not have his subject "on the couch." True enough; in this field, the analysand's collaboration in the study of his life history is replaced by the empathic responses of a succession of analytic scholars. Just as successive analysts discover ever-novel insights about the same person who consults them in turn, so the biographers who study a given set of historical materials will arrive at differing interpretations. As the psychoanalytic consensus about human nature evolves, the interpretations acceptable to the scholarly community slowly change in their turn.

Liebert's portrait of Michelangelo, as well as mine, is typical for a segment of American psychoanalysis in the 1980s. Beyond our theoretical and clinical commitments, however, there lie differences in our human response to this enigmatic figure. Liebert writes movingly about the child Michelangelo's terror "in the silent darkness of the motherless night" (p. 180); I suspect that such a description grossly underestimates the peculiarities that must have foreshadowed Michelangelo's *terribilità* in adulthood. Like Leo X, I find the man unpalatable; his awesome sculptures and paintings astonish me but leave me cold. As was Bernini, I am most impressed by Michelangelo's architecture—but as a patron, I would have preferred to deal with Bramante. I am confident that Robert Liebert would follow the example of Paul III in naming Michelangelo the premier artist of Christendom. And that is the reason for his devotion and success in writing this exciting book about his heroic subject.

ADDENDUM: As this essay goes to press, Professor Leo Steinberg's review of Liebert's book has appeared (*New York Review of Books,* June 28, 1984). Although I cannot incorporate my reactions to Steinberg's cogent discussion into the body of my paper, I trust that a few brief comments will not be out of place here.

First, I should like to note that Steinberg's jocular "reconstruction" of Michelangelo's blissful childhood at his mother's side, though purposefully preposterous, parallels my own efforts to demonstrate the perils of Liebert's specific approach to psycho-analytic biography—my effort to outline an alternative vision of the artist's emotional development. Steinberg's successful reductio ad absurdum of the risky reconstruction method also illustrates my point that each biographer necessarily finds in his materials the character he prefers to attribute to his subject. Steinberg is not fully in earnest about his portrait of Michelangelo as a robust and confident personality, but he makes a good case for paying more attention than any commentator has done to the artist's ruthlessness in matters of money and love. I am, of course, pleased that he also cites new documentary evidence validating my conviction that Michelangelo's homosexuality was overt.

Second, I wish to underscore the significance of Steinberg's brilliant *aperçu* that the visage of the Virgin in Michelangelo's *Manchester Madonna* (in London) mirrors the artist's own disfigurement. Not only does this support my contention that the fracture of his nose was a profoundly meaningful experience for the adolescent Michelangelo; more crucially, it buttresses a major theme of this essay—the artist's lifelong identification with the Virgin. I am therefore glad to be able to modify my conclusion (p. 291) that this identification is nowhere to be discerned in Michelangelo's early work.

Notes

1 According to Lucco (1980), about a dozen of Sebastiano's works postdate his loss of Michelangelo's assistance in 1534 (nos. 90–102, pp. 121–

122). Sebastiano was always a notoriously slow worker; scarcely over 100 paintings by him are known in an active career that spanned 35 years. Lucco comments on the recent tendency, largely "correct and opportune," to "detach Sebastiano from Buonarroti's tutelage," whereas formerly he was "condemned to the role of an eclectic reworker of ideas by the Florentine" (p. 121, my translation). It is not my intention to take sides in this complex scholarly controversy—only to point out that, in view of these uncertainties about the extent of Sebastiano's dependence on Michelangelo's assistance, Liebert's espousal of one position appears to represent a wish to credit Michelangelo with a greater share in Sebastiano's total accomplishment than he may deserve.

2 Liebert seems entirely to ignore the fact that Pontormo's apparently bizarre behavior, which he interprets as an aspect of his relations with Michelangelo, took place about a dozen years after the latter left Florence, ending their collaboration. In the interval, Pontormo produced an impressive body of distinguished work in fresco, portraiture, and tapestry design.

3 Liebert cites Kavka's (1980) thesis that the *Moses* represents an angry mother surrogate. I believe that this interpretation misses the main purport of this work by going "too deep." Michelangelo wanted only *father* surrogates, for reasons I shall try to specify below.

4 In line with his understanding of Michelangelo as forever looking for reunion with the lost nurse of his infancy, Liebert once again correlates this remark with a putative wish to resurrect that prehistoric mother surrogate, rather than the artist's lost patron in the present.

5 Liebert is surely right in detecting the same theme in the Sistine *Temptation of Adam and Eve,* as well as in two early self-portrait drawings (Hartt, nos. 16, 17). I also concur with Liebert's judgment that the naked youths in the background of the *Doni Tondo* constitute the earliest reference in Michelangelo's commissioned works to this aspect of the artist's inner life. It should be recalled that in 1503–05, when he produced this painting, Michelangelo did not have a relationship to a single, idealizable patron. The reference to his passive longings *almost* hidden in the depths of the painting was probably evoked by the cumulative frustration of these emotional needs.

6 Incidentally, Michelangelo probably presented Tommaso with at least three other drawings: *Children's Bacchanal* (already discussed), *Dream of Human Life,* and *Archers Shooting at a Herm. Bacchanal* may be read as a retrospective account of Michelangelo's childhood, with its outcome of dwelling in an exclusively masculine world of attempted self-sufficiency, lewdness, and aggression, as Liebert states (p. 290). Contrary to Liebert, I believe Michelangelo wanted Tommaso to rescue him from all this, not to join him in such a life! The *Dream* is centered on the attainment of fame, which can rouse the virtuous from falling into the vices, emblematically represented in a circle around the main figures. Liebert's interpretation of this work (pp. 307–310) is diffuse and unconvincing, and he fails to discuss the *Archers* altogether. Should the entire series of presentation drawings be understood as autobiographical? If so, the *Dream* might be interpreted as the expression of Michelangelo's hope that his creative accomplishments would permit him to overcome his sins, and the *Archers,* enigmatic as it is, would somehow represent the artist's concerns about love and death (see Hartt, 1970, pp. 252–253).

7 Hartt, nos. 410, 416, 427, 428, 430.

8 Hartt, nos. 421, 423–426, 429.

9 Hartt, nos. 451–454, 456, 457.

10 Along these lines, we might understand Michelangelo's dissatisfaction with the *Florence Pietà* (which he intended as a marker for his own grave)

as a sign that he could no longer abide masking his wish for Divine merger by showing himself as Nicodemus and relegating the opportunity for fusion to a third person (the Virgin), as he did in that work. The death of Vittoria Colonna, until 1547 Michelangelo's intercessor for Christian Grace, may have emboldened the artist to present his Ganymede fantasy within a Christian context in his last carving.

11 A handful of earlier drawings on this theme (Hartt, nos. 57–59, 177–179) exist, one or two of which depict mother and child in a more affectionate interaction; in the main, however, they confirm the evidence of the later works.

12 It is true that Michelangelo probably relegated the production of this area of the fresco to an assistant, but the conception is surely his.

13 These images constitute the sole instance about which Liebert transmits the dubious judgments of earlier authorities. He echoes the view that *all* the Ancestors are "isolated" in private anguish, presumably reflecting the artist's mental state during his solitary labors. I cannot follow Liebert's conclusion that these images suggest an identification with Jesus on the part of their creator.

14 It may be pertinent to note here that the peculiar bisexual genital anatomy Michelangelo depicted in his *Rape of Ganymede* (as Liebert notes, a discovery made by K. R. Eissler [1961]) was not unprecedented in his art. Hence it cannot be a copyist's error, as suggested by those who doubt that Michelangelo's original of the drawing is extant. The bisexual genitals are also present in *The Drunkenness of Noah,* as a feature of one of the naked sons. This is presumably an allusion to Michelangelo's fantasy of his own bisexuality.

15 If we can trust Vasari's later report (1912–15, v. IX, p. 116) that the artist sometimes kept his boots on for such long periods of time that, when he removed them at last, he pulled off some of his own skin in the process, the flayed St. Bartholomew may also represent an actuality of his adult condition, i.e., some form of eczema or ectopic dermatitis. Is it possible that he may have suffered from infantile eczema as well? The earliest months of individuals with this condition are sometimes characterized by continuous overstimulation even if their caretakers are benign and competent.

16 We should note, however, that Michelangelo's propensity for paranoid thinking may also have represented an identification with his father, at least if we may judge on the basis of the artist's letter of 1521 (in Liebert, p. 34) in which he tried to soothe Lodovico who had apparently accused him, without foundation, of turning his father out of the family house.

17 By no stretch of the imagination can such activities be seen as "transitional" in the sense of that word introduced by Winnicott, as Liebert would have us believe about Michelangelo's work in stone (p. 222).

18 I am indebted to Jack Spector for putting at my disposal his then-unpublished review of Liebert's book; for the interpretation of Michelangelo's flayed image, I have leaned on Spector's work.

References

Ackerman, J. (1961). *The architecture of Michelangelo.* Harmondsworth: Penguin.

301

Andersen, W. (1971). *Gauguin's paradise lost*. New York: Viking.

Clements, R. (1968). *Michelangelo: A self portrait*. New York: New York University Press.

Condivi, A. (1553). *The life of Michelangelo*. Transl. A. S. Wohl; Ed. H. Wohl. Baton Rouge: Louisiana State University Press.

Eissler, K. (1961). *Leonardo da Vinci: Psychoanalytic notes on the enigma*. New York: International Universities Press.

Fischel, O. (1948). *Raphael*. London: Springs Books, 1964.

Frank, G. (1966). The enigma of Michelangelo's Pietà Rondanini: A study of mother-loss in childhood. *American Imago, 23*:287–315.

Gedo, J. (1983). *Portraits of the artist*. New York: Guilford.

Gedo, M. (1980). *Picasso: Art as autobiography*. Chicago: University of Chicago Press.

Gilbert, C., & Linscott, R. (1965). *Complete poems and selected letters of Michelangelo*. New York: Modern Library.

Hartt, F. (1970). *Michelangelo drawings*. New York: Abrams.

Kavka, J. (1980). Michelangelo's *Moses:* Madonna Androgyna. *The Annual of Psychoanalysis, 8*:291–316. New York: International Universities Press.

Kernberg, O. (1975). *Borderline conditions and pathological narcissism*. New York: Aronson.

Liebert, R. (1977a). Michelangelo's mutilation of the Florence Pietà. *Art Bulletin, 59*:47–59.

———— (1977b). Michelangelo's Dying Slave. *The Psychoanalytic Study of the Child, 32*:505–544. New Haven: Yale University Press.

———— (1983). *Michelangelo*. New Haven: Yale University Press.

Lucco, M. (1980). *L'Opera Completa di Sebastiano del Piombo*. Milano: Rizzoli.

Moraitis, G. (1985). The psychoanalyst's role in the biographer's quest for self-awareness. In S. H. Baron & C. Pletsch (Eds.), *Introspection in biography: The biographer's quest for self-awareness*. Hillsdale, NJ: The Analytic Press, pp. 319–354.

Oremland, J. (1978). Michelangelo's *Pietàs*. *The Psychoanalytic Study of the Child, 33*:563–591. New Haven: Yale University Press.

———— (1980). Mourning and its effect on Michelangelo's art. *The Annual of Psychoanalysis, 8*:317–351. New York: International Universities Press.

Spector, J. (1978). Letter to the Editor. *Art Bulletin, 40.*

———— (1983). A review of R. S. Liebert, *Michelangelo. Italian Quarterly* XXIV, no. 94, 113–19.

Sterba, R., & Sterba, E. (1956). The anxieties of Michelangelo Buonarroti. *Int. J. Psycho-Anal., 37*:7–11.

———— (1978). The personality of Michelangelo Buonarroti. Some reflections. *American Imago, 35*:156–177.

Vasari, G. (1568). *The lives of the artists*. Transl. G. de Vere. London: Medici Society, 1912–1915.

Wind, E. (1969). *Pagan mysteries in the Renaissance* (rev. ed.). New York: Norton.

Wohl, H. (1982). Discussion of Liebert's presentation to the Boston meeting of the American Psychoanalytic Association, May 1982.

Earl E.
Rosenthal,
Ph.D.

Review of Robert S. Liebert, *Michelangelo: A Psychoanalytic Study of His Life and Images.* Yale University Press, 1983.

Robert Liebert's stated purpose is to supplement the art historian's observations on style and iconography with a study of the intra-psychic conflicts that he believes determined both form and content in Michelangelo's art. He explained, "My approach has been governed by the basic assumption that there are certain invariable laws of human behavior which operate in all individuals, irrespective of period or culture" (p. 3). While historians of art may find it difficult to accept the validity of "universal psychiatric laws," they will be pleased that Liebert (unlike most psychiatrists writing on art) is familiar with their research and also that he has avoided unnecessary psychoanalytic terminology.

Information on the artist's life was drawn from a wide range of literary sources. The author listed 480 letters and 327 poems written by Michelangelo and 800 letters written to him and, of course, the two biographies by his friends, Vasari and Condivi. He also cited incidental comments and characterizations by contemporaries, but he gave less attention than I should have expected to statements that reveal Michelangelo's theory of art.

The study is restricted to the artist's painting, drawing, and sculpture, because the author saw no way of applying psycho-analytic techniques to architecture. Apparently form itself has little to tell us of Michelangelo's unresolved and repressed conflicts. Their detection depends on a related subject or theme that the author believes "resonated" in the artist's psyche.

Liebert began with the two childhood events that are cited by all psychiatrists writing on Michelangelo: his separation after two years from his wetnurse and the death of his natural mother within four years of his return to his family in Florence. Twice abandoned, Michelangelo is believed to have suffered a disruption of the process of individuation, and uncertainty as to his "ego boundaries" and sexual identity. As a result, he developed matricidal, patricidal, and homosexual inclinations that led to guilt feelings as well as fear of bodily destruction. He seems to have turned to a series of protective males or father-figures that included Lorenzo il Magnifico, Francesco Aldovrandi, Piero Soderini, Julius II, several later Popes, and, finally, the handsome, young Tommaso de' Cavalieri. All failed him and so did the accommodation of his homosexual inclinations to the current fashion for Neoplatonism; so, late in life, he turned to a preoccupation with death and salvation, and he sought reconciliation and reunion with his natural mother. It is in the context of this psychiatric history that Liebert discusses Michelangelo's works in a generally chronological order.

Beginning with the teenage artist's first representation of the Madonna and Child, the relief sculpture *Madonna of the Stairs,* he cites De Tolnay's suggestion that the seated, profile position of the Madonna is reminiscent of Greek grave stelae depicting a deceased mother bidding farewell to her children (pp. 18–20). That unusual motif touched Michelangelo, Liebert explains, because he had lost both his surrogate and natural mothers. While his explanation cannot be proved or disproved, it provides a reason for the choice of the odd motif, whereas De Tolnay simply noted that a stele of the type was in Florence in the 16th century. The fixed forward stare of the Madonna (unusual at the time but taken by historians to be an indication of her foreknowledge of the sacrifice of her son) is interpreted by most psychiatrists as inattention or indifference to the Child. To be sure, inattention is characteristic of all Michelangelo's representations of the Madonna and Child until his very last year, when he did the chalk drawing of an affectionate Madonna now in the British Museum, which Liebert believes signals a belated reconciliation with his natural mother.

Other early works are given little attention. The impressive relief *Battle of the Lapiths and the Centaurs,* probably Michelangelo's second known work, is simply mentioned without comment, and so are the youthful sketches after figures by Giotto and Masaccio. These boldly drawn figures seem to have nearly filled the original sheet and they are notable for the marked articulation of the joints (beyond those of his models) and also a predominance of densely cross-hatched shadows. Is there no psychiatric interest in these formal traits? Must we first link the subjects (Masaccio's St. Peter and Giotto's St. John the Evangelist) to one or more of Michelangelo's unresolved conflicts? It is surprising that of approximately a dozen extant works assigned to Michelangelo's first 20 years, only the *Madonna of the Stairs* was analyzed at length.

Special attention was given to the *Doni Tondo* in which Michelangelo depicted the Holy Family with young St. John the

Baptist in the middle-ground and six androgynous youths lounging in a semicircular recess in the background. The unusual position of the Child, who holds onto Mary's hair while He is passed by Joseph over her shoulder, is thought to have been inspired by the infant Dionysus on the shoulder of a satyr in one of the roundels of the Medici palace courtyard. Liebert suggests that it was the image of a male caring for a boy that attracted Michelangelo, because of his own transfer from maternal to paternal care. Of course, the male satyr in the Medici roundel was replaced by the Madonna in Michelangelo's tondo, but Liebert holds that transmutations of this sort were typical of the artist. In the case of the Child frightened by the bird in the *Taddei Tondo,* Liebert accepts the general belief that the motif was inspired by the action of one of Medea's children in the sarcophagus of that designation in Mantua, but the murderous and terrifying associations that first attracted him to the pose were then disguised by the playful context of childlike behavior. The assumption of disguises of this sort introduces considerable flexibility in the identification of "controlling unconscious forces" in the selection of models. Another limitation is revealed when a figural motif was used for a series of very different biblical and mythological personages. For example, the configuration of Raphael's Heliodorus (struck down while robbing the temple) was used by Michelangelo for Ganymede carried off by Jupiter; Tityus beset by vultures who devour his ever-renewed liver; Venus with Cupid; Christ of the Resurrection; the Dreamer surrounded by the seven deadly sins; Phaethon in the final version of his fall; and Saul (St. Paul) struck down on the road to Damascus. With each added personage the associations become more entangled and less convincing. Most art historians would, I believe, explain the persistence of the Heliodorus motif as an instance in which Michelangelo (like so many of his contemporaries) was attracted to a figural "invention" or a "difficult" pose and explored its formal possibilities, with little evident concern for the original personage or function. While Liebert seems to be thoroughly familiar with art historical literature, he does not often weigh the psychiatric explanation against the historical. Even so, Liebert's explanations for Michelangelo's attraction to particular motives are of special interest.

Psychiatric explanations are also offered for more general questions about Michelangelo's life and works. One is his predilection for the theme of the bound and struggling captive, first found in the rather sedate male nudes in the project for the tomb of Julius II in 1505 and the essentially heraldic *Ignudi* in the first bay of the Sistine ceiling, begun in 1508. As Michelangelo progressed across the ceiling, the *Ignudi* became more animated and often more victimlike; and, when he returned to the sculpture for the tomb in 1513 and again in the 1520s, the struggle of the captives became more intense and anguished. Most readers will accept Leibert's suggestion that Michelangelo's intrapsychic conflicts gave special meaning to the tethered captives of 1505 and also the hopeless struggle of the Laocoön group discovered in 1506. Less convincing is the author's citation of Michelangelo's statements that he had executed most of his work "under duress and against my will" and that he had spent most of his life "chained to the tomb of Julius II." These complaints were made in his 60s, but at age 30, when he first took up the captive motif, he had not yet suffered coercion of this sort.

Students of Michelangelo have wondered about the extraordinary amount of time he spent at the quarries supervising the cutting of marble blocks for his many ambitious projects and also the unusual number of sculptural works that remained unfinished. Liebert has a common answer for both questions. The quarries reminded him of his first two years in Caprese with his wetnurse, the wife of a stone quarrier and, more specifically, Liebert accepts Sterba's suggestion that the great stone cliffs were identified with maternal breasts (p. 220). Thus, for Michelangelo stone was a "transitional object" or, in more popular terms, a "security blanket." His attachment to stone also explains his leaving so many sculptural works unfinished. He was not able to sever that bond with a block of marble.

In a surprisingly brief (page-and-a-half) conclusion Liebert summarizes his psychiatric analysis of Michelangelo, without grouping or classifying the many works of art analyzed separately and without delineating patterns in the operation of the unconscious in the conception of his work. Also, because the author states that his findings are intended to supplement stylistic and iconographic analyses, the reader has reason to expect an evaluation of the interrelation or the relative validity of psychiatric and historical explanations. The closest Liebert comes is the claim that Michelangelo's "nuclear yearnings for protection and sustenance from an idealized male endowed with tender qualities . . . provided *much of the energy* for specific images in painting and sculpture as well as the overall programs for such major works as the Sistine Chapel frescoes and the Tomb of Pope Julius II" (p. 417, my italics). Even so, Robert Liebert has provided a well-researched and thoughtful psychoanalytic account of the life and oeuvre of Michelangelo and, I believe, historians of art—even those who think they know his art very well—will benefit from the reading of this book.

Robert S.
Liebert, M.D.

Response to John E. Gedo's Essay-Review and Earl E. Rosenthal's Review

I

I should state at the outset that it is not without conflict that I accepted the invitation to respond to Dr. John Gedo and Professor Earl Rosenthal's reviews. My more high-minded side holds that the fundamental dialogue resides between the work being reviewed and the review. Moreover, the book, once "out there," must lead an independent life and not rely on its author to take arms in its defense when challenge is voiced. Nevertheless, like most authors with whom I have compared experiences, when anything less than a fully praising review appears, I spend the night tossing in bed, composing elegant, irrefutable letters— epistolary gems that put the matter back into proper perspective. But somehow they pale as the circulating adrenalin diminishes and the dawn mercifully arrives. Thus, the invitation to respond proved a temptation beyond my capacity to resist. I will address myself first to Dr. Gedo, then to Professor Rosenthal.

II

John Gedo is a psychoanalyst with an uncommonly fertile and broadly interested intellect. It is, therefore, a particularly rewarding experience for me to encounter the outgrowth of his study of my work on Michelangelo. In what follows, I will confine my comments to one theme in Dr. Gedo's review—an aspect of the methodology of psychoanalytic biography and criticism. It concerns the ways in which the personal psychology of the investigator affects the conclusions that he or she draws from the data. And, directly related to this question, to what extent should the

307

biographer make explicit to the reader those elements of his or her private self that bear on the subject at hand. Dr. Gedo and I have strong disagreement in this realm.

In restricting my remarks to this theme in Dr. Gedo's review, I do not do justice to the richness of many of his own formulations about Michelangelo and his art—ideas that certainly expand our understanding of both the artist and the creative process in general. Of course, substantial differences remain between us on many matters of interpretation and reconstruction, and so it should be. If we were easily to agree down the line it would only reflect the narrow and impoverished character of the working constructs provided by psychoanalytic theory and clinical experience.

III

The question about Michelangelo that has been by far most frequently asked of me, both after presenting papers to professional groups and in ordinary conversation, has been—was he overtly homosexual? The issue, not surprisingly, arouses strong feelings of various sorts. And it is in the course of discussing our different conclusions with respect to this aspect of Michelangelo's life that Dr. Gedo states: "In my judgment, a biography aspiring to be called 'psychoanalytic' should show awareness, preferably explicitly, about the nature and sources of the author's personal bias toward his subject" (p. 275).

We are fortunate in that a wealth of material has come down to us—in the form of Michelangelo's letters and poetry, letters written to him, contemporary accounts of him, as well as painted, sculptured, and sketched images—that appear to yield some understanding of the artist's sexual fantasies and behavior, and their role in his art. There is *not,* however, one piece of evidence that is conclusive about the nature of his manifest sexual behavior. And every "one-liner" that firmly points in one direction is contradicted by another which points toward the opposite. Scholars through the years have been divided in opinion. Thus, in the context of everything else I know about the man, tempered by common sense, and my outlook as a psychoanalyst, I tentatively developed the view that Michelangelo did not consummate his intensely homoerotic relationships and yearnings. Dr. Gedo, on the other hand, is convinced that the artist did have sex with quite a few young men (although not with Tommaso de' Cavalieri).

How does Dr. Gedo account for our drawing different conclusions? He proposes that my reasoning is the outgrowth of my "idealization" of the artist. Thus, he states, "perhaps Liebert's judgment that Michelangelo was not overtly homosexual is another consequence of such idealization" (p. 276). Dr. Gedo is quite forthright is asserting that he finds Michelangelo, the man, "unpalatable," and Michelangelo's art "astonishes" but leaves him "cold." Clearly, Dr. Gedo and I are drawn to different sorts of people and have different aesthetic sensibilities.

Dr. Gedo assumes that I share what emerges as *his* system of values; namely, that homosexuality is necessarily a reflection of psychic impairment, if not frank psychopathology. And that if one is nevertheless so inclined, restraint is more admirable than indulgence. Not only do I not share this belief, but the interpretation that Dr. Gedo offers about *why* I have reached the conclusion that I have, attributes to me the notion that not to consummate one's deepest passions is "ideal"—a notion that I would scarcely subscribe to.

In my long chapter on Michelangelo's relationship with Tommaso de' Cavalieri and the artist's sexuality, I attempted, first of all, to present all of the significant written and pictorial data related to the issue. Then, I indicated the contradictory interpretations that have and could be given to the data. And finally, I offered the reasoning that brought me to my final conclusion. Obviously, I cannot recapitulate my final reasoning here, but suffice it to say that the data and arguments leading to either conclusion are sufficiently compelling that I would allow that Dr. Gedo (and Dr. Jerome Oremland, 1980) might be correct and I (and Drs. Richard and Edith Sterba, 1979) not. That room still exists for multiple well-reasoned conclusions on this issue is demonstrated by a scholarly, full-length study of homosexuality in Renaissance Italy by Professor James Saslow (soon to be published by Yale University Press). In a long chapter on Michelangelo, Saslow examines all of the relevant primary data within the social practices and intellectual currents of the time. He, too, arrives at the conclusion that Michelangelo was probably abstinent.

My central point in this discussion of Michelangelo's homosexuality is that Dr. Gedo believes himself to be correct and so, with less certainty, do I. Readers will judge for themselves and, no doubt, end up divided in opinion. The same will obtain for future scholars reexamining the primary data. The division will reflect the intellectual rigor, theoretical base, and the individual psychology of each student of the subject. It is more intellectually useful to marshal evidence in support of one's own conclusion than to make interpretations about the motives underlying the espousal of the alternative position. Dr. Gedo's form of criticism of my reasoning in this matter comes precariously close to dissolving the boundaries between psychoanalytic dialogue and *ad hominem* argument.

IV

Pursuing Dr. Gedo's contention that my idealization of Michelangelo interferes with accurate scholarship, I turn to our very different views of the fate of Sebastiano del Piombo after his abrupt and cruel rejection by Michelangelo in 1535. Here, Gedo attributes to me an "unduly harsh" attitude toward the Venetian Master, growing out of an unreasoned identification with Michelangelo's long-standing complex and ambivalent relationship with his loyal follower. Dr. Gedo states: "Liebert asserts that Sebastiano became unable to paint after Michelangelo broke with him; this claim is not sustained by some recent historical research" (p. 276).

My first question is—what is the "recent historical research" that Gedo alludes to? Apart from other evidence, my assertion of Sebastiano's decline following the break in 1535 comes from three main sources: Vasari (1568), Hirst (1961), and Freedberg (1970).

Vasari, who knew Sebastiano personally and was in residence in Rome during many of Sabastiano's last years, wrote that as a result of the rift: "Being finally brought to a state wherein he [Sebastiano] would neither work nor do any other thing than but just attend to his office as Frate del Piombo. . . until he resigned his soul to God" (p. 345). Vasari does not specify the onset of Sebastiano's withdrawal from painting. S. J. Freedberg, however, who is widely regarded as the leading scholar of 16th-century Italian painting, wrote: "Apparently he [Sebastiano] ceased to paint after 1539; he died in 1547" (p. 151). And finally, Hirst offered the same view of Sebastiano's dearth of works in his later years.

After reading Dr. Gedo's piece, with its allusion to recent research, I examined some of the Sebastiano literature that has appeared since I completed my chapter on Michelangelo and Sebastiano. First, Hirst, in his 1981 book on Sebastiano, held that only two works—the *Nativity* for Santa Maria del Popolo and the *Visitation* for Santa Maria della Pace—are from the late 1530s. With respect to the *Nativity*, which was commissioned in 1530 and on which Sebastiano intermittently continued to paint for a few years beyond the 1535 rift, two points are crucial. One, Sebastiano was unable to complete the work for no apparent external reason; it had to be completed by Francesco Salviati. And, two, the project (like so many of Sebastiano's earlier ones) was primarily based on studies that Michelangelo had originally provided for Sebastiano. Hirst wrote about the *Visitation*: "we know even less than in the case of the Popolo *Nativity*. No reference to the work appears in any of Sebastiano's surviving letters. And even its site in the church is open to doubt, and the date when it was removed from the church unrecorded" (p. 144). Hirst based his late dating of the *Visitation* entirely on considerations of the style of copies and the three surviving fragments of the painting. Dr. Gedo relies on Lucco's 1980 catalogue of Sebastiano's paintings. I have reviewed this catalogue, written in Italian, with Professor James Beck. Our reading is quite different from Dr. Gedo's, as he presents in his Note 1. We understand Lucco to have taken a clear position on only three other paintings as having been executed after the rift between the two artists, but even one of these (*Ritratto di Donna*) is of questionable attribution. Finally, Beck, in his book *Italian Renaissance Painting* (1981), stated that Sebastiano "virtually stopped painting" during the period under question. Professor Beck told me that he had examined the documentation of Sebastiano's paintings before arriving at his conclusion.

Now there may be another reconstruction and interpretation of Sebastiano's artistic activities and enthusiasm after 1535 than the one I have offered. If so, it must be based on a set of facts or authorities different from those on which I have relied. I find Dr. Gedo unconvincing in this regard. Thus, he ends by employing his version of Sebastiano's late career as if it were proven and widely accepted, and as evidence, therefore, of my distortion of the facts. And again, Dr. Gedo suggests that my idealization of Michelangelo prevents me from seeing the Sebastiano affair as he does. There are quite plausible explanations, other than mine, of why Sebastiano's work so diminished in his late years. But such an explanation must firmly rest on documentation, and this Dr. Gedo has not sufficiently given us.

V

I turn now to another area in which Dr. Gedo is convinced that my idealization of Michelangelo leads me into an otherwise inexplicable, serious error—this time, of omission. I am referring to the fact that I did not elaborate on what Dr. Gedo calls "the most notorious incident from Michelangelo's early life." The incident was a fracas during pre- or early adolescence, in which a young fellow artist, Pietro Torrigiani, broke Michelangelo's nose, leaving it thereafter flattened. I must say that I think that Dr. Gedo becomes slightly hysterical on the matter when he talks of Michelangelo's "*poisonous* provocativeness toward direct competitors" (p. 276, my italics). Gedo then offers the assertion, unsupported by a single line of documentation, that "the injury left Michelangelo permanently disfigured—a matter that *must have had enormous impact* on a young man forever obsessed by the ideal of masculine beauty" (p. 276, my italics). Again, I think the facts as they are known about this incident have to be reviewed before Gedo's analysis of my motives can be given credence. I described the disfiguring effects of the broken nose in the third sentence of the book, in the text facing the *frontispiece* of Daniele da Volterra's bust of the aging artist, but thereafter never returned to this boyhood incident. Why? In answer to this question it might be useful for me to trace the reasoning which led to my not according great significance to the matter.

So far as I can learn, there are only three contemporary mentions of the incident. The first is Condivi's (1553) passing comment, in describing Michelangelo's physical appearance, that the nose was broken by Torrigiani, "a bestial and arrogant person." Nowhere else in all of Michelangelo's writing is there any allusion to Torrigiani or his disfigured nose, nor are there direct projective evidences of conflict in the treatment of noses in his artistic imagery. This alone does not, of course, necessarily nullify Dr. Gedo's contention; perhaps the conflict over his nose was symbolically displaced to other body areas. The next contemporary reference appears more than a half-century after the incident, in the autobiography of Benvenuto Cellini (1562), who related his encounter with Torrigiani more than 30 years after the event. Torrigiani's version, as he related it to Cellini, was of Michelangelo's "habit to banter" with the other youthful students who came to draw at the Brancacci Chapel, and his particular annoyance on the occasion of his punching Michelangelo in the nose. Our final source is Vasari (1568), who, it must be noted, is rarely neutral when Michelangelo's behavior is called into question. Vasari, nevertheless, places the blame squarely on Torrigiani. According to Vasari, the two were close friends, but as Michelangelo's art emerged as singularly distinguished, Torrigiani filled with envy, following by "jeering," and finally, assault. Vasari's version of the fight is supported by what he states to be fact—that young Torrigiani was banished from Florence for his assault on his early teenage friend. This harsh punishment, if true, is striking, inasmuch as the Torrigianis were an aristocratic Florentine family.

What more do we know about Torrigiani that is relevant to the matter under discussion? He matured into a sculptor of major rank, who chose not only to leave Florence, but Italy altogether, and devote himself to working in England and Spain. His migration raises the question—was it simply opportunity abroad, or was it that Torrigiani also found the competitive situation in his native Florence intolerable and resolved his conflict by moving elsewhere—a question, but hardly evidence. But then we learn how Torrigiani died. Symonds (1887) informs us that he starved to death in a Spanish prison, a victim of the Inquisition. His crime, however, was a startling one. He carved a statue of the Virgin for a nobleman and, not receiving the pay he expected, Torrigiani smashed the sculpture. This act of sacrilege in that religious-moral climate predictably brought him to his tragic end at 58 years of age. This fact leads me to consider that Torrigiani was impulsively given to violent action and, in this instance, under circumstances that betray a gross suspension of self-preservative judgment. Given these few facts about Torrigiani, I have trouble concluding that it was necessarily Michelangelo's "poisonous provocativeness" of Torrigiani that cost him his original facial structure. Perhaps one can say that it was motivated bad judgment on Michelangelo's part to banter with the likes of a hothead like Pietro, who was, incidentally, three years older. But, for lack of other documentation, like with so many other events in Michelangelo's life, what actually took place that day in the chapel of the Carmine between the two youthful artists must remain hazy.

Dr. Gedo's assignment of the broken nose to a role of singular importance in the artist's youth implies that Michelangelo's art, behavior, or inner life would have been demonstrably different had his nose not been flattened. It was, no doubt, traumatic at the time and regrettable throughout life. The dearth of mention of the event in contemporary Renaissance documents or confirmation from Michelangelo himself, suggests to me that the nose affair did not have the formative importance that Dr. Gedo postulates. Again, Dr. Gedo's speculation, and it is pure speculation, may be correct and advance our understanding of the artist. At this point, however, he cannot endow his speculation with the status of fact, and then use this speculation as if it were fact as a basis for demonstrating my wishful distortions of Michelangelo. For my part, I prefer to consider Dr. Gedo's position on the nose an interesting thesis, but one that for me remains unpersuasive. Dr. Gedo's conviction with respect to the nose incident may or may not, incidentally, be colored by his personal feelings about Michelangelo, feelings about his own appearance, fights in his own youth, or whatever else. I am interested in Dr. Gedo's hypothesis, his documentation, and his psychoanalytic reasoning; but not in what motivated his thinking.

Dr. Gedo's concern with "evidence" of my idealization of Michelangelo takes what, from my point of view, are other tendentious turns. For example, where I refer to Michelangelo's quotation of Masaccio's *Fall* in his Sistine ceiling panel, Dr. Gedo faults me for not referring to Michelangelo's need to turn to his Florentine predecessor. I am perplexed inasmuch as earlier in my book (chap. 3) I explore at some length Michelangelo's need to create a powerful mythological family ancestry for himself, and then extend that discussion to the basis of his choice of the masters of the monumental style of Italy's past, including Masaccio, as models for his own artistic style.

VI

In sum, I am not different from other biographers. For a period of years we are immersed in studying the life of one individual, selected from all others for reasons we are never fully aware of. The relationship to that individual is profound, ambivalent, fluid, and always subject to distortion. I had the conviction that I "knew" Michelangelo in some respects, while in others he remained as much a mystery as he was 10 years earlier, when I embarked on the project. Thus, my story of Michelangelo is my personal version, which is to say nothing more than everybody knows.

It is my impression that where authors tell readers "where they are coming from," what they reveal is a circularity; that is, formulations about themselves that are selected from among many because they happen to be consistent with the thesis put forward. At worst, there is a self-aggrandizing pseudo-honesty, which is irrelevant and an attempt to pacify and seduce the reader, and serves to obscure the validity of the ideas and arguments that follow. If Dr. Gedo was faithful to his own canon, he would have to tell us a lot more about himself than he has in his essay. I, for one, am pleased that he chose not to.

I have responded to one dimension of Dr. Gedo's essay. Having said my piece on the subject, I do want to conclude by underscoring the contribution that he has given us. It is far more than a review of my book. It is an important contribution to the growing body of Michelangelo studies by psychoanalysts.

VII

My response to Professor Rosenthal's review is basically one of appreciation of his thoughtful engagement with a body of ideas from another discipline, many of which may well have been unfamiliar and even uncongenial to him.

He raises questions at several points with respect to my lack of attention to certain subjects: Michelangelo's theory of art, architecture, earliest surviving drawings, and early sculpture. I would only say that it was not among my intentions to produce a catalogue of his works or study all aspects of the man. Therefore, I did not address issues and works about which I felt I had little to contribute or that had already been said by others. There are works that I could have discussed more fully, but what I would have said would only have replicated what I was to say about other of Michelangelo's works. Thus, for example, I did not discuss the *Bruges Madonna* because in the course of lengthy discussions of two other Madonna—the *Madonna of the Stairs* and the *Holy Family,* a shorter discussion of the *Taddei Madonna,* and a little bit about the *Medici Madonna,* I said all that I would have to offer about the Bruges statue.

Professor Rosenthal's cautionary note is well-taken with respect to my potential for overemphasizing the narrative theme in works or parts of works by others that probably struck dominant unconscious chords in Michelangelo, thereby making them compelling to him as models. I regard this approach as holding heretofore unexplored rich possibilities. But the method does lend itself to overreading, to the relative neglect of the challenge of the more formal elements in the model. Perhaps Professor Rosenthal's note of my discussion of Michelangelo's use of the composition of Raphael's *Heliodorus* is such an instance. I do think, however, that given Michelangelo's lifelong envy and enmity toward Raphael, the fact that Heliodorus was by Raphael, and not another artist, made it irresistibly attractive to him as a competition piece.

References

Beck, J. (1981). *Italian Renaissance painting.* New York: Harper & Row.

Cellini, B. (1562). *Autobiography of Benvenuto Cellini* (J. A. Symonds, Trans.). New York: Dolphin Books, 1961.

Condivi, A. (1553). *The Life of Michelangelo* (H. Wohl, Ed., A. S. Wohl, Trans.). Baton Rouge, LA: Louisiana State University Press, 1975.

Freedberg, S. J. (1970). *Painting in Italy: 1500–1600.* Harmondsworth: Penguin.

Hirst, M. (1961). The Chigi Chapel in Santa Maria della Pace. *Journal of the Warburg and Courtauld Institutes, 24:* 161–185.

_____. (1981). *Sebastiano del Piombo.* Oxford: Oxford University Press.

Lucco, M. (1980). *L' Opera Completa di Sebastiano del Piombo.* Milano: Rizzoli.

Oremland, J. (1980). Mourning and its effect on Michelangelo's art. In *The Annual of Psychoanalysis, 8:* 317–351.

315   Sterba, R., & Sterba, E. (1979). The personality of Michelangelo: Some reflections. *American Imago, 35:* 158–177.

Symonds, J. A. (1887). In B. Cellini, *Autobiography of Benvenuto Cellini* (J. A. Symonds, Trans.). New York: Dolphin Books, 1961.

Vasari, G. (1568). *The lives of the artists,* 2 vols. (Mrs. J. Foster, Trans.). New York: Hermitage Press, 1967.

William
Conger,
M.F.A.

Review of Laurie Wilson, *Louise Nevelson: Iconography and Sources.* Garland Publishing, 1981.

When the early abstractionists like Kandinsky and Dove put together their shapes and colors it did not bother them at all that new images, not actually depicted, would be brought to mind by apparently abstract form. But in our recent past much was said and done to eliminate all reference from abstraction and the dominant aesthetic guidelines asserted that the quality of an abstract work was at least partly defined by its capacity to remain itself and not evoke otherness at all. Now our perceptions are changing again and new abstraction, although often adhering to formalist concerns, is once more full of reference, if not actual depiction. Boundaries are blurred and even the "pure" formalist or nonreferential abstractions of a decade or so ago now seem to be less than completely themselves. Everything looks like something else. In the midst of this it is clear that the subtleties of meaning long recognized in figurative art should also be found only slightly less quickly perhaps, if one is willing to look, in abstract art, too, where seemingly nonreferential form can symbolize deeply personal or autobiographical content.

In this crisply written analysis of Louise Nevelson's art, Laurie Wilson begins with the recognition that although Nevelson's art is abstract, its thematic and allusive titles suggest a meaning beyond purely formal concerns. She examines Nevelson's biographical history—her youth, family, and friends (often through interviews), and matches it to an analysis of the formal, historical, and critical contexts of the artist's work—her artistic influences and aspirations. From this Wilson concludes that three interrelated themes—Royalty, Death, and Marriage—can provide access to the autobiographical content in Nevelson's art and show how it, in turn, is symbolized by the found objects, the wooden pieces of things, painted black or white, that make up the artist's grandly meditative sculptures.

In presenting Nevelson's formal and artistic concerns as a basis for her later iconographic interpretation, Wilson gives particular attention to the artist's several thematic exhibitions between 1943 and 1960. Central to her discussion is "Moon Garden + One," 1958, Nevelson's first fully mature exhibition which established her career and signature style.

Importantly, however, Wilson does not ignore Nevelson's earlier work and here one is reminded of the highly playful work of the 1940s (*Menagerie Animals,* for example) which, in their similarities to the circus figures of Calder and the whimsical constructions by Picasso, display Nevelson's confident intuition and her alertness to artistic interests. Although the expressive character of her work became more and more somber as it matured, there was no loss of wit, intuitive quickness, and compositional rightness. Furthermore, Wilson does well in emphasizing the theatrical and environmental aspects of Nevelson's art not only by showing her artistic relationship to painters such as Pollock, Rothko, and Still, but also by discussing the artist's association with the multitalented designer Frederick Keisler, sculptors Isamu Noguchi and Louise Bourgeois, and dancer Martha Graham. Agreeing with Thomas Hess, who considered Nevelson's work theatrical, artificial, and sculpturesque, Wilson is convincing in showing that those are, in fact, the very qualities which give the work its distinction. They reflect the artist's early ambitions for a theatrical career and dance. They also convey the environmental interests of the artist in which a work imbues a space, or redefines it, with its own expressed sensibility. Wilson does not say that Nevelson's constructions are formal representations of dance itself, but one can hardly ignore the association when being reminded by Wilson that Nevelson frequently danced in the midst of her work. The association is completed in facing a work like *New Continent* (1967), and seeing the linear movement of edges, the twisting of columns and spindles, the extensions outwards and inwards, the whole organic rhythm that becomes so kinetic in perception. The formal connections in Nevelson's work to theater and environment bring to mind the interests of the Dadaists and Pop artists to blend art and life. Wilson notes similarities, for instance, linking Nevelson to Duchamp and Kaprow and thus by implication one is led to distinguish between an art like the "Happenings" which accomodate life and an art that, like a Nevelson environment, replaces life. In denying the original identities of the found pieces she uses by painting everything a uniform black (or white), Nevelson actually prepares them for new symbolic meaning or at least gives priority to that. The neutralizing effect of the black paint, for example, gives equal potential to all associated meanings evoked by the sculptural pieces. It is a kind of artistic imperialism in which, again, life (in this case being represented by the original identities of Nevelson's found things) is replaced by art, the new symbolic meanings those pieces acquire through the medium of the neutralizing paint. "In darkness there is oneness," Nevelson said. Perhaps she was thinking of how the black paint might make disparate pieces seem to blend together but her statement may also apply to the equality of possibilities with respect to symbolic meaning provided by the neutralizing effect of overall blackness or "darkness."

Wilson notes that Nevelson "has often claimed that she built an empire," and Wilson's interpretation of that claim suggests that for Nevelson, an empire of her own artworks is an expression of deeply personal needs. Thus, having outlined in sufficient detail the formal and historical facts, and what critics and writers had to say about Nevelson's work (and none of them said anything about iconography), Wilson reviews the artist's biography and shows the correspondences between Nevelson's personal life and the expressive intent of her work—notwithstanding its subconscious source.

Throughout Wilson's detailed commentary, she makes Nevelson's notion of her art as "empire" a continuing reference, a point of origin as in perspective drawing, one might say, that gives coherent shape and depth to the whole. Nevelson's interest in native art of the Americas, ceremony, ritual, and especially the ancient Mayan culture is regarded seriously. It is part of a formal and experiential matrix, Wilson suggests, that expresses the artist's sense of building an empire and reflect possibly subconscious childhood fantasies. For example, some early Nevelson sculpture evokes urban architecture. Later works look like encrusted houses with open doors. Having learned from Wilson that Nevelson's father was acquisitive both in regard to houses (buildings) and furnishings (antiques)—his was a sort of imperialist ambition—and that Nevelson regarded her mother as ill-adjusted, misplaced, closed in, we can conclude that the city and houselike sculptures symbolized more than what might be determined on the basis of their allusions to native American or Mayan art alone. The open-door, houselike sculptures not only "open the door" for her mother (and herself) but together with the citylike sculptures express the acquisitive sense of domain, her father's and, again, her own. In speaking of her mother Nevelson said, "I always felt so sympathetic to her that I was determined to open every front door . . . I didn't care if I had to build the house myself." Nevelson's predominant use of wood, of course, almost certainly relates to her childhood in Maine, her father's lumber business, his antique collection, and even the shipyard near her family's home. But these connections between Nevelson's art and her childhood recollections are not so unusual or complex. Wilson is able to show their deeper importance (and much more) by specifying what she regards as the three principal themes of Royalty, Death, and Marriage that weave through Nevelson's six thematic exhibitions in the 1950s.

In Wilson's discussion of Nevelson's second thematic exhibition in 1956, entitled "Royal Voyage," the artist's symbolic content of royality is explained. The dominant pieces here are two tall totemic works, the royal couple, the *King* and the *Queen*. The formal similarities these pieces have to modernist form (one thinks of Brancusi) and ceremonial art, Mayan or northwest coast Indian, veils their true identities as the memorialized mother and father of the artist an as dual representations of the artist herself. Nevelson is the *Qoeen* mother who surveys her domain presented by the accompanying sculptures, *Undermarine Scapes, The Indian Chief,* and *The Forgotten City,* says Wilson, and she is also *King* father who has built the empire. Continuing, Wilson shows how numerous works by Nevelson are really self-representations that symbolize the artist as reigning monarch of her realm. She is aided by Nevelson's own revealing remarks such as the quoted statement that she, the artist, is the "Queen of the black-black" and that black is the color of "royalty and aristocracy." Empire, royalty, and black all interrelate for Nevelson and ultimately become her self-personification and identification with her parents.

Nevelson's important exhibition, "Moon Garden + One" (1958), not only brought her long awaited critical success but it also displayed her mature style for the first time. Its principal theme, as Wilson points out, was death. Part of the sculptural ensemble included tall, boxlike constructions, some with half-open lids (doors?) and containing intuitively arranged abstract pieces (are they antiques?) that strongly evoke skeletal remains. Clearly, they are coffins and corpses and among them is *King II,* an allusion, in Wilson's intrepretation, to the artist's interred father. As with the theme of royalty, Wilson expertly leads us through a labyrinth of works and associations, not excluding Nevelson's childhood experiences, her fascination with Mayan sculpture and its funereal suggestions, and the ever-shadowy nature and meaning of black. Although Wilson is right in saying that Nevelson's poetry lacks the aesthetic quality of her sculpture, there are exceptions: "Daylight has form; Darkness is oneness." For Nevelson, death means completeness and so does black. Darkness, black, completeness, oneness are Nevelson's synonyms for death. In presenting "Moon Garden + One," Nevelson insisted on keeping the exhibition space dimly lit, saying "it was really for my visual eye," and Wilson claims the environment actually represented a churchyard cemetery, and more specifically, the private cemetery of the artist's family in Maine.

Nevelson's strong identification with her mother, expressed in such statements as "I dedicated my life to her" and her ambivalence toward marriage are fully expressed in Wilson's examination of the marriage theme in Nevelson's art. "The Forest" exhibition of 1957 included the extraordinary *First Personage,* an acknowledged self-portrait more than six feet high. Although freestanding, it was made to be placed by a wall partially hiding its second component, a series of projecting daggerlike shapes that seem to jut from the "spine" of the personage piece. The work expresses extreme emotional pain but in a passive, quiet, and enduring kind of way. Toward the top of this wood piece there is a woodknot and Wilson quotes Nevelson's dramatic recollection of making the work and imagining the knot to be a moving mouth and being terrified by it. At the same time, Nevelson was creating two other pieces, *The Black Wedding Cake* and *The Wedding Bridge.* Wilson shows how these three pieces were interrelated and centered on the artist's pessimism and fear concerning marriage. We learn, for instance, that *The Wedding Bridge* probably symbolized an episode in her mother's life when she could not "escape" the amorous youth who would become her husband and Nevelson's father by crossing a river to live with a sister. That was the one year in a hundred, Nevelson said, that the river did not freeze. For Nevelson, *The Wedding Bridge* was a representation of something dangerous and she did not consciously relate it to her mother's experience and consequent unhappy marriage. But Wilson urges us to make that relationship by claiming that the "moving mouth" of the *First Personage* may also represent a vagina. That subconscious association by Nevelson, she concludes, evoked the artist's fears and fantasies about marriage and sexuality because it occured as a result of the *First Personage* being created in the same context as *The Black Wedding Cake* and *The Wedding Bridge.* Nevelson's deeply felt anxieties about this complex mix of marriage, mother, and sexuality caused her, Wilson says, to exclude *The Black Wedding Cake* and *The Wedding Bridge* from "The Forest" exhibition. After that, Nevelson began to create more secretive enclosures as in the walls of constructed boxes that represent her signature style.

In *Dawn's Wedding Feast* (1959), a seemingly exhuberant white work of many parts including totems, a wall (*Dawn's Wedding Chapel*), and a horizontal piece (The Wedding Pillow), there is a theatrical aura of an imminent marriage. But the implication that Nevelson's anxieties are now calmed (the white paint) is instead best regarded as a new self-awareness or acceptance, if we take the suggestion of Wilson's arguments. Two totem figures, the *Sun* and the *Moon,* seem prepared for their marriage before *Dawn's Wedding Chapel.* Considering all of Wilson's interpretations, they are the Mayan gods, the royal couple, the mother and father (moon and sun), the interred parents, and the artist herself, who is also the presence of the whole work as a feast, the white dawn. Here, Wilson shows the links between the *Moon* goddess and its parallel role as the artist's mother and self. She asserts that this unity of mother and self in Nevelson's subconscious is what ultimately urged the artist to show the *Moon* as Bride alone facing *Dawn's Wedding Chapel,* but turned away from the *Sun.* So, in *Dawn's Wedding Feast,* there is no wedding, just the "feast" of the whole environment and the narcissistic union of artist as self and mother to her work, implicated by the *Moon* facing a "mirror" in the *Chapel* construction. Thus is Nevelson wed to her art and empire. This book concludes with a Nevelson poem titled, "Narcissus."

The complexity of Wilson's book has only been slightly revealed here. The numerous relationships between Nevelson, her art, and other artists such as Cornell, Dali, Duchamp, Giacometti, Moore, Gottlieb, are woven into the fabric of her work in ways that truly express the actuality of how artists interact and remain aware of what is going on. Surrounded by that complexity, Wilson does not lose sight of her thesis and by approaching the content of the three themes of Royalty, Death, and Marriage in different ways she presents the reader with a clear view of the artist and her art. The iconographic explanations are clear enough, in fact, for one to extend them to newer works by Nevelson that are chronologically beyond the scope of the book.

As a Garland publication of the author's dissertation, one must accept the fact that Wilson's work was prepared for a small academic audience. There is little in its organization or style to make an appeal to the larger interested public which is conditioned to respond best to romanticized and glossy treatments. Wilson's language is suited to its academic purpose and, happily, it is lively, clear, and without pedantry. The many photographs following the text are a great aid, especially where they show gallery installations. A listing of some dimensions for works shown would be helpful and considering the many references to artists, an index would be useful, too. There is, however, an excellent, extensive bibliography.

Beyond its obvious value in adding to our understanding of Nevelson, Wilson's book provides a good example of the likelihood that abstract art symbolizes significant personal or autobiographical content even as it presents purely formal concerns. That is an issue of importance in today's art.

Jerome D.
Oremland,
M.D.

Review of Laurie Wilson, *Louise Nevelson: Iconography and Sources*. Garland Publishing, 1981.

Professor Laurie Wilson has given us an unusually well-documented and complete study of a dramatic, brilliant, though somewhat cryptic presence in the art world. Remaining true to its title throughout, *Louise Nevelson: Iconography and Sources* shows the restraint associated with its origin as a dissertation. Because of its purpose, Wilson showed admirable caution when it came to interpretation of the personal motivations represented in Nevelson's oeuvre. Although there is no doubt that Wilson's psychoanalytic knowledge would allow her to delve into Nevelson's personal life and its influence on her art, Wilson's restraint provides pristine material that can be usefully mined by the author herself and by successive generations of those who study creativity and the relationship of personality to the creative enterprise.

The book, a photo-offset of typed pages, is clearly written with an interesting organization. The beginning chapter is entitled "Major Monuments and Cultural Reaction." "Personal History" and "Artistic Development" are treated in subsequent chapters and the Nevelson oeuvre is discussed in three chapters: "Empire," "Theatre and Dance," and "The Ceremonial." The text ends with an epilogue discussing recent works and exhibitions, reminding us of Nevelson's living and continuing productivity. The book concludes with 191 black-and-white illustrations of selections from Nevelson's works and a number of companion pieces by other artists. There are two interesting appendices: a chronological listing of exhibitions at the Museum of Modern Art, New York, devoted to children's art (1938–48) and to dance and theater

(1943–48). The selected bibliography is useful and full, and the listing of interviews with and on Nevelson will be particularly helpful to future students. Unfortunately, the book does not have an index; tracing specific people and themes through its pages is difficult.

Apart from her art, Nevelson appears in these pages as a not unfamiliar, if unusual, mid-20th-century woman. Striking to the psychoanalytic reader are the hysterical stigmata—including a dramatic, histrionic, and colorful personal appearance; oracular statements; impulsive actions; flirtations with metaphysical experiences; and severe, prolonged, periodic, disabling depression.

As one reads Wilson's account of Nevelson's childhood and reflects on the artist's demeanor and style, one thinks of the peculiar combination of being a part of and yet separate from others that characterized growing up as a daughter of middle-class, foreign-born, Jewish parents in a small Yankee community in the early part of the 20th century. Yet of more determining significance were the peculiarities of Nevelson's mother, Minna. Strongly implied is that the mother was a tentative, fearful, chronically depressed woman, who was idealized by her husband for her "beauty." Minna sounds "doll-like," controlled yet controlling, hiding from the world behind make-up and clothes in a meticulously kept home, protected from life by her ambitious, somewhat self-centered husband. As a couple, they sound all too typical of the post-Victorian era.

Of most importance in understanding the mother is realizing the significance of her having been "forced" to follow her husband into the New World and leaving behind in Russia her family, in particular, her own mother. It seems clear that Minna's imperfect separation from her mother became catastrophically enhanced by knowing that she probably was never to see her mother again. For Minna, the New World was not the land of opportunity that it was for her husband; for Minna, it was a land of loneliness, fearfulness, depression, and an unrelenting sea of psychosomatic and hysterical ills.

Much can be made of the fact that the father dealt in lumber, was a near compulsive collector and storer of antique furnishings, and that the family lived on Linden Street in Rockland. Such enticing tidbits, of course, arouse the psychoanalyst's desire to tie together Nevelson's own "collecting," her choice of wood as her material, and her most characteristic art form, "environments," with an identification with or an attempt to be close to her father. The importance of the father, however, quickly pales as we fully realize the curious, complex, and enduring relationship with her pitiful mother.

As is often the case with creative people, Nevelson seemed to manifest her talents early. Siblings recall her early and continuing, sometimes driven, attempts to rearrange furniture. Such fleeting glimpses into the early life of creative people, although tempting, are often misleading. The recollections regarding early evidence of a talent by those associated with creative people are heavily influenced by the knowledge of the subsequent development of their special abilities.

Nevelson is a contemporary personality. Studying her psychoanalytically presents the problems of evaluating "the interview" with all its spuriousnesses, unreliabilities, and incompletenesses. Such studies provide a sobering perspective for those of us who study the more ancient creative people: although availability provides invaluable data for the art historian, it presents the psychoanalyst with yet another order of difficulties that comes with evaluation of self-appraisal and recollections in the non-psychoanalytic setting. In all psycho-biographical studies, how the psychoanalyst longs for the transference reenactment as corrective and guide.

Nevelson is one of the group of creative people who talk a good deal, if not about themselves, at least about their work. However, most of what she says is oracular, cryptic, and contradictory. She seems less the artist who despairs when asked about a work or works—feeling that the work is itself the expression or else it is unsuccessful—and more an artist who is evasive, enigmatic, and seemingly keeping some secret that will not be shared. For example, in a recent interview, she responded, "I'm not a searcher for truth or any of that, because, well, you see truth moves for each person. It shifts. You can believe in it and each one can believe in what ever they feel" (A.P. release, Jan. 26, 1984).

In that Nevelson's long life has truly spanned the development of modern art in the United States, it is not surprising that Wilson presented a great deal of information about 20th-century American art with numerous references to many of the most influential and intriguing artists of all time. Of special interest is the considerable material from interviews with Nevelson; her son, Michael; her surviving siblings; members of the art world who knew and know her; and Wilson's extracts from art reviews and catalogues of Nevelson's gallery openings. The few existing minor biographies of Nevelson wisely are used sparingly, and there is interesting material from the W.P.A. federal arts projects in New York which for a time was a major supporter of Nevelson.

Collectively, these materials create the impression of a minor talent during a period of monumental change in the nature and locus of artistic creativity. Nevelson seems more reflective of than integral to the art world. One finds oneself tending to be interested in her association with, for example, Isamu Noguchi, Hans Hofmann, Diego Rivera, more for what it tells us about them than about her.

The material from the reviews and the gallery openings reminds us in a striking way of how important discovery and exposure are to art and the artist and how crucial are the critics. Women, ironically, in view of the ambivalent relationship with her mother, were to play an extraordinary role in Nevelson's recognition. Of vast importance in her eventual acceptance were the art critic Dore Ashton, and Colette Roberts, the director of the Grand

Central Moderns Gallery in New York. Further, it was Dorothy Miller, the assistant to Alfred H. Barr, Jr., the director and curator of painting and sculpture of the Museum of Modern Art, New York, who persuaded Barr to include Nevelson in the museum's 1959 major exhibition, "The Sixteen Americans." It was this exhibition that launched Nevelson's work into significance.

As previously mentioned, the three chapters on Nevelson's works are enticingly captioned; sub-heading the "Ceremonial" chapter is "Loyalty," "Death," and "Marriage." Such headings remind us of the high drama in Nevelson's presentations. In fact, much of her early work consisted of dramatic sets for the work of others. Gradually her presentations became unpeopled, ritualized settings. These large-scale, highly compartmentalized relief sculptures, though often called environments, are not settings for humankind. Her totemic and elaborate ornamental figures are seemingly from another world. These exalted personages, rarely more than humanoid in form, are archetypical expressions of the elements of but not of life itself. Even in her representation of the celebration of wedding, *Dawn's Wedding,* the wedding pillow (Fig. 1) is ordered forms, barren, and unused. It is Dawn's wedding, but it is ambiguous whether Dawn is a state, a person, or an allegory. Similar to Nevelson's recent statement, "I am married to the world," her sculpted representation of marriage, though global, is an unpeopled aloneness (A.P. release, Jan. 26, 1984).

Much emphasis has been placed on Nevelson's development of shadows and the role of black on black. Her use of black, as noted by her, is not an expression of mourning. Unnoted but likely is her use of black as the color of the aloneness of night, curiously still, accepted, and never fearful. Hers is not a world from which *objects* have departed, rather it is an *objectless* world. (*Object* is italicized in that it is used to refer to a complex psychoanalytic concept, essentially an external presence—early a part of a person, later, a person—that is associated with need

Fig. 1. Louise Nevelson, *Dawn's Wedding Pillow.* 1959. White painted wood. Private Collection. U.S.A.

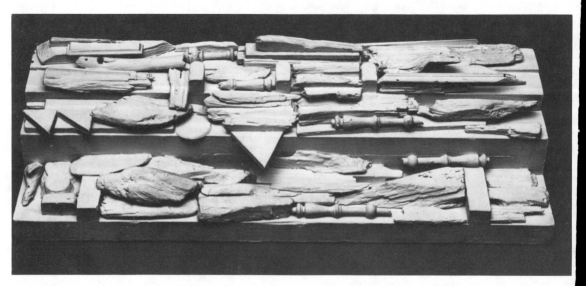

gratification and becomes endowed with meaning and intra-psychically represented.)

Wilson traced the development of Nevelson's sporadic productivity, emphasizing nodal events often related to associations with artists and geographical sites. Strikingly, family seems to play little part in Nevelson's life and art. Indeed, her marriage at age 18 seems to have been one of convenience, almost Victorian in form. Charles Nevelson—short, wealthy, 15 years her senior—appears to have been selected to provide her with life on a grander scale, a Gentile-sounding name, financial security, and social prominence. When the last two attributes failed in 1931, she abandoned the marriage, retaining his name. Her son, Michael, is rarely mentioned. She left him at age nine in the care of her chronically unhappy, emotionally incapacitated mother. Care for him on her return is little discussed. The impression is that even her time with him was sporadic and minimal. One is fascinated to realize that this is one of those curious women of the early 20th-century who abandoned husband and child for art with little in the way of explanation, justification, or apparent remorse. Hers became an almost nunlike life devoted to her art.

The chronicle of Nevelson's life is replete with artistic influences, and her art markedly reflects the great contemporary artists. Yet, in the artist's own account, one of the most consistent features is her dismissal of the influence of other artists, with the exception of Picasso. The discrepancy between the effect on her art and Nevelson's acknowledgement of the effect is highlighted by Wilson's careful research. For example, by Nevelson's account, she studied less than two months with Kenneth Hayes Miller of the Art Students' League. In fact, it was over two years. This parthenogenetic view of her creativity, seeing it as coming forth fully formed from within, might become the central organizing theme for a psychoanalytic study of this complex personality and her works. Within such a view of her capacities, perhaps, can be seen seeds for a thesis pivoting on the intensity of the ambivalence towards her parents, particularly the psychologically incapacitated, psychologically unavailable mother, and Nevelson's ambivalent capacity to trust and integrate another within.

As disavowing as Nevelson is of the influence of other artists, there is some acknowledgement of the influence of environment on her work. Her fascinating, often internally compartmentalized totemic figures are clearly influenced by the Mayan stelae seen on her two visits in the late 1940s to Mexico and Central America, particularly the Guatemalan site of Quiriguá. These highly sophisticated, often dramatically beautiful Mayan sculptures are ritualistic studies of figures within figures within figures. Perhaps keyed by these monuments from an enigmatic culture, Nevelson developed uncanny visual depictions of the subjective experience of highly fragmented and unintegrated *object* and self concepts—in the psychoanalytic lexicon, "unintegrated introjects." Perhaps our fascination with this aspect of her work (and with these curious figures from a civilization that seemingly arose as mysteriously as

Nevelson thinks of her own creativity) is that they provide expression and recognition of the split-off, unintegrated introjects that "inhabit" each of us.

The role of "unintegrated introjection" becomes particularly compelling as we hear about Nevelson's response to her mother's death helping us understand the unattended funeral. Her simple statement, "She died, *so to speak* and I never give it a thought" is a vivid and telling description of defense against loss through "introjection" (Wilson, 1981, p. 186, my italics). The lost mother is maintained, that is, internalized but not integrated. Nevelson's now lost *Audience Figure* (see Fig. 3, p. 236, this volume) possibly closely followed the mother's death in March 1943. *Audience Figure,* with its figures residing in figures, is, perhaps, a clear depiction of this complex defensive kind of preservation of the lost *object* within. The *object* remains an "unintegrated introject" rather than an "identification," an integration of the *object* that is self-enhancing. Metaphorically speaking, the "interior" is "occupied," yet the self is "empty."

This is not to say that Nevelson was unreactive to death. The death of her friend, sponsor, and patron, the gallery owner Karl Niererdorf, in October 1947, the year following the death of her father, was marked by profound, prolonged, and debilitating depression, anaclitic in nature. From this six months of severe, work-inhibited depression, she arose phoenixlike with a sudden fury of near maniacal but nonetheless creative productivity. Important to my thesis is the idea that it was at this time that she made her two visits to Quiriguá and became fascinated with the monolithic Mayan stelae that she had been introduced to earlier by Rivera (Fig. 2). In short, I suggest that these monumental sculptures with their curious figures within figures may have particularly captivated Nevelson at this time for they, like her own *Audience Figure,* depict ancestral images telescoped within.

Among the fascinating relationships that Wilson mentions that need further exploration are Nevelson's friendships with the actress Princess Norina Matchabelli, and the dancer Martha Graham. These dramatic, independent, creative, powerful females seem like natural fellow travelers. Of interest to the psychoanalyst is their mutual fascination with metaphysics. As one reads Wilson's list of the various psychic fads that engrossed them, including Scientology, Dianetics, Christian Science, New Thought, Zen, and the teachings of Edwin Burnell, Gurdieff, and Krishnamurti, psychoanalysis is striking by its absence, particularly in that psychoanalysis during their era was a fad, especially among experimental artists. Nevelson's proclivity was toward situations that gave her a feeling of being in relationship with something or someone that provided, in fact, only relationship with split-off, projected aspects of herself. Psychoanalysis, perhaps, carried the threat of true relationship.

As one reads the unfolding of this life and its products, one cannot help but wonder if the interest in Nevelson is not increased by her enigmatic, histrionic qualities coupled with our

Fig. 2. *Stela F,*
North face,
Guatamala. 761 A.D.
Sandstone. The
American Museum of
Natural History.
Photo: Courtesy The
American Museum of
Natural History.

present interest in female artists and their art. Aside from important investigations regarding the sociohistorical encumbrances
placed on the creativity of the female, there are unplumbed
important considerations regarding basic relationships between
creativity and the female. For this reason alone, Nevelson's life
and work are worthy of full examination as a study of basic
incompatibilities and enhancements among her concepts of woman, motherhood, and herself as a creative individual.

Yet there is an inspiring quality as one fully appreciates Nevelson's perseverance despite severe discouragement by such
greats as Hans Hofmann and the critical audiences of New York
in the 1930s. Though one admires her courage, one questions the
wisdom of a young Jewish woman traveling alone to Nazi Germany in the early 1930s to study art! In regard to her per-

severance, one wishes to know more about the relationship with "Miss Cleveland," the high school teacher who early gave recognition to Nevelson's creativity. Initial recognition is of vast importance to creative people. Again it is fascinating and in a way ironic, as one considers the complexity of the relationship with her mother, that Nevelson's recognition first came from a woman. Nevelson's creativity being discovered and acknowledged by a woman was to be reexperienced many years later in the person of the critic Dore Ashton.

In summary, Laurie Wilson has presented the psychoanalyst with much refined data and the art historian with careful research about the iconography in and sources of the work of an eccentric, curious, creative woman, who came to be acknowledged in the second half of her life, strangely at the very time her style of living was becoming anachronistic. Carefully avoiding premature closure through interpretation, Wilson has provided us with choice material to consider regarding certain themes in Nevelson's life and art. Further study may confirm that the thesis briefly offered here, namely, that the intensity of the ambivalence towards her psychologically crippled, psychologically unavailable mother helps account for Nevelson's parthenogenetic view of her creativity, and helps us understand her dramatic, compartmentalized, unpeopled "environments" for which she is most noted. These "environments" and some of her totemic figures depict in a way almost without parallel, perhaps, a subjective sense of inner emptiness, an inner vacuousness that is at the same time compartmentally "inhabited." Her works suggest a self largely composed of unintegrated introjects rather than self-enhancing identifications. Perhaps, this sense of lack of integration and inner compartmentalization is autobiographically depicted in her 1964 sculpture, *Self-Portrait, Silent Music IV* (Fig. 3), unfortunately not included among Wilson's illustrations.

In the "Coda," in a rare moment of giving rein to her psychoanalytic interpretive bent, Professor Wilson invoked the concept of *narcissism* with regard to Nevelson. In explication of the relationship of the artist to his art, I called for caution in applying the concept narcissism to the artist (1975, 1984). Based on investigations by Phyllis Greenacre (1957, 1962) and Donald Winnicott (1953, 1967) into the origins of creativity, I suggested that the artist responds to a different order of *object* than the ordinary interpersonal *object*. I held that the artist looks to his art for the self-realizations, self-validations, and self-transcendence that the ordinary person finds in interpersonal relatedness. Of more importance, I suggested that the artist's art provides for him the promise of continuity (immortality) parallel to the promise of continuity that progeny provide for the more ordinary person. I argued that the artist's relationship to his art is a variant of *object* relatedness with similar motives, directions, and vicissitudes, and quite different from the stunted development of *object* relatedness loosely called narcissism. I suggested that it is the artist's lack of interest in and regard for the interpersonal *object* world as opposed

Fig. 3. Louise Nevelson, *Self-Portrait, Silent Music IV*. 1964. Black painted wood. Photo: Courtesy The Pace Gallery, New York.

to his intense interest in a broader panoply of *objects* that unjustly earns him the appellation, narcissistic.

Studying Nevelson from this point of view might be rewarding, for as one gets a sense of her self-preoccupation and "into-her-selfness," her art increasingly seems to be largely repetitious and limited presentations of herself, suggesting that narcissism heavily informs *and* limits her art. Perhaps, her struggle with narcissism (and anaclitic depression) accounts for the long and laborious period that transpired before she found her artistic place and the limited range of themes, forms, and new directions to her art despite her long career. One might hope that psychoanalytic study of Nevelson's life and works would fruitfully explicate the particulars of that complex self-state, narcissism, as informing, sometimes dominating, and possibly limiting her art. Indeed, Wilson's brief suggestion of the importance of narcissism in understanding Nevelson is given much evidence by Nevelson's short but revealing poem,

Narcissus

I dared to look
I like what I see
Good i good i good i for me
I like what I see
Good i good i good i for me
I like what, I see
(Wilson, 1981, p. 223).

References

Friedman, M. (1973). *Nevelson wood sculptures.* Minneapolis: Walker Art Center.

Greenacre, P. (1957). The childhood of the artist. *The Psychoanalytic Study of the Child,* 12: 47–72. New York: International Universities Press.

_____ (1962). Discussion and comments on the psychology of creativity. *Journal of the American Academy of Child Psychiatry,* 1: 129–137.

Oremland, J. (1975). An unexpected result of the analysis of a talented musician. *The Psychoanalytic Study of the Child,* 30: 375–407. New Haven: Yale University Press.

_____ (1984). Empathy and its relation to the appreciation of art. In J. Lichtenberg, M. Bornstein, & D. Silver (Eds.), *Empathy I.* Hillsdale, NJ: The Analytic Press.

Winnicott, D. W. (1953). Transitional objects and transitional phenomena. *International Journal of Psychoanalysis,* 34: 89–97.

_____ (1967). The location of cultural experience. *International Journal of Psychoanalysis,* 48: 368–372.